THE WORLD'S BEST
WHISKIES

THE WORLD'S BEST
WHISKIES

750 ESSENTIAL DRAMS FROM TENNESSEE TO TOKYO

DOMINIC ROSKROW

Stewart, Tabori & Chang
NEW YORK

Published in 2010 by
Stewart, Tabori & Chang
An imprint of ABRAMS

Text copyright © 2010
Dominic Roskrow

Library of Congress
Cataloging-in-Publication Data

Roskrow, Dominic.

The world's best whiskies :
750 essential drams from
Tennessee to Tokyo /

Dominic Roskrow.
    p. cm.
Includes index.
    ISBN 978-1-58479-886-6
    (alk. paper)
1. Whiskey. 2. Distilleries–
Anecdotes. I. Title.
TP605.R66 2010
641.2'52–dc22

2010016621

This book
is dedicated
to friends, family,
and whisky drinkers
everywhere.

Editor: Wesley Royce

Designer: Robin Rout

Production Manager: Tina Cameron

The text of this book was composed
in Joanna MT Pro

Printed and bound in China

10 9 8 7 6 5 4 3 2 1

Stewart, Tabori & Chang books are
available at special discounts when
purchased in quantity for premiums
and promotions as well as fundraising
or educational use. Special editions
can also be created to specification.
For details, contact
specialsales@abramsbooks.com
or the address below.

115 West 18th Street
New York, NY 10011
www.abramsbooks.com

Contents

THE WORLD'S BEST WHISKIES

INTRODUCTION

Adventures with whisky

When one whisky distiller heard about this project, he said, "Does the world really need another whisky book?"

The immediate answer may appear to be: "Er…no, not really." Or at least it doesn't need another book that rehashes the history of each distillery, regurgitates a mass of statistics about the number, size, or capacity of its stills, or reproduces figures showing the volume of spirit it produces.

But I have never been big on history, and right from a very young age I was up there painting the wagon with Lee Marvin, always looking forward to the next adventure.

It's why I became a journalist and, indeed, why I love whisky. And make no mistake—whisky is an adventure, an ever-changing map composed of new roads to explore and new people to meet.

Whisky shouldn't be about cold copper or sterile steel, nor about dull dates and horrible history. As important as provenance and heritage are, evolution and innovation interest me more. Whisky should be a living, dynamic thing. It is a dichotomy: a simple mix of grain, yeast, and water, crafted and shaped into a complex drink that is constantly evolving and continues to perplex. Most of all, though, whisky is a proud representation of the people who produce it, an integral part of the community from which it comes.

This book, then, is an attempt to capture some of the wonder of whisky and the magic of malt. It is more than a list of the world's best whiskies. Rather, it is a collection of some of the stories and anecdotes behind the drink, and an introduction to at least a handful of the characters that have played key roles in creating a craft in a glass.

And not just in the obvious territories, either. Never has there been a more exciting time for whisky; new versions of the spirit are appearing in the unlikeliest places across the globe, from Austria to Australia, and Wyoming to Wales.

Whether you're a seasoned whisky expert or a novice just starting to dip your fingertips into the glass, this book is an attempt to lead you on a colorful tour through the world of whisky, to point you toward some new roads to explore, and to give you a glimpse of the passion that produced it and the limitless pleasure that it can give. It's a wagon ride, if you like, into whisky's wildest new frontiers.

So when you're ready, Mr. Marvin, let's move 'em on out.

Dominic

History

Pinpointing when whisky distilling began is like trying to spot shining pebbles in the murky depths of Scotland's Loch Lomond.

History points us to the Far East, Middle East, and Northern Africa. The earliest stills were found in Taxila in Pakistan and in Cyprus, while there is some evidence that distillation was used in these regions for medicine and perfume. We know, too, that a heavy form of beer was fermented in Mesopotamia, in the region now covered by Iran and Iraq. Exactly when grain-distilled drink was first consumed for pleasure is lost in time. I like to think, though, that an Irish priest stumbled upon it and, being Irish, didn't bother waiting to be ill to start to appreciate its redemptive qualities.

Clues to whisky's origins are all here, though. Much of the language of drink is derived from Arabic, for instance, including the word "alcohol." The link between distilled drink and distilled medicine is borne out by the large number of drinking toasts that refer to good health and happiness.

And, of course, the Church has had a long and fruitful relationship with alcoholic beverages. It is highly likely that priests brought the techniques of brewing and distilling back first to Ireland, then to the west of Scotland. The monasteries became thriving centers for beer and spirits production. Monks and priests were among the few sectors of society able to flee from the ravages of the Black Death, taking their distilling skills with them farther afield. When England's Henry VIII consigned many of them to the unemployment line by decommissioning their places of worship, a great number changed careers and became brewers and distillers instead. So thanks, Henry—not great on the women front, but on the plus side a big help for the British drinks trade.

The Irish make many claims when it comes to whisky, but maintaining that they brought grain spirit to Scotland is probably among the more credible ones. Ireland can also boast the world's oldest licensed distillery in Bushmills, which was registered in 1608, and Irish whiskey, the choice tipple of the nobility, was established on the high table of gentry long before its Scottish counterpart was. Scotch whisky, meanwhile, rapidly gained a foothold among the tenant farmers and landed masses of Scotland as both a libation and a currency, with communities trading it for clothes and shoes with traveling salesmen. That in turn attracted the attention of the authorities, who quickly saw a chance to make money through taxation, and so began a cat-and-mouse game of tax avoidance between the governments in Edinburgh and London and the local Scottish populace, who saw it as a patriotic duty to avoid paying the tax.

One of the driving forces behind the Jacobite uprisings of the seventeenth and eighteenth centuries was a campaign against malt tax. When those uprisings finally ended in defeat for the Jacobites and the brutal slaughter of Culloden in 1746, and in the ensuing Highland Clearances that drove crofters from their lands, many Scots took their distilling skills to the farthest corners of the world. In North America, they were joined by Europeans such as Johannes "Jacob" Beam, by Irishmen, and by Welshmen forced from their homeland by the Temperance movement. Among them were Kentucky's Evan Williams and the Scottish and Welsh grandparents of Jack Daniel of Tennessee whiskey fame.

Scotch whisky's journey to the drink cabinets of first England, then the Empire, and finally the world was to be defined by a remarkable 50-year period between 1825 and 1875. The foundations had already been laid in the decades beforehand, with the start of the Industrial Revolution and the technological advances that came with it. The Industrial Revolution brought railways to Scotland, and with them the means and fuels for greater and better-quality production. Highland whiskies began to be smuggled to the pubs and drinking houses of Edinburgh and Glasgow, and their reputation rapidly spread well beyond these environs.

Three events would promote Scotland to the position of world leader in whisky. First, Scotch whisky makers and the authorities called a truce in their battle over taxes, reaching a compromise. From 1823, distillers began to turn their trade into a legal one, providing quality malt.

Second, Scotsman Robert Stein developed a completely new way of distilling grain in a continuous process. The system would be improved upon by Irishman Aeneas Coffey, but the new column-still process was eschewed by the Irish while being gleefully seized upon by the Scots, who found that when coupled with their rough malts it made for a smoother, easier-to-drink style of whisky.

Finally, Scotland's whiskies were to benefit massively from a disaster that struck across Europe in 1860. A destructive aphid by the name of *Phylloxera vastatrix* began a 15-year feeding frenzy that was to wipe out the vineyards of France and beyond, destroying the wine and brandy industries in the process. Scotch was ready and willing to replace brandy.

It has never looked back. Scotch whisky reinforced its new status in the twentieth century, finding its way to the Prohibition-era speakeasies of the United States and into the affections of American servicemen stationed in Great Britain during World War II. By contrast, Irish whiskey has undergone a century of decline, although it has pulled out of its tailspin in recent years.

Canadian whisky, a dominant player in the North American market for many years, has been treading water of late, and Japanese whisky, established more than a century ago, has made massive advances in recent years, and Japan is arguably now the world's number-five whisky nation. But the competition from other countries is fierce; France, Belgium, Germany, Switzerland, Austria, Australia, England, and Sweden have all scratched a significant mark on the whisky map. It's hard to keep up and, indeed, during the production of this book a new player arrived from nowhere—Taiwan.

Whisky already has a proud and glorious history to point to, but it's clear that the story has only just begun. The history of this great drink is being written by the day.

LEFT Scotland's history and whiskies are intrinsically linked to each other. This is the ruined castle at **Balvenie** near Dufftown.

ABOVE A snapshot of the past: workers at what is now the **Buffalo Trace** distillery in Franklin County, Kentucky.

Making whisky Water, malted barley, and yeast

Water, malted barley, and yeast are the holy trinity of whisky—three ingredients that are bland individuals, yet their whole is very much greater than the sum of their parts. They are to the world of drinks what certain household items are to homemade explosives: innocuous until combined by an expert into a combustible mix. So what role do they play?

WATER

If you have visited a distillery pretty much anywhere in the world, you have undoubtedly sat through one of those cutesy documentaries where clichéd local folk music accompanies pictures of gurgling brooks and vast waterways, and a portentous über-voice melodramatically explains how centuries of evolution and geology have combined to provide the perfect water for producing the distillery's liquid gold.

These movies can be unintentionally hilarious. In one, made by a Scottish island distillery, the celebrity actor hired to narrate the distillery's story looked positively ill as he concluded his dramatic speech and sipped at his dram. It turned out that midway through filming he had suddenly discovered that he had an allergy to malt whisky and was violently ill on set. Rather than dispense with his services, the filmmakers carried on, replacing his dram with a glass of cold tea. It didn't stop him from looking dreadful, though.

But we digress. These movies, as well as occasionally being awful, may be guilty of being economical with the truth. Much store is put on the importance of water. Distillery owners sometimes go to extreme lengths to protect their sources by buying up neighboring land, and undoubtedly the bond between pure, clean water and the resulting malt spirit is an important one. The source of water has long been held in reverence by whisky makers, and many claims have been made for it. And to some extent the facts support the romance. Soft water, with low mineral content, may help the malting process and make for better absorption of water by the grain and therefore result in higher-yielding barley. Undoubtedly, the peaty journey experienced by water on Islay, in particular, influences the island's malt.

But the science works against the argument, too. Many would maintain that the nature of distillation is such that the influences of the water are all but removed. And, if they aren't, then how is it that some distillers—although they don't like to shout about it—have used treated and chlorinated water in their production process on occasion, and yet have continued to make great whisky?

Most of Scotland's water is soft, and the country's distillers understandably argue that this is a key factor in the excellence of Scottish single malt. But there is an argument, too, that nutrients and minerals feed yeast and therefore aid fermentation. Single-malt whisky is successfully made in other countries, including Wales and England, where the water is hard. Also, when it comes to brewing, the best British source is considered to be around Burton-on-Trent, in Staffordshire, where the water is rich in minerals. The waters of Kentucky in the United States are deemed essential to the bourbon-making process because they contain calcium—the same reason that the state produces strong-limbed Thoroughbred racehorses. And while it is true that you can count on one hand the distilleries in Scotland that use hard water, on that short list are true heavyweights Highland Park and Glenmorangie. How does that work?

Moreover, water can be, and is, treated these days to be whatever it needs to be. Some argue that mashing, fermenting, and finally distilling mean that the difference between soft and hard water in the end flavor is negligible.

That's not to say water is not important—of course it is. Pure water—water free of microorganisms—is crucial to ensuring that the rest of the process passes off correctly.

But today, in the twenty-first century, the most important factor governing water source is not whether it is hard or soft, or whether it contains certain minerals or not, or even whether it passes through flavor-imparting peat beds. No, the most important factors governing water are that there is plenty of it and that it is of sufficiently cool temperature.

In recent years, climate change certainly seems to have made its mark on whisky production. In Scotland, for instance, there have been an alarming number of instances where water shortages have forced distilleries to stop production. The picture is far from predictable, however. After a series of mild winters in Scotland that saw water levels as low in April as they would usually be in September, the winters of 2007–2010 were all exceptional for their long and deep snowfalls.

A further problem stems from the generally warmer climate. If water is not cool enough for condensing, it means either longer closed seasons for distilleries or an investment in expensive cooling equipment.

RIGHT Cereal thriller: whisky at its embryonic stage.

FAR RIGHT Barley being turned in a traditional floor maltings. Barley matured in this way, on a wooden floor, is said to provide better flavor for whisky.

MALTED BARLEY

Barley is nature's answer to Doctor Who's Tardis—a simple telephone box on the outside, a complex giant engine room within. It has been part of brewing and distilling history for centuries, a durable grain capable of growing on harsh, infertile terrain, seemingly the simplest of grains, loved and cherished by generations of folk living off the earth since medieval times. But science has caught up with barley, and on a regular basis laboratories create a new strain that moves the goalposts when it comes to yield. Some argue that higher-yielding barley produces barley that results in a sacrifice of flavor and some distillers stay loyal to particular barley strains, but attempts to stem the tide of commercialism will ultimately prove fruitless. Macallan and Glengoyne, for instance, both extolled the qualities of Golden Promise and chose it despite its relatively low yields. In 2009, Golden Promise ceased to exist.

Some argue that, as long as barley meets certain production criteria, it does not matter where it comes from. Others contend fiercely that provenance of the barley is of crucial importance. Some take the default position that while Scottish barley is ideally best for making Scotch whisky, the practical realities are that there is not enough of it. Certainly, a fair proportion of barley used in Scotch whisky production is imported, particularly from the East of England.

And nothing makes a Scottish distiller pale quicker than when a Scottish National Party politician calls for Scotch whisky to be made with only home-produced ingredients.

YEAST

Yeast is the great unknown in whisky, rarely talked or written about, or fully understood. A living microorganism, yeast can lay for years in a dormant state, but in the right wet and warm conditions and with the right food—sugar— it will rapidly multiply, feed ravenously, and produce carbon dioxide and alcohol. This fermentation process can be an impressively aggressive and violent one, and can make a huge and sturdy washback rock with the force.

Thousands of yeasts occur naturally, which is why fermentation can take place without any yeast being added, and when a successful strain is created artificially it must be stored carefully to avoid contamination. Exactly what effect yeast has on flavor is the subject of fierce debate, and the degree of attention given to yeast production varies from one distiller to another. Most yeasts used in whisky production are a combination of brewer's yeasts and yeasts created in the lab, and in some cases—particularly in the United States— both brewers and distillers fiercely guard details about the exact nature of their yeasts.

The role of peat and oak in the production of single-malt whisky

Single-malt whisky may be made only with malted barley, yeast, and water. Apart from supposedly flavorless caramel for coloring, nothing else is allowed to be added.

That said, though, there are two other major influences on the flavor of a single malt—peat and oak—and for a full appreciation of single malt it is essential to understand their role in the overall flavor of the finished whisky.

PEAT

Peat is made up of decaying vegetation and grasses that have formed over centuries in boggy and wet marshland areas. It has been used as a burning fuel in communities across the world for centuries. In Scotland, in particular, peat has played a central role in the drying of barley for Scotch whisky making. When the Industrial Revolution brought trains and they in turn carried coal across the country, many distilleries abandoned peat as a fuel, but it remained in use in the islands—and it is on the islands that it is still most widely used today.

Most of the big phenolic, smoky-flavored whiskies derive their taste from this process, and not from the water that has traveled through peat bogs.

Peat in Scotland is graded into three categories. The deepest layer looks like dark chocolate fudge cake when it is wet, and dries into a hard fuel that resembles coal and burns slowly. The top layer, made up of the least decayed or suppressed vegetation, crumbles in the hand when dry and burns rapidly, but produces high quantities of peat smoke.

The three layers are cut from the ground in spring and dried naturally during the summer, before being collected in the fall. A distillery such as Highland Park on Orkney will cut just enough peat to see it through the ensuing year.

Peat differs from place to place because it is made up of vegetation. This is significant because the vegetation in a country such as Australia will be vastly different from that found in Scotland, so while the raw ingredients would seem to be the same, they have different effects on the whisky. In Sweden, some of the peat was submerged under the Baltic Sea at one time, and is therefore very salty. Furthermore, the rules governing malt whisky production do not dictate what exactly barley should be dried over, so in Sweden Mackmyra has incorporated the traditional drying method of using juniper twigs in the drying of malted barley. This process makes a further distinction from the usual whiskies produced in Scotland.

OAK

If geographical differences affect the flavors that peat gives to malt, then oak from different parts of the world results in even greater variations. The differences between oak from Europe and its cousin in North America are so pronounced that you can discern them with the naked eye. Even within Europe there is variance, with Swedish and Spanish oak imparting different flavors to spirit.

It takes 100 years or more to grow an oak big enough to turn into a cask and, while some environmentalists are critical of an industry that fells trees for whisky making, more oak is being planted in the second decade of the new millennium than at any time in the past 1,000 years, and most distillers are keenly aware of their environmental responsibilities and the need for sustainability. Certainly, few countries face the acute shortages of oak that resulted in the Middle Ages after the great warring nations had felled the trees for ships, fortifications, and weapons in the desire to build empires.

Oak is in such demand because it is very strong but still malleable, as well as being waterproof yet porous, and able to let oxygen (and indeed water and alcohol) molecules pass through it. Additionally, it is rich in flavor compounds that are easily accessible by charring or toasting the wood.

On its own in a brand-new cask, the spirit contained within would be quickly dominated by the spiciness of the wood; the maturing process is therefore improved by using a cask that has been used previously for maturing a different spirit. Most malt spirit is matured in casks that have already been used for the production of sherry in Europe or bourbon in the United States. While all bourbon casks will be made of American wood (even though there is no law saying that they have to be), it does not follow that all sherry produced in Spain is matured in European oak. Sherry styles such as oloroso are matured in American oak, so there are on the whole three main types of cask for whisky making: bourbon cask, European oak sherry, and American oak sherry.

SPECIAL FINISHES

The rules governing the production of single-malt whisky do not stipulate what the cask had to have contained before, and considerable experimentation has taken place in recent years. It is not unusual to find whiskies that have been matured in part in wine casks, port pipes, or casks used for the production of Madeira or rum. Although the rules forbid the addition of anything to a single-malt whisky, some do take on distinctly ruddy and pink hues from their contact with the spirit- or fortified wine–soaked wood; such casks can have a major impact on flavor.

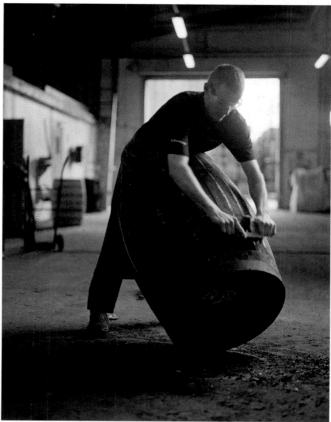

RIGHT Coopering skills are much in demand again now that barrels are such a valuable commodity. This cooper is at William Grant's own cooperage on the site of **Glenfiddich** and **Balvenie** in Scotland.

How to make single-malt whisky

The magic of single-malt whisky lies in the fact that it contains just three simple ingredients: malted barley, yeast, and water. The process of making single malt and the equipment needed to make it are pretty much the same throughout the world. And yet such a simple and uniform production process produces a vast array of different flavors and aromas.

Whisky is like a collection of seemingly identical landscape paintings; each picture looks the same from a distance, but study them closely and there are countless differences between each one. The first step in whisky making is to turn barley into malted barley by tricking it into growing, which is done by soaking the barley in water. The grains will start to produce shoots, breaking down the grain husk, and this in turn gives access to the enzymes and starches contained within each barley kernel.

After a few days, it is necessary to halt the growing process, and this is achieved by drying out the barley over a heat source. Traditionally, barley was dried over fire fueled by peat. This process imparts the smoke and peaty flavors that produce the phenolic medicinal styles of whisky for which Scotland's west coast is famous. Nowadays, though, most barley is malted in large commercial maltings, and most malt is dried in modern electricity-fueled ovens.

Once dry, the malted barley is ground into flour, known as grist, and mixed with hot water in a vessel known as a mash tun. The water removes the starches and enzymes that are needed to produce alcohol. The process is known as mashing, and it is exactly the same as the one used to steep a pot of hot black or green tea. The spent grains are removed from the process at this point, leaving a sweet brown nonalcoholic liquid known as wort.

The wort is moved to a large vessel called a washback, and yeast is now added to the mix to start the process of fermentation. Yeast feeds on the wort, converting the starches to sugars and the sugars to alcohol and carbon dioxide. After a period of two to three days, the wort is converted into a beer with an alcoholic strength of about 7% to 9% alcohol by volume (ABV). Unlike beer produced in breweries, which is made under sterilized conditions, distillery beer is sharp and sour—not unlike Belgian lambic beer. This is due to the presence of bacteria and is crucial to the success of the whisky-making process.

Distillation is the process of separating water from alcohol through the use of heat. For malt whisky, this involves boiling the beer solution in large copper kettles known as "pot stills." Alcohol evaporates at a lower temperature than water and, once in vapor form, will pass up the copper still. It is condensed back into liquid by passing through a condenser cooled by cold water, lowering its temperature so that it returns to a liquid state. The copper plays a pivotal

ABOVE The size and shape of pot stills vary from distillery to distillery, and often affect the taste of the spirit made. You will find these stills at the **Glendronach** distillery in Speyside, Scotland.

role in the process, catching fats and oils as they pass over it and reacting with the spirit to influence flavor and removing unwanted sulfur compounds from the vapor.

Malt distillation is usually—but not always—carried out twice. The first process is carried out in a wash still and produces a solution known as "low wine" with an alcoholic strength of a little over 20% ABV. This is mixed with the rejected residue from the previous distillation, raising its alcoholic strength to the high twenties, and this is distilled in the spirit still.

This is where the first major piece of magic takes place. The spirit collected in the second distillation is the spirit that will be put into casks to make whisky, so its composition needs to be considered carefully. Unlike the first distillation, where all the condensed liquid is retained, much of the second run will be rejected. As the liquid is heated, the first alcohols to evaporate are by definition the most volatile. They have the highest alcoholic content and tend to be, at worst, poisonous and at best, foul-tasting. They are not desirable. So the first part of the run, known as "heads" or "foreshots," is collected in a holding vessel and rejected.

Over time, the strength of the alcohols in the vapor will fall and flavorsome spirit worthy of keeping will be produced. So this spirit is collected in a second vessel. This is known as the "cut" and is the part of the run that will be put into casks for maturation. Finally, the condensed spirit will reach a point where the alcohols are weak and unpleasant to taste. This portion will also be rejected and is known as the "tails" or the "feints."

The whole process was once vividly described to me as like cutting the head and tail off a fat fish and retaining the juicy, fleshy part in the middle. Where exactly that cut is made varies from distillery to distillery, and in some cases it is little more than a sliver. At the end of the run, the middle cut forms the "new make" spirit, which will be stored to make whisky. The rejected parts of the cycle are recycled and used in the next distillation, then the whole process begins again.

To make whisky, the new spirit—which is clear, but has a distinctive and strong flavor—must be stored in oak casks and matured. In Europe, this process has to be for a minimum of three years. Malt spirit is not robust enough to fend off the dominant spicy flavors of new oak over this time, so it is matured in casks that have already been used for something else, most often bourbon or sherry.

Malt's greatest mystery lies in how it matures. No two casks will produce exactly the same whisky and, although recognizable distillery characteristics may be found in each one, there will be significant variations on the central theme. Casks of different sizes will be used, and they will have previously contained different liquids. But even two identical casks containing spirit from the same run and stored side by side in exactly the same conditions and for exactly the same period of time may well produce different whiskies.

So the bottle of 12-year-old single malt that you eventually buy will contain a marriage of whiskies from an array of different casks, cleverly combined by a whisky maker so that, whether you taste the distillery's malt in New York today or London next year, you will not notice any great variance in taste, even though the two bottles will have been produced from different batches. The word "single" in single-malt whisky refers to the fact that the whisky is the product of just one distillery, rather than referring to it being from a single cask or batch.

How to make blended whisky

Blends are to whisky what fast food is to catering: immensely successful across the world, popular and enjoyed by the mainstream, but rarely truly loved or cherished; often unfairly dismissed as bland and unexciting; and only occasionally garnering the positive press bestowed elsewhere.

There are two principle reasons for this. First, because while the world of single malts is all about variety, and new expressions are constantly being added to the menu, fueling the enthusiasm of aficionados, blended whiskies are all about consistency and reliability, and new releases in the category are few and far between. As a result, blends rarely create news. Second, while the rules governing the production of single malts are rigid and ensure an extremely high standard, the rules governing blends are more flexible. Poor-quality blends can be made within the rules, so a vast number of ordinary or poor blends have sullied the reputation of the category as a whole. This is a shame because blended whiskies at their best can be stunning and require a level of craftsmanship that not even the very best malts can match.

Scotland actually produces four styles of whisky, but it is blended whisky that has given the country its status as the world's best and leading producer of whisky. Most single-malt whisky is produced with the intention of forming part of a blend, rather than for being consumed alone. Even with all the current focus on single-malt whisky, blended whisky still accounts for nine out of ten glasses of Scotch whisky consumed across the world.

Blended whisky not only constitutes an important export market for Scotland, but also for Great Britain. Not surprisingly, therefore, Scotch whisky makers take blends very seriously indeed. The biggest ones—Johnnie Walker, Chivas Regal, Bell's Famous Grouse, Teacher's—are made to exacting standards and are supported by huge marketing budgets. They might not be anywhere near as sexy as a premium single malt, but they're the industry's bread and butter and are quality products. Trouble is, there are plenty of inferior brands that cannot make the same claim.

FAR RIGHT Checking on the blending process at **GlenDronach**.

RIGHT **GlenDronach** (single malt), **Johnnie Walker** Black Label (blended whisky), **Compass Box** Spice Tree (blended malt), and **The Snow Grouse** (grain whisky) exemplify types of Scotch.

SCOTLAND'S FOUR STYLES OF WHISKY

• **Single malt:** made from malted barley, yeast, and water, and the product of just one distillery.

• **Blended whisky:** a combination of different malts and grain whisky usually—but not always— mixed together after the individual whiskies have been fully matured separately and brought together by the whisky maker before bottling.

• **Blended malt whisky:** the confusing name given to a mix of malts from different distilleries, but one that contains no grain whisky. This category is different from blended whisky, and its whiskies used to be known as "vatted malts."

• **Grain whisky:** made with a variety of grains, including corn, wheat, rye, and malted and unmalted barley. It is usually produced in a continuous process in a different style of still than that used for malt whisky and is known variously as a "column," "continuous," or "coffey" still.

Blended whisky's inconsistent reputation stems from the inclusion of grain whisky. Grain plays an essential role in rounding off some of the more extreme flavors of single malt, making the drink more palatable to a greater cross section of people. Grain has a less distinctive taste than single malt, and much of the flavor it does have is given to it by the cask. The rules governing blends do not dictate what proportions of grain and single malts need to be in the blend, so often a higher proportion of less tasteful grain is used. Moreover, grain is often matured in old and much-used casks, where the wood has little to offer the spirit, further making for a bland and characterless whisky. Buy a cheap bottle of Clan Bagpipe McTavish, and chances are you're going to get a low-quality grain-heavy blend colored with caramel to make it more impressive than it actually is.

But it does not have to be that way, and the great names of blended whisky have obtained their status through generations of blending perfection and the employment of the finest malt and grain whiskies. A good blend is a lovingly constructed oil painting, balanced and in harmony, and bursting with color and style. It may include more than 40 malts and grains, and the number might actually be considerably higher. The Scotch whisky industry has cleverly adopted an exchange system by which each whisky company swaps its malts with other producers, so that each one has the widest possible range of flavors with which to work.

Master blenders understand the characteristics of different malts and know how to construct beautiful blends with them. A great blend is like a professional or college football team; there are big-name heavy-hitting stars in the lineup, but many of the most important jobs are done by lesser-known names. If they weren't there, the team would fall apart. When the whole team is firing, the result is a study in excellence. When they're not, it's one big unholy mess.

Although each brand of blended whisky is designed to be consistent time after time, different blends can be suited and tailored to satisfy the palates of different people in different countries. For this reason, blends are often created for specific markets with specific tastes, and are not sold elsewhere, making it a difficult, bordering on impossible, task to monitor them all.

How to make bourbon

Bourbon is whisky because it is made with grain, yeast, and water. But these three ingredients vaguely connect it to single-malt whisky in the same way that a bat, ball, and the participation of two teams link baseball to the English game of cricket. Beyond basics, the two have little in common and, where there is an opportunity to head off in a different direction, Americans have tended to take it.

Although bourbon and single-malt whisky follow a template under which grain is converted to beer and the beer is distilled, the raw materials, the distillation process, and the maturation of the spirit differ significantly.

Single malt is made using malted barley alone. Bourbon, meanwhile, is made with more than one grain in the mix and must include at least 51% corn, although in practice this percentage is much higher. While some malted barley will probably be included in the process because malted barley is a good catalyst for aiding the conversion of sugars to alcohol, it is also probable that there will be some wheat, rye, and/or unmalted barley in the mix, which is known as the "mashbill."

As with malt whisky, American whiskey makers at different distilleries will tweak the process so that each distillery has its own whiskey DNA, but in broad strokes the process is similar across them all.

As with malted barley, the aim of the whiskey maker is to release the sugars and starches from the grains so that yeast can convert them to alcohol through fermentation and, as with malted barley, the process is known as "mashing" because hot water is used to flush out the sugars. The three grains are crushed into flour individually, before being added to boiling water in what is known as the "three-step process." Each distillery will have its own view on what temperature the water should be when each grain is added, but generally corn, which is a tough grain with a hard outer shell, will be added at the highest temperatures, with wheat, unmalted barley, and rye being added at slightly lower temperatures; malted barley, the most delicate of the grains, is added last and when the water has cooled significantly. When mashing is complete, the entire solution, spent grains and all, goes forward to the fermentation stage.

THE SOUR MASH PROCESS

The sour mash process plays a key role in the production of American whiskey, and it is a further point of difference from Scotch whisky production. At the end of each bourbon distillation process there is stillage, a residue made up of the used grain from the process. This is known as "backset," and is made up of the last of the solution left after distillation and the remnants of the grain with all its sugars removed. It has a sharp, sour taste—hence it is "sour." This stillage is added back to the mash before the yeast is added. Its purpose is to provide a chemical balance to the solution and control bacteria, creating a fermentation process that is conducive to distilling spirit that is clean and full of character.

When fermentation is complete, the beer—a thick viscous solution that is completely different from the wash that is produced in Scotland—is ready for distillation. Whereas the distiller's beer in Scotland is thin, sour, and fruity, in bourbon production it is rich, creamy, and sickly, more akin to warm milk on soggy cornflakes.

THE CONTINUOUS STILL

Single-malt whisky is produced in batches, with a quantity of single malt converted to beer, and the beer distilled in two stills before the process starts again. Bourbon is produced in a continuous still, in which the distillery beer is passed in at one end and comes out as a spirit at the other. The continuous still is just that, allowing an ongoing distillation, and it is capable of producing larger quantities of spirit in a more efficient and commercial manner. But far less copper is involved, the separation of spirit from water is done differently, and the resulting spirit has a higher alcoholic strength but none of the depth and variety of flavor that single-malt distillation produces. Whereas single-malt whisky spirit is created by boiling the beer solution in a glorified copper kettle, the continuous still works by forcing the distiller's beer down pipes containing a series of sloping plates and into a wall of pressurized and very high temperature steam, which converts the alcohol to vapor and drives it out. It is recondensed and channeled out of the still at different points during its downward journey, is collected, and undergoes what is effectively a second distillation process by being passed through a simple pot still known as a "doubler." The resulting spirit is clear and is known as "white dog."

ABOVE **Woodford Reserve**'s stills in Kentucky are unconventional because they're pot stills, like those used in Scotland. Bourbon is normally distilled in column stills.

LEFT Open top fermentation at **Maker's Mark** in Kentucky.

MATURATION

Even the maturation process in the United States is different. The spirit that continuous distillation produces is less distinctive than new-make single malt, and hence maturation is particularly important to the overall process. While U.S. law requires that an oak barrel be used, it also dictates that a new barrel is used for each production run. When you consider the size of Jack Daniel's, the world's biggest whiskey, and Jim Beam, the world's biggest bourbon, and the huge number of barrels that they are using that by law must be discarded each year, it explains why so much single malt is matured in ex-American whiskey casks.

The new barrels are charred or toasted to varying degrees on the inside before spirit is added, helping to release all the qualities in the wood that will impart flavor and character as the spirit matures. Once more, bourbon maturation is to single-malt whisky maturation what baseball is to cricket: an altogether more brash, aggressive, and less time-consuming affair. Kentucky is, in every sense, a state of extremes, and the weather is no exception. It has long, extremely hot, and high-humidity summers and viciously cold, sharp winters. When the sun is at its hottest temperatures at the top of the tower block warehouses, it can hit the 100-plus mark on the Fahrenheit scale. In winter, fierce frozen winds from the Appalachians bring temperatures in the thirties and below.

The effect on the spirit is to provoke rapid and dramatic distillation. As with all chemical reactions, heat makes change happen faster. The extreme changes in temperature make the spirit expand and contract faster, and to move more rapidly in the cask, regularly bringing all the spirit into contact with wood and accelerating the transfer of flavor and color from wood to spirit.

For these reasons, bourbon reaches maturity much faster than malt whisky does in Scotland.

There is one final difference between the ways in which the two whiskies reach their destinations. In Scotland, alcohol evaporates from the maturing spirit, escaping from the cask and providing the angels with their share. This gradually reduces the alcoholic strength of the spirit in the cask. Alcohol also evaporates from the cask in Kentucky, but in the vast majority of cases not as fast as water does.

The humidity makes a crucial intervention, and in most cases the alcoholic strength of the bourbon spirit gets higher during maturation, although this process is not uniform and in some Kentucky distilleries there are areas where spirit in the cask remains at about the same strength throughout the process, and in some cases actually declines as it does in Scotland. U.S. law requires that bourbon is matured for a minimum of two years. Unlike the case in Scotland, where coloring may be added to the finished product, nothing at all may be added to bourbon.

THE WORLD'S BEST WHISKIES

WHISKY BASICS

Key whisky questions answered

While the vast majority of people on the planet have heard of whisky and have an inkling as to what it is, there remains a huge level of ignorance on the subject and some great myths have grown up surrounding it. It is not the purpose of this book to look in any great detail at the styles of whisky and the detailed aspects of their production, but nonetheless there are a few questions that arise time and time again. Here are some of them—and their answers.

Why do Scotch single malts vary from region to region?

Scotch malt whisky is the result of a combination of culture, history, politics, and economics. Scotland is effectively three countries in one: the Highlands, Lowlands, and Islands. The differences in the histories and cultures of each region are reflected in the whisky that they produce, although it should be noted that there are exceptions to every rule, increasingly so nowadays as whisky makers strive to find new flavors by dispensing with as many barriers as possible. Each of the regions can be divided again, with the island of Islay off the west coast of Scotland demanding its own category within the Islands region, the area around the river Spey separate to the rest of the Highlands, and the Campbeltown region distinct to the Lowlands region.

Regional variation

The Lowlands With the invention of the continuous still came the golden age of blended whisky and the need for a big supply of malt whisky. Big commercial malt stills were built in the Lowlands, close to the ports of Glasgow and Leith, and where there was a plentiful supply of barley because of the better farming climate. The bigger the still, the lighter and more floral the style of spirit produced because the spirit vapor has to travel farther over the copper, giving it more time to remove impurities and making the longer journey for the heavier and more flavorful oils and congeners more difficult and less likely. Hence, the Lowlands is known for light, floral apéritif-style whiskies. Triple distillation was also commonplace in the Lowlands, further producing light and smooth malts.

The Highlands It is harder to grow barley in the Highlands, which means that traditionally there was less of it to distill and so smaller stills were adequate. Much Highland malt was distilled illegally, and so it helped to have a still that was easy to conceal or portable. Small stills allow more heavy compounds and oils to pass over to be condensed, creating a heavier, richer, and more flavorful malt spirit.

The Islands The Industrial Revolution brought trains to the whisky regions of mainland Scotland, and with them came coal. Most distilleries therefore abandoned the use of peat and replaced it first with coal and eventually with oil and gas heating. This did not happen on the Islands, so more traditional methods of whisky making continued there. Today, the Islands produce a wide range of whisky styles, with peat used prominently across all the islands, but cleaner, lesser peated whiskies coming from the islands of Jura, Mull, Orkney, Arran, and, in one or two cases, Islay.

Speyside About two-thirds of all Scotland's distilleries are based in the northeastern region between Aberdeen and Inverness, alongside the River Spey or one of its tributaries. They sprung up here to take advantage of the soft river water, which is considered ideal for producing sweet, fruity malts ideal for blending.

Islay The island of Islay has eight distilleries and is world famous for the big, peaty phenolic whiskies from distilleries such as Laphroaig, Lagavulin, and Ardbeg. All eight distilleries produce a peated style of whisky though three also make considerable volumes of whisky where peat is not the dominant characteristic.

Campbeltown The Mull of Kintyre peninsula to the west of Glasgow used to boast a large number of distilleries and was a principal base for export of whisky to North America. Today, whisky production there survives by a thread, made up of a distillery that produces intermittently, a new distillery, and the iconic three-for-the-price-of-one distillery **Springbank**, which houses the eponymous malt, the peated Longrow, and the triple-distilled Hazelburn. Hard to pinpoint a regional style, then, although the words "rustic" and "traditional" come to mind.

Is older whisky better than younger whisky?

No, not necessarily. The longer spirit is in the cask, the more flavor it will have. But there will come a point at which the wood not only is no longer contributing to the flavor, but also will be impacting in a negative way, with the wood overwhelming the subtleties of the spirit. When this process happens varies from cask to cask and whisky style to whisky style. Meaty, oily Highland malts are likely to resist the wood for longer and continue to improve into their third, fourth, and occasionally fifth decades. Lighter whiskies may not be able to hold off the effects of wood for more than 15 years.

Age is only a guide to quality, and younger whiskies can be zesty and zippy, refreshing, uncomplex, and fruity. These are desirable traits. Moreover, while a young peaty whisky will be rawer and spicier, this may well be what the drinker wants. It is like cooking chili; the longer you leave it, the more integrated and balanced the flavors become. But if you are after a big, raw, and spicy hit of heat, time is not necessarily your friend.

Can you tell the age of a whisky by its color?

Not really. A sherry cask will turn whisky a deep reddish brown very quickly, while a bourbon cask makes it a rich yellow. If it is the first time that the cask has been used for making whisky after being used for something else, the effects of the cask will be more pronounced than when it is used for the second or third time. Some casks naturally work on spirit better than others. And at the end of the process, some whisky makers add caramel to enrich color, making the visual guide to age redundant. So color is not necessarily a lot of help when it comes to judging how old a whisky is.

ABOVE At the foot of the Mannoch hills, beside the Rothes Burn in Speyside, the **Glenrothes** distillery makes use of water from two local springs for the distilling process.

What does cask strength mean?

Simply that the whisky has been put into the bottle at the strength at which it came out of the cask.

What does the age on the label refer to?

If there is an age on the label, this refers to the youngest whisky in the mix. Most bottles of whisky contain whiskies of various ages, but just one drop of 12-year-old whisky in a bottle of 25-year-old malt makes that bottle 12 years old. No, age statement does not necessarily indicate an inferior whisky. Some great blended whiskies (**Johnnie Walker Blue Label**, **Dewar's Signature**, **Royal Salute 100 Cask Selection**) use small amounts of young whisky to pep up the grand old malts that they are mainly made up with—and have no age statement because the small volume of young whisky that would have to be stated on the label would not do justice to the composition of the rest of the blend.

What does "non chill-filtered" mean?

Naturally produced whisky clouds when it is cold because the fats in the solution solidify at lower temperatures. To prevent this and ensure clear whisky, makers have tended to chill the whisky and filter out the solidified fats. But in recent years there has been a trend toward leaving these fats in because they also contain flavor.

So "non chill-filtered" is regarded as a statement of quality and reflects the fact that drinkers are becoming increasingly demanding and knowledgeable about their drinks.

Tasting whisky

Whisky suffers from an identity crisis, particularly when it comes to nosing and tasting it.

Whisky is a simple drink made of grain, yeast, and water, and is effectively distilled beer. It is the drink of the tenant farmer and the common man. In its crudest form, it is harsh firewater; at its most sophisticated, it is an ideal lubricant for socializing, celebrating, bonding, and peacemaking. It should have no airs or graces, and most of the time it doesn't.

But the world of whisky is split between those who accept whisky as the drink of the people and those who would prefer it to sit on an altogether higher table. They prefer to link it not with the grain but with the grape, and they dress it in the livery of wine and of wine language. There was even a magazine that brought the two together. It failed.

And it is from this that the identity crisis stems. For while many whisky books are broadly in agreement as to how whisky should be nosed, tasted, and appreciated, scratch below the surface and there is little common agreement among writers and experts on the subject. Some believe that water should be added; others not. Professional "nosers" or tasters add lots of water. Some say that you should spit

whisky; others that you cannot appreciate the full experience without swallowing it.

My view is that whisky is not wine and therefore should not be treated as such. Whisky is three or four times as strong, for a start, and the process of distillation takes spirit several steps away from the provenance of the ingredients from which it is made. While many flavors and aromas can be found in whisky, it does not command the same degree of nuance or subtlety that wine does and therefore does not demand the same indulgences of language. Whisky is made all the more attractive because, on the whole, it is free of the pretentiousness that goes with wine tasting, and snobs and drinks bores would not be tolerated in the distilleries of Scotland, Kentucky, Ireland—or anywhere else for that matter. Whisky is all about independence and free spirit, and for this reason nobody should tell you how to taste it. That said, though, while how you travel down the whisky road is a matter entirely for you, it certainly does not hurt to have some signposts along the route. Here are a few pointers.

TASTING SEQUENCE
First, look at the whisky, note the color and whether it has "legs"; approach at arm's length. Breathe in the aromas through both nostrils, then one at a time. Finally, taste it.

VIEW

APPROACH I

1. WHAT GLASS TO USE
It is one of the great ironies of whisky writing that no matter how many book chapters are written explaining the best glass for whisky nosing, the publishers often feature a tumbler on the front cover. Tumblers are fine for blended whisky or bourbon, when mixers or ice might be added. They are useless for nosing single-malt whisky. For the record, the whisky industry favors a tulip-shaped glass with a tapered neck because this concentrates the aromas into the nose. You can buy them from most whisky shops at a modest cost. Champagne flutes, sherry glasses, or small red wine glasses are all better than tumblers for tasting whisky.

2. BEWARE HIGH-VOLTAGE ALCOHOL
Approach a glass of neat whisky with caution. Whisky has a strong alcoholic content and should be respected. Nose a strong spirit too quickly, and it will hurt your nostrils. Not only that, but your senses will batten down the hatches as well if they perceive that they are under threat, making further sensory perception redundant, at least in the short term. Approach a new glass of whisky in the same way that you would approach an unfamiliar animal: at arm's length at first, then with caution, until you are both happy in each other's company. Taste a very small amount of the spirit neat before you do anything else to it.

RIGHT The Glencairn whisky glass shape is perfect for nosing whisky. Ignore anyone who says you should not add water—it is a personal choice. Drink water between whiskies to refresh the palate.

3. WATER OR NOT?

If any so-called expert tells you that should not add water to your whisky, tell him that the whisky industry started the practice. New spirit comes off the still with an alcoholic strength in the high sixties or low seventies. Until recently, when warehouse space and barrel shortages became an issue and casking smaller quantities of liquid at higher strength became fashionable, most distillers brought the strength at which the spirit entered the cask down to about 63% ABV by adding water. After maturation, the whisky has a strength of anywhere from 55% to 65% and, again, water is added to bring the strength down to the bottling strength of normally 40%, 43%, or 46%. In other words, more than one-third of the whisky in your bottle is added water. Who's to tell you that you should not add a bit more? Blenders will take samples down to just 20% ABV, and water is crucial for breaking down the whisky and releasing an array of aromas, thereby making appreciation of the drink easier.

But it is not for everyone. A few tasters dislike adding water and only do so when tasting strong whiskies.

4. SPIT OR SWALLOW

Whisky is a strong spirit, which means that the palate will tire quite rapidly when swallowing it, and after three or four samples further tasting is impossible. It therefore makes sense to spit if you intend to be judging or appraising whisky for more than just fun or personal reasons. But that doesn't happen very often, does it?

There are two compelling arguments for swallowing and not spitting. One is the fact that whisky is a drink. There is a clue in the title. The other is that when describing whisky we talk about the finish. How can we do this if we do not finish it? It is like watching a movie, then leaving 15 minutes before the end. Surely, the warming feeling as the spirit passes down the throat and the taste left in your mouth afterward are crucial to the whisky-tasting experience. For this reason, it is best to sip and savor any whisky that you have not tasted before, in order to fully appreciate the sight, aroma, flavors, and finish of the drink. This is the way to gather a complete profile.

APPROACH 2

NOSE

SIP

Flavor categories

While whisky is not wine, identifying flavors will enhance your enjoyment of it, at the very least because you will be able to identify the specific flavors that most appeal to you.

THE MAIN CATEGORIES

Perhaps the easiest way to improve your tasting and nosing skills is to start with the broadest and most general of categories. When you are happy with those, introduce subsectors, then subsectors of those, and so on. I base my subcategories around retail stores.

PEATY/SMOKY—OR NOT

This is the most fundamental split, certainly in Scotch whisky. Drying barley over peat fires imparts smoky and peaty flavors that some people hate and some would kill for. The characteristics are:

SWEET OR SAVORY?

In whisky, these two are not mutually exclusive, but at the same time there are many in which these are defining characteristics. Most American and Irish whiskey, many Speyside and Lowland whiskies, and some Highland whiskies fall into the sweet category; a number of Highland and Island whiskies and a proportion of Japanese whiskies could be considered to be in the savory spectrum.

PEATY
Mild antiseptic/medicine
Tar, coal, and engine oil
Iodine and salt
Seaweed
Chili and pepper

SMOKY
Barbecue
Grilled meat
Bonfire
Charcoal
Tobacco

SWEET
Exotic canned fruits in syrup
Maple syrup
Candy sticks
Banana caramel pie
Vanilla ice cream
Sweet ginger barley
Christmas or rich fruit cake
Summer pudding

SAVORY
Mushrooms
Meat
Earthiness
Olives
Nuts
Cheese
Poached fruits
Forest walk, damp leaves
Fall bonfires
Seaside and beach
Fish and seaweed

SUBCATEGORIES

From these three broad categories, I like to take a stroll down a neighborhood shopping street:

THE PRODUCE STORE (SWEET)
Green fruit
Apples, pears, gooseberries, grapes, and unripe fruit such as banana and melon
Orange fruit
Marmalade, blood oranges, mandarins, tangerines
Sweet yellow fruit
Ripe melon, canned pears, plums, bananas, pineapple
Red and berry fruits
Summer fruits, raisins, currants, blackberries, strawberries, raspberries
Citrus and exotic fruits
Grapefruit, limes, lemons, kiwis, guavas, lychees
Nuts

THE FLORIST
Scented flowers
Heather
Lavender
Powdery and sherbety, zingy
Handbag, perfume, lipstick
Grass and hay
Christmas trees, firs, forest walk

THE CANDY STORE (SWEET)
Candy sticks
Parma violets
Toffee
Banana caramel pie
Vanilla ice cream
Maple syrup
Licorice
Candied ginger

THE BAKERY
Dough
Yeastiness
Fresh bread
Toast and melted butter
Cookies and biscuits
Creme brûlée and cake

THE PET STORE
Muskiness
Breakfast cereal
Oatmeal
Pencil shavings, wood chips, sap, sawdust

THE FURNITURE STORE
Furniture polish
New wood
Cleaning products
Pine

THE HIPPIE JEWELER
Sandalwood and incense sticks
Nutmeg, cinnamon, and sweet spices
Spent matches
Leather

THE HARDWARE STORE
Oil and lubricant
Rubber
Creosote
Charcoal

THE TOBACCONIST
Tobacco and cigars
Cigar box
Saddle leather
Smoke

The art of drinking whisky

TRADITIONAL QUAICH

It may not be politically correct to say it these days, but alcohol has played a major and positive role in society for hundreds of years. It has been used for medicinal purposes and as a tonic.

It was consumed before battle to give warriors courage and taken by defeated armies to drown their sorrows or by conquering armies to celebrate victory. Former enemies coming together to make peace blessed their deals with alcohol.

In Scotland and Ireland, clans shared whisky at the end of conflict, passing around a shared cup—a quaich—in a communal ritual that is echoed in many Christian churches to this day. But whisky stands apart from many other drinks. it takes years to make, and centuries to make well, so it deserves respect, like wine.

A culture has grown up around whisky. Today, there are different glasses for different occasions, but in short, if you want to appreciate whisky by nosing it, you need a narrow, relatively short glass like those illustrated below. While a tumbler is fine if you are adding ice, it is not a glass that is particularly suited to nosing.

GLENCAIRN TASTING GLASS

MODERN TASTING GLASS

CLASSIC TUMBLER

TRADITIONAL SNIFTER

CLASSIC TULIP TASTING GLASS

CLASSIC TASTING GLASS

Whisky styles

All whisky is made with grain, yeast, and water, but under that umbrella are many variations. Here are the main ones.

Ardbeg Nasda SINGLE MALT

Compass Box Hedonism GRAIN WHISKY

Johnnie Walker Blue Label BLENDED WHISKY

Monkey Shoulder BLENDED MALT

Redbreast 12 year-old POT STILL WHISKEY

The Irishman IRISH BLENDED WHISKEY

SINGLE-MALT WHISKY

Whisky made only of yeast, water, and malted barley that is the product of only one distillery. Scotland is the leading player in this sector, but single malts are made across the world, in countries including the United States, Japan, Australia, South Africa, and many European nations.

In Europe, malt must be matured for a minimum of three years in oak casks, and it must also be of at least 40% ABV (alcohol by volume).

GRAIN WHISKY

Whisky made with grain or grains other than malted barley only. Grains might include wheat, corn, unmalted barley, and rye. In Europe, the minimum maturation period of three years also applies. Great Scottish examples include **Cameronbrig** from Fife, **Imperial** from Morayshire, and **Compass Box Hedonism**, produced by a young Edinburgh company that specializes in artisanal blends.

BLENDED WHISKY

A combination of single malts from different distilleries mixed together with grain whisky. Look out for **Johnnie Walker Black, Red, Gold,** and **Blue** labels, **Famous Grouse,** or **Ballantine's** for a taste of blended whisky that steers away from the bland and is rich in flavor.

BLENDED MALT WHISKY

Whisky made using malted whisky from a number of different distilleries. **Monkey Shoulder**—which is made from a blend of single malts from Glenfiddich, Balvenie, and Kinivie—and **Johnnie Walker Green Label** from Scotland exemplify the style.

POT STILL WHISKEY

An Irish style of whiskey, which in its purest form is made using malted barley and another grain, usually unmalted barley, mixed to form the grist before mashing, then fermentation. Although the term has been used to describe any whiskey made in a pot still, this does not do this unique style of whiskey justice.

IRISH BLENDED WHISKEY

Most commercial Irish whiskeys are blends, and are usually made up of pot still whiskey mixed with grain whiskey—although **The Irishman 70** is made up of 70% single malt and 30% Midleton pot still whiskey, a unique north-meets-south whiskey that may be described as a blend, but is in effect in a category of its own.

Buffalo Trace BOURBON

Jack Daniel's TENNESSEE WHISKEY

Sazerac Rye RYE

Bernheim Original WHEAT WHISKEY

Mellow Corn CORN WHISKEY

Glen Breton CANADIAN RYE WHISKEY

BOURBON

Whiskey made in the United States using grains including at least 51% corn, although in practice the amount is usually considerably higher. Bourbon is produced under strict guidelines and must be matured in fresh oak barrels for at least two years. The most celebrated bourbons are **Jim Beam, Maker's Mark, Buffalo Trace,** and **Woodford Reserve.**

TENNESSEE WHISKEY

Whiskey made in the state of Tennessee in a similar style to bourbon, but which differs from bourbon because it has undergone the Lincoln county process—where the spirit is passed through maplewood charcoal before it is put into the cask. Jack Daniel's is the most famous example.

RYE WHISKEY (UNITED STATES)

Whiskey made in a similar way to bourbon, but with a minimum of 51% rye in the grist. It must also be matured for more than two years. Look out for **Rittenhouse Rye** and **Pappy Van Winkle's Family Reserve 13-year-old Rye,** both produced in Louisville, Kentucky, as well as **Sazerac Kentucky Straight Rye** from Frankfort, Kentucky.

WHEAT WHISKEY

Whiskey made in a similar way to bourbon, but including a minimum of 51% wheat. It must be aged for at least two years. One of the best-known wheat whiskeys is **Bernheim Original,** a relative newcomer to the scene, originating from Louisville, Kentucky.

CORN WHISKEY

Whiskey made up of at least 80% corn. There are no aging requirements and, if corn whiskey is aged, it is usually for no more than six months. **Heaven Hill's Mellow Corn** and **Georgia Moon** are key examples of the style, as is **Dixie Dew** from the same distillery.

RYE WHISKY (CANADA)

"Canadian rye" is a term used to describe any whisky that has the "aroma, taste, and character" of Canadian whisky, whether it contains rye or not. There is an irony here because rye produces aggressive and spicy whiskeys in the United States, and Canadian whisky can be soft, rounded, and quite characterless. In practice, Canadian whisky will probably have a number of different whiskies in it, with only a small proportion of rye among them. Canadian whisky also permits a small amount of a totally different liquid and this may include American bourbon and fruit juice. Count **Canadian Club, Glen Breton,** and **Forty Creek** among the main contenders here.

Whisky and food matching

The idea that you can match whisky to food appalls some people. Traditionalists, in particular, have a problem with it. Their loss—and here's why.

It is all about perceptions. Mention the idea of cheese and wine, and most of us accept the pairing as naturally as we do salt and pepper, or Laurel and Hardy. But for years beer and food as a match were not widely accepted at all, and this pairing is only now making headway through the dedication and hard work of people within the beer industry. And so it is with whisky. Yet talk to food scientists and they will tell you that the grain is a far better suitor for many foods than the grape is. The fats in cheese, in particular, react more comfortably with beer and whisky than they do with wine or brandy. Seafood is the other natural partner for whisky.

In recent years, there have been commendable attempts to bring whisky to the dining table, and there have been some wonderful dinners featuring six food courses and six whiskies. What we learned from these is that whisky is generally most successful when served with one course or with one particular food type during a meal.

Here are a few tried-and-true combinations.

ARDBEG WITH CROTTIN

LAGAVULIN WITH ROQUEFORT

FIVE WINNING COMBINATIONS

ARDBEG WITH CROTTIN **Ardbeg** is a big, peaty Islay whisky and, when combined with this pungent, slightly nutty goat cheese, the result is wonderfully loud, rustic, and spicy. Works best when the crottin is crumbling.

LAGAVULIN WITH ROQUEFORT Quite possibly the best whisky–cheese combination of them all. The **Lagavulin** brings out the saltiness of the cheese; the Roquefort batters down the sharp whisky taste and leaves smoke and fruit. Astounding.

RITTENHOUSE RYE WITH PARMESAN Don't skimp on the cheese here—fork out for one of the better quality Parmesans. The fully spicy rye and the more delicate hard cheese make for a stimulating pepper-and-salt mix.

GLEN ELGIN WITH CHEDDAR Be careful with the Cheddar—nothing too strong. This combination works with most fruity Speysiders, but **Glen Elgin** is an eloquent and rounded malt, ideally suited to finding the sweetness in the cheese.

BRUICHLADDICH WITH SHRIMP Much is made of seafood with peated Islay whisky, but this is a more elegant partnership: the gentle salty taste of the shrimp contrasts with the fruity notes of the whisky, but rides on its maritime qualities.

RITTENHOUSE RYE
WITH PARMESAN

GLEN ELGIN
WITH CHEDDAR

BRUICHALDDICH
WITH SHRIMP

Making a meal of a whisky

The notion of whisky and food going together may be alien to some, but let's lay that to rest by starting with four worthy and well-tested combinations sufficient to change anyone's opinion.

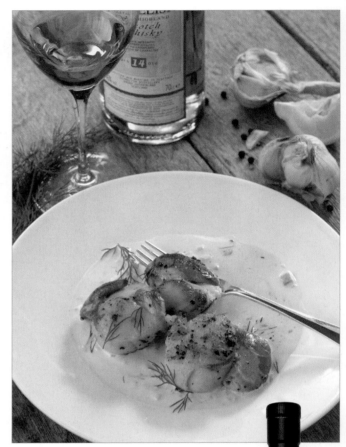

Rich, fruity Speyside whisky
with foie gras

It is not that many years ago that there was nearly a riot at a Whisky Live London tasting event staged by **Laphroaig**, at which the brand owners dared to pair up the malt with cheese, horrifying some people in the room, who were there for Laphroaig and Laphroaig alone.

Whisky, though, is remarkably flexible when it comes to accompanying food. On the face of it, foie gras would seem ill-suited as a whisky accompaniment, but it works surprisingly well with a rich and fruity Speysider, with the whisky taking the place of a fruit compote with certain roasted meat dishes, and the fats and oils in the foie gras bringing out the flavors in the malt. Try **Cardhu** or Laphroaig for starters.

Spicy or peaty whisky
with seared scallops

Seafood and whisky are a marriage made in heaven. Langoustines and oysters suit a peated whisky such as **Bowmore**; the saltiness works well with seaweedy and seaside notes in the whisky. The peppery, spicy nature of **Talisker** also works well with seafood, giving it a salt-and-pepper tang. For a slightly more subtle and sophisticated pairing, try a robust whisky such as **Clynelish** with shrimp, mussels, or seared scallops. It's a more balanced pairing than some peaty whisky and seafood ones.

Actually, Clynelish is a very versatile single malt for food pairings. Amazingly, it works well with roast beef and mustard or horseradish sandwiches, and with spicy chicken dishes.

Fruity Speyside whisky
with egg rolls

Perhaps unsurprisingly, much of the work in the
area of food and whisky pairing has come from
France, and in particular from the great French
whisky writer Martine Nouet. Her whisky
dinners, using a varied range of malts from
Ardbeg to **Aberlour,** are legendary. She is at
ease with using whisky as an ingredient and
with serving it to go with food.

  Her advice: experiment with different foods,
and look for pairings that either complement
each other or that contrast.

  You would not necessarily expect a
combination of Chinese egg rolls and a fruity
malt such as **Cragganmore** to work, but the
whisky contrasts with the filling, bringing out
the flavors in both, particularly ginger.

Big, sweet Highland whisky
with desserts

Dalwhinnie is alcoholic bottled honey,
and it works extremely well with a whole
range of desserts and sweets. Try it with a
chocolate bar and you will be amazed.

  Bread and butter pudding would not
seem to have the guts for a malt whisky
pairing, but with Dalwhinnie it is like
eating honey sandwiches, with the
currants in the pudding adding an
extra dimension to the flavor.

  If you don't have a sweet tooth
and would prefer to go for the
cheeseboard instead, then a big
peaty whisky such as **Lagavulin** with
a strong-tasting blue cheese such as
Roquefort is stunning.

Classic whisky cocktails

Whisky traditionalists don't hold much truck with cocktails either, which is a bit bizarre, really.

Why? Well, the malt whisky produced in the Highlands a few hundred years ago tasted so awful that they added anything—mint, honey, heather—to hide the taste. The story goes that Bonnie Prince Charlie handed over the recipe to Drambuie as a thank- you to the people who saved him—a lot of old balderdash, admittedly, but the point is that it is plausible that in the mid-eighteenth century whisky was served with flavorings—and that's all a cocktail is, after all. These days a good cocktail is not about concealing the taste of whisky; it's about showing it off. The classic and longest-surviving whisky cocktails, therefore, are the simplest and the ones that add a twist to the whisky.

The **old-fashioned**, possibly the first- ever cocktail, is served in a lowball glass.

The **Manhattan** is always an elegant apéritif. Serve in a martini glass.

The **Mint Julep** works best in a squat lowball glass.

The **Waldorf** cocktail first appeared at the start of the twentieth century, at the Waldorf-Astoria bar.

The **whisky sour** is bourbon-based. Serve in a low fluted glass.

Old-fashioned

1 sugar cube
2 or 3 dashes of angostura bitters
2 fresh orange slices
3 fl oz (90 ml) bourbon
maraschino cherry, to garnish

Put the sugar cube at the bottom of an old-fashioned, or lowball, glass. Saturate with the bitters. Add 1 orange slice. Muddle these ingredients, then fill the glass with ice cubes. Add the bourbon. Stir well. Garnish with the second orange slice and a maraschino cherry.

Manhattan

4 drops of angostura bitters
2 fl oz (60 ml) Grant's Family Reserve blended whisky
1 fl oz (30 ml) Noilly Prat Rouge
2 teaspoons juice from maraschino cherries

Pour the ingredients into an ice-filled cocktail shaker. Shake well. Strain into glass.

Mint Julep

4 fresh mint leaves, plus a sprig of mint, to garnish
1 teaspoon superfine sugar
1½ fl oz (45 ml) bourbon

Lightly muddle together the 4 mint leaves and sugar with a few drops of water in the bottom of the glass. Next, almost fill the glass with crushed ice, and pour the bourbon over the ice. Garnish with the sprig of mint.

Waldorf

¼ fl oz (8 ml) absinthe or substitute
2 fl oz (60 ml) rye whisky
¾ fl oz (25 ml) sweet vermouth
2 dashes of angostura bitters

Pour the absinthe into a mixing glass, and swirl it around to coat the sides. Toss out any excess. Add the remaining ingredients and ice. Stir well. Strain into a chilled cocktail glass.

Whisky Sour

1½ fl oz (45 ml) bourbon (such as Maker's Mark)
1½ fl oz (45 ml) lemon juice
25 ml (¾ fl oz) sugar syrup
maraschino cherry, to garnish

Pour the bourbon, lemon juice, and sugar syrup into a cocktail shaker with ice cubes. Shake well. Strain into a chilled sour glass. Garnish with the cherry.

Contemporary whisky cocktails

These modern takes on traditional whisky cocktails deliver a new twist to hip whisky drinking.

Whisky is to bartenders—or mixologists—what Mount Everest is to the climber: the ultimate challenge. Mix a cocktail with vodka, and the spirit quietly goes under without a struggle, providing an alcoholic kick, but giving the mixologist free license to paint pictures. Whisky—especially single-malt whisky—does not do that. It is the untamed tiger of the drinks world and, if you're going to work with it, you're going to need a lot of patience.

In the early part of the millenium, *Whisky Magazine* held a cocktail competition that divided the room between those who made good cocktails despite having whisky in them and those who made good cocktails because they had whisky in them. Things have moved on since then, and here are five specially created whisky cocktails made by the some of the sector's hottest drinks makers.

Pure Bard by Esther Medina Cuesta of Bureau Club, London.

The Broadmoor by Stuart Hudson of Viajante, London.

Watermelon Smash by Nidal Ramini of Brown-Forman Spirits.

Bonnie Blush by Alistair Malcolm of Lab, Soho, London.

Cool Walker by Vamsi Putta of Salt of Salt Whisky Lounge and Dining Room, London.

Pure Bard

1 fl oz (30 ml) *Talisker single malt*
1 fl oz (30 ml) *Noilly Prat Rouge*
1 fl oz (30 ml) *Guignolet de Dijon cherry liqueur*
1 fl oz (30 ml) *blood orange juice*
strip of orange zest

Shake together the liquid ingredients, then fill an elegant tumbler with ice cubes and pour everything in. Garnish with a twist of orange zest and enjoy the flavors.

The Broadmoor

2 fl oz (60 ml) *Dalwhinnie 15-Year-Old single malt*
scant ½ fl oz (12.5 ml) *Chartreuse liqueur*
2 teaspoons *sugar syrup*
3 dashes of *orange bitters*
star anise

Stir over ice, and strain into a coupette glass. Garnish with a star anise.

Watermelon Smash

½ lemon
2 fl oz (60 ml) *Woodford Reserve bourbon*
8 fresh mint leaves
1 bar spoon vanilla sugar or 4 teaspoons vanilla syrup
large piece of watermelon, sliced

Cut the lemon into quarters, squeeze, and add the juice to an ice-filled cocktail shaker. Add the bourbon, mint, and vanilla. Shake together, strain, and garnish with melon.

Bonnie Blush

1 fl oz (25 ml) *Johnnie Walker Black Label*
½ fl oz (12.5 ml) freshly squeezed lemon juice
½ fl oz (12.5 ml) crème de mûre (blackberry liqueur)
3 bar spoons blackberry jam or conserve
high-quality Champagne
fresh blackberry, halved, to garnish

Shake together all ingredients except the Champagne and berry. Half-fill a tall Champagne flute with Champagne. Slowly add the contents of the shaker. Garnish.

Cool Walker

1½ fl oz (45 ml) *Johnnie Walker Black Label*
½ fl oz (15 ml) Drambuie
2 teaspoons lime juice
2 teaspoons gomme syrup
ginger ale
slice of fresh lemon

Pour the Johnnie Walker, Drambuie, lime juice, and gomme syrup into a Boston shaker, and add ice. Shake and strain into a highball glass filled with ice. Top with ginger ale, and garnish with a lemon wheel.

THE WORLD'S BEST WHISKIES

A WORLD OF WHISKY

A world of whisky

Whisky is now produced across the entire world, ensuring an even greater range of tastes to enjoy.

Making the selection

Keeping a tab on the number of whiskies available across the world is like counting leaves in the garden during a hurricane. The world of whisky is not only in a permanent state of evolution, but segregated, too, with Scottish blends, in particular, finding favor in certain territories, but unavailable elsewhere.

If counting the number of whiskies is extremely difficult, then picking a definitive 750 best whiskies has been, if the truth be told, quite a challenge. You simply could not taste every single one, but, even if you could, deciding which should and should not make the cut is an entirely subjective and deeply unscientific process.

What would be hard to do in any drinks category is made all the harder in the field of whisky because of the presence of independent bottlers. These are companies that buy up casks of whisky, then bottle them under their own labels, often in tiny quantities because they are the product of one, two, or three casks. Every cask produces slightly different whisky to the next, so independent bottlers do not seek to produce uniform representative malt from the distillery in question, but rather offer the whisky lover a variation of it. If an official distillery bottling is to whisky what an official CD release is to a rock band, then the independent bottling is a live bootleg: often a rougher and rawer version, clearly by the same artist, but reproduced differently; sometimes better than the original, sometimes not—but highly attractive to the true fan nonetheless.

As independent bottlers often bottle just one cask and produce only 250 or 300 bottles from it, many whiskies are literally gone before they can be written about, and are rapidly replaced by another wave of bottles. This area of the industry is an ever-changing quicksand, and for this reason many great whiskies produced even a couple of years ago by independent bottlers have had to be ignored because they have gone forever, although I have touched on this area in a bid to recognize the biggest and best independent bottlers.

The selection process can be simplified further by ignoring the scores of poor-quality drinks passing themselves off as whisky that are made outside the guidelines laid down by the Scottish (and therefore European) and American whisky industries. Both continents work to a code where the highest standards are maintained, and they provide a good base camp from which to work. While some rare whiskies are included, other extremely exclusive ones haven't made the cut.

But that does not mean that the net has not been cast far and wide: it has, and there has been a conscious effort to include some of the most esoteric whiskies and to recognize countries where the whisky light has only just been switched on. Some of them are distinctly weird; others are a shock to the palate that has grown used to the finest Scottish malts and the tastiest bourbons. But every whisky mentioned in this book has been well made by a master craftsman and is included on merit. For ease of reference, whiskies are listed by country of origin, with the biggest regions of Scotland and the United States to the fore. Within each country section, whiskies are listed by whisky style; within these sections, brands and/or distilleries are listed in alphabetical order. The symbols are designed to help make selection and categorization of each whisky easier. Each entry includes tasting notes, but I've tried to avoid being too prescriptive. More importantly, I have attempted to capture some of the personality of the whisky, and the people or events that shaped it, to give it greater context and interest.

While everything possible has been done to ensure accuracy, the pace of evolution in the world of whisky inevitably means that some whisky distilleries and whisky brands will have changed, or changed hands. Some will have been swallowed up, some closed, new ones opened. A significant number of the whiskies included here are produced by small independent distillers and might be hard to find. I haven't deliberately attempted to be obscure, but, on the other hand, I have had considerably more time and greater resources to seek out these whiskies. If you struggle to find some of them, my apologies in advance.

Tasting symbols

The following symbols have been used in the whisky listings to help describe each of the 750 listings, from classic blends to special cask-aged bottlings. They correspond to the following definintions listed below.

CONNOISSEUR CLASSIC
Cult or classic whiskies that should be high up the wish list for a whisky connoisseur.

SESSION SIP
Everyday whiskies that often feature in the cupboard at home.

PREMIUM TIPPLE
Special whiskies for occasional drinking or best reserved for celebrations.

OLD AND VENERABLE
Whiskies aged 25 years or more.

SUPER STYLE
Whiskies that exemplify a particular style of whisky.

FOR PEAT'S SAKE Whiskies whose smokiness or peaty phenolic flavor is a major component of the overall taste.

MIND HOW YOU GO Whiskies bottled at the strength they came out of the cask or at more than 50% ABV, 100 poof.

A LITTLE UNUSUAL Quirky or unusual whiskies with a unique taste or featuring an unusual or unique aspect to their production.

RAREST OF THE RARE
Hard-to-find and very special whiskies.

GONE BUT NOT FORGOTTEN
Whiskies from a distillery that has closed.

The face of modern whisky

New distilleries, new whisky–making nations, and new marketing–savvy companies are ensuring that whisky looks as exciting and varied as it tastes.

It was not so long ago that buying a whisky meant either selecting from a weak and predictable selection of bottles and labels at the supermarket or liquor store or venturing into a "specialist" shop for something more exciting. But whisky packaging has evolved in leaps and bounds in recent years. If you like the formal, somewhat grandiose and elegant style of the traditional whisky bottle, that's fine. There are plenty of them still out there, such as the iconic names and iconic packaging of **Glenfiddich**, **Johnnie Walker**, **Jack Daniel's**, and **Jim Beam**, pretty much unchanged. But these days a new generation of whisky companies such as **Penderyn** and **Compass Box** has helped to transform the shape of packaging, and companies across the world have adopted bottles in such a range of shapes and sizes that whisky shelves are as vibrant and colorful as those of any other drink product. The traditional qualities are now being served up in a modern context.

THE WHISKY LABEL

There are rules as to what can be stated on whisky labels, varying by country. Generally, if there is an age on the label, that age refers to the youngest whisky in the mix. There may be many older whiskies, but one drop of 12-year-old whisky is enough to "age" the overall bottle.

LABROT & GRAHAM

WOODFORD RESERVE

DISTILLER'S SELECT

Personal Selection

Dominic Roskrow   45.2% ALC/VOL

PENDERYN

SINGLE MALT WELSH WHISKY

Aur Cymru

70cl 46%vol

TRIPLE DISTILLED SINGLE CASK WHISKY

Telsington

Distilled in May 2006
Bottled in distillery
50cl, 42% Vol.
No. 210/560

HANDCRAFTED IN THE PRINCIPALITY OF LIECHTENSTEIN

GLENCADAM

ESTᴰ 1830

TALISKER

THE ONLY SINGLE MALT SCOTCH WHISKY
FROM THE ISLE OF SKYE

*From the western shores of the Isle of Skye, in the tall shadows
of the Cuillin Hills, comes a single malt like no other.
An alluring, sweet, full-bodied spirit with a warming afterglow,
so easy to enjoy yet, like Skye itself, so hard to leave.*

AGED **10** YEARS

SINGLE MALT SCOTCH WHISKY
TALISKER DISTILLERY CARBOST ISLE OF SKYE

45.8% vol   70cl

THE WORLD'S BEST WHISKIES

SCOTLAND

Scotland

When it comes to whisky, it all starts and ends with Scotland.

We can jet all over the world searching for great whisky, and there is no doubt that in Kentucky, Ireland, and Japan we can certainly find plenty of it—and even some that is better than a good proportion of Scotland's. We can marvel at the whiskies of distilleries such as **Lark** and **Bakery Hill** in Australia, **Amrut** in India, **Mackmyra** in Sweden, **Blaue Maus** and **Slyrs** in Germany, **Millstone** in the Netherlands, and **The Belgian Owl** in Belgium. But when all is said and done, we always return to Scotland.

Why? Well, because not only does Scotland produce a breathtaking quantity of stunning whiskies, but also it effortlessly seems to be setting the pace for whisky as we go forward, celebrating its traditions, but looking toward the next goal and challenge as well. And because overall the standard of its whiskies, blends, vatted malts, and grains—as well as single malts—is consistently so high.

While it's true that from time to time another nation will produce a whisky that is a match for the very finest from Scotland, it does not happen every day. Scotland's whiskies are like the New Zealand national rugby team the All Blacks—they can be beaten, but rarely, and over any era they still dominate their field.

When choosing the 750 whiskies for this book, there was no pre-planned decision over numbers. Lists were made of all the potential candidates for inclusion, then they were tasted and chosen on their merit. The fact that about two-thirds of the final number should come from Scotland is down to quality alone. The proportion is spot-on.

There are just over 100 single-malt distilleries in Scotland, more than the rest of the world put together, and there are hundreds of single malts. Probably thousands. For that reason, single malt is the dominant style and is reflected here by the largest number of entries. But it should also be remembered that 90%-plus of all Scotch whisky sold is blended whisky, and most of it conforms to the same high standard as malts. You do not get to be a global household name such as Johnnie Walker or Chivas Regal by being average. Some blends go even further, using the finest aged malts and commanding the same very high price tags that even the rarest malts do.

Scotland is the home of whisky, where every whisky lover returns eventually. No matter what is happening elsewhere, that will not change anytime soon. If ever.

KIRKWALL ● **8**

INVERNESS ●

ROTHES ● **7**   KEITH ● **12**

DUFFTOWN ● **3**

FORGUE BY HUNTLY ● **5**

KENNETHMONT ● **2, 6**

ABERDEEN ●

S
C
O
T
L
A
N
D

OBAN ● **10**

ISLAY

EDINBURGH ●

BOWMORE ● **4**

PORT ELLEN ● **1, 9**

GLASGOW ●

CAMPBELTOWN ● **11**

ABOVE Some of Scotland's whiskies are matured in the most extreme parts of the country, such as on the Orkney Isles, where severe winds are commonplace.

Single malt

Scottish single-malt whisky is the world's most exciting, dynamic, and complex spirit. While wonderfully diverse concoctions exist in the fields of rum, tequila, and to some extent brandy, no other drink style can amaze and delight so consistently and so frequently as Scottish single malt does. And no other drink exhibits its qualities quite so flamboyantly and stylishly.

Single malts are now produced in a number of countries, but none of them can hold a candle to the better Scottish malts. If you are not convinced, line up a world selection of malts alongside the best of Scotland, and taste them. Even if they match up in the first instance, add a few drops of water, leave them for 20 minutes, and compare again. You can almost guarantuee that a proportion of the non-Scottish malts will have fallen apart.

The attention to detail in production, the involvement of copper, the craftsmanship honed over centuries, the calm and patient maturation, and the loving attention to detail all combine to form what is nothing less than a fortress in a drink. To you and me, it is a glass of whisky. To a scientist, it is a feat of molecular engineering, a complex, unyielding liquid that is so well structured that it delivers on the palate every time you approach it.

There is an air of mystery and romance about Scottish single-malt whisky. Produced from the simplest of ingredients, it serves up tastes and aromas that really have no right to be there. How is this? And why is it that wine matches or outperforms beer in terms of diversity of flavor, and yet brandy comes nowhere near malt whisky when it comes to taste?

Scottish single-malt whisky as a hobby is still in its infancy. Most malt whisky is produced as a component for blended whisky, and only a handful of malts are widely recognized in their own right. A good number of malts have never or have rarely been bottled singly, and many have never had the chance to show off because they have always been stored in average wood on their journey to the blending room. But that may change as interest grows, and there are many cases of distillery owners recasking malt in order to give it a chance to shine in the future.

Much has been made of the growth of new whisky-making nations. Indeed, in this book, a strong argument is made for a number of countries and why they deserve to be on whisky's highest tasting table.

The head of that table is Scotland, however, and year after year the country serves up a feast of fresh single-malt whisky. and it is a trend we will continue to see.

ABERFELDY
www.dewarswow.com

Drive through Aberfeldy distillery and up the lane beyond it, and you will find, high up in the hills, a group of cottages that are available for rent. In the morning, the cloud gathers in the valley below, and you can watch golden eagles dip in and out as they swoop to find breakfast. You can then walk down to the village with the distillery below you to the right. I am not sure that there is a better way to start the day.

Aberfeldy distillery lies in the village of the same name, to the north of Perth and not far from Pitlochry. It is also the home of Dewar's World of Whisky, an excellent visitor facility telling the story of the Dewar family and its famous blended whisky. The distillery itself is kept in pristine condition and is also open to the public. There are enough interactive facilities to keep the children occupied, too, although whether it is a good thing that my youngest son now knows how to blend a whisky and is, according to one machine in the center, better at it than me is up for debate.

The distillery—of course—also produces a great malt.

Aberfeldy 12-year-old 40% ABV

Rich, oily, and honeyed, this malt has lots of orange and exotic fruits, some soft spices, and a soft, earthy peat carpet.

Aberfeldy 18-year-old single cask 59.6% ABV

A very recent addition to the range, this is an absolute stormer. It is a smooth, rich malt with honey, nuts, vanilla, and spices, but best of all it has a weighty punch to it.

Aberfeldy 21-year-old 40% ABV

Rich honey is often a defining characteristic of Aberfeldy bottlings, and here it is at its most potent. But there are also some lovely orange notes, a little bit of peat, and just enough oak to give the proceedings some gravitas. I wish it was bottled at a higher strength, though.

ABERLOUR
www.aberlour.com

Of all the tours offered by Scotland's malt distilleries, Aberlour's is among the very best. Owner Pernod Ricard has several distilleries in the Speyside region, and it seems that those involved sat down way back and thought about how they could offer the visitor a different experience at each. **The Glenlivet**, with its smuggling past and large visitor center, looks after itself. **Strathisla** is the home of Chivas, and that provides an obvious angle. And Aberlour? Well, there are those of us who regard the distillery as Speyside royalty. VIP tours are commonplace now, but Aberlour was offering them years back. Today, your visit will be a lengthy one, with knowledgeable guides. At the end, you can taste the whisky, pour an exclusive cask-strength version from a bourbon or a sherry cask, and bottle it.

Aberlour 10-year-old 43% ABV

This is classic Speyside, with an emphasis on the green fruit end of the Speyside spectrum. Crisp, fresh, and distinctive, with traces of trademark mintiness and elements from both bourbon and sherry casks used for production. Creamy on the one hand, red berries on the other. World-class.

Aberlour 15-year-old Cuvée Marie d'Ecosse 43% ABV

Mainly sold in the French market, where Aberlour and *amour* are two sides of the same coin, this comes from a mix of bourbon and sherry casks. It is delicate and flowery on the nose, with lingering toffee and licorice notes, late spice, and a smooth finish.

Aberlour 15-year-old Sherry Wood Finish 40% ABV

Another beautiful mix of sherry and bourbon, with butterscotch, candy, tangerine, and red berry fruits, all delivered on a gossamer-light pillow, with some trademark mint and spices late on.

Aberlour 18-year-old Sherry Wood Matured 43% ABV

Most Aberlour expressions are akin to elegant ladies dressed in finery, but this is altogether more fiesty. Think Nicole Kidman on horseback in the movie *Australia*. OK, any excuse. The 18 years in the cask and the fact that the casks in question are all sherry go a long way to explaining this one. Nutty, spicy, and fruity in equal measure, this is a complex malt, bright orangey amber in color, that ebbs and flows, but ultimately leaves the oak and sherry in charge.

Aberlour a'bunadh ("The Origin")
NO AGE STATEMENT 59.6% ABV BATCH 21

In Gaelic, "a'bunadh" means "the origin," and it is the name given by Aberlour's owners to a series of malts released in batches. Each batch varies, but the overall effect is the same—simply, these probably represent the best value for money malts on the market. Indeed, they seem to be well underpriced.

Each batch is a vatting of sherry-cask Aberlours, with a range of whiskies aged from very young to more than 15 years old. The batches vary in strength, but often tip over 60% ABV—that's one and a half bottles of standard 40% whisky. The flavors are intense, with frequent whiffs of smoke and sulfur over concentrated red currants and blackcurrants, cherries, blood orange, nuttiness, spice, and some mint. Each one is rich and elegant, almost liqueur-like, and unforgettable. You would think that such big flavors would appeal only to committed malt lovers, but I met a woman on a bus once who hated whisky of all types except this one. What's more, this one she drank regularly. Can't blame her.

Aberlour 16-year-old Double Cask Matured 43% ABV

Fluffy apples and fruit crumble on the nose, green fruits, vanilla, and mint on the palate, with a refreshing and moreish finish. Almost a palate-cleanser, this one.

ARDBEG
www.ardbeg.com

Could this be my nomination for the best whisky moment ever? Drinking cask-strength Ardbeg at the distillery after two days of a sponsored charity event that comprised traveling from Jura to Ardbeg by cycling 30 miles, walking 30 miles, and rowing 3 miles from Bruichladdich across Loch Indaal to Bowmore. The first day went fine until lunch, when we collected our bikes at Bunnahabhain and started up the long hill from the distillery. A nightmare that was not helped by Bunnahabhain's distillery manager John MacLellan, who insisted on sharing a couple of cask-strength malts just as we were leaving. Problem was that I had not been on a bicycle for 35 years. By the time we reached Bruichladdich for the first stop, I could barely walk. So the rowing—and that's another story—and the lengthy walk from Bowmore were a blistery nightmare. Worth it, though—for those Ardbeg drams. It is hard not to love Ardbeg regardless. The distillery is known for its big, peaty whiskies, it is one of the prettiest distilleries in the world, and as a bonus it provides some of the best food on Islay.

Ardbeg 10-year-old 46% ABV

The distillery reopened in 1997, but it was only a couple of years ago that the standard ten-year-old, made of all new spirit, was first released. This is a humdinger of a whisky, big, oily, tarry, and sweet, with wave after wave of solid peat. Awesome.

Ardbeg Corryvreckan 57.1% ABV

Corryvreckan is one the most violent and dangerous whirlpools in the world, and it lies close to the islands of Islay and Jura. You can pass over it safely only at certain times of the day during low tide, and even then it is an experience—a wide stretch of small eddying pools making up a collective monster. With such a raw display of nature come countless fables and legends, but undoubtedly it has claimed many lives. The writer George Orwell is among the many people who had to be rescued after an encounter with it.

The whisky is like the reputation. Calm and placid on the surface, underneath it is dense, rich in plummy jam fruits wrapped in intense smoke, with citrus notes running through it. Wonderful.

Ardbeg Uigeadail 54.2% ABV

Named after the source from which Ardbeg takes its water, this is almost the definitive distillery bottling. Bottled at cask strength, it is a hugely flavored whisky, with all the rich, tarry, and phenolic peat tones at which the distillery excels. But behind the curtain is a malt of sublime complexity. You will find sweetness, citrus fruits, earthy and astringent notes, smoked fish, seaside flavors, and dark cocoa.

Ardbeg Almost There 54.1% ABV

Some distilleries are like baseball teams—they have a group of diehard supporters who were into them before the current managers, and will still be there whoever takes charge in the future. As a result, they act like custodians, not shy of offering their views if anyone messes with their malt. Ardbeg is one such distillery. When Glenmorangie bought and reopened it, the move was obviously greeted positively, but there was curiosity—and some concern—as to what the new owners might do to their beloved malt. To help reassure them, whisky-maker Bill Lumsden and his team released a series of works in progress—Very Young at six years old, Still Young at seven and a half years, and this one at nine years. The first two bottles have pretty much disappeared, and this one is not far behind it, so they are true collector's items. But if you find one, consider drinking it—peated whiskies as young as four years old can be excellent and, while this one might have the odd rough edge, the intense fruit and coal-like tarry smoke make it a treat.

Ardbeg Renaissance 55.9% ABV

This is the fourth and final whisky in the "works in progress" and is effectively a cask-strength version of what has become the standard ten-year-old. What a great moment when this was released. Few Ardbeg fans would have tasted this and been disappointed. It is undeniably vintage Ardbeg—lots of sweet and sour, and fruit and peat notes to compare and contrast.

Ardbeg Airigh Nam Beist 46% ABV

All but disappeared now and replaced by Corryvreckan, the name is another reference to the area where Ardbeg is produced and is pronounced *arry nam bayst*. If you find a bottle, it is worth exploring because it has a soft vanilla-influenced heart and the usual citrus flavor is replaced by rounder, softer yellow fruit.

Ardbeg Blasda 40% ABV

This very nearly did not make the cut, but finally made it through after an intense second round of tasting. The problem here is that approaching it as an Ardbeg is like going to see heavy-metal band Motorhead and lead singer Lemmy playing along to a string quartet. You want the volume up to 11. You should bang your head to Ardbeg, not tap your feet. And this is a muted toe-tapper, with the peat turned well down and the strength at only 40%. The name means "sweet and delicious," which says it all, really. It is truly delicious—it just doesn't taste like Ardbeg, so bear this in mind when you approach it.

Ardbeg Supernova 58.9% ABV

From the faintly ridiculous to the truly sublime. If Blasda were acoustic Motorhead, then this would be Motorhead with your head stuck in the bass bin, the peat scale turned to max. The oily coal-like notes form a tsunami, crashing over the palate into the throat, then refusing to budge. Licorice and cocoa appear, too.

Ardbeg 17-year-old 40% ABV

You rarely see this anymore, but it does come up at auctions from time to time. It is included here because it has reached iconic status, but it probably has more value as a collectible than as a drinking whisky—like Blasda, it is underpowered and peat-lite.

ARDMORE
www.beamglobal.com

If there were any justice in the world, Ardmore would be a household name. It is a Highland distillery situated to the south of Speyside, and it makes a great deal of malt—one of the few distilleries at the time of writing that was still in full production as the rest of the industry slowed up a tad. Most of its output goes into Teacher's, a malty, rugged blend with more character than many of its competitors. But now, under the ownership of Beam Global, the single malt is becoming known in its own right. Realistically, it probably will not ever become as familiar as the Glenlivet or Glenfiddich because it is altogether more challenging. But I do not think that I have been to any distillery where the folks who make the whisky are more proud of their product—and rightly so because Ardmore tastes like no other dram. It is the backbone of a great blend and is winning new admirers by the month.

Ardmore Traditional 46% ABV

A few years ago, the previous owners of this distillery, Allied, launched an experiment under the watchful eye of a skilled team of whiskymen including Robert Hicks and Michael Cockram. The idea was to put a number of malts into small quarter-sized casks, as would have been the way a couple of centuries ago. The small casks mean more interaction between spirit and wood, and a faster process of reaction and flavor absorption. Of the several malts involved in the experiment, only two worked out well: Laphroaig and Ardmore. When Allied broke up, Beam took Teacher's, Ardmore, and Laphroaig, as well as Cockram and Hicks. And here is the first properly backed single-malt offering from the distillery for several years—and the quarter casks are included in the mix.

This whisky is not an easy ride. It has a rootsy savory, bamboo-like nose, and on the palate it is the whisky equivalent of a delicatessen, with savory flavors, olive and artichoke, and waves of grungy peat. It is oily, full, and demanding. Still, it really grows on you, and the grungy brine and peat finish are a delight. Do not try it after the ice cream and chocolate sauce dessert, though.

Finish: delightfully peaty, briny, long, and full.

ARDBEG DISTILLERY

Port Ellen, Isle of Islay, Argyllshire PA42 7EA
www.ardbeg.com

As shards of sunlight pepper the broody, inky–blue waters around Islay, the bows of the boat rise and dip in the swell, and the white walls of the distillery appear and disappear with each surge as sea spray cleans the pores and alerts all the senses.

It is an invigorating and exciting way to arrive on the Hebridean island of Islay and at the three great distilleries that hug its rugged southeastern shoreline.

If whisky were the music industry, Ardbeg and its neighbors Laphroaig and Lagavulin would be its big industrial heavy metal bands, the Metallica, Iron Maiden, and Motorhead of malts. For whisky lovers, this compact two-mile stretch of coastline is a peaty paradise, unrivaled anywhere else in the world.

Of the three, Ardbeg is easily the most cherished. While its neighbors flourished, healthily supported by the international drinks companies that owned them, Ardbeg struggled, stopped producing on a couple of occasions, and was nearly lost entirely.

It was eventually bought and rescued by the Glenmorangie Company, who took it on 12 years ago. It was in a sorry state, its farmhouse-like still houses and production areas badly neglected, in need of some serious repair work. Since then, the distillery has been restored to its full glory, and not only is it a delight to visit, but can also now boast the best food on the whole island, produced in the delightful Old Kiln Cafe.

Like the distillery, the remaining whisky was not in great shape, either. Stocks of whisky in the warehouses were, by any standards, no more than ordinary.

For these reasons, what Glenmorangie's director of malts, Bill Lumsden, and his team have achieved with Ardbeg is nothing less than extraordinary. Unearthing a number of diamonds in the dust, they set about mixing old and new

Most of the buildings at Ardbeg, including the striking main building (opposite page), were built in the nineteenth century, and stand at the head of a protected inlet on the southern side of the beautiful Isle of Islay, an essential shelter from the North Atlantic.

malts throughout the first years of the new millennium to produce malt gems such as Airigh Nam Beist and Uigeadail. But it was not until 2006 that the distillery properly qualified for whisky's Champions League, and it has not looked back since. That year saw the launch of Very Young, a six-year-old whisky made entirely with malt produced since the reopening, and the awards have been pouring in on a regular basis ever since. By 2008, its flagship ten-year-old was being made with all-new malt.

Ardbeg is small—making just over one million liters (264,170 U.S. gallons) a year on one pair of stills, a tenth of the amount that Glenfiddich is capable of, and the new owners show no signs of messing with quantities, having stuck doggedly to the traditional way whisky is made here.

This, though, comes with its own set of problems. The stills are stubborn old beasts, unpredictable and untamable, regularly throwing tantrums and sulkily refusing to play along with the stillmen. They are, literally, high maintenance, but don't dare suggest that the distillery could do with a new pair.

When they do decide to work properly, they produce a complex, distinct, sweet, and peaty spirit. It is matured on site in warehouses just a few yards from the shoreline. The debate over whether coastal maturation influences the flavor of the whisky has been going on for as long as Scotland has been making whisky and is never likely to be resolved, but the warehouses in Ardbeg put up a great argument for those who believe it does—their walls are caked with salt, and you can taste the saline in the air. It is a whisky every bit as exciting as the sea crossing to Islay.

WELL, FANCY THAT . . .

Ardbeg Corryvreckan is named after a large and vicious whirlpool off the coast of Islay and close to the island of Jura. The third-largest of its kind in the world, the Corryvreckan is actually a series of small whirlpools that form over a shelf on the seabed. During certain tides and at certain times of the year, waves more than 30 feet high and traveling at high speed crash noisily through the narrow straits nearby. The whirlpool can usually be crossed only at certain low tides. It has claimed scores of lives over the years and wrecked dozens of boats. The writer George Orwell was left stranded by the whirlpool on Jura while writing the novel *1984*.

ARDMORE DISTILLERY

Kennethmont, Aberdeenshire AB54 4NH
www.ardmorewhisky.com

When Queen Elizabeth embarks on her Diamond Jubilee tour in 2012, perhaps they will reopen the railroad line up to Ardmore distillery for the occasion. The Queen and Prince Philip stayed in the railroad sidings during the Golden Jubilee tour in 1992, the very last people to use the line. Whether they had a glass or two of Ardmore is not recorded.

"John Campbell at Laphroaig goes on about his distillery's link with Prince Charles, but we just tell him we don't muck around with princes—we deal with queens," laughs Alistair Longwell, Ardmore's manager. "When she came, they put down new tarmac for the caterers, so, if you're the queen, it's not just a new lick of paint which greets you.

"She isn't the only royalty we have had here, either. In 1906, the king of Spain, Alphonso XIII, came here after he and his bride survived an assassination attempt on their wedding day. There was a connection to here because one of the local lairds had links to González Byass. The distillery has a rich royal history."

It also makes fine whisky. Ardmore is a rugged, earthy Highland malt that plays a key role in Teacher's Highland Cream, both as a main component in the blend and as a

brokering malt to exchange for the many other malts that help to give Teacher's its signature high malt content.

Since the distillery became part of Beam Global, it has enjoyed considerable success in its own right. Ardmore Traditional has been partly matured in quarter casks in the same way that one of the expressions at sister distillery Laphroaig has.

"It doesn't work for all whiskies because it reinforces the sweetness, so if the whisky is already sweet it can be too much," explains Longwell. "But with a whisky such as Ardmore, it smooths off some of the rugged edges and has a delicious mix of sweetness and spice."

Ardmore may be a traditional distillery on the face of it, but it has never been afraid to experiment, and this year saw the launch of Teacher's Origin, the first new version

Ardmore Distillery in the Scottish Highlands lies at the highest point of what was the Aberdeen-to-Inverness railroad line and has its own sidings. It is one of the few passing points on the line. The line was used to bring coal to the distillery and to transport casks off toward Glasgow. It was used up until the early 1990s, when the distillery stopped using coal.

KEY WHISKY

Ardmore Traditional Cask 46% ABV

BELOW LEFT Some of the casks used to mature spirit at Ardmore, including the quarter cask on the right.

BELOW Ardmore's stills make a weighty, peaty, and savory spirit unlike anything else in Scotland.

of Teacher's for well over a decade. It is a piece of creative genius that stems from the quarter-cask trialings.

"We took the vatted malt for Teacher's and the grain for Teacher's, but kept them apart," says Longwell. "Then they were sent back here to Ardmore, where they were matured separately to each other for a further two or three years in quarter casks. Then the grain and malts were brought together just before bottling. It makes for a full-bodied and rich-tasting blend."

The new Teacher's will be rolled out worldwide into 2011, and there are more plans for Ardmore as a single malt in the pipeline after that.

And, who knows—maybe a Diamond Jubilee bottling in 2012 that is fit for a queen?

ARRAN

www.isleofarrandistillers.com

If you are an Elvis Presley fan, you will know that the only time he set foot in the United Kingdom was when he landed very briefly at Prestwick Airport on Scotland's west coast.

Why Prestwick? Well, that's because back in the day it served as Scotland's main international airport, the airport most likely to stay open, because of the fact that it rarely freezes there or struggles with snow.

If you want to travel to the distillery at Arran, you can fly to Prestwick and take a train to Ardrossan for the ferry crossing. And the moderate climate that the airport and the island have in common has a great deal to do with the whisky that is produced on the Isle of Arran.

There are palm trees on Arran. Really. The island sits slap bang in the middle of the Gulf Stream. The distillery itself, built only some 15 years ago, sits in a sun trap, and all of this has had a profound effect on the whisky.

Every new distillery faces a dilemma. After three years, you have whisky and you can sell it as such, but is it up to the job? How long can you afford to leave it? On the one hand, in the short term, the investors want some money and you have to keep shelling out for wages, fuel, and so on; on the other, the short-term damage of bottling immature whisky may fatally impact your reputation in the longer term.

Some of Arran's early efforts were very poor indeed. But then something wonderful happened. Around seven years old, the malt went from ugly duck to beautiful swan, it took on a rich, creamy texture, and the distillery started to bottle a wonderful malt that not only tasted different from anything else coming out of the islands, but also tasted like nothing else on earth.

Isle of Arran 5-year-old 46% ABV

Young and zesty, with some sherbet, straw, and flour on the nose; sweet, zingy citrus notes on the palate. Overall, a clean and fruity whisky with a touch of cinnamon spice.

Isle of Arran Robert Burns 250th Anniversary Edition 43% ABV

Floral, with Parma violets and some perfume notes on the nose, and a very sweet taste, reminiscent of squidgy melon and canned exotic fruits. Clean and refreshing on the palate.

Isle of Arran 10-year-old
46% ABV

Full and creamy in feel, with some butterscotch and spearmint on the nose, a big chunk of chewy barley, rich melon and sweet candy on the palate, and a gentle and rich medium-long finish.

Isle of Arran 12-year-old

43% ABV

A coming-of-age for Arran, but slightly disappointing because there is less of the buttery richness and more orange and mandarin notes, some ginger, barley, and spice. It has a good finish, though, which is almost liqueur-like.

Arran 8-year-old St Emilion Finish 50% ABV

This has a sugar-and-spice nose, with some rosehip syrup and fresh flowers, but then blueberries, and earth roots, with almost putty-like notes. The taste is a strange mix of grape, green banana, and plum, and it all finishes well with some savory but rich tones.

Arran 8-year-old Madeira Finish 50% ABV

Madeira finishes can go two ways—and there is a danger that the big dose of sweetness will be too much. Not here, though. This is an outstanding expression of Arran. The irresistible nose is of strawberry soda, sweet lime, and exotic fruits, the palate is a refreshing mix of fruit Starburst candies, stewed apple and pear, and a topping of vanilla ice cream. Clean, summery, and guaranteed to have you reaching for another.

Arran Malt Fontallaro Finish 55% ABV

Another sweet, fruity delight, this time with mandarin notes joining the parade of citrus fruits on the nose, and a full and oily mix of canned fruits in syrup on the palate. Not too much, though. This is not oversweet and has a nice balance throughout.

Arran Moscatel Finish 55% ABV

The nose on this one is a little odd, with roses, old lady perfume, lavender, and toffee all popping up. Tastewise, it is equally intriguing: sugared (Jordan) almonds, apple peel, and some pepper combined with a certain oiliness make for a surprisingly agreeable overall package and a pleasant and warming peppery finish.

Arran 8-year-old Chianti Finish 55% ABV

Here you will find a powdery light and elusive nose, with traces of Parma violets, and a contrast on the palate, with savory and rootsy notes and some olives and stewed plums. The finish is unassertive.

Arran 100 Proof 57% ABV

This is Arran in all its pomp and finery, and one of the distillery's very best bottlings. The 100 proof refers to the British proof system of measurement, equating to 57% ABV, and not the American one, which would be 100 proof and a corresponding 50% ABV. The British one is all to do with the ability of the spirit to set fire to gunpowder, apparently.

Expect a grapey-green-apple nose from this, some chewy barley and highly attractive sweet lime on the palate, and a creamy finish.

Arran Single Sherry Cask No. 96/1754 59.4% ABV

By rights, I am not sure that a brutish cask such as this should work with a malt such as Arran. It does, though, and brilliantly so—a Little and Large double-act combination with lots of kitchen pantry odors, rich fruitcake mix, and mouth-coating rain, red berry, and orange fruits on the palate. It is surprisingly astringent, too, the oak sucking back the malt and making for a drying finish. A surprise all around.

AUCHENTOSHAN
www.auchentoshan.co.uk

When the distillers at Auchentoshan started making a beer last year, it may have been that they were completing a circle, for Auchentoshan is built on the site of an old monastery where the monks were almost certainly into brewing—another link between whisky and the Church. Auchentoshan is something of an oddball. Once a wee rural distillery (the name means "corner of the field"), it is now part of the Glasgow urban sprawl, the city's freeways reaching out to it like gigantic tentacles. It can therefore lay claim to being Glasgow's distillery. It is unusual in other ways, too. It is a Lowland distillery, but draws its water from Loch Katrine some six miles away in the Highlands. It triple-distills, too, one of the few establishments to do so in Scotland. It could be that the distillery's time has come because owner Suntory has invested heavily in visitor and conference facilities, the brands got a makeover, and a new 12-year-old was introduced a couple of years back. This is a beautifully maintained distillery.

Auchentoshan Select 40% ABV

This is Auchentoshan at its fruitiest and freshest, suggesting that it is young. Some citrus notes, some berries, and a clean, refreshing barley taste all reflect its young age.

Auchentoshan 12-year-old 40% ABV

Introduced two years ago to replace the standard ten-year-old expression, this is a big improvement, with the extra two years giving it a new dimension. Still quite light, but with a nicely balanced fruit and malt taste and just enough spice to pep it up.

Auchentoshan 18-year-old 43% ABV

Not nearly as woody as you might expect, but the influence of sherry casks gives this a richness and spiciness, and the slightly higher strength reflects a significant step up in quality.

Auchentoshan 21-year-old 43% ABV

Without a doubt, this is the best of the range. You would never know that it was 21 years old, and the wood certainly has not overwhelmed the Lowland malt. This is zappy—all grapefruit and zesty citrus, with a touch of oak and spice. Very drinkable and utterly irresistible, it is right up there with the very best of the Lowlanders Rosebank and St. Magdalene.

Auchentoshan Triple Wood 43% ABV

A rep for Auchentoshan was sitting at a bar once when a New Zealander working behind it started explaining the background of different single malts to an American guest.

"The barman was doing fine until he got to Auchentoshan," he recalls. "The guest asked him about Three Wood, and he said, 'Oh, that's a special bottling for golf clubs. Auchentoshan do a Seven Iron, too, and I think this summer they're launching a Putter.' I nearly fell off my seat."

The name actually refers to the oloroso, Pedro Ximénez, and bourbon casks used in maturation.

AUCHROISK

The Singleton is a generic name that means different things in different countries. Buy a Singleton in Europe, and the malt is Dufftown. In the Far East, it's Glen Ord. In the United States, it's Glendullan. But the original Singleton, and the one that commanded the most loyalty, was the Singleton of Auchroisk. When it was launched in the 1980s, anybody listed in the phone book with the name Singleton received a free miniature of it. It is now bottled under its own name as a single malt, but you don't see it too often because most goes into the blended whisky J&B.

Auchroisk 10-year-old 43% ABV

Orange, lemon, a touch of smoke, and a savory undertaste make this more than just a "me too" Speyside malt. The light and refreshing notes make it a good summer whisky.

BALBLAIR
www.balblair.com

Balblair is a Highland distillery sited on the Dornoch Firth, very close to Glenmorangie. This is a region steeped in ancient history, stone monuments, and the remains of dwellings from ancient races and tribes. Clach Biroach—the sharp stone—is not exactly Stonehenge, but it proves that a race of people who predated the Picts by 2,000 years understood the moon and stars because the stone is aligned against the nearby hills and marks the summer and winter solstices, giving guidance to the people as to when to plant and harvest crops. The Picts adopted the stone, too. Four thousand years on, it has been adopted as a symbol of the distillery.

The whisky here is fresh, clean, and sweet, but relatively unknown, although owner Inverhouse has recently rebranded the range.

Balblair 1997 43% ABV

This is like drinking an alcohol-soaked serving of Del Monte canned fruits.

It is all kicking off here in the sweet fruit department: mouth-coating vanilla, lime cordial, kumquat, and orange peel, with rich barley and a trace of sweet pepper to finish.

Balblair 1990 43% ABV

More fruit here, but from a different bowl this time. The trademark vanilla is there, but also pineapple and green fruits on the nose, a mix of canned pears and confectioners' sugar–like spices, plus an oak finish.

Balblair 1989 43% ABV

As succinct as one of the truly great Tamla Motown tracks, this is simple and to the point, but quite perfect in its delivery and execution. Lots of sweetness and vanilla from the bourbon casks, sherbet fruits and strawberry Starburst candies on the nose, then lots of sweet barley, exotic fruits, sweet lime, and citrus candy. Not into dessert? Have one of these instead.

Balblair 1975 46% ABV

The increased age of this bottling gives it considerably more depth than other expressions. There are all sorts of aromas coming from this one, including orange marmalade, vanilla, cherry, berries, and some oak. The taste is wonderful—almost liqueur-like—with dark chocolate, cherry, orange liqueur, sweet fruits, and oak.

BALVENIE

www.thebalvenie.com

Balvenie is the Jack Daniel's of Scotland—a big malt-producing distillery that has somehow successfully managed to convince the world of whisky that it is a small artisanal one, producing handcrafted small-batch malts. It is, in fact, a Speyside whisky producer owned by William Grant, and occupies the same site as sister distillery Glenfiddich. And it does seem small in comparison. It has its own floor maltings that produce a fraction of the malt it requires, and it sits next to Grant's traditional labor-intensive cooperage, so you get a sense that it is from a different era. Balvenie is another distillery, like Aberlour, offering outstanding VIP tours. You will be shown around in small groups, often led by someone who has 30 years' experience in the industry. The tour is as thorough as it gets.

Balvenie DoubleWood 12-year-old

40% ABV

Matured first in American oak, then in sherry casks, this is the whisky equivalent of a show home. Everything is in its place, immaculate, and well put together, but it is a house, not a home, and does not exude the warmth you get from the great Balvenies. That said, there are some pleasant fruit notes and a sherry richness that make it an acceptable everyday dram.

Balvenie Signature 12-year-old 40% ABV

The nose here is complex, dry, and woody, like pencil shavings, but with some satsuma and orange notes. On the palate, there are fruitcake and orange fruits. The finish is medium, pleasant, and fruity.

Balvenie Roasted Malt 14-year-old 47.1% ABV

Butter and praline on the nose, some dry woodiness, then a rich palate of burnt toffee, dark treacle, some spices, and toasted oak. The finish is long and toasty.

Balvenie Single Barrel 15-year-old 47.8% ABV

This varies from barrel to barrel, but the intention is to pick the sweetest, most dessertlike Balvenie. There is lemon and lime, and fruit Starburst candy in the mix, combined with sweet barley and zingy spice. The standard of these bottlings has been consistently high, and this is another right up there with the very best of Speyside. This has fruit syrup dusted with confectioners' sugar on a delicate oaky base. Enjoy.

Balvenie Rum Cask 17-year-old 43% ABV

Yo, ho, and indeed ho, rum is influential from the off here, with dark rum and raisin notes, some oak, plus all sorts of exotic fruits thrown in for good measure, including apple and citrus fruits. Complex and curious, this is but another triumph from a very impressive distillery.

Balvenie PortWood 21-year-old 40% ABV

An absolute masterpiece of a whisky and arguably the finest port finish available. There are traces of oak that reflect its age, a good nuttiness, and big lashings of fruit. This is wonderful in every respect.

Balvenie Vintage Cask No. 6570, 1976 52.8% ABV

A cask-strength bottling, this is a very big whisky, with a fruitcake mix, dense honey, and hazelnuts on the nose. The texture is thick and mouth-coating on the palate, where wood and spice battle against prune juice and melon, with the fruit just about going the distance. An altogether rather marvelous experience.

THE BALVENIE DISTILLERY COMPANY

Dufftown, Banffshire AB55 4BB
www.thebalvenie.com

In theory, making single-malt whisky is the same process no matter which distillery you visit. But variety is the spice of life, and one of the great joys of Scotland's distilleries is the way in which the process is tweaked, making each different from the next. Sometimes the differences are considerable and brought into stark focus by their proximity to one another—never more so than on the site of William Grant's three distilleries at Dufftown, in the beautiful setting of Speyside.

At one extreme is Glenfiddich, an amusement park of a distillery with the warmest of welcomes for all the family to the home of the world's biggest single malt, multilingual tours by smart and smiling guides, an interactive and state-of-the-art guide to the malt's history and production, and support facilities that include an outstanding café. It also has the most luxurious ladies' restroom in Scotland—take my word for it.

At the other end of the scale, and buried deep in the heart of the site beyond the barrel skyscrapers and the noisy and business-like cooperage, is Kininvie, an anonymous malt factory that produces spirit targeted entirely at the company's blended whiskies. There are no visitor facilities here, little information to impart, and no whisky to try. Kininvie is not bottled as a single malt, but it is the pumping heart of the worldwide William Grant success story.

And then there is Balvenie, a whisky-lover's whisky, with its distillery that is a whisky-lover's distillery. No whisky enthusiast should ever forget how much Glenfiddich has done for the single-malt category, or take for granted the qualities that have made it the world's number-one malt. But, let's be honest, it is to whisky fans what the Harry Potter franchise is to movie fans: you respect its success, acknowledge its quality, and, if pushed, concede that it has played a leading role in bringing in thousands of new faces and introducing them to the endless possibilities the category has to offer. But, for all of that, it does not excite the enthusiasts, does it? Balvenie, on the other hand . . .

For a starter, it would seem to be pretty much everything Glenfiddich is not. It is a traditional, old-fashioned, and slightly ramshackle distillery and is definitely high-maintenance, demanding considerable hands-on love and care. It still malts a proportion of its barley in its floor maltings. Only

WELL, FANCY THAT . . .

Monkey Shoulder, which has successfully converted a new generation of drinkers to whisky, is made up of three malts: Glenfiddich, Balvenie, and Kininvie.

ABOVE The traditional and charming Balvenie distillery in Banffshire is an essential destination for any whisky lover visiting Scotland.

a proportion, though. Let's not get too carried away—for all of its rustic charm, it is still one of Scotland's biggest distilleries. It is also capable of producing some of the most delicious of all Speyside malts, some rich and sherried, others intensely fruity and laced with vanilla, like tasting a bowl of alcohol-steeped canned fruit and ice cream in a glass.

Although acclaimed by whisky writers for some time, Balvenie has been relatively hard to find as a single malt until recent years, and it is only now starting to enjoy a deserved place in the sun.

But any budding whisky enthusiast wanting to get under the surface of malt-whisky production should take time away from the glitz and glamor of Glenfiddich up the road, and set aside half a day to do the VIP tour at Balvenie. At the beginning, you will be taken to the old distillery manager's office for an introduction, and you will enjoy a vertical tasting through pretty much the entire Balvenie range at the end. And in between you will spend most of your time as part of a small group in the company of a highly knowledgeable guide who has spent his life in distilleries, often at senior levels. If you're lucky, he will regale you with anecdotes stretching back four decades, providing a unique insight into whisky's past.

It is priceless stuff, and it not only adds up to one of Scotland's very best tours, but also ensures that, once you have completed the rounds, Balvenie will have carved a special place in the corner of your heart—one you'll return to again and again. Every time, in fact, you pour yourself one of the distillery's wonderfully distinctive whiskies.

KEY WHISKIES

Balvenie DoubleWood 12-year-old 40% ABV
Balvenie Signature 12-year-old 40% ABV
Balvenie Roasted Malt 14-year-old 47.1% ABV
Balvenie Single Barrel 15-year-old 47.8% ABV
Balvenie Rum Cask 17-year-old 43% ABV
Balvenie PortWood 21-year-old 40% ABV
Balvenie Vintage Cask No. 6570, 1976 52.8% ABV

ABOVE The team behind the production of Balvenie.

BELOW Four core malts from the Balvenie portfolio: DoubleWood, Signature, Single Barrel, and PortWood.

BEN NEVIS
www.bennevisdistillery.com

Fort William feels as if it is the last outpost before you get to Scotland's Wild West. You can cut across country to Speyside from here, head up to the Isle of Skye and the far north, or take the scenic route along Loch Ness. But whichever way you go, it gets pretty bleak and desolate.

The Ben Nevis distillery, in the shadow of the mountain, is an odd one. Owned by Japanese company Nikka, it has a checkered stop–start history, and it is not well known as a single malt. Much of the distillery's output goes into blends, and it is one of the few whiskies that uses the same name for both a single malt and a blend. If you can source it, though, Ben Nevis is a weighty, robust, and complex malt.

Ben Nevis 10-year-old 46% ABV

A big and oily Highland whisky, this offering tastes as rugged as the environment that produced it. Here, you will find attractive orange-flavored rich dark chocolate notes, chunky malt, and exotic fruit.

BENRIACH
www.benriachdistllery.co.uk

It may be only a small distillery, but, like Bruichladdich on Islay, BenRiach sure does make a hell of a lot of noise. BenRiach used to belong to Pernod Ricard, and the company set about experimenting with peated whiskies here in the heart of Speyside because it did not have an Islay malt. It did not release any of them, but since a consortium fronted by Billy Walker took over bottlings have come thick and fast, and some of the peated releases have been magnificent. The distillery is something of a dream for malt fans—small and farmlike, it has its own floor maltings that Walker has started using again, and the big fires have been back in action, too, peating the barley. The whole place is in immaculate condition, and all sorts of unusual casks are maturing in its warehouses, maintaining its history as a test distillery. Add to that a wide range of always interesting bottlings, and we are talking serious whisky heaven.

BenRiach Heart of Speyside 40% ABV

The distillery's entry-level malt is classic Speyside—lots of sweet fruit and vanilla on the nose; pineapple, barley, and citrus fruits on the palate; and an agreeably sweet medium-long finish, with just a touch of spice.

BenRiach 12-year-old
43% ABV

A more intense version of Heart of Speyside, this has lots of sweet fruit, honey, and vanilla, and a delightfully summery finale.

BenRiach Curiositas 46% ABV

Not sure where the trend comes from, but the team at BenRiach seems to have a lot of fun coming up with Latin-derived names for their peated whiskies. This, at ten years old, has been bottled at 46% and 40% ABV; get the higher strength if you can because it is a growling monster of a malt. Acrid charcoal smoke and soot mix with lemon and cocoa on the nose, while on the palate there is a stunning mix of melon and peach on the one hand and diesel smoke and coal dust on the other. There is a slightly acerbic wet-fire finale, but overall this is a corker.

BenRiach Dark Rum Finish 15-year-old 46% ABV

If you like your whisky sweet, this one's for you. On the nose, it is all milk chocolate, honey, and caramel bar; on the palate, it is rum-and-raisin ice cream, vanilla, and exotic fruits. There is a touch of spice and oak coming through late on, but overall this is a one-trick pony.

BenRiach Madeira Finish
15-year-old 46% ABV

Another dessert whisky, this boasts melon, pear, and vanilla on the nose. It tastes like chocolate lime bonbons at first, with some influence from the wood and a touch of pepper and spice late on. All in all, though, this is sweet and lingering.

BenRiach Pedro Ximénez Finish 15-year-old 46% ABV

There is no doubt about the quality of the whisky-making on show here. The nose is quite restrained, with some toffee apple and fruit mince pie, but on the palate this is a mouth-coating and rounded malt, elegantly unveiling a procession of flavors including grapes, nuts, spice, some oak, and marzipan. Sophisticated and seriously classy.

BenRiach Sauternes Finish
16-year-old 46% ABV

Another whisky with a curio for a nose, with stewed bamboo shoots, dough balls, and a musty sweetness not selling the malt particularly well. But the taste is much better. It is a zippy whisky, with grape, berries, and vanilla all vying for attention, some pluminess coming to the fore, and distinctive sweet pepper and oakiness toward the end. It is a bit of a Tango taste sensation, this one, with its rich orange syrup color.

BenRiach Tawny Port Finish
15-year-old 46% ABV

What a weirdo! The nose is all over the place, with rosehip syrup, chestnut, and dark coffee notes. The palate is something else again, with fresh, clean soft fruit and barley, and a charming and clean finish.

BenRiach Aromaticus Fumosus
12-year-old 46% ABV

This is finished in a rum cask, but of all this series it is the least affected by its finishing school. What we have here is a peaty monster, with lots of grungy smoke. The rum-cask aging gives it a nice sweet core, but really this one is for lovers of Islay.

BenRiach Heredotus Fumosus 12-year-old
46% ABV

Well, you cannot accuse the whisky makers of playing safe here. This is one of a number of peated whiskies finished in casks used to mature other drinks. It has the potential to taste like too many paints mixed together—a browny black mess. In fact, all four bottlings in the series work. This one is full, oily, and peaty, with a soft yellow citrus and blackcurrant center, like a smoky, liquid Turkish delight. A long, smoky fruit finish is exceptional.

BenRiach Importanticus Fumosus
12-year-old 46% ABV

Not quite reaching the dizzy heights of the previous whisky, this one is still exceptional. The nose is a challenge, with brine and peat, as well as vanilla, fruits, and some floral notes, but the taste saves it, with port and lemon, grapefruit and smoke, and a long finish.

BenRiach Maderensis Fumosus
13-year-old 46% ABV

This one makes the claim that it is heavily peated, and it is—so much so you can write your name in it, the whisky equivalent of a live steam meet. The "spoonful of sugar helping the medicine go down" comes courtesy of soft pear and melon notes, and a lemon color. The finish has all the classic BenRiach sootiness you could want.

BenRiach 16-year-old 40% ABV

Back to classic Speyside malt, and the next step up from the 12-year-old. This offers a pretty straightforward journey from honey, vanilla, and sweet fruit on the nose to a sweet and clean medium finish at the end, passing through apple crumble and vanilla ice cream. Late spices add depth, but this is about as far from the Fumosus bottlings as you can get.

BenRiach 20-year-old
43% ABV

This whisky is a bit shy on the nose, and you have to work hard to find grape, apple, pear, and marzipan. The palate, though, is an elegant delight—a subtle and sophisticated marriage of fresh yellow fruits, vanilla, oak, and honey. A slightly higher strength and the oak influence give it shape and a sense of purpose.

BenRiach Authenticus 21-year-old 46% ABV

The pick of the bunch from this great distillery, this Authenticus pulls off the rare feat of balancing rich fruit and intense peat and smoke. There is East Anglian Cromer crab and fried cured bacon on the nose, but also apples and peach. On the palate, sweet canned fruits and milk chocolate are wrapped in a wall of peat and smoke. Some astringency, an oaky influence, and a spicy bite lead to an oily, charcoal finish.

BenRiach 30-year-old 50% ABV

The age shows through significantly with this one, where the honey and citrus of younger bottlings are joined by dusty wood so that the overall effect is like a big oak-paneled office that has recently been polished. On the palate, citrus and orange fruits give way to wood and spice. The finish is quite sharp, but the orange fruits just about hold their own.

BENROMACH
www.benromach.com

Benromach lies close to Forres, to the north and west of the Speyside region. It is a small, rustic distillery now owned by independent bottlers Gordon & MacPhail, who bought it, invested heavily in it, and saved it from demolition. The distillery was reopened 12 years ago, which means that recent bottlings have contained spirit made since the reopening. Although classed as a Speyside distillery, the spirit produced here is varied, but much of it has a distinctive peaty earthiness. Profilewise, it fits better with Highland distilleries such as Glen Garioch, Ardmore, and Glencadam. Benromach was the first distillery to produce an organic single malt approved by the UK Soil Association. This entailed stripping down all the equipment and cleaning it to an approved standard, and using only organic oak barrels.

Benromach Traditional 40% ABV

The nose suggests youth, with grassy and viney notes, but also some smoke and oil. The palate is agricultural, cereally, and earthy. When I was 16, we used to go out into the fields, chew barley husks, and smoke roll-up cigarettes. This whisky reminds me of those lazy days in rural England.

Benromach 10-year-old 43% ABV

Malty Ovaltine, sappy damp straw, and flour dough balls on the nose, a savory wave of peat and smoke on the palate at first, then a delicatessen smorgasbord, with touches of cocoa and fruit. This ten-year-old is intriguing, challenging, different, and— overall—worthwhile.

Benromach 21-year-old 43% ABV

Apple, pears, and some prickly peat on the nose, with lime, guava, and kiwi fruits on the palate. Overall, this is sweet and clean, with some vanilla and marmalade notes. Later spice arrives, and stays until the conclusion.

Benromach 25-year-old 43% ABV

Lemon and lime jelly bonbons to the fore on the nose, but backed by some spice, peat, and oak. You just know from the aroma that this is going to be a treat. And it is—like a heavy metal band with three egotistical lead guitarists trying to outperform one another. While oak, spice, and peat are all to the fore here, it is the fruity rhythm section that holds it together and prevents a random mess. "Free Bird" in a glass.

Benromach Organic 43% ABV

This organic dram is softer and sweeter on the nose than the Traditional or the ten-year-old, but with oak and some toffee and mashed pear. With time, there are hints of raspberry and blackberry sherbet. The palate is big and bold, with oak and blackcurrant cordial, quickly followed by a wave of pepper so that overall it is a sweet and spicy treat. The finish is long, spicy, and liqueur-like.

Benromach Organic Special Edition
43% ABV

Benromach goes to the seaside. A perfectly coastal nose that boasts salt, seaweed, and shellfish in the mix. On the palate, it is oily and fishy, with plenty of peat. Soft and rounded, with little or no spice in evidence.

Benromach Origins
50% ABV

You have to reset your radar for this one. The nose is very odd and disconcerting, with some sulfury notes, then milk chocolate. It is intriguing more than off-putting, but you do wonder what it is going to taste like. The sulfur soon gives way on the palate, and you are left with a liqueur-like treacley malt, with sweet brown sugar in the mix.

Benromach Peat Smoke Batch 2 45% ABV

Lemon drizzled on grilled sole and barbecue wood chips on the nose, this is a charming mix of creamy lemon and feisty peat. All in all, a big, fat, and fishy peaty treat.

Benromach Sassicaia Wood Finish 45% ABV

The nose is a bowl of overripe fruit, resinous, with oak and peat vying for attention. On the palate, there is chunky melon and the pleasant interplay between peat and oak remains. Yet another individual whisky from this intriguing distillery that has sailed down a little flavor creek all of its own making.

Benromach 1968 43% ABV

The aroma of this one is reminiscent of a church sacristy, with incense, fresh flowers, and polished oak. Maybe a Spanish one, at that, where the priest likes fruit because there is some Seville orange marmalade in the mix, too. And it is orange marmalade that dominates the palate, while the oaky tannins give the whisky a hint of astringency.

Benromach 1955 42.4% ABV

There are few distilleries that could age a cask for more than half a century and end up with a whisky as sublime as this. It comes from a cask that was laid down and cared for by a team of people, many of whom are no longer with us, from the days before pop and rock music as we now know it had yet to be invented, before Elvis and the Beatles, before computers and moon landings. Mind-blowing. The whisky is delicate and subtle, with mandarin and tangerine fruits, together with traces of peat, oak, and spice.

BLADNOCH
www.bladnoch.com

Bladnoch takes some getting to. It is tucked away in the southwest corner of Scotland, about as far from Edinburgh as Aberdeen is. But the Dumfries and Galloway region is well worth a visit, offering beauty and a more varied landscape than much of Scotland, with its coastline rugged and Celtic. The distillery, in the renowned book town of Wigtown, is unlike any other in Scotland, coming over like a cross between a small cotton mill and a rural arts center. Owner Raymond Armstrong is a free spirit and thinks outside the box, too, so you can buy a range of malts from other distilleries at almost ridiculously low prices. In the warehouses, there are casks from Scotland because the distillery rents out space at very favorable prices. Look hard enough, and you will find several lesser-known malts maturing in top-quality casks. Some of them have been recasked and are quietly maturing away now. Could these be the star names of the future?

Bladnoch 6-year-old Lightly Peated
58.5% ABV

You need to add water to pry open the nose, but once you do you will find blackcurrant and sweet peat. The palate is multilayered and sophisticated, with apple, pear, and other soft fruits, then some peat smoke and spice. Toward the end, the peatiness still comes through, but there are some savory and earthy flavors, and even pine needles.

Bladnoch 15-year-old 40% ABV

The nose here is reminiscent of Irish whiskey, with delicate, clean fresh fruit, especially pear. The palate is mostly apple and pear, but with some oak coming through and some marzipan-like apple pip. Overall, this is a refreshing, fruity summery whisky, with the merest hint of spice and a pale lemony color with a greenish hue.

Bladnoch 16-year-old 46% ABV

This has a fall garden of a nose, with some green fruit and delicate smoke. The taste is of canned pears with ice cream, all wrapped in an earthy and peaty blanket. The finish mixes smoke and spice, liked canned pears in ash. This is a good thing.

Bladnoch 18-year-old
55% ABV

Gooseberry, barley sugar, oak, and grape on the nose, rich sweet fruit and sweet peppers on the palate, with oak and spice appearing toward the satisfying finale.

BLAIR ATHOL
www.malts.com

Blair Athol is a pristine, well-maintained Diageo distillery close to Pitlochry, and this is an ideal base for a whisky lover with a less interested family. Blair Castle is only up the road, and there is plenty to do and see, great walking, and a handful of distilleries and whisky attractions within easy reach. This distillery is the spiritual home of Bell's. There is a small exhibition, but it pales alongside the efforts at Aberfeldy (Dewar's World of Whisky) and Glenturret (the Famous Grouse Experience). All very pleasant, but it is so well maintained that you can forget that they make whisky here.

Blair Athol 12-year-old
Flora and Fauna 43% ABV

One of those single malts that feels as if it was intended for blending. It is a surprisingly full and fruity malt, rich and thick, with some pleasant fruit notes.

BOWMORE

www.bowmore.co.uk

Bowmore lies halfway up the island of Islay on the sea loch, Loch Indaal. It faces Bruichladdich, which is about three miles away on the other side of the loch. Each summer, there is a swimming event across the loch, but can I suggest that you don't row it unless you have taken advice on tides. This comes from bitter experience. We did it for a charity event and grew a little concerned when a fishing boat came alongside and the six lads on board told us that they were escorting us for our own safety. They were bluffing, though, and were in fact a bunch of distillery workers led by Kevin Campbell, out for a laugh. We did well for three-quarters of the crossing, but then realized that Bowmore wasn't getting any closer. As we struggled to row harder, the boat crew passed along a flask and tried to curb their raucous laughter. Finally, they took pity on us and towed us in. Kevin asked me to join the annual round-island row for charity after that, but I never did, deciding I would be better off preserving what dignity I had left.

Bowmore 12-year-old 40% ABV

If Lagavulin, Ardbeg, and Laphroaig are the Iron Maiden, Metallica, and Motorhead of whisky, Bowmore is its Bon Jovi. The whisky from here is peated, but not so fully as that of the southern distilleries—altogether a more mainstream taste. Bowmore can rock when it wants to, though, and this expression might be a lightweight, but it is still a classic—a sort of "Keep the Faith" or "Livin' on a Prayer" for malt drinkers. A peaty, seaspray nose leads to a fruit and spice palate.

Bowmore 16-year-old Limited Edition Sherry Cask 53.8% ABV

This is very hard to find, and I think that there may have been a bourbon-cask version of it, but if you can find it then this is a treat, a mix of big sherry notes and intense peat delivered at cask strength. Sherry and peat can be a disastrous mix, but when it is right—BenRiach Authenticus, Compass Box Flaming Heart, Laphroaig 27-year-old, and this—it works for me.

Bowmore 18-year-old 43% ABV

I believe that everybody who discovers the joys of whisky will have an enlightenment moment, the point at which you cross the threshold from interest to passion. I remember vividly the first time I went to an evening soccer match at Filbert Street, Leicester, some time around 1968. I remember walking up the steps to our seats and the pitch coming into view. I remember the sheer excitement and wonder of the bright green pitch illuminated by dazzling floodlights, the noise of the crowd, the sense of anticipation. It was the beginning of a lifelong love affair. The whisky equivalent to that for me was my first taste of Bowmore 17-year-old, with its distinctive Parma violet notes and weird fruit and peat mix. Sadly, the 17-year-old has been discontinued, and this isn't a patch on it. The Parma violet notes are just about still there, though, and there are enough positives to hold the attention, even if it is all a bit too slick and clean these days.

Bowmore 25-year-old 43% ABV

Surprisingly clean, light, and delicate for a whisky of such an age, most of the distinctive flavors here are sherry-influenced, with berry fruits and some citrus in the mix. It is all rich and chewy—a very pleasant experience.

Bowmore Legend 40% ABV

Vanilla, sweetness, and as big a wave of peat and smoke as you will get from any Bowmore. There are also some lemon and orange in the mix.

BOWMORE DISTILLERY

School Street, Bowmore, Islay, Argyllshire PA43 7JS
www.bowmore.co.uk

There is no finer place to drink whisky than when sitting on the sea wall at the waterside Bowmore distillery.

In summer, the view across Loch Indaal to Bruichladdich is a dynamic and colorful one. Gulls drift in the clear blue sky, sunlight flits off the waves in the loch, and bracing crisp wind caresses your face. You can smell fish and seaweed in the breeze. Sipping a strong, peated malt in such circumstances is an exhilarating and vital experience, and it is made all the more so by the knowledge that just below you some of Bowmore's most treasured whisky stocks are sleeping peacefully.

The wall is part of the town's sea defenses, but also forms the outer wall of warehouse one, the legendary warehouse that has stored some of the distillery's finest malts. While angry seas vent their frustration against the wall in winter, the casks rest in blissful tranquility on the other side. Part of the warehouse is below sea level, and you can smell the salt in the air, see it encrusted on the walls alongside the black mold that is proof positive that the angels are taking their share. If you do not accept that malt matured in coastal distilleries is affected by its environment, then ten minutes here may just be enough to make you change your mind.

It was warehouse one that produced the malt used in the Bowmore Trilogy, which was completed last year with the launch of Gold Bowmore. The bourbon and oloroso casks used for maturation were laid down under the stairs in 1964, and gave up their final treasures 45 years later.

"You never know exactly how casks are going to mature, and many are ready at 18 or 20 years," says distillery manager Eddie McAffee. "But we have areas of that warehouse where we know there is a chance of the casks doing something special. There was always something exceptional about those casks. Even in the early 1970s, when it was still the practice for distillery workers to take a dram from the cask, the warehousemen would not let anyone touch those ones. And the whisky inside them just kept getting better and better. It is the best malt I have ever tasted."

Eddie joined the distillery in 1966, when the casks were just two years old and their contents were still too young to be called whisky. He is a week younger than whisky legend Jim McEwan, and went to school with him. His appointment as Bowmore manager four years ago meant that every distillery manager on Islay was born on the island. He is clearly proud of his career at the distillery and acutely aware of the responsibility of being its custodian. But he believes a combination of a good young team and an investment by the parent company in quality casks will ensure a bright future for the distillery.

"Bowmore always had good spirit but in the past there was an inconsistency in the wood," he says. "But about 15 years ago a decision as taken to put the spirit in to better wood and the 12-year-old coming through now is getting better and better. Some of us older ones will be leaving the distillery soon so it is important that we pass on our skills."

If you take the VIP tour of the distillery you will be offered new-make spirit to try and a sample from one of the casks. The remains of the cask sample will be returned to where it came from, but the new-make spirit will be thrown on the floor. "We do it to ward off bad spirits" says Eddie. "It's to ensure nothing bad happens to the casks."

On the evidence of the 1964 casks it seems to be working. Without doubt more stunning casks will appear in the future. Sitting on the sea wall soaking in the splendour of the view is the perfect way to appreciate Bowmore.

KEY WHISKIES
Bowmore 12-year-old 40% ABV
Bowmore 16-year-old 53.8% ABV
Bowmore 18-year-old 43% ABV
Bowmore 25-year-old 43% ABV
Bowmore Legend 40% ABV

MAIN PICTURE An old photograph showing the jetty at Bowmore and the view across Loch Indaal, one of the most exhilarating places in the world to sip whisky and daydream.

BRORA
www.malts.com

The Brora distillery no longer exists, having been demolished some years ago. It was on the same site as Clynelish in the far northeast of Scotland, in the village of Brora. It is included here because in recent years Diageo has released a series of 30-year-olds and, although they vary significantly from one to the next, they have been consistently excellent.

Brora 30-year-old 2008 Release   52.4% ABV

This whisky lies somewhere between the tobacconist, the florist, and the fresh produce store, with big orange and soft fruit notes and waves of peat, with a rounded spice and peat finish.

Brora 30-year-old 2006 Release   55.7% ABV

This expression is defined by a drier, woodier nose than the 2008, with wood dust, spices, pepper, peat, and peach to the fore on the palate, with a long, peaty finish to distinguish it.

BRUICHLADDICH
www.bruichladdich.com

Reopened at the start of the millennium, Bruichladdich has proved itself a very twenty-first-century distillery ever since. Its smart packaging and distinctive sky-blue livery have made it instantly recognizable, and a large range of different and diverse bottlings, a good proportion of which are outstanding, has won it a loyal fan base across the world. The team at the distillery, which includes legendary Ileach whisky maker Jim McEwan, has never been slow to exploit a marketing opportunity or to promote itself, nor has it minded being Islay's maverick distillery, and undoubtedly bizarre things have happened to it. Like the time the distillery was allegedly spied on by the U.S. Defense Threat Reduction Agency because it was worried that the distillery was actually making weapons of mass destruction, rather than whisky.

Bruichladdich Laddie 2001   45% ABV

Here you will find stewed vegetables, noodles, and bean sprouts on the nose, and a highly unusual and provocative mix of sweet and savory, peat, raw vegetables, and delicate floral notes.

Yellow Submarine
46% ABV

A few years back, a fishing boat discovered a bright yellow mini submarine packed with high-tech surveillance equipment floating a few miles from Islay. It had "MoD" on the side. At first, Britain's Ministry of Defense denied that it was theirs, then implied that it had been stolen. For ten days, the submarine was left abandoned, until eventually a Royal Navy mine hunter arrived at Islay and hastily removed the submarine. This whisky commemorates that occasion.

There is honey, soft melon, and sweet plum on the nose, while on the palate are green fruits and some clean malty, peppery notes. The finish is savory with some pepper.

Bruichladdich 12-year-old   46% ABV

This has a very fresh and enticing nose, with vanilla, citrus, and yellow fruits. The palate is a can of exotic fruits in syrup, with vanilla ice cream for good measure. Soft and rounded, it is a very moreish whisky.

Bruichladdich Links 15-year-old Birkdale   46% ABV

This is one of a series of releases named after classic golf courses. Not quite sure why. But this is very different from the last bottlings, with its earthy, wet grass, and autumnal roots on the nose. It has a challenging but not unpleasant mix of clean barley and grape on the one hand, and some tannin and spice on the other. The finish is medium, with wood, spice, and some dryness.

Bruichladdich 3D The Peat Proposal
46% ABV

Cross the fields toward the coast for this one, where the nose is seaweed, barbecue, and salt, the flavor comes from gooseberry and young green fruits, and barbecue and peat are on the palate, with a spicy finish.

Bruichladdich 10-year-old Oloroso Finish 46% ABV

Caramel, toffee apple, red berries, and sweet fruits on the nose, and soft canned fruits, particularly melon, on the palate. This is all sweet and fruity, and a rich golden brown color, with sugar dusted on for good measure.

Bruichladdich Waves 46% ABV

On the nose, it is like being in a fishing port when the tide has just gone out, with fish, seaweed, and saltiness all in the mix. The taste of this one is a real delight—barley, rich plummy stewed fruit, and smokiness all battling in the mix, with the sweetness winning through.

Bruichladdich 16-year-old Bourbon/Latour 46% ABV

Vanilla ice cream, soft melon, and pineapple on both the nose and the palate; apart from a touch of oak and some sweet pepper late on, that is it. This is simple, blemish-free, very palatable, and sweet.

Bruichladdich Bourbon 16-year-old
46% ABV

Rich, sweet, honeyed, and with vanilla on the nose, lots of bourbon, candy, and vanilla notes, masses of fruit, and again with a touch of spice very late on.

Bruichladdich Bourbon/Lafite 46% ABV

There are several other wine finishes in this range, and to my mind not all of them work, but, then again, I do struggle with some wine casks. This, though, is a beauty. There are most welcoming butterscotch and vanilla on the nose, and a rich and full mouthfeel. On the palate, the whisky changes direction sharply but thrillingly midway, with orange marmalade and dark chocolate cherry liqueurs at first, then a sharp astringency to give the malt structure. The finish is a mix of chili, bitter cocoa, and wood.

Bruichladdich 1998 Manzanilla 46% ABV

Flighty, wispy nose with tangerine and cocoa, but on the palate this is like a fruit-and-nut milk chocolate bar, with some honeycomb candy thrown in for good measure. The finish is short, soft, and pleasant, and leaves you wanting another sip.

Bruichladdich 18-year-old 46% ABV

The nose is grungy and rootsy, with stewed chestnuts reminiscent of Chinese food. The palate is savory, with grape and clean barley, some chili, and a salt-and-pepper finale.

Bruichladdich 20-year-old 46% ABV

The nose is complex, with some mustiness and tannin kicking out at a flavor combination of fruit compote of date, dried apricot, and canned pear. The palate is clean and refreshing, with some peppermint, oak, and traces of peat among candy fruits and fluffy apple. All very soft and subtle, with some sweet pepper and spice at the finish.

Bruichladdich 35-year-old
Legacy Series 40.7% ABV

A bit laid-back this, but cajole it and there are some good flavors here. Candy and sweet nougat on the nose, with sherbet–citrus lemon-and-lime combos on the palate. The whisky dries in the mouth, before a peppery conclusion.

Bruichladdich Peat 46% ABV

Does it do what it says on the can? Sure does, with beach barbecue and burnt fish on the nose; the most wonderful cheesecake palate of stewed sweet pear and apricot on top; a creaminess with wispy smoke in the middle; and a rugged cookie base at the bottom. Total harmony.

Bruichladdich PC6 61% ABV

Port Charlotte is the little town close to the distillery, and the whiskies using the name have come to mean intense and highly peated wonder beasts. This has deep tar and strong coastal notes on the nose, and is oily and rich in the mouth, with the full range of peated flavors, from diesel engine to tarry rope, smoky barbecue, and seaweed. It roars in like a lion, but is a pussycat in the finish, with a long and gentle purring mix of fruit and smoke. Sublime.

Bruichladdich PC7 60.5% ABV

Not quite what you might expect, with a damp wood and lighter peat attack, much more subtle and restrained than PC6. On the palate, you will find more tarry peat and growly smoke, but the predominant flavor is canned stewed strawberries. As with PC6, the finish is long and impressive, with fruit and smoke dancing around each other to marvelous effect.

Bruichladdich 21-year-old 46% ABV

The aromas here are rich, with dried fruits and some softer citrus candy notes. The taste is big, rich, and bold, with the age of the cask adding gravitas, while peach and apricot are enhanced by a polite level of pepper and oaky tannins. Astringent in the finish and a deep autumnal brown in color, with a greenish hue.

Bruichladdich 40-year-old 40% ABV

This is light, clean, and sherbety in flavor, with sweet pineapple on the nose and an assortment of exotic fruits on the palate. The finish here is mainly sweet and sugary, but the drying tannins and spices prevent it from becoming too cloying.

Bruichladdich Blacker Still 50.7% ABV

A whisky the size of a dump truck, with a tidal wave of prunes, sultana raisins, and pantry spices on the nose. The taste is big and heavily sherried, with great spoonfuls of overripe fruit, a big oak hit, and spices that dip in and out of the mix. It is like the sort of whisky the Japanese make, and it is utterly seductive—a bit of a roller coaster, but by the finish it has slowed right down and delivers you safely and gently back to earth.

Bruichladdich Infinity 52.5% ABV

Here, you will find an Islay coastline on the nose, with brine and seaweed. Tastewise, it is like eating a can of exotic fruits while smoking. Very sweet and smoky, this is yet another Bruichladdich that is all too easy to fall in love with.

Bruichladdich Octomore 63.5% ABV

This comes in stylish and very unusual packaging and is out-and-out Islay, with big waves of charry tar, barbecued bacon, and grilled fish on the nose. A big, oily whisky that needs water. Once unlocked, it is a charmer—trout drizzled with lemon, playful phenols, a very sweet peat center, and a stunning finish.

Bruichladdich Redder Still

50.4% ABV

Dandelion and burdock soda—a bit like root beer or sarsaparilla—is on the nose here, only with alcohol. Blackcurrant cordial and floral notes are also present. On the palate are lots of intense candy fruits: lemon, lime, and orange. A clean, intense malt-stormer, this.

BUNNAHABHAIN

Kilchoman and Bruichladdich might be farther west, but Bunnahabhain on Islay feels like Scotland's last malt outpost.

To reach it, you drive pretty much to the end of the island and, just before Port Askaig, set off down a long, sloping pathway. The distillery hugs the shore under the shelter of the cliffs, and the view out across the sound of Jura and toward the Paps (hills) is breathtaking. The distillery itself is a little weatherbeaten, the offices dated, but, as with a lovable scruffy mongrel, the friendliness of the welcome here makes up for the tatty appearance. Bunnahabhain promoted itself as the "gentle taste of Islay" because its core brands have only a light peatiness. Within the distillery's warehouses, however, there are some stunning peated casks. And, recently, the distillery's owner has allowed some of the peated stock to be bottled, most notably Toiteach, meaning "smoky."

Bunnahabhain 12-year-old 40% ABV

Only lightly peated it may be, but this 12-year-old is a rugged and coastal malt, and there are salt and a nutty earthiness among some solid fruit notes. Late on, a rapier-sharp barley spice hit welcomes in a hint of sherry trifle, adding sweetness to an otherwise savory malt.

Bunnahabhain 16-year-old
Manzanilla Sherry Wood Finish 53.2% ABV

Limited to fewer than 3,800 bottles and bottled at cask strength, this is an example of the distillery letting some of its buried secrets out of the bag. Hopefully, it will be suitably encouraged to do more. This is the distillery on a day out at the fair, sacrificing discipline for big flavors—wine, cocoa, red fruits, and brine.

Bunnahabhain 18-year-old 43% ABV

In some ways, this is another departure for the distillery, but something of a star nonetheless. This is rich and full, and there are some big, fruity sherry notes, plenty of oak, and traces of citrus.

Bunnahabhain 25-year-old 43% ABV

The malt and salt that you expect from a Bunnahabhain are in place, but this is an altogether bigger, more lavish whisky than others in the portfolio. The fruits are rich and chewy, the oak influence is big and bold, and the core barley is delightfully full and sweet. Very good indeed, but whether I would trade three bottles of 18-year-old for one of these is a moot point.

Bunnahabhain Toiteach 46% ABV

Anything the other Islays can do . . . Here is public proof that Bunnahabhain can do peat. The nose is quite shy, although the peat is there, but on the palate there is a fascinating mix of sherry fruits, peat, and pepper.

CAOL ILA

www.malts.com

Caol Ila is one of the fastest-growing of all Scottish malts and, as people discover it, that growth might well accelerate. Despite the fact that it turns up in scores of independent bottlings, it has been something of an industry secret because a high proportion of it goes into blends, particularly Johnnie Walker. Its emergence as a single malt in the early part of the millennium may have stemmed from an accounting mistake. Caol Ila is owned by Diageo and is one of two distilleries owned by the company on Islay. The other is Lagavulin, which was one of the original six Classic Malts that were sold together to pubs in a display plinth. A few years ago, the company realized that it had miscounted its stock of Lagavulin and, once the Classic Malt allocation had been dealt with, there was not much left for everyone else. So Caol Ila stepped into the breach. Much of the output from the distillery going into blends is unpeated and occasionally appears as such in the form of special bottlings.

Caol Ila 12-year-old 43% ABV

One of the reasons Caol Ila is such a good blending malt is its oiliness, and this is oily—but in the nicest possible way. At this age, it is a lively malt, with sooty peat and some citrus fruits, as well as some burnt bacon rind, all adding to a rich tapestry of flavors.

Caol Ila 18-year-old 43% ABV

There is a view that peat is at its liveliest and most expressive when it is young and that, once it has been aged for more than 15 years, it loses some of its effect. The imperious Lagavulin 16-year-old, however, provides a big counter-argument to that view, the release of the Laphroaig 18-year-old last year demolishes it off entirely, and this mix of age, sophistication, and oily smoke demonstrates that a peated whisky need never be too old to rock and roll.

Caol Ila 25-year-old 59.4% ABV

An Islay classic—with the oils, sea spray, smokiness, barbecued trout with lemon, burnt bacon, and oak all in evidence and all playing a role in making this one of the very best malts that you can buy.

Caol Ila Cask Strength
61.6% ABV

The battering-ram strength of this one demands water, but that in turn unlocks some sweet fruits among the oil, seaweed, and smoke. They tell you on the bottle to mix this one part whisky to two parts water. Do not be tempted to do so. This should be three parts whisky to one part water, so that you are drinking it in the high forties ABV and are able to appreciate the full pepper and peat attack of the whisky. When it comes to this unmissable classic, you can take the responsible drinking theory too far, you know.

CARDHU

www.malts.com

Cardhu's main claim to fame in recent years has stemmed from an unholy row caused when its owners, Diageo, added malt from other distilleries to it and branded it as Cardhu Pure malt. That story has been regurgitated ad nauseam elsewhere, so let's not bother with it here.

Cardhu is in Speyside, and it makes the best 12-year-old malt in the region. The distillery is the symbolic home of Johnnie Walker, and it has an amazing history. Originally founded by whisky smuggler John Cummings and his wife, Helen, at Cardow farm in 1811, it was run by first Helen, then her daughter-in-law Elizabeth, who became famed for her whisky-making and marketing ability, and who expanded the distillery into a major operation. This example remains one of the few times that women have run whisky distilleries, made all the more amazing given that it happened during the Victorian era, when women tended to play a far more submissive role in society.

Elizabeth's son, John Fleetwood Cummings, took over from her and was the first person in Speyside to own a car. He was driving it back to the distillery when he encountered

Willie, the distillery's handyman, coming the other way on his bicycle. Willie, who had imbibed a few drams of Cardhu and had never seen a car before, did not quite know how to avoid it, so steered first left, then right, before riding off the road altogether and ending up in a ditch.

Cummings stopped his car and, rather than check to see whether Willie was all right or to apologize for driving him off the road, unfairly berated him for being drunk instead. "Yer a disgrace to yersel', yer a disgrace to yer family, and yer a disgrace to my distillery," he said, to which Willie replied, "It's a wonderful thing, this whisky. It puts some of us in big, flashy cars, and it puts others of us in the ditch."

The license plate of that first car can still be seen in Speyside on a blue Mercedes. A few years ago, the owner turned down an offer from London-based porn magazine and sex-show promoter Paul Raymond for the license plate. Raymond had realized that, if the number was attached to a car with the rivets in the right place, the number "SO11O" would look very much like "Soho."

Cardhu 12-year-old 40% ABV

Hard to find outside Spain, but this an absolute must for fans of Speyside malts. This is the whisky equivalent of the chocolate factory of Johnny Depp's Willy Wonka in the 2005 movie *Charlie and the Chocolate Factory*: an oral mass of happy, bright colors and an overdose of the sweetest, fruitiest, most delectable flavors you could ever imagine.

Cardhu Special Cask Reserve
40% ABV

Fuller and with an added third dimension over the 12-year-old, this expression has some nuttiness among the malt. Vanilla and oak both make an appearance here, in another very palatable malt.

CLYNELISH

The coastal road from Inverness to Wick has been described as Scotland's forgotten coastline, but it is home to a string of excellent distilleries, including Glen Ord, Glenmorangie, Balblair, and Dalmore. Clynelish is here, too; a distillery that is sometimes not given the credit due to it. This is partly because it is a relatively new distillery built in the 1960s and is overshadowed by the ghost of Brora, which occupied the same site for a few years, but was finally put down and replaced by Clynelish. Shame, really, because it produces very good whisky. No doubt its day will come.

Clynelish 14-year-old 46% ABV

With green fruit and some melon on the nose, and zippy lemon sherbet and fruits on the palate, this expression is given an extra dimension by its strength, together with traces of pepper and peat to round it all off.

Clynelish Distiller's Edition 46% ABV

This has been put into big sherry casks—and it shows, with the Clynelish at the heart of the mix struggling to keep its head above the influence of the cask and just about succeeding. Arguably, Clynelish does not need this treatment, but it is worth trying because I suspect some people will fall in love with the unusual mix.

CRAGGANMORE

www.malts.com

Depending on how you define the region, well over half and up to two-thirds of Scotland's distilleries are in Speyside. We associate distilleries there with fruity, sweet, honeyed whiskies, but it was not always that way. Before the Industrial Revolution, distilleries would have used peated fires to dry the barley. But Scotland's whisky has a long and close association with trains and, as the railways spread into Scotland, they brought with them cheaper commercial fuels such as coal. On the mainland, peat was made redundant and its use continued on the islands only because trains do not generally travel through the sea.

Cragganmore was one of the first distilleries to build a railway siding into the heart of the distillery, ensuring an efficient method of bringing in supplies from the mainland and shipping out malt.

The distillery's whisky was chosen by Diageo to represent Speyside in its Classic Malts collection.

Cragganmore 12-year-old 40% ABV

If you are of the view that Speyside whiskies tend to be predictably fruity, easy-drinking, and unchallenging, then this should change your mind. It is a surprisingly complex malt, with heather and spring meadow on the nose, while on the palate you will find deep fruits, oak, and wisps of smoke.

Cragganmore Distiller's Edition 43% ABV

This is Cragganmore finished in a port cask, and such a sympathetic extra maturation works well, giving the already complex malt additional red berry and cherry flavors and an extra sweetness.

DALMORE

www.thedalmore.com

You know those signs that say: "You don't have to be mad to work here, but it helps"? Well, they were invented for places such as Dalmore.

The year 2010 marked the fiftieth anniversary of the distillery being part of the Whyte & Mackay stable. It is located in the northeast of Scotland on the Cromarty Firth, and it is as wacky and kooky as a whisky distillery gets. While many distilleries are logically constructed and contain a balance of wash and spirits stills, Dalmore is anything but. Its stills come in a range of shapes and sizes, and distilling is a hit-and-miss affair, with different runs coming off at different strengths. Making malt here is the whisky equivalent of flying a kite in a gale. It is a demanding process made more complicated by the unpredictable water supply. Water travels down to the distillery from a little reservoir, but the seawater must travel over a wall. When the water levels fall below the level of the wall, the water stops flowing completely. Global warming, therefore, is not the distillery's friend.

Making spirit here is a tough ask, so you can excuse a certain degree of ordered chaos. The resulting spirit, though, is robust, fruity, and the starting point for some of the finest malt whisky to be found in the Highlands.

The Dalmore 12-year-old 40% ABV

A burnt caramel, rich orange, and mandarin taste and some oaky notes make this seem older than its 12 years, but it is a big, full malt with lots of flavor, most notably a sprinkling of cocoa powder and some charming spicy notes.

The Dalmore 15-year-old
40% ABV

The nose is reminiscent of a church on Easter Sunday morning, with polished oak, fresh flowers, and a hint of sherry. On the palate, there are bucketloads of fruit, with tangerines and satsumas in the mix. Vanilla, cinnamon, and some woody tannins all contribute to a big, bold, and spicy whisky. Delicious.

The Dalmore 18-year-old 43% ABV

[1]

Released late in 2009, this is a step up for Whyte & Mackay because it is bottled at 43% ABV instead of the company's favored 40% ABV. It has a bold and meaty nose, with a trace of sulfur, then intense orange and red berry fruits. The palate is a big and busty mix of fruit, chewy malt, oak, and spice—all rather wonderful. This is a heavyweight of a whisky.

The Dalmore Gran Reserva 40% ABV

[star] [1] [S]

A sort of Dalmore greatest hits package, with some creamy walnut-and-date cake, dried fruit and tangy spice on the nose, and a sharper and fuller spiciness on the palate, with some pleasant fruit notes.

The Dalmore 40-year-old 40% ABV

[star] [1] [grid] [S]

Historically, whisky stills in the Highlands are small. While barley was in abundance in the Lowlands and big commercial malt stills were built to produce the volumes of malt needed to service the growing blended whisky market, in the Highlands barley is harder to grow, so there was less of it to turn into whisky. Smaller stills also suited the illicit distillers because they could be transported or hidden from the gaugers more easily. But the more the spirit comes into contact with copper, the more fats, oils, and flavor compounds are removed, creating lighter, more floral malts. Short, squat stills allow more to pass through into the final spirit, making for an oilier, meatier, and fuller malt. Robust malt is better suited to standing up to the influence of the cask, and that is why you can get the likes of Dalmore and Macallan maturing 40, 50, and even 60 years, and they still taste good. This has a shy nose at first, and you do not want to be adding water to a whisky this old, so work with it. Eventually, there are some orangeade and lemonade notes. The taste is elegant, delicate, and citrusy. Added to this are some dark chocolate, nutmeg, and plummy notes for good measure.

Dalmore 1263 King Alexander III 40% ABV

[1]

Legend has it that one of the Mackenzie clan saved Alexander III, King of Scots, from death during a hunting trip, and as a way of thanks he granted the Mackenzies the right to use the royal stag's head in its livery. When the Mackenzies became involved with the Dalmore, the stag's-head emblem was taken up and now appears proudly on all bottles. In commemoration of this, whisky maker Richard Paterson has married casks of the Dalmore of different ages and of different types. As a result, the whisky has all sorts going on, with plums, red licorice, vanilla, and red berry fruits on the nose, and a big hit of stewed fruits, oak, cherry, and spice on the palate.

Dalmore 1974 45% ABV

[1] [grid]

If the Dalmore was the Beatles, then this is Ringo Starr, the least charismatic and stylish of the bunch, but a Beatle all the same. Actually, it is a bit of a weirdo, with milk chocolate, soft yellow fruit, and some oak in the mix. The finish is long and fruity, but it does not taste as if it belongs in this company. Odd, but intriguing nevertheless.

Dalmore Sirius 45% ABV

[star] [1] [grid] [S] [glass]

An extremely limited 1951 malt, making it more than 50 years old. Unsurprisingly, it is rich and venerable, full of burnt oak, toffee, and deep orange marmalade notes—and surprisingly aggressive and robust for such an old boy. Pretty special, but at about $15,000 a bottle it ought to be. I tasted my small sample during the second half of the thumping that New Zealand's All Blacks rugby team gave to France in Marseille—this was a super-premium malt moment, if there ever was one.

DALWHINNIE

www.malts.com

Arguably the funniest sign in the United Kingdom is the one that greets you at the tiny village of Dalwhinnie, just off the A9 on the road up to Aviemore.

"Dalwhinnie—twinned with Las Vegas," it says. In winter, when the snow is several feet deep and the icy gusts from the Cairngorms reach into your soul, the village is a remote and barren place, and really as far removed from the glitz and glamor of Las Vegas as you can get. Thankfully, God invented whisky for such occasions, and the malt at Dalwhinnie is the ideal tonic for such extreme conditions. The distillery can no longer claim to be the highest in Scotland, now that Braeval has reopened, but sipping a 15-year-old at altitude is a marvelous experience.

Dalwhinnie's sign is not the funniest I've ever seen. That honor goes to a house door near Cork in Ireland. It says: "This is the back door. The front door is round the back."

Dalwhinnie 15-year-old 43% ABV

Dalwhinnie does not come in a range of ages, but that is because its owners discovered long ago that its perfect age is 15. This is one of the truly great malts, traditionally part of the Classic Malts range. It is a rich, full, and mouth-coating malt defined by two very different traits: intense, honeyed sweetness wrapped around the fruit and malt center, and a peaty earthy carpet to rest it all on. That combination—sweet and earthy—is what great Highland whiskies are about.

Dalwhinnie Distiller's Edition 43% ABV

Tasting this after the 15-year-old is like watching the Rolling Stones do "Start Me Up" for an encore after they have ended their set with "Jumpin' Jack Flash," "Satisfaction," and "Sympathy for the Devil." It is perfectly fine, better than many other malts, and you wouldn't turn it down—but you have just pretty much experienced perfection, so this cannot help but be a tad disappointing. That said, the oloroso influence does work well, and there is still plenty to enjoy, particularly for fans of the core whisky.

DEANSTON

www.burnstewartdistillers.com

It is cool to be green these days, so Deanston has an advantage over many of its competitors, one that its owner has hit upon and taken full advantage of.

The distillery is like no other. It lies beside a fast-flowing river and is a tall, foreboding eighteenth-century cotton mill of the dark satanic variety. It was founded by the great industrialist Richard Arkwright, and it channels water from the river to drive a wheel and power its own electricity plant, so successfully that it provides light and heat for both the distillery and the local community.

The old Deanston sold very well in the United States a while back, but was not stunning. The new 12-year-old is an altogether richer, fruitier affair. It is like Speyside, with spicy, nutty notes and eco-friendly packaging.

Deanston 12-year-old 46.3% ABV

The new 12-year-old Deanston is a vast improvement on the original standard Deanston, with a softer and more rounded fruity palate and a longer finish.

DUFFTOWN

www.malts.com

Clever people, the malt marketing folk at Diageo. Having backed down in the row over Cardhu a few years ago, they came up with another way of spreading their limited stocks farther afield by encouraging people to drink malts they might not otherwise have chosen. A few years back, the Singleton of Auchroisk built up a considerable following before it was eventually withdrawn. Now the Singleton is back—but what you are drinking depends on where you drink it. In Asia, the malt in the bottle is a sherried version of Glen Ord. In the United States, it is Glendullan; in Europe, Dufftown.

It is a clever ruse because many customers are drawn to the words "The Singleton," which appear on the label in bold capitals. The distillery name is in light italics. In many whisky shops, you will find it under S for "Singleton," not D for "Dufftown" or G for "Glendullan." The whole package is cleverly designed to encourage people who would never buy a Glendullan or Dufftown to do so by purchasing a Singleton.

Is this a con, and does it matter? Not really, especially if the customer ends up with a quality bottle of malt. And, actually, you cannot help but admire Diageo's chutzpah.

Singleton of Dufftown 40% ABV

This is a bit like the quiet bloke who comes down to the bar to watch baseball with the guys. All perfectly pleasant and harmless, but you would not really miss him if he was not there. This is a workmanlike Speysider with nothing worthy of criticism, but nothing to get excited about, either. It is included here, though, because it is an easy-drinking entry-level malt—a tame pony to teach novices how to sit in the saddle.

EDRADOUR

www.edradour.co.uk

Few distilleries command as much love and devotion as Edradour. This is partly due to the fact that is very small and perfectly formed. Production at the distillery is just 90,000 liters (23,775 U.S gallons) a year, a drop in the whisky ocean compared to Glenfiddich and Glenlivet, both of which can produce 10 million liters (2,641,720 U.S. gallons) of spirit annually. The whole production process is housed in one small outbuilding, although the site has grown in recent years with the addition of a bottling hall, visitor center, and shop. Until recently, Edradour was Scotland's smallest distillery, now Kilchoman and the new Isle of Lewis distillery match it. Tour-bus drivers love this pretty distillery because it is an easy drive from Glasgow and Edinburgh, and a good stop-off for the Highlands.

Edradour 40% ABV

An attractive mix of lemon, lime, and gentle spearmint on the nose; soft fruits, honey, and vanilla on the palate; and a lingering, pleasant finish with a hint of peat.

FETTERCAIRN

Fettercairn is a rustic Highland distillery that has not had the best press in the past. This is a little unfair. One celebrated whisky writer was so critical of the malt from here that he has not been invited back. Which in turn means that he has never updated or reassessed his criticism. Perhaps he should. About 14 years ago, the distillery replaced the old stainless-steel condensers with copper ones, and over the past couple of years the 12-year-old has been made with spirit from after the change. Some of the whisky in casks at

the distillery suggests that Fettercairn has a lot to offer as a single malt, including some sparkling new packaging and a new range of four malts. The malt has adopted a unicorn emblem as a reference to the Ramsays, distillery owners who were noted for their philanthropist tendencies. Fettercairn was sold on to the Gladstone family, and Liberal Prime Minister William's familiarity with whisky led to legislative reforms that abolished the malt tax, allowing the sale of whisky in bottles to the public, and tax laws, so distillers were no longer taxed on the "angel's share," the 2% of spirit that evaporates during maturation.

There is plenty to thank this distillery for, so the Fettercairn fightback starts here.

Fettercairn 24-year-old

44.6% ABV

An awkward malt, which initially hides behind a slightly rubbery, sulfury nose, but in time gives way to a taste of tangerine and grapefruit, some cocoa, and some prickly spices. It is like prising conversation out of a sulky adolescent schoolboy, and finding that he is remarkably bright and interesting—just lacking in confidence. A strange but ultimately worthwhile experience.

Fettercairn 30-year-old 43.3% ABV

The best of these three old releases is a delight: surprisingly young-tasting, with zest of red apple and soft pear, some melon and orange fruit, and eventually a subtle wave of spice. The age starts to make itself known only very late on. In the finish, there is blackcurrant sherbet. Fettercairn—poor? Oh, no.

Fettercairn 40-year-old 40% ABV

Classic old Highland whisky without a blemish. Early on, it is surprisingly soft and gentle, with grapefruit and lemon, and some savory notes, but it builds, with oak and spice adding to the body, and gives way to raspberry and glacé cherry. The finish is long but gentle, with spice and oak.

GLENCADAM

www.angusdundee.co.uk

The traditional view of a distillery setting up close to a primary water source is turned on its head by Glencadam. The Highland distillery, close to Brechin on Scotland's coast, pipes water 30 miles to meet its distilling needs, but the malt made here does have a distinctive creaminess. Glencadam is a notably creamy malt, using unpeated malt.

Glencadam 10-year-old 46% ABV

Sweet strawberries with ice cream on the nose, pleasant and easy malt and spice on the mouth, with some raspberries, strawberries, and red currants. The spiciness remains into the finish.

Glencadam 15-year-old
46% ABV

Arguably the definitive Glencadam bottling, here the extra age gives the malt a fuller and richer mouthfeel. The berry notes are still prevalent on the nose, but on the palate the oak makes its presence felt, and with time tannins and spices battle against the berry fruits, leaving a long oaky and spicy finish.

Glencadam 25-year-old 46% ABV

A rare and unusual bottling of Glencadam because there are some distinctive sherry influences. Indeed, this is a classic big Christmas pudding of a whisky, with sherry-soaked raisins and mulled wine on the nose, leather, raisins, plummy fruits, and spices on the palate, and tasty strawberries and ice cream in the fruity finish.

GLENDRONACH

www.glendronachdistillery.com

Talk to people with long memories in and around Huntley, and they will talk of GlenDronach as a big, proud, and dark sherried whisky, a million miles away from the somewhat anemic 12-year-old that kept the brand's name alive. For many years, the distillery's owners, Allied Domecq, did not seem to know what to do with it, and it seemed to drift, unloved and uncared for. When Allied was broken up, Teacher's and Ardmore went to Beam Global, while GlenDronach, a key component in the blend, went to Pernod Ricard. It felt like a divorce, and the distillery's wretchedness was summed up on the quaint maltings floor, where cardboard figures had been placed to show visitors what a working maltings was like. But a couple of years ago, the team behind BenRiach got its hands on the distillery and wasted no time in restoring the distillery to its former glory. A new range of standard bottlings and a number of special releases—yes, big, dark sherried ones—has helped to put GlenDronach well and truly back on the distillery map.

GlenDronach 12-year-old 40% ABV

Some mint toffee on the nose, with sherry, berries, and citrus fruit. The taste is reminiscent of blackcurrant and cranberry, and there is some pepper and an earthy undercarpet, so that the overall effect is not too sweet. The finish is savory, with some peat.

GlenDronach 15-year-old 46% ABV 2009 RELEASE

The new version of the 15-year-old is deep brown, leaving the drinker in no doubt about what is coming next. There are distinctive wisps of sulfur on the nose, but this does not detract from a grandiose and complex nose that includes sherry, floral notes, and chicory coffee. The taste is also intense and challenging, with sweet fruitcake at first, then a wave of chili and paprika, and finally some woodiness, astringency, and plummy smoke. The finish is about three Ps: plums, peat, and pepper. Wonderful.

GlenDronach 18-year-old

46% ABV 2009 RELEASE

Not for the fainthearted, this. You want big old-fashioned sherry cask malt? You've got it. There are earthy and rootsy aromas, with some distinctive sulfur on the nose, but don't be too put off—the taste is all about plum, stewed fruits, and raisins. There is some astringency from the wood late on, some peat and menthol, and some spices in the finish.

GlenDronach 33-year-old 40% ABV

Here, there are Kahlúa and dark coffee on the nose, with raisins and mince pie filling. The taste at first is fruity, with peach in the mix, then tannins and spices come through. It is all ordered and rounded, with a long, soft finish.

GlenDronach Cask No. 483 1971
Single-Cask Batch 1 49.4% ABV

A classic example of the sort of weighty whisky we might come to expect from GlenDronach, with rich sherry, spice, and earthy peat notes on the nose, blood orange, dark chocolate, espresso coffee, and woody tannins. This is to malt whisky what Batista is to world wrestling.

GlenDronach Cask No. 4424
1988 Gaja Barolo 54.3% ABV

Thinner and less sweet than the previous cask, and much spicier, with orange marmalade, some lemon, and clear honey in the mix.

GLEN ELGIN
www.malts.com

Several towns lay claim to being the "capital" of Speyside, but Elgin's claim is as good as any. Elgin is, according to its website, Scotland's smallest city and its friendliest, and has a fascinating history based around its cathedral. But it also lies close to several distilleries and is home to outstanding independent bottling company Gordon & MacPhail. The company's large store in the town is well worth a visit if you are in the area, especially if you're looking for something different, whiskywise. Glen Elgin distillery lies in a small village on a road into the town and has been long associated with the White Horse blend. It has a substantial following as a single malt, too, and its reputation as a rich, fully flavored, and honeyed malt has been enhanced by some special bottlings in recent years, including a cask-strength bottling as part of Diageo's Manager's Choice series in 2009.

Glen Elgin 12-year-old 43% ABV

This is an example of classic Speyside at its best. You do not see it very often, but, if you like clean, sweet, malty, and plummy whiskies, then you need to seek this one out. An unsung hero.

Glen Elgin 16-year-old 58.5% ABV

A lovely rich nose with a touch of sherry, blackberries, and blueberries. The taste is big, sherried, and intense, with some stewed fruits, oak, spice, and aniseed.

THE GLENDRONACH DISTILLERY

Forgue by Huntly, Aberdeenshire AB5 4DB
www.glendronachdistillery.co.uk

Visit the GlenDronach these days, and you will quickly pick up on the positive sense of purpose. New facilities, fresh paint, happy staff, and some great malts all contribute to the feel-good factor.

But it was not always this way. Three years ago, a brooding black cloud of gloom hung over the stills and warehouses. It was a moribund, directionless distillery with its heart ripped out, the victim in a messy divorce when parent company Allied Domecq was broken up. Long a key malt in the makeup of Teacher's, it was split from the blend and sister distillery Ardmore when they passed to Beam Global. GlenDronach went to Pernod Ricard, a company that already had more than enough distilleries in the region. Unloved and uncared for, it started to look shabby and weather-worn, its visitor center felt dated and irrelevant, and it was all but ignored by the whisky-loving public.

Perhaps the most potent symbolism of all, though, came courtesy of a whisky bottle that is framed in the old wood-paneled boardroom.

The whisky was bonded in 1884 and bottled in 1913, and was one of three purchased by three friends. When World War I was declared, the men signed up and decided to hold their whisky for when they returned from a victorious war a few months later.

It never happened. Two of the friends were killed, and the owner of this bottle put it away in a cupboard, unopened. In the 1960s, when the owner of the bottle died, his family rediscovered it and handed it back to the distillery.

Did that old soldier ever look at the bottle again, or was the memory too painful? Did he often hold it and think about his fallen friends? Did he consider opening it in their memory, but find that he could not bring himself to take out the cork? Three years ago, that bottle epitomized GlenDronach itself: a wretched story at the heart of a wretched distillery.

Now, three years on, GlenDronach is going places. Now owned by the same team that owns BenRiach, it has taken a new lease on life. New signs have been put up, everything has been painted, and the old 1960s-style visitor center and offices have been completely upgraded. Not, it has to be said, without a struggle.

"One of our major projects last year was to develop a brand-new visitor center and shop," says Kerry White. "This we achieved, but the distillery was badly flooded shortly after completion, and much of the work was ruined, so we had to restore it all over again. But we managed to do this for the tourist season in 2010."

A little woods at the back of the distillery dedicated to the Gordon Highlanders is also being restored to its former glory, to give ex-soldiers a memorial their families can be proud of, and the run-down brewers' house has been refurbished to provide accommodation for visitors to the site.

Best of all, though, is the flow of new and exciting bottlings. Managing director Billy Walker is determined to restore GlenDronach's reputation as a distillery producing the finest sherried whiskies and, to this end, 2010 alone saw the launch of a 21-year-old, a 31-year-old, and a number of special finishes.

LEFT Under the distillery's new owners GlenDronach is returning to its rich sherried roots. This is a vintage bottling.

RIGHT Whisky supremo Billy Walker inspects a glass of malt from his new distillery. Walker has already restored the fortunes of BenRiach.

ABOVE RIGHT The pretty distillery at GlenDronach, now being restored to its full glory.

KEY WHISKIES

GlenDronach 12-year-old 40% ABV
GlenDronach 15-year-old 46% ABV
GlenDronach 18-year-old 46% ABV
GlenDronach 33-year-old 40% ABV
GlenDronach Cask No. 483 1971 49.4% ABV
GlenDronach Cask No. 4424 1988 Gaja Barolo 54.3% ABV

WELL, FANCY THAT . . .

One of the buildings that the new owners of GlenDronach have restored is the two-story warehouse—one of the few of its kind in Scotland. The warehouse has always been part of the traditional maturation process at the distillery and, while two stories in the Highlands is not quite the same thing as the multi-storied warehouse in Kentucky, lovers of GlenDronach believe that the two floors do affect the way in which the spirit matures.

GLENFARCLAS

www.glenfarclas.co.uk

Glenfarclas is to whisky what Bentleys are to cars—excellently made, to the highest standards, in the traditional manner. You do not mess with classic style, so there are no gimmicky finishes from the distillery, no malt alchemy in its labs. Glenfarclas is one of the last family firms still making whisky in Scotland, and it survives by simply being the best at what it does. And what it does is to produce big, bold, and fruity sherry-influenced Speyside malts.

Much of the day-to-day management is handled by father-and-son team John and George, with George very much in the front line. After several years of traveling the world promoting his malts, George may well be cutting back on the globetrotting. It is not all it is cracked up to be, he says, especially when you are detained at immigration in the Far East twice—once for carrying a plastic bag full of white powder, which turned out to be barley flour, and once for carrying a suspicious-looking lump of peat.

Glenfarclas 10-year-old 40% ABV

There are some orange and lemon on the nose here, followed by Christmas fruitcake, rich malt, some orange notes, and a warm and delightful finish.

Glenfarclas 105 60% ABV

A weighty, intense classic malt, and the epitome of clean and crisp sherried whisky. Clearly, you need some added water, and this releases raisin, date, and plum flavors, sweet spicy orange notes, and some delicious crystallized maltiness at the end.

Glenfarclas 12-year-old 43% ABV

A rich and full sherry influence here, with stewed plums and apricots, honey, cinnamon, and nutmeg. This is a perfect winter-warmer.

Glenfarclas 15-year-old 46% ABV

The extra strength and age add another dimension to the malt here. Tangerine, marzipan, and red berries complement the sherry trifle and Christmas fruitcake mix. Some oak adds tannin and spice, to give the overall flavor balance and shape.

Glenfarclas 21-year-old
43% ABV

A slight departure from what has gone before, the intensity of previous bottling is replaced by a candyish flavor, less sherried, and perhaps with more vanilla and yellow fruit notes.

Glenfarclas 25-year-old 43% ABV

Glenfarclas responds well to old age. I was given a small bottle of whisky from the year of my birth by John Grant at a Speyside festival. From 1961, 44 years old, it was sublime, one of the best whiskies I've ever had—toasty, spicy, and fruity. I am saving my bottle for when England next wins the soccer World Cup: a heady and happy day, for sure.

Glenfarclas 30-year-old 43% ABV

The nose is surprisingly soft and rounded, with some marmalade and oak notes. The oak is noticeable in the taste, too, with crystal barley, pepper, and earthiness.

Glenfarclas 40-year-old 43% ABV

A big wave of pink grapefruit, burnt toast, and chunky lime marmalade on the nose, with rich orange marmalade, dark orange chocolate, and Turkish delight on the palate. A very lucid flavor for one so old.

Glenfarclas Family Cask

Glenfarclas might not be experimenting with weird casks and strange finishes, but that does not mean that it is not capable of being a pioneer in the world of malt.

The Family Cask range has no parallel in whisky—43 single-cask bottlings covering 43 consecutive years from 1952 to 1994. This is the equivalent to the long-awaited complete archive set of recordings that Neil Young has been promising and which has been appearing in dribs and drabs—a chance to plot the complete history of a distillery. Unsurprisingly, over such a lengthy period of time, there is a huge variety on display.

Among the casks are these:

1952 ED2 Cask 2115 46.5% ABV
Nose: Herb garden, plums, raisins.
Palate: Sweet, salt, and spice. Tannins.

1954 Cask 444 52.6% ABV
Nose: Chestnut, oak, root vegetables.
Palate: Cocoa, dark chocolate, bitter oak.

1957 Release III Cask 2 46.2% ABV
Nose: Stewed fruits, date, oak, dark treacle, nutty.
Palate: Intense marmalade, menthol.

1959 Release III Cask 3227 50.9% ABV
Nose: Polished mahogany office.
Palate: Dark chocolate, treacle, toffee.

1962 Cask 2647 52.0% ABV
Nose: Dry sherry. Cocoa, dark chocolate, orange, and limes.
Palate: Rum-and-raisin chocolate, mint, sherry, cocoa, oak.

1969 Cask 3188 55.6% ABV
Nose: Spent-match sulfur, toasty, candy, shrimps.
Palate: Sweet, metallic. Raisins, dark cherry, menthol.

1972 Cask 3546 51.1% ABV
Nose: Dusty and musty, smoky, resinous.
Palate: Mint. Sharp spices. Wood. Hot.

1975 Cask 5038 51.4% ABV
Nose: Blood orange, hot fruit mincemeat pie filling.
Palate: Orange fruits, licorice, soft toffee.

1976 Cask 3111 49.4% ABV
Nose: Ginger cookie. Date. Cake batter. European-style fruit.
Palate: Sweet, full, and fruity. Dates and late pepper.

1978 Cask 587 50.3% ABV
Nose: Linseed oil, nuts, mandarin.
Palate: Rapier-sharp spice, bitter fruit, liqueur-like.

1979 Cask 146 52.8% ABV
Nose: Sweet, honey, and sherbet.
Palate: Honey and lemon, smooth and rounded.

1981 Cask 29 52.4% ABV
Nose: Chinese spices, tingling.
Palate: Plum fruit, menthol.

1988 Cask 7033 56.3% ABV
Nose: Odd, herbal, oil paints.
Palate: Soft fruit, pear, licorice.

1989 Cask 11721 60.0% ABV
Nose: Powerful, rich orange, fruitcake, sulfur.
Palate: Rich, sweet, rounded, and very fruity.

1991 Cask 5623 57.9% ABV
Nose: Almost European liqueur-like fruit, sweet.
Palate: Rich, mandarin orange, creamy, oak.

1993 Cask 11 58.9% ABV
Nose: Metallic, sulfur.
Palate: Sherry, sharp astringent oak, dark, intense finish

ABOVE A lineup of all 43 expressions of the Glenfarclas Family Cask collection, covering the years 1952 to 1994, makes for an impressive sight—and an even more impressive collection of tasting experiences.

GLENFIDDICH
www.glenfiddich.com

Lovers of whisky have a great deal to thank William Grant and his number-one malt Glenfiddich for. Familiarity breeds contempt, and it is understandable that experienced malt lovers might feel the overwhelming urge to move swiftly on, but please don't. Pause for a minute, and pay tribute to the malt that kicked it all off.

Talk to family member Peter Gordon about how William Grant & Sons has consistently sensed the way the wind is blowing and continually gotten it right when making big make-or-break decisions, and he will modestly tell you that it has been through luck, rather than design.

I don't buy that. It is a bit like the "lucky" fisherman who keeps catching the best fish because, by chance, he is always in the right place at the right time. And from the 1960s, when the company set about putting single malt under the spotlight, right up to the launch of cool and trendy Monkey Shoulder, William Grant has been instrumental in the development of modern-day malt whisky.

It is hard to believe now, but 50 years ago there was no real single-malt market. Single malts were sold in Scotland and close to the distilleries where they were produced, but their influence was minimal. But William Grant & Sons had a problem. To make its blended whiskies, it relied on grain whisky from its rivals. So what would happen if the suppliers turned off the tap?

The company made two huge decisions in the early 1960s: It built its own grain distillery at Girvan, and it bottled Glenfiddich as a single-malt whisky. It had already come up with the distinctive three-sided bottle. To help to explain the world of whisky, the company also opened up the very first distillery visitor center.

The rest, as they say, is history. But Glenfiddich was no pacesetter, leading from the front, then falling away to let bigger and stronger competitors get out front. Glenfiddich has held on to the top spot in the single-malt market ever since. If you cannot get excited by the standard 12-year-old, then the distillery offers all sorts of more esoteric and special releases, culminating with a remarkably delicate 50-year-old in 2009.

Glenfiddich 12-year-old 40% ABV

One of the things that the whisky industry rarely talks about is the way malt whisky changes over time. Better cask management and a greater understanding of production and maturation on the one hand, and better yielding but arguably blander and more homogeneous barley strains on the other, mean that the spirit in the bottle today will not be the same as it was 20 years ago. Booms and busts affect whisky, too. There will be times when a standard 12-year-old contains more rare and aged whisky than at others, for instance, depending on malt supply and demand.

There is no doubt that this has changed in recent years and is now a better whisky than it used to be. This well-made but unchallenging entry-level malt is fresh and fruity, with vanilla malts.

Glenfiddich 15-year-old Solera Reserve
40% ABV

Unfortunately, this whisky will always remind me of a prospective candidate for the British Conservative Party who joined a group of whisky writers for a short leg of a sponsored walk from Glenfiddich to the Craigellachie Hotel in Speyside. I got stuck with the Tory, an Englishman who bemoaned the fact that he had been banished not just to the north, but to Scotland. As I walked with him, he argued that we should not be raising money for Africa anymore because everyone was so rich there now they all had sunstrips on their cars thanking the British for their new wealth; he thought that whisky would be a more viable product if the Scots just added flavorings to industrial alcohol.

A fine example of Speyside malt, this has a vanilla creaminess, plus soft fruits, sweet barley, and a touch of oak. It is beautifully crafted.

Glenfiddich 18-year-old 40% ABV

A full fruit bowl of overripe, squelchy fruit, with plums, raisins, apricots, and grapes all in the mix, as well as some toasty oaky notes, make this a sophisticated and stylish drinking treat.

Glenfiddich 21-year-old 40% ABV

Many of my favorite whiskies are aged 17 or 18 years, but for some reason Glenfiddich does not seem to fully hits its stride until this age. This would probably be my pick of the entire core range, although there are some beauties in the rarer and older vintage range.

Hard candies, new office, and lemon cleaner or polish on the nose, and lemon and honey on the palate, plus sweet malt, oak, and a touch of menthol. The finish is quite zingy, with lemon and grapefruit in evidence.

Glenfiddich 1983 Cask 10888 53.4% ABV

Big sherry notes on the nose, with rich Christmas fruitcake, sweet spices, and some nutty notes. The taste has lots of big fruit, mince pies, sweet pepper, and oak, and there is a licorice and hickory twist, too.

Glenfiddich 1975 Cask 15354 47.3% ABV

The aromas here are soft and welcoming, with vanilla, honey, and hard-candy fruits. The taste is diverse and complex, with spearmint and chili mixed among soft yellow fruits. The finish is balanced between fruit, oak, spice, and honey.

Glenfiddich Vintage Reserve 1975 Cask 287
51.1% ABV

An odd rootsy and earthy nose here, but the taste is much better—it is a full, oily malt with grapes, prunes, pear, and soft peach. Gentle spices arrive toward the end.

Glenfiddich Rare Collection 40-year-old
43.6% ABV

This whisky does not give up its treasures lightly, and you have to chase the nose a bit. But it is a surprisingly soft and subtle whisky, with some lovely yellow fruit flavors, as well as honey and vanilla. There are few signs of age, no negative oak or spice notes, and a lingering and lovely finish. Quite outstanding.

Glenfiddich 50-year-old 46.1% ABV

Should a whisky that retails at $15,000 a bottle and that is pretty much all gone anyway be included in a book such as this? That's a big debate, and one to be held over a dram or two, although probably not with this particular whisky.

OK, I'm there—yes, it should. Once this is gone, it will have gone forever, and there should be a record of it somewhere. William Grant & Sons invited people from all over the world to the launch of this. One bottle arrived accompanied by a piper, then guests were invited to swoon over it. We had songs and a dramatic and quite brilliant recital of Robert Burns's "Ode to a Haggis" by Glenfiddich public relations manager, Libby Lafferty. All this was in honor of one whisky.

It could have been a disaster, an overdose of sentimentality resulting in a massive anticlimax. But it wasn't, simply because this whisky is stunning. At 50 years old, it is imbued with spritely sweet grapefruit, honey, and citrus. Amazingly, you can trace the thread of this malt all the way forward to the petulant teenager that is Monkey Shoulder. It is like watching the scene in Martin Scorsese's *Shine a Light* when Mick Jagger upstages Jack White, the master showing the pupil how it should be done.

Is whisky ever worth $500 a shot? Of course not. Is this a blemish-free, perfectly matured piece of art in a glass and history in a bottle? Very much so. This was distilled before the age of single-malt whisky had fully dawned—and it is an honor to have tasted it.

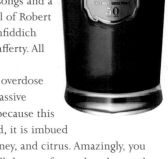

GLEN GARIOCH

www.glengarioch.com

Glen Garioch—pronounced *geery*—is a hidden gem, the unsung sibling in the Morrison Bowmore stable, although that might be changing. Having rebranded and repackaged Auchentoshan, the company seems to be turning its attention to this highly underrated distillery. You will find it north of Aberdeen, off the main road to Speyside in the village of Old Meldrum. It is a small but perfectly formed distillery with a smart, newish visitor center.

Glen Garioch is a Highland whisky, but it has had something of an identity crisis, with a distinctive peaty note playing hide and seek. It is back, in spades, in the latest bottling—but for how long?

Glen Garioch 15-year-old 43% ABV

A Jekyll-and-Hyde malt, with heathery light and almost floral notes on the nose, and a fuller, earthier, and eventually drying prickly taste, with some smoke. The oak makes a fleeting appearance, too, just for good measure.

Glen Garioch Founder's Reserve

48% ABV

Crikey! A new bottling focusing on the fact that this distillery was originally established in the late eighteenth century. If, however, Morrison Bowmore is keen to win over new drinkers to this malt, it sure is taking a difficult route. This is a true Highland laddie, dominated by big spicy, peaty, and earthy notes. Easy it is not, but for me it sits in a special category of old-fashioned Highlanders, along with Ardmore, Benromach, and Glencadam. No bad thing at all, in my book.

GLENGLASSAUGH

www.glenglassaugh.com

In the heady days of 2008, when malt was at its most buoyant and everybody and their dog was after a distillery, Glenglassaugh was snapped up by a private consortium. Its new owners inherited a distillery in a stunning location (it has access to a small private beach), but with virtually no stock at all and with a serious vandalism problem. But they are not messing about—they have recruited two top talents in the form of managing director Stuart Nickerson and former Glenmorangie and Scapa distillery manager Graham Eunson, and have released limited quantities of aged Glenglassaugh (see below) and a couple of "works in progress," including one called the Spirit that Blushes to Speak Its Name and tastes a lot like raspberry liqueur and nothing at all like whisky. Give it time, though . . .

Glenglassaugh 21-year-old 46% ABV

With lemon hard candy and vanilla on the nose, this has a core taste of orange, citrus fruits, and crystallized barley, and supporting roles for mint, cinnamon, chili, and oak. The finish is disciplined and polite.

Glenglassaugh 30-year-old 55.1% ABV

The pick of the bunch, with all the ducks lined up in a neat and balanced row. There are lots of delicious orange marmalade, stewed fruits, and plums on the nose, and it has a zesty, sherbety taste, with pineapple and melon up front and tannins and spices later. The finish is long and fruity, with just the right amount of oak to balance it all up.

Glenglassaugh 40-year-old 44.6% ABV

Dark berries, fruitcake, and plum on the nose, and a creamy toffee and vanilla heart on the palate, with berries, chili, and tannins in the mix. The finish is refined and very long, with the plum and oak holding out longest.

GLENGOYNE

www.glengoyne.com

Glengoyne is Glasgow's other distillery, but it is located a few miles north of the city, straddling the Highland line—the distillery being in the Highlands, the warehouses across the road in the Lowlands. The distillery is owned by independent bottlers Ian MacLeod. Its Islay malt, Smokehead, is currently enjoying some success among younger drinkers and rock fans, which is ironic because for a long time Glengoyne has made an asset of the fact that it is peat-free. A few years back, it even hired a luxury boat and sailed to the Islay festival with a banner that urged whisky fans to drink peat-free whisky—the real taste of malt.

Glengoyne is a lovely distillery, and it employs some of the most charming people in the industry. It offers a comprehensive range of tours and whisky experiences, from the basic tour to a blending course.

Burnfoot 40% ABV

Something of a victory for style over substance, although full marks to the owners for trying to do something genuinely different with the packaging and presentation. Subtle, this isn't. There is no age statement, and it tastes young and two-dimensional. But in its favor, it is a clean and robust whisky, with some endearing sweet and malt notes.

Glengoyne 10-year-old 40% ABV

Another entry-level malt with a clean and crisp malt bite; very refreshing. Wet straw and heather give way to a touch of oak and sweet crystallized ginger, as pure as the water that tumbles down the rocks at the back of the distillery.

Glengoyne 12-year-old Cask Strength

57.2% ABV

This is an intense and pure version of Glengoyne, but not as uncluttered or pure as other bottlings. There is plenty to delight here, though, including cooking-apple notes, apple pip/marzipan, and some vanilla. The malts eventually give way to pepper spices.

Glengoyne 12-year-old 43% ABV

A recent addition to the Glengoyne stable, having been launched a year ago, this has a clean and refreshing green apple taste, lots of crisp barley, and just a small amount of spice late on. This is a beautifully made malt whisky, with flavors all working at their cleanest and sharpest limits.

Glengoyne 16-year-old European Hogshead 52.3% ABV

Clean, fresh straw and barley field on the nose, with crystallized ginger, chewy barley, a big oak hit, and some hickory and red licorice on the palate.

Glengoyne 17-year-old 43% ABV

A great Glengoyne, this one, with dense sherry notes on the nose and palate, the odd swirl of sulfur playing the role of pantomime baddie, but enlivening proceedings in the process, and some butterscotch, maple, and vanilla lurking just below the surface. They like big, smelly browny-black sherried casks here—we know that because a while back each of the team was allowed to choose a cask for bottling, and without exception they were sherry monsters. This is a happy compromise.

Glengoyne 21-year-old Sherry 43% ABV

Again, restraint is the order of the day, and this is a delightfully juicy mix of succulent barley, rich raisins, and black grapes on the nose, and dried fruits, grapefruit marmalade, and a wave of oak and pepper on the palate. The finish is a long-distance jog, featuring honey, red fruit, and oak.

THE GLENLIVET

Ballindalloch, Banffshire, AB37 9DB
www.maltwhiskydistilleries.com

On my first day at work as editor of *Whisky Magazine*, I received a letter of complaint from an outraged reader. Apparently, the magazine had published a picture of a pair of pot stills, which we said were at Bunnahabhain, but were actually from Bruichladdich. I nearly resigned on the spot.

At the time, it was beyond me how anyone could tell the difference between one pair of pot stills and another. And I felt that there was something unhealthy about a grown man identifying two lumps of copper at one place over two lumps of copper down the road. This was, it was clear, obsessive—the whisky geek's version of the page three photograph in the British tabloid *Sun* newspaper. But, of course, every distillery's stills are different; each still room unique. Like

the whiskies they make, distilleries have much in common with one another, but we thrive on the differences between them. And while they all go through the same process in pretty much the same order, the differences between them can be vast.

One of the main differences can be found in atmosphere, created in part by size, in part by the layout, and in part by the noise, or lack of it. So while Bunnahabhain, say, or

Pulteney, clatter and clang, others such as the Macallan or the Glenrothes seem to hum. The former are bustling and busy; the latter, calm and graceful.

I have always put the Glenlivet in the "quiet" category. But if the old still room is relatively silent, nothing quite prepares you for the new still room, which in 2010 effectively doubled the distillery's output and made it the biggest single-malt distillery in Scotland. It is like a library.

Where once malt spirit production required several people with a number of skills, today the modern distillery can be operated by one person. If health and safety regulations allowed it, he or she could run it from their living room and not come into the distillery at all. Modern computers have taken on so much of the burden of production that, at the Glentauchers distillery, everything has been maintained in the traditional way, so that staff can be trained in skills that might otherwise become redundant.

At the Glenlivet, the new still room is like something from a science-fiction film. There is only one desk, placed at an angle on a raised platform, to oversee the new stills. It has a bank of computers telling the operator exactly what is going on in the room. Nevertheless, just in front of the desk are the traditional spirits banks you would find in any distillery.

"When we were planning the new still room, we involved staff in decisions as to where to put the desk and that sort of thing," says Chivas distilleries manager Alan Winchester. "It's not often you get the chance to include people in that way. They wanted the spirits banks where they could see the spirit flowing, even though the computer tells them that it is. It's a link to the old ways."

They do not want to make much about their size, pointing out that all the company has done by reopening Braeval and Allt-a-Bhainne and extending the Glenlivet is to replace the volumes it lost when it was forced to sell off Glen Grant and Ardmore during the purchase by Allied a few years back.

But it makes what is one of Scotland's most impressive distilleries even more so. It also produces some of the world's finest whiskies and some which pretty much define Speyside. A ridiculous pricing policy in British supermarkets may have devalued the Glenlivet 12-year-old, but expressions such as the 15-year-old French Oak Reserve, the 16-year-old Nadurra, the 18-year-old, and the 21-year-old are all heavyweight champion malts.

But there are other reasons to visit here, too. A small but beautifully executed interactive visitor experience is a highlight of one of the most charming visitor centers in the industry, and the Glenlivet is trading on its historical role as the birthplace of the modern Scottish malt whisky industry, by opening up a series of smugglers' trails so that you can relive more dangerous times for whisky while immersing yourself in the beauty of the Glenlivet valley.

KEY WHISKIES

The Glenlivet 12-year-old 40% ABV
The Glenlivet 15-year-old French Oak Reserve 40% ABV
The Glenlivet Nadurra 16-year-old 48% ABV
The Glenlivet 18-year-old 43% ABV
The Glenlivet 21-year-old 43% ABV
The Glenlivet XXV 43% ABV

Add to all of this a calm and not-too-noisy tour, and there is an argument that the Glenlivet is actually the epitome of rest and relaxation. Oh, and if you are interested, there are some pretty distinctive pairs of stills, too.

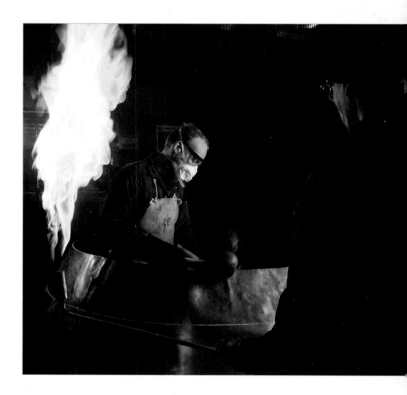

OPPOSITE TOP The new stills were installed in the winter of 2009–2010, despite the worst conditions for a generation.

OPPOSITE The Glenlivet distillery is located by the banks of the river Spey in Laggan, in Scotland's Central Highlands.

ABOVE Glenlivet's new stills take shape at the Forsyth's foundry, where they were made.

GLEN GRANT
www.glengrant.com

One of five distilleries in the Speyside town of Rothes, Glen Grant is now owned by Campari and continues to enjoy immense popularity in Europe and particularly Italy. It would surprise many in Scotland to learn that it is one of the five top-selling malts in the world. It is a lovely distillery to visit, particularly in late spring or early summer, because it has extensive gardens. By the side of a little bridge, there is a safe built into the wall. Major Grant kept a bottle of whisky here, and would take guests out for a dram among the flowers and trees. The house style may be described as light and soft. The Italians like it at five years old (probably because at such a young age it is the nearest that Scotch gets to grappa), but the ten-year-old is more suited to most malt lovers' tastes.

Glen Grant 10-year-old 40% ABV

Dry and shy on the nose, followed by a crisp, herbal, and light fruity taste on the palate, with a medium-long finish to enjoy.

GLENKINCHIE
www.malts.com

The nearest distillery to Edinburgh can be found at Pencaitland and is a Lowland distillery making light, gingery whisky.

Glenkinchie 12-year-old 43% ABV

The nose is cereally and sweet here, with some damp straw and a hint of spice. The taste is distinctly spicy, but rounded and smooth, with some ginger notes. This is one of those single malts that works as an apéritif whisky.

GLENLIVET
www.theglenlivet.com

A few years back, Glenlivet's owners announced that it intended to challenge Glenfiddich for the number-one malt spot, but the claims were regarded by most of the cynical journalists present at the press conference as marketing bluster. In 2010, though, the distillery put the finishing touches to an expansion program that now allows it to produce pretty much the same amount of spirit each year as Glenfidddich and Diageo's "super distillery" at Roseisle.

The Glenlivet was already a big player, up there as one of the three great Glens, alongside Glenfiddich and Glenmorangie. It is a great distillery that produces fine malt—a shame, then, that its fine 12-year-old has been so badly devalued by years of discounting into the supermarket trade. Only Glen Moray has fallen farther from malt's high table.

The Glenlivet 12-year-old 40% ABV

This is another classic Speysider, with aromas of fresh green apples and a touch of grapefruit, and a soft, sweet fruity taste with a pleasant and clean finish.

The Glenlivet 15-year-old French Oak Reserve
40% ABV

Now we're motoring. This is an outstanding expression of Glenlivet, all zippy spice from some virgin French oak, and scattergun oak and malt, like a couple of playful kittens tumbling each other. Feeling depressed and into rock music? Then get yourself an album by Australian cosmic rock giants Wolfmother (either will do, but the debut album is easier to come to grips with), pour a weighty (but obviously responsible) glass of this, turn off the lights, and listen to the Black Sabbath–Zeppelin hybrid while the spices zip about your mouth. Try not to smile until you have swallowed. There. Everything seems better now, doesn't it?

The Glenlivet Nadurra 16-year-old 48% ABV

There is a cask-strength version of this, but this is the one to go for. You have to hunt for the Glenlivet characteristics because this malt is a law unto itself, a mix of ginger, paprika, white pepper, and chili, all sprinkled over ginger barley. You know how trendy chefs are into mixing pain and pleasure, and creating egg and bacon ice cream and that sort of thing? Well, this is whisky's answer to that—a sort of chili-flavored chocolate, with ginger wine in the mix.

The Glenlivet 18-year-old 43% ABV

If the Nadurra is a fun pillow fight of a whisky, this is the sensible big brother asking you to keep the noise down. This is exactly what you would expect the 12-year-old to grow up to be, with some oak, honey, and spice adding a sophistication not found in the younger malt. But the fresh apple fruit is still there.

The Glenlivet 21-year-old
43% ABV

Very rich and chewy, the flavor here is much fuller than in younger bottlings. If the 18-year-old is a fit athlete of a whisky, this is it with a beer gut, less disciplined, but fun to spend time with—a soft and smooth malt with citrus fruits, a nuttiness, and some oak. Yet another twist to the Glenlivet story.

The Glenlivet XXV 43% ABV

This is a rich and enveloping malt, with big candy, toffee, and vanilla notes alongside the trademark fruits. Oak and spice give away clues to the whisky's age—but overall it is a sublime and enjoyable whisky.

GLENMORANGIE
www.glenmorangie.com

The latticework symbol on the Glenmorangie bottle is an image of an old Pict standing stone, which you can go to view in a field close to the distillery. The images on it show female warriors on horseback, symbolizing power and high rank, and suggesting that the Picts were a matriarchal society. Sitting at the foot of the stone with a glass of fine Glenmorangie such as this one is, without doubt, a special and spiritual experience, and is throughly recommended.

There are plenty of people who will tell you that a few years back Glenmorangie was driving fast toward a brick wall, its warehouses full of inferior whisky going nowhere quickly. The turnaround since then has been nothing short of remarkable. Taking full advantage of the skills of whisky genius Dr. Bill Lumsden, Glenmorangie has become the industry leader in wood management. Spirit was put in better wood, and existing whisky was finished and transformed in a range of different casks. The result: "Glenmorangie" is now synonymous with "quality whisky."

Under the new ownership of French luxury company Louis Vuitton Moët Hennessy (LVMH), a new range of core malts and three finishes was introduced in ultra modern bottles. More recently, Lumsden, ably assisted by Rachel Barrie, has started to experiment with new whiskies such as Astar and Signet—with astounding results.

Glenmorangie Original
40% ABV

This is the original ten-year-old repackaged, and it is as reliable as a Harley-Davidson. There is a lot going on in this whisky, with a honeyed nose, sweet malty center, and candy-like core. Rounded, easy-drinking, characterful whisky, with hints of orange and nuts.

Glenmorangie 18-year-old 43% ABV

Sharper than the ten-year-old, with clean citrus fruits on the nose and the overall taste a mix of orange, oak, and citrus fruits. The finish is clean and lengthy.

Glenmorangie Nectar d'Or 46% ABV

Putting malt in a cask that has been previously used for wine, rum, port, or Madeira for the last few months of its maturation is a delicate and complex skill. Many such finishes are clumsy, at best making for a disjointed and confused whisky, and at worst brazenly trying and failing to hide poor-quality malt. Glenmorangie's finishes, though, are exemplary. This whisky is finished in Sauternes casks—sweet white wine—and some of the big French red wine casks are more of a challenge to a whisky maker. But the sweetness, cinnamon, and spices take what was a great whisky to an even more glorious place.

Glenmorangie Quinta Ruban 46% ABV

Here, the finishing cask is port, and again the lovely orange and barley core is enhanced by sweet fruit and an extra richness, so that sweet and dry battle for attention, to pleasing effect. This is up there with the wonderful Balvenie 21-year-old as the best port finish available.

Glenmorangie La Santa 46% ABV

OK, enough's enough. This is finished in sherry, which is fine and the whisky is perfectly palatable, but what's with the name? What on earth were they thinking? Actually, it is pretty obvious. Some marketing team headed by someone called Tristan or Sebastian, and with little understanding of Scottish malt whisky, its culture, or its heritage, got carried away by the LVMH connection and went to town relabeling the malt finishes, coming up with the wheeze of each name coming from the same country as the finishing cask—French for Sauternes, Portuguese for port, and Spanish for sherry. Nectar d'Or is just about OK, but Quinta Ruban is contrived and pretentious, and La Santa is meaningless and forgettable. Compare these names with the stylish and sympathetic but complex names given to the malts at sister brand Ardbeg, and you realize exactly what a road crash these names are.

Glenmorangie 25-year-old 43% ABV

If you are going to splash out for a whisky of this age, you have to be sure that it steps up a level. Without doubt, this does—up there with Macallan 25 and Highland Park 25 as a monumental malt worthy of every one of its 25 years. This is stately, dignified, and complex, with a honeycomb-candy heart, enough oak and spice to give the whisky shape, orange and stewed fruits in the mix, and a dusting of cocoa.

Glenmorangie Signet
46% ABV

This is not so much a roller-coaster ride as the whole amusement park in one glass. What has happened here is that Bill Lumsden and his team have thrown away the Genmorangie rule book and set out on an adventure, exploring every channel within the tight rules of whisky-making. They have used toasted and chocolate malt, virgin oaks to add spiciness, casks of different types and sizes. And they have come up with the most exquisite and hedonistic malt imaginable. It is rich and gloopy, and is whisky's equivalent of those handmade boutique dark chocolates you get that have been infused with fruit flavors and aromatics. Awesome whisky-making, and there is more to come. Dr. Lumsden has just shared another "work in progress" with some of us, and it is a different beast altogether. We live in exciting times.

Glenmorangie Astar 57.1% ABV

On the face of it, another experimental departure for Glenmorangie, an intense barley-fueled cask-strength malt. If Signet is all about urban sophistication, then Astar on the face of it would seem to be all about rustic gruffness. Add some water, though, and the Glemorangie characteristics come flowing through, with a range of barley and honeycomb candy in evidence. The spices that make an appearance early, then just keep popping up, are a big plus.

GLEN MORAY

www.glenmoray.com

I wonder if the LVMH folk reading the Glenmorangie notes just listed will glance down and feel just a tad ashamed. Glen Moray has been the ugly duckling of Scottish malt, or at least in its younger forms it has, wandering from supermarket shelf to supermarket shelf, before, "Quack! Get out of town. . . .

   Hopefully, all this will change. The distillery is located in the Speyside town of Elgin, tucked back at the end of a standard residential area. It is a dinky, pleasing distillery, and it makes perfectly fine 12-year-old and some rather special older releases. But the distillery has been criminally undervalued, its 12-year-old sold at under half its market value through supermarkets. So let's look at this: You distill fine spirit, put it into quality oak casks, and mature it to the same standards as other malts for a minimum of 12 years. You then flog it off as a cheap supermarket brand. What does that do for the morale of the talented team at the distillery? LVMH finally sold the distillery so that it could focus on its more premium malts, and Glen Moray is under new ownership. It has been very quiet in recent times—and hopefully a reappraisal and repositioning process is underway.

Glen Moray 12-year-old 40% ABV

This defines a Speyside malt—plenty of sweetness, plenty of fruit, plenty of crystallized barley, and a blemish-free and pleasing mouthfeel, taste, and finish.

   There has been a series of distiller's editions from this distillery that has been truly outstanding over the years. These are extremely hard to find, but, if you do stumble across one, it is definitely worth investigating. A limited-edition 1974 pot-finished malt is particularly recommended.

GLEN ORD

www.malts.com

Glen Ord is something of a hidden gem, occupying a site to the north of Inverness overlooking the Black Isle, and it has suffered from something of an identity crisis over the years, having been bottled under several different names. Most recently, it has been reformulated to include a higher proportion of malt matured in sherry wood, and bottled as the Asian representative of the Singleton range.

The Singleton of Glen Ord 40% ABV

Soft, sweet, and very drinkable, this is more sherried than the usual bottlings of Glen Ord, but none the worse for it. There are traces of nuts and flowers among the soft fruits, as well as the gentlest trace of oak.

The Singleton of Glen Ord 12-year-old
43% ABV

Glen Ord is located close to Inverness in the northeast of Scotland, and it has become quite difficult to find as a single malt because Diageo has used it as its Singleton malt for the Far East and particularly Taiwan. If you do find this version, expect a robust, fruity, and reasonably sherried malt, with some plummy fruits. The Singleton version, should you come across it, is sweet and has even more sherry. There is little evidence of an earthy Highland backbone, but this is pleasant enough all the same.

Glen Ord 25-year-old 58.3% ABV

Wow. A gem of a whisky, with sweet and savory in perfect balance. On the one hand, there are green and exotic fruits; on the other, just the right level of earthy, peaty fruit. And wrapped around the whole shebang are some oak and spice notes.

Glen Ord 28-year-old 58.3% ABV

Hickory, surprisingly youthful barley, and some estery notes on the nose here, with a full and sweet taste, combined with some cocoa and coffee notes. Late on, some tannin and spice, but it is all well balanced and ordered. A revelation.

GLENROTHES

www.theglenrothes.com

You would struggle to find two places that have less in common with each other than the sprawling state of Texas on the one hand and St. James Street in Mayfair, London, on the other—but they do have a bizarre link.

St. James Street is home to Berry Bros. & Rudd, a traditional wine merchant with a long and colorful history, at the heart of affluent London. In recent years, it has added fine spirits to its offerings, and it has the long-term rights to the outstanding Speyside Glenrothes distillery.

A few years ago, Berry Bros. company director Christopher Berry Green was made a freeman of the state of Texas by the then governor George Bush Sr.

"Between 1842 and 1845, Texas was the Lone Star republic and had embassies and legacies across the world," says Glenrothes ambassador Ronnie Cox. "In London, it was on the first floor of our offices in St. James. So in recognition of this, in 1996, Mr. Berry Green, who was a six-feet-four former Grenadier Guard and very British, was presented with a pair of garish cowboy boots and a ten-gallon Stetson, which I doubt he ever wore. In return, he gave George Bush Senior an unpaid invoice from 1845 for three months' rent."

Glenrothes is a big distillery—they call the still room the "cathedral"—but most of its output has traditionally gone into blends. Now, though, it is being recognized in its own right, partly because of the quality malts it is putting out and partly because of its distinctive grenade-style bottles with handwritten labels.

The people behind Glenrothes are not above having some fun with the brand, and they like matching each vintage with music of different styles, including jazz, blues, new wave, Americana, and rock. So, in the spirit the company intended, here are some classic rock pairings.

The Glenrothes Robur Reserve
40% ABV

The aromas here include apricot jam, some lemon zest, and honey. The creamy taste has citrus and yellow fruits, as well as some soft spices. Very pleasant, very Speyside, and very ordered.
Soundtrack: "Make Me Smile (Come Up and See Me)" Steve Harley & Cockney Rebel

The Glenrothes Select Reserve 43% ABV

This is a mix of various vintages and is therefore more consistent than some of the distillery's other malts and at the same time is something of a greatest hits package. Sweet barley, vanilla, mince pie, sherbet, and orange on the nose; dried fruits, spice, sugar, and sherry on the palate; and a gentle pruney finish.
Soundtrack: "Purple Rain" Prince

The Glenrothes 1994 43% ABV

This is reminiscent of a freshly cleaned dining room, with aromas of lemon cleaner and polish. The whisky is oily and rich in the mouth, with flavors of melon and lemon, and some toffee. A breezy summertime whisky.
Soundtrack: "Made of Stone" The Stone Roses

The Glenrothes 1992 43% ABV

Another light and easy-drinking malt, with a flowery nose sprinkled with sherbet and fruit. The taste is rich and fruity, with pineapple, melon, licorice, and melon.
Soundtrack: "Dancing in the Dark" Bruce Springsteen

The Glenrothes 1991 43% ABV

An enticing malt, with some welcoming aromas that include soft toffee, vanilla, black currant, and blueberries. The taste has caramel, some tannins, cherry, and red currant, and stewed fruits, and the color is chestnut bronze.
Soundtrack: "Solsbury Hill" Peter Gabriel

The Glenrothes 1987 43% ABV

Probably the least complex and most predictable of all vintages, but that is not a criticism—this is floral and almost perfumey, with orange and grapefruit notes and a simple medium-long but pleasantly sweet finish.
Soundtrack: "I Want You to Want Me" Cheap Trick

The Glenrothes 1985 43% ABV

A different Glenrothes to what has gone before, it has an earthy, savory nose, with chestnuts, apple core, and mushroom. The taste is much more attractive, with overripe peach and apricot, honeycomb candy, burnt toffee, and a distinctive oakiness in the delicious mix.
Soundtrack: "In the Evening" Led Zeppelin

The Glenrothes 1984 43% ABV

This is a more delicate example of Glenrothes, with delicate vanilla and wood sap. The taste is sweeter than you might expect, with sugary barley, vanilla ice cream, and some caramel sauce. Ends with a pleasant dash of oak and spice.
Soundtrack: "Wrecking Ball" Emmylou Harris

The Glenrothes 1981 43% ABV

The oddest of the Glenrothes vintages, this has some sulfur and cask vagrancies on the nose, reminiscent of stewed bean sprouts. The taste is woody, with some dried fruits and, after a sweet start, thins out and leaves a peppery and woody finish. Not an easy malt this one.
Soundtrack: "Welcome to the Machine" Pink Floyd

The Glenrothes 1978 43% ABV

The nose is a bit off-kilter, with a strange mix of sherbet fruits and earthy chestnut flavors, but the complex taste makes up for it—with lots of fruits, licorice, aniseed, and vanilla. The finish goes on and on, and it is very pleasant.
Soundtrack: "More than a Feeling" Boston

The Glenrothes 1972 43% ABV

Another vintage that starts off with rootsy and earthy aromas reminiscent of stewed vegetables, but the malt is creamy and full in the mouth, with fruit, vanilla, and licorice, and some late spice and tannins. The finish is the best part—long and balanced, with sweet fruits, spices, and oak.
Soundtrack: "Nice 'n' Sleazy" The Stranglers

The Glenrothes 30-year-old 43% ABV

This takes no prisoners, after a slow-burn start. At first, there are damp leaves and faintly musty aromas on the nose, then some sherry and citrus fruits. But it explodes on the palate, with lemon sherbet, aniseed, sweet mint, and some drying astringency. The finish is long and intense.
Soundtrack: "Mistreated" Deep Purple

The Glenrothes 25-year-old
43% ABV

Here you will find a truly adorable nose, including sweet candy fruits, lemonade, orange and lemon rind, and spearmint. The taste is pretty extraordinary, too—tropical fruits, some sugarlike spice, and an oaky carpet. The finish is long and sweet, with fruit and spice.
Soundtrack: "California Dreamin' " The Mamas and the Papas

Glenrothes John Ramsay Legacy 46.7% ABV

This was produced to mark the retirement of Edrington's master blender John Ramsay, the man responsible for Famous Grouse, among other things. What makes this special is the clever mix of some stately and old malt and some refreshing and spritely younger ones, making for a crystal-clean but sophisticated and complex mix. Most of this release was snapped up on release, but it is a fitting tribute for John Ramsay to go out on.

GLENROTHES DISTILLERY

Rothes, Morayshire AB38 7AA
www.theglenrothes.com

When whisky maker Edrington and wine merchants Berry Bros. & Rudd announced that they had struck a deal over the future of single-malt Glenrothes and historic Scottish blend Cutty Sark, it was a bittersweet moment for whisky expert Ronnie Cox.

He is the international brand ambassador for Glenrothes, and he has dedicated a good part of his life to promoting both that brand and Cutty Sark.

"The deal gave Berry Bros. control over Glenrothes, but at the same time Cutty Sark has gone to Edrington. That was a sad moment for me because I started at Berry Bros. & Rudd on that side of the business, promoting it into South America—not always totally successfully, I might add, because it's a light blend and not easy to sell in that part of the world. It's a blend with an amazing history and is very special."

History is important to Ronnie Cox, and it seems to surround him—in the brands he works on, at the distillery, and especially at the premises of Berry Bros. & Rudd on St. James Street, London. Here they still have the scales that were used to weigh the leading lights of society, and there are wine collections in the cellars stretching back decades and generations. If you are really fortunate, you can dine in Napoleon's Cellar, where there is an escape tunnel that was built as a quick getaway for Emperor Napoleon III, who took refuge there while in exile in the 1840s, when he lived in fear of assassins and used it as a base to plot his return to France.

If I were to pick a table for the perfect dinner party, Ronnie Cox would be among the guests—probably sitting between English politician Tony Benn and the wonderful American crime writer James Lee Burke. Cox is a genial host, a wonderful raconteur—and as batty as a fruitcake.

Give him half a chance, and he will tell you great stories about how Cutty Sark was designed as a peat-free alternative whisky for Berry Bros.' wine customers, who wanted to taste fine Scotch, but did not want to taint their palates. He will tell of how Sam Bronfman, larger-than-life

American head of Seagram, rudely burst in on a company lunch to demand to buy the business and was politely and firmly rebuked, and how, just over 20 years ago, the management approached Highland Distillers to ask if they could develop one of its whiskies that had not been bottled as a single malt before, thus starting the Glenrothes–Berry Bros. partnership.

Then there's the story of how Mr. Berry traveled on the same ship as Prohibition advocate Pussyfoot Johnson, how they had an altercation, and how Johnson wrote a letter of rebuke on ship's paper urging Mr. Berry to train his son for the cloth, rather than the wine trade, which he assured him was a "vanishing business."

Cox is one of the whisky industry's true gentlemen and, although you would not necessarily sense it from his educated accent and attire—he is more of a tartan trews sort of guy, rather than a kilt-wearing one—he has Scotland and whisky running through his veins, distilled and matured over generations.

It is fitting that he is the face of Glenrothes because he has an association with the town of Rothes stretching back to when he was a little boy. Indeed, the house the distillery owns brings back memories from his childhood.

"It was the old manse, and I had been there as a boy," he says. "When I was six, I got a three-inch rocket on a spring as a gift from a cornflake packet; with it I managed to hit the Presbyterian minister on the head right in the middle of a sermon—a frightening moment."

That Glenrothes will be tied to Berry Bros. and Ronnie Cox for many years to come is great news. With such a marriage of outstanding talent, the malt cannot fail to go from strength to strength.

LEFT Rothes is an ancient crofting village and a popular destination for anyone following the malt-whisky trail map.

BELOW The stunning Moray coastline provides breathtaking views and a beautiful backdrop to the five local whisky distilleries.

BELOW INSET The river Spey, known for its pure waters, runs close to the Glenrothes distillery.

KEY WHISKY

The Glenrothes Robur Reserve 40% ABV
The Glenrothes Select Reserve 43% ABV
The Glenrothes 1994 43% ABV
The Glenrothes 1992 43% ABV
The Glenrothes 1991 43% ABV
The Glenrothes 1987 43% ABV
The Glenrothes 1985 43% ABV
The Glenrothes 1984 43% ABV
The Glenrothes 1981 43% ABV
The Glenrothes 1978 43% ABV
The Glenrothes 1972 43% ABV
The Glenrothes 30-year-old 43% ABV
The Glenrothes 25-year-old 43% ABV
The Glenrothes John Ramsay Legacy 46.7% ABV

GLEN SPEY

One of several Speyside distilleries that exists primarily to provide malt for blending. It is not easy to find as a single malt, but Diageo did release a 12-year-old as part of its Flora & Fauna range.

Glen Spey 12-year-old 43% ABV

Full and sturdy fruity malt, with a spicy fencing and solid malty base. Smooth, honeyed, and tasty.

GLENTURRET
www.thefamousgrouse.com

Glenturret is one of Scotland's oldest, most rustic distilleries, but it is also home to the Famous Grouse Experience, a completely interactive family outing. The overall effect is akin to dressing a farmer in a space suit. The distillery itself is small and traditional. Much of the malt goes into the Famous Grouse, but there is a hard-to-find single malt, too.

Glenturret 10-year-old 40% ABV

Solid enough although somewhat two-dimensional Highland malt, with honey, crystallized barley, and gentle oaky tones.

HAZELBURN
www.springbankdistillers.com

If Springbank is the scuzzy street punk of Campbeltown and Longrow is its salty sea dog, then Hazelburn is its dapper young gentleman, a triple-distilled unpeated and sweet malt on a day trip down from the northeast. It is not easy to find, but is a treat if you do.

Hazelburn 8-year-old 46% ABV

Hazelburn is triple-distilled at Springbank in Campbeltown, so the overall taste is smooth and rounded. This is a Malteser (or Whopper)-in-a-glass, with honey flowing throught it.

HIGHLAND PARK
www.highlandpark.co.uk

Everyone should visit the Orkney Isles at least once in their life. The islands are littered with burial sites, ruins, and stone circles, signposts to history are at every turn, and you can trace human sacrifice and suffering from the earliest settlers thousands of years ago, to the protected war grave in Scapa Flow. The islands are also home to two distilleries.

Highland Park is whisky's greatest all-rounder, its malts noted for the balance of peat, oak, fruit, honey, and spice, making it easy to put up an objective argument as to why the 18-year-old and 25-year-old, in particular, can lay claim to being the world's greatest malts. The 21-year-old won best single-malt whisky in the World Whisky Awards.

In recent years, the distillery's owners have started putting out unconventional and surprising expressions of Highland Park. For this reason, new releases are always exciting.

Highland Park 12-year-old 40% ABV

The standard 12-year-old Highland Park is like a colorful fashion show featuring a number of different designers. You get honey and barley first, then fruit, a touch of wood and spice, and a sexy, sensual peaty smoke finale. Some performance.

Highland Park 15-year-old 40% ABV

Again, trademark honey to the fore and a support act of oak and smoke, but the extra years give the malt more of a caramelized toffee center.

Highland Park 16-year-old 40% ABV

This is more restrained than the younger bottlings, and the nose has developed some range and citrus notes. The honey is there on the palate, but this time with some toasty, cereally notes, an orange candy center, then some pleasant smokiness. The malt ends as it started, with a finish that is delicate and short.

Highland Park 18-year-old 43% ABV

Malt whisky's equivalent to rock band REM's "Man on the Moon." Loud bits, quiet bits, passion, and perfect harmonies—a little bit of something for everyone and, as a whole, somehow instantly familiar while different to everything else in its field. Perfect.

Highland Park 21-year-old 40% ABV

Brought down from a higher strength, but still a masterpiece, with the oak playing a big role, but malt and honey still the dominant tastes.

Highland Park 25-year-old 48% ABV

This has changed significantly from the big, heavy fruit-and-oak-driven 25-year-old from a few years back. With lemon cold-and-flu powder and grapefruit on the nose, it is quite delicate overall. And a game of two halves on the palate: First up, there are honey and hard candies, followed by some citrus notes. Then a triple whammy of spice, peat, and oak takes your taste buds to a different place altogether. The finish is an intriguing amalgam of all that has gone before.

Highland Park 30-year-old 48% ABV

It seems that there are two very different styles of old Highland Park. This one, like the 25-year-old above, comes from the citrus stable, but this is an altogether more assured bottling than its slightly younger sibling. The citrus fruits dominate the nose, but there are some peat and honey there, too. Honey and vanilla dominate the taste, but there is enough oak and peat to prevent it from being too sweet and wispy.

Highland Park 40-year-old 43% ABV

Another twist again. On the nose, there are scented wax candle, potpourri, and sweet citrus fruits. The palate combines exotic and citrus fruits, honey and peat. The big five—peat, fruit, spice, oak, and honey—face up to one another in the finish, to see who can go the longest without blinking. Peat wins.

Highland Park Vintage 1998 40% ABV

Surf and turf, this. A surprisingly farmyard version of Highland Park, with soft and mellow peat smoke and barley sap on the nose, and a fresh, playful, and easy malty taste, with plenty of honey at first, then a Highland-style peat carpet.

Highland Park Vintage 1994 40% ABV

Highland Park sails around to Islay with barbecued fish, chili, brine, and deli aromas. Just as Ardbeg Blasda is akin to heavy rock band Motorhead playing acoustic with a gospel choir, this is poptastic English pop band Take That playing a set of Nirvana songs. Nothing necessarily wrong with that, but be prepared. As the popular British Old Speckled Hen beer advertisement would put it, "Very interesting, but it's not a hen . . ."

Highland Park Vintage 1990 40% ABV

All change. This time, there are toffee apple and vanilla ice cream on the nose, and the fruity apple and pear make it through to the taste. It is quite amazing that this and the 1994 vintage come from the same place. This is clean and sweet, with rumtopf apple and pear, and honeycomb candy bar in the mix. Oh, and to wrap it all up, a touch of confectioners' sugar late on in the spice.

HIGHLAND PARK DISTILLERY

Holm Road, Kirkwall, Orkney KW15 1SU
www.highlandpark.co.uk

Over the past five years or so, Britain has lost a number of top–class beer breweries, each of them shut because they were considered "economically unviable."

This excuse has become depressingly familiar in the past quarter of a century, and reflects a sizable shift away from culture and community, and toward the relentless and selfish pursuit of money. And as we increasingly try to trade and/or compete with nations who pay their workers a pittance and can mass-produce components for next to nothing, uncaring capitalism will grow stronger.

Next time someone tells you that the local factory or business closure is inevitable, say two words to them: "Highland Park." Truth is, when companies are committed to something beyond the cash figure at the bottom of the page, miracles can happen. Whisky is full of them. And when it comes to economics, how can it make sense to produce whisky on the tiny islands of Islay, Jura, and Skye?

And, most of all, what sort of business model allows for a regular convoy of vehicles to travel the full length of Scotland on narrow roads to its farthest point, then take sail through rough northern waters to a group of islands best suited to sheep rearing, and all for the sake of an alcoholic drink?

It is because distillery owners—and this includes giants such as Diageo and Pernod Ricard—are committed to maintaining a malt whisky industry noted for its diversity and regional variations.

And Highland Park is a case in point—a malt distillery that makes no sense whatsoever until, that is, you taste the whisky that comes from it. Highland Park is Scotland's most northerly distillery, and it is sited at the heart of a group of islands where history is marked out by archeological sites, stone circles, and ruined villages that predate Egypt's pyramids. The islands are characterized by wind and water, and there are few trees due to the unforgiving climate. The surrounding seas are littered with wrecks, including much of the German fleet scuppered toward the end of World War 1, and that of HMS *Royal Oak*, which was sunk by a U-boat, with the loss of more than 800 lives. You can still see the masts of fishing vessels sunk to block channels and stop U-boats from entering Scapa Flow, and some of the islands are linked by roadways placed over massive concrete slabs that were piled up in the narrow waterways by Winston Churchill, to thwart the submarines when the fishing boats failed.

The distillery itself is a cozy dark-brick distillery with twin working pagodas, a haven of warmth and welcoming aromas set in the harshest of environments. Owner Edrington has been investing heavily in it over the past couple of years, so new pagoda roofs, a modern and stylish distillery shop, and a smart tasting room sit next to old traditional stone walls and cozy but antiquated offices.

The beating heart of the distillery, however, lies high up in the distillery's maltings. Here, in a forgotten and dusty room full of crumbling old distillery equipment, is a rectangular window. Through it is a room illuminated in eerie orange. Wispy smoke wafts across it, and on the floor golden nuggets of barley feed on the peat smoke that is rising up to them. This is the honeycomb heart of the distillery and its whisky, and it is utter magic.

Honey is at the heart of Highland Park whisky, but so is the peat, which is cut from a moor close to the distillery. You can see it being cut in spring, and drying in the fields over summer, an umbilical cord between the malt and the land on which it is produced. And if the sun shines and the sea turns a Caribbean turquoise color, then grab a hip flask full of 18-year-old, head to the port, and watch the procession of ships bringing in barley and carrying away waste products and whisky spirit.

It is enough to have the bean counters sweating in their sleep. And it is testament to how whisky makers are committed to investing in their industry.

WELL, FANCY THAT. . .

The Pictish village at Skara Brae consists of eight dwelling areas dating back to 3200 BC. Huge stones used to create ancient stone circles are not from the islands, but no one knows how they were transported there.

ABOVE The Orkney Isles are rich in history and spiritualism. This is the Ring of Brodgar, made with stone not native to the islands.

BELOW Quiet . . . whisky sleeping.

Highland Park 12-year-old 40% ABV
Highland Park 15-year-old 40% ABV
Highland Park 16-year-old 40% ABV
Highland Park 18-year-old 43% ABV
Highland Park 21-year-old 40% ABV
Highland Park 25-year-old 48% ABV

Highland Park 30-year-old 48% ABV
Highland Park 40-year-old 48% ABV
Highland Park Vintage 1998 40% ABV
Highland Park Vintage 1994 40% ABV
Highland Park Vintage 1990 40% ABV

JURA

www.isleofjura.com

Highland Park on Orkney might claim to be the most "uneconomic" whisky distillery, but Jura can give it a run for its money. It is not fashionable to say it these days, but there are more important things than the blind pursuit of money. Such things include happy communities, the dignity of honest labor, and an expectation that the state has a duty of care to its people. Many, many businesses would not survive without being subsidized, but what is and is not helped out financially is the essence of politics. So Britain's coal mines, for instance, central to the communities of all working-class Britain, were not helped, but farming and, most recently, the banks have been. The distillery on Jura makes no sense economically because it is on an island off an island. Great big semitrailers must negotiate little back roads and a feisty car ferry to ship in grain and ship out spirit, as well as effluent because the distillery's wastage cannot just be dumped offshore. But it is thanks to distilleries such as Jura that the world of whisky is so diverse and stimulating.

Jura has a lot of deer, even more adders, and the most bolshy cows in Britain. If you go there, they will remind you that you are the visitor by refusing to get out of the way.

The whisky has been changed and improved in recent years, and repackaged. It is clean and unpeated, but the new and quite pricey Prophecy suggests that the distillery can give Islay next door a run for its money.

Jura 10-year-old 40% ABV

A soft and unassertive malt, with a sweet and fruity backbone. The abrasive tangy notes and "baby sick" notes have gone, so if you were put off in the past, it might be time for a revisit. That said, it continues to be quite two-dimensional and unexceptional, apart from the well-designed packaging.

Jura 16-year-old 40% ABV

This is a step up from the ten-year-old expression, with more malty cereal, oak, and honey, and some nutty notes. It is still a bit timid, though.

Jura Prophecy 40% ABV

Some years ago, while sailing down the Sound of Jura, the captain let me take the helm. I will never forget the excitement of that moment, the sun shining, the wind whipping up the spray, the feeling of power and control. Then fellow traveler and whisky writer Dave Broom gave me his iPod and played me Alabama 3's "U Don't Dans 2 Tekno Anymore." I've got a lot to thank Mr. Broom for, but introducing me to Alabama 3 (known as A3 in the United States) and the album *Exile on Coldharbour Lane* is up there with the best of them. A blast of this album and a sizable (but obviously responsible) dram of Islay malt remain my 6 p.m. Saturday evening treat. Throw in a few favorable soccer results, and the weekend truly starts here.

This whisky is a revelation. As with my sailing experience, it has salt spray in its face and finds itself somewhere between Jura and Islay, its big peatiness ensuring that it can hold its head up high when mixing it with the big boys from the other island. At last, an assertive, aggressive malt from Jura, which seems to have grown tired of having sand kicked in its face and has struck out with the same sort of rich, peaty vein that the outstanding but very rare Jura five-year-old had.

Jura Superstition 43% ABV

The addition of peated malt to a mix of different aged Jura whiskies is akin to adding salt and vinegar to an ordinary piece of cod—it brings it on in leaps and bounds, but not necessarily for all the right reasons.

KILCHOMAN

www.kilchomandistillery.com

The launch of whisky from Islay's first new distillery for more than 100 years was some occasion. Representatives from all of Islay's other distilleries were there, friends traveled across the world, whisky writers and enthusiasts rubbed shoulders, and the whisky arrived on a tide of emotion. For the team behind the project, its arrival was greeted with relief—successfully overseeing the birth of a new whisky takes blood, sweat, nerve, and very deep pockets. Kilchoman, though, is on its feet and starting to run, and all the indications are that it will go from strength to strength.

The distillery lies to the west of the island and is a pretty, dinky operation, complete with a small shop.

Kilchoman 3-year-old 46% ABV

Young and aggressively peated, this whisky is vindaloo curry in a glass— quite sharp and fiery, but with sweet malt and charcoally peat just starting to make friends.

KNOCKANDO

www.malts.com

Knockando is something of an enigma. Not a particularly large distillery, it is the core malt in J&B, but it has a surprisingly big fan base of its own. Fans are drawn to its complexities— nuttiness and floral notes, honey and an engaging earthiness—which all contribute to a fascinating malt.

Knockando 12-year-old 43% ABV

Like being out in the long grass on a summer's day, with light grassy and heathery notes, some sweet fruit, and a dry and brittle malt.

KNOCKDHU

www.ancnoc.com

Knockdhu is owned now by Inver House, but when the company bought it from Diageo it agreed to change the name of its malts to An Cnoc to avoid confusion with Knockando. It is a Highland distillery, but sits right on the boundary of Speyside; its postal address is in Speyside, although the distillery is not.

An Cnoc 12-year-old 40% ABV

This is an interesting malt. Taste it in isolation when you have had nothing else to confuse your taste buds, and it is quite rugged, with clean-cut barley, some herbal notes, and a rising crescendo of spices, before a long, complex conclusion. Taste it after a meal, and it can flounder. Overall, though, an impressive whisky.

An Cnoc 16-year-old 46% ABV

Pineapple candy, vanilla, and crystallized barley on the nose, lots of citrus and yellow fruits in the center, and a long spicy-sweet conclusion.

An Cnoc 1994 46% ABV

A real dessert of a whisky, with rich vanilla ice cream and butterscotch sauce, deep sweetness, and summery malt.

An Cnoc 1993 46% ABV

More oak and spice than the 1994, but otherwise this is from the same stable—clean, sweet barley, with cotton candy and ice cream after.

An Cnoc 1975 50% ABV

The nose is subtle and sophisticated, with citrus fruits, noticeably lime, vanilla, and honey. A pleasant mix of balanced flavors on the palate, with berries, honey, and gentle oak and spice.

LAGAVULIN

Lagavulin is one of Islay's holy trinity of big peated whiskies, and the distillery lies in the southeast of the island, hugging the shoreline. It does not go for lots of different expressions, but that is because, once you have gotten to where the 16-year-old is, the only place to go is down, and there is not much room on the tasting ledge for anything else.

Lagavulin 12-year-old Cask Strength
56.4% ABV

Intense, sharp, and peaty, with the odd citrus note on the nose, and a full and mouth-coating peat and oil hit in the mouth. The finish crackles and flares with peat and fruit.

Lagavulin 16-year-old
43% ABV

Up there with the very best whiskies in the world and a place in my personal top ten, Lagavulin 16-year-old has a nose that floats like a butterfly and stings like a bee, with some sweetness on the nose and palate, but a sledgehammer punch, with big peat and some brine. Salty seaweed lingers, giving way to sensational oily grilled bacon and an exquisite smoky conclusion. As with Miles Davis, you either get it or you don't.

Lagavulin Distiller's Edition 43% ABV

To continue with the music analogy, would you add an orchestra to a definitive Miles Davis track? Messing with this malt is like playing pontoon and twisting on 20. Lagavulin lovers fall into two camps. The traditionalists argue that you do not dance with the devil, no matter how good the moonlight, so leave this well alone. And then there are those that argue that this is indeed the extra ace to give you what you need to make the score up to 21. Sherry casks give this a rich intensity and some extra sweetness, but remarkably none of the peat is lost.

LAPHROAIG
www.malts.com

Quite possibly the least subtle of the Big Three, Laphroaig is still hard not to love if you like peated whisky. There has been a debate among lovers of this malt about whether it has been "dumbed down" in recent years. But there is plenty to be encouraged about. The Quarter Cask bottling is an intense heavy-hitter and does not break the bank, the weak 15-year-old has been replaced with a storming 18-year-old, and a truly remarkable 27-year-old has been added.

Laphroaig 10-year-old 43% ABV

A classic iodine-charged medicinal and peaty nose, with big, grungy taste and, through the brooding clouds of peat, some sweet and succulent barley. The finish is long and peaty.

Laphroaig 10-year-old Cask Strength 57.3% ABV

Restrained peat, salt, and tar on the nose, but a firecracker of a taste, particularly with a little water. This is a sort of scorched-earth policy of the mouth, with hot chilis flattening the few taste buds still standing after the peat has jumped up and down on them a few times. It is the oral equivalent of soccer hooligans running riot. When the peat and pepper depart, you can still hear them chanting, out of sight.

Laphroaig Quarter Cask 48% ABV

After about six years of maturing, the whisky is put into smaller casks, increasing the amount of contact between wood and spirit. This leads to speedier maturation, but more importantly it intensifies the flavors in the whisky. So that by eight years and maybe a bit more, you have all the flavors of a ten-year-old, but with the volume turned up and, better still, you retain some of the youthful barley at the core.

Laphroaig 18-year-old 48% ABV

Sometimes the best whisky moments come when you least expect them. Somebody recently gave me a CD by Soulsavers, a band whom I knew nothing at all about, beyond the fact that the lineup features Mark Lanegan, of the Screaming Trees, various dreamy solo albums, and Queens of the Stone Age fame. I tasted this while watching out of my window as the snow fell, when the fifth track "Some Misunderstanding" came on. It is eight minutes long, mixes dreamy, beautiful interwoven vocals; rolling, sludgy bass lines; and sharp, twisted gritty guitar. Just like this whisky, the music mixes pure sweet grist and grain, sludgy licorice and hickory, and growling pepper and peat. Quite possibly the best whisky and music match that I have ever experienced. And this is quite possibly one of the best-ever whiskies.

Laphroaig 25-year-old 50.9% ABV

Be warned: The age of this whisky means that the peat has not only been tamed, but also cowers back for a good part of the drinking experience. That is not necessarily a bad thing, because there are plenty of pleasant and sweet directions in which the core malt takes you. The nose is almost grapey, and on the palate there are some oak and dark chocolate. When the peat does arrive, it crashes over the palate like a spring tide crashing past the harbor walls and swamping the beach with frightening speed.

Laphroaig 27-year-old 57.4% ABV

An extraordinary, exceptional, and unusual malt. The nose is earthy, rich, and intensely sherried, with some winey, floral notes for good measure. The taste is an oral double whammy, with stewed fruits and overripe berries on the one hand, and intense smoke and peat on the other. They batter tannins and spices back and forth between them, like some form of demonic tennis match, and let go very, very slowly, leaving a long mouth-coating fruit and smoke aftertaste. Truly unforgettable.

Laphroaig 30-year-old 43% ABV

Hard to find, but the age has imparted a complexity that you rarely see in Laphroaig. It has a full, rich taste, and the peat still sits at the head of the table, but is surrounded by oak, fruit, and spice.

LINKWOOD
www.malts.com

Linkwood's output is mainly used for blended whiskies and, in particular, Johnnie Walker. Occasional single-malt bottlings do emerge, however, and these are surprisingly refined and floral on the palate.

Linkwood 12-year-old 43% ABV

If you have a good imagination, you could describe the St. Andrew's area of the English city of Norwich as the Soho of the east (London's Soho, that is). OK, a very good imagination. It has a store selling Chinese food and drink, a Sinsin's Love Store, and an Ali Bongo's, so that's sort of like Soho, isn't it? But it also has a great pub, the Rumsey Wells, run by brother-and-sister team Dan and Katie. On the one hand, it is a traditional boozer, with great Adnams ale and a sausage and pie menu. On the other, it puts on great live music and attracts a cool student crowd. It is also where the Norwich Whisky Club meets. I tasted this whisky for the first time at a club meeting while world-class saxophonist Snake Davis played soprano sax for us. Snake has appeared on recordings by Take That, M People, and Heather Small, and has toured with everyone, most recently Annie Lennox and George Michael. To taste a new whisky while listening to such sublime music guarantees a relationship with that whisky for life.

This is ideal for sax-fueled jazz—a summery Speyside malt with green pear and apple notes, and some clean and fresh barley notes . . . until, that is, a sharp wave of pepper arrives late on. Utterly irresistible.

LAGAVULIN DISTILLERY

Port Ellen, Isle of Islay PA42 7DZ
www.discovering-distilleries.com

It is a late summer's evening on the western Scotland whisky island of Islay, and darkness has shrouded the distillery in darkness.

On the far side of a pretty courtyard, pictures of sailing boats, whisky tastings, and impromptu parties are being beamed onto one of the walls. In the courtyard itself, there is laughter, the babble of chat, and the sound of tinkling glasses. The whisky is flowing liberally, and around the courtyard revelers help themselves to an impressive buffet of local cold meats, shellfish, and seafood. Later, Islay's finest choir will entertain the guests.

This is Lagavulin hosting a *céilidh* to mark the end of the Classic Malts Cruise, an annual three-leg three-week pleasure sail that attracts up to 1,000 boats and brings the world together for a celebration of whisky and sailing, linking up the distilleries of Oban on the mainland, Talisker on Skye, and Lagavulin on Islay. Speak to anyone who has taken part in the cruise, and they will talk of new friendships, the thrill of sailing on Scotland's wild western waters, and the fun and laughter of it. But even by the Classic Malt Cruise's standards, the final *céilidh* at one of Scotland's most magisterial distilleries would be intoxicating, even without the whisky.

We had arrived by boat into Lagavulin bay by sea earlier in the afternoon, our boat bobbing wickedly as an increasingly ashen-faced skipper battled to steer us through two posts marking the only section of waterway deep enough to let us into the natural harbor.

The sense of history is all-encompassing. When the Lords of the Isles ruled the western waterways, they made their home here, and the ruins of their castle lie close to the distillery. The prominent white walls and bold black lettering of the distillery itself are seen to be carved deep into the land, and there is evidence of several distilleries in the region stretching back to the time of the Jacobite uprisings. Savor the craggy shoreline, and you cannot help but feel that little has changed geographically in the ensuing 275 years.

Lagavulin is the centerpiece of Islay's holy trinity of peated whiskies, all lying within a couple of miles of one another. It sits between Ardbeg on one side and Laphroaig on the other. If Islay is to whisky what heavy metal is to rock music, then Lagavulin is its Led Zeppelin, a loud battering ram of a whisky, but with nuance, subtlety, and sophistication if you look for it. This mix of "volume to 11" peatiness and rich

vein of fruity sweetness stems from the long maturation period and the use of selected sherry casks. Unusually for any malt, but especially for a peated whisky, where old age is not necessarily a friend, the standard Lagavulin is aged for 16 years, although a cask-strength 12-year-old has teasingly been drip-fed in limited batches on several occasions in recent years. Blink and you will miss it, though.

For all its majesty and charisma, Lagavulin is actually a dinky, intimate distillery, where the emphasis is on quality rather than quantity. Owner Diageo has Caol Ila at the other end of the island geared up for large-scale production. Here, the emphasis is on quality. The year 2010 may well be regarded as a pivotal one for the malt, too. In the 1990s, the distillery started producing a malt with a phenolic content of 50ppm, but reverted back to the original formula of 35ppm a while later. The heavier 50ppm was bottled throughout the first decade of the millennium, but 2010 saw the first 35ppm whisky complete its 16-year maturation journey and arrive in the bottle.

There is one word of warning about the tour at Lagavulin. While the warehouses are a highlight, do not be taken in if the guide talks about the whisky maturing here. Only a tiny amount is stored in those warehouses, mainly for show, and Diageo takes virtually all its new-make spirit away in tankers to be matured on the mainland—not very romantic, but practical. And as anyone familiar with Lagavulin can testify, there is no discernible negative effect on the final whisky. Sipping a glass of it on the deck of a sailing boat in front of the distillery as the sun sets is right up there as one of my favorite whisky experiences.

ABOVE The stills at Lagavulin produce the distinctive rich and peaty spirit that characterizes the final whisky after it has undergone 16 years of maturation.

RIGHT Lagavulin is one of the holy trinity of peated distilleries that are located next to one another on the southern shores of Islay.

KEY WHISKIES

Lagavulin 12-year-old Cask Strength 56.4% ABV
Lagavulin 16-year-old 43% ABV
Lagavulin Distiller's Edition 43% ABV

WELL, FANCY THAT . . .

The rocky shoreline is a challenge to even small boats, so in times gone by casks had to be floated out to a puffer ship, which would carry the stock over to the mainland.

LONGMORN

Iconic single-malt whiskies enjoy the same sort of loyalty that sports teams or rock bands do. Mess with the whisky at your peril, as the owners of Longmorn found out. Longmorn enjoys cult status, or at least its 15-year-old expression does, made all the more intense and perhaps charismatic by the fact that the distillery is usually closed to the public. So opening the distillery and launching a new expression at one Speyside festival made for a major event. I bet Pernod Ricard wishes that it had not bothered. What should have been a celebration turned sour as die-hard fans of the 15-year-old rounded on the people unveiling the new premium-priced 16-year-old and roundly rejected it. They had a point.

I was first introduced to Longmorn by the French whisky writer Martine Nouet, who passed me a glass and uttered the immortal, Gallic-inspired: "Let me introduce me to your new mistress . . . " Since then, it has all gone very quiet on the Longmorn front, and the mistress has become a dowdy madam. Pity.

Longmorn 15-year-old 45% ABV

Hard to get now, but definitely the expression to go for from this distillery. It is one of those malts where the age is not reflected in the whisky. The oak is held back by the juicy, grassy, and green fruity center. Balanced and refreshing, Speyside-style.

Longmorn 16-year-old 48% ABV

Considered by some as a blatant attempt to take advantage of the growing market for premium malts, the 16-year-old is bigger and fruitier than the 15-year-old, but is in some respects flabbier and less focused. There are no negatives here; the whisky is good, but not like the original.

Longmorn 17-year-old Cask Strength 49.4% ABV

Apple, pear, maple, and vanilla on the nose here, with yellow and apple fruits on the palate, plus custard, toffee, and some oak. Spices arrive later.

LONGROW
www.springbankdistillers.com

Longrow is the name of the heavily peated phenolic whisky made at Springbank in Campbeltown.

Longrow 10-year-old 46% ABV

An oddball this, where smoky peatiness and a sweet barley core work side by side, but never totally in harmony. Intriguing, though, and worth investigating because it is distinct from the peated island malts.

Longrow 10-year-old 100 Proof 57% ABV

This one is much more like it. An earthy, rootsy flavor underpins a rich, intense, and very oily mouth-coating mixture of sweetness and malt. Water lets the smoke out.

Longrow 14-year-old 46% ABV

Smoke and peat on the nose here, as well as fudge, but the taste is coal tar, peat, and bonfire. Distinctive seaside notes, too, make for another deli of a whisky for savory malt lovers. Oak and spice are a late showing.

Longrow CV 46% ABV

Arguably the best of the Longrow range, with a proper charcoal peat delivery and a delightful oily and downright rustic note—tastes as if it is handcrafted by artisans. Funny that . . .

Longrow Gaja Barolo 55.8% ABV

I have a problem with whisky and red wine, and think that as a rule they prove that, while you can mix the grain and the grape, you have to keep them at arm's length much of the time because they will fight like cat and dog. But this is an example of a puppy and a kitten rolling about in playful abandon. Lots of smoke flavor, lots of wine flavor, and a totally original taste. The whisky here is only seven years old, so it is untamed. It works very well.

THE MACALLAN

www.themacallan.com

Will the real Macallan, please, stand up?

On the one hand, there is the iconic gilt-edged Speyside distillery that has few equals when it comes to special and rare collectible bottles; the distillery that has been capable of commanding more loyalty than almost any other and that has consistently sat at the very head of the premier cru Scottish distilleries. And on the other is the one that seems to have lost its way in recent years, partly through bad luck and partly through bad judgment.

Having for years based at least part of its reputation on exceedingly well-made spirit using Golden Promise barley and the finest sherry casks, it has had to move away from Golden Promise because there is none left, and it is trying to move European customers away from sherry casks because of their limited supply due to the demands from Taiwan and Southeast Asia. The argument made by the distillery's owners that European drinkers want lighter spirits and have therefore moved naturally to its Fine Oak range of malts does not hold any water when you look at trends in dark spirits generally and the success of the likes of Glenfarclas and GlenDronach in particular.

Macallan also lost a great deal of respect when it first denied that it had fallen victim to forgers, as every other company had, then tried to spin its way out of the mess in which it found itself when tests showed that some of its special bottles were indeed fakes.

For all its recent problems, some of the world's best whiskies still come out of the distillery, and the Fine Oak range contains some expressions that easily outshine their sherried counterparts, showing off whisky maker Bob Dalgarno's outstanding skills to great effect.

So, still a distillery very much in credit. You just wish that it would throw off the marketing claptrap.

The Macallan 10-year-old 40% ABV

The original ten-year-old punches well above its weight, dripping in style and sophistication without commanding a premium price. A bottle of this, a bottle of Aberlour, and a bottle of BenRiach 12-year-old, and you have a pretty good cross section of Speyside styles. This is sherried with orange, red berry, and plum fruits.

The Macallan Fine Oak 10-year-old 40% ABV

The Fine Oak range marked a radical departure for the Macallan, and offered a lighter version of what had always been a full sherried malt. A higher percentage of bourbon cask whisky in the mix works remarkably well, showing off the malt craftsmanship. Clean barley, cedarwood, and orange on the nose; citrus and spice to taste.

The Macallan 12-year-old 40% ABV

Rich Christmas fruitcake, fruit crumble, and spice, with some orange in the mix and a taste shaped by toffee and candy notes.

The Macallan Fine Oak 12-year-old 40% ABV

This has aromas of butterscotch, vanilla, orange fruits, and other citrus fruits. The taste is of grapefruit and orange before a big wave of spices arrives. In all, a great example of how sherry and bourbon casks can perfectly complement each other.

The Macallan Fine Oak 15-year-old 43% ABV

A soft nose with squidgy yellow fruit, a big mouth-coating taste of ginger barley, canned peaches, and some oak and spice late on. Altogether, this is a rich and satisfying malt, and proof positive that the Fine Oak concept can be every bit as rewarding as the other traditional Macallans.

The Macallan Fine Oak 18-year-old 43% ABV

The nose is soft and mushy, and not very impressive, but the taste is much better, with a sweet and sour one–two, rich fruit and chewy barley giving way to intense pepper and oaky tannins. It all pulls around, however, for a pleasant finish.

The Macallan 18-year-old 43% ABV

This is another contender for the title of the world's best single malt, whatever that means. There are plenty of Macallan lovers who will tell you that this is not the heavyweight it once was, more of a David Beckham than a Wayne Rooney. I could not tell you because I do not get this expression at all and do not have a long enough history with it. Undoubtedly, this is premier league stuff all the same—lots of sherry, oak, and spice.

The Macallan Fine Oak 21-year-old 43% ABV

An ideal whisky for warm summer days, this one, it has lots of playful barley and zippy citrus fruits on both the nose and the palate. Very refreshing, and the oak very much takes a backseat.

The Macallan 25-year-old 43% ABV

Venerable old-boy whisky, with rich sherry, plenty of oak, and a clean orange core.

The Macallan Fine Oak 25-year-old 43% ABV

An assertive nose, this combines stewed fruits, dark chocolate, and cocoa, plus summer berries. The taste is a Ferris wheel of flavors, with all sorts of sweet exotic fruits, ordered and pleasant spices, hickory and licorice, and just enough oak to give the whole shebang some weight.

The Macallan 30-year-old 43% ABV

Christmas in a glass, not just because of the big sherry and fruitcake notes, but also because of the spicy aromas of clove and cinnamon-laced punch and licorice allsorts at its center. If the Macallan is the Rolls-Royce of whiskies, this is its Silver Cloud, an aging, classy model.

The Macallan Fine Oak 30-year-old 43% ABV

This is no slouch either, a slightly sleeker but not so stylish and elegant old whisky, the Rolls-Royce Silver Shadow perhaps? The sherry and red berry notes are all present and correct, but there are some notes of yellow and citrus fruit, too, and on the palate it's all about chunky orange marmalade and oak. Heady stuff that is rich and golden in color.

The Macallan Select Oak 40% ABV

Like a great Beatles song—short and perfectly formed, with lots of honeyed and sweet notes. There are aromas of honey, wood sap, toffee, and fruit; on the palate, there are hints of soft pastille fruits, the gentlest spices and oak imaginable, and a soft, gossamer-like conclusion. An elegant lady of a dram and a fine example of blemish-free whisky-making.

The Macallan Whisky Maker's Edition 42.8% ABV

Do not add water to this. It is gentle on the nose, with some aromas of fruit gums. Some oak, grape, and spice appear, too. On the palate, the citrus fruits are matched by a delightful woodiness and some hot chocolate notes. Spice wraps it up. A traffic light of a whisky, changing as it unfurls in the mouth. A delight.

The Macallan Estate Reserve 45.7% ABV

Dried orange peel, marmalade, gingery spice, and some woodiness on the nose; blood orange, toasted barley, and burnt oak on the palate. The whole ball game is wrapped up with creamy toffee.

MILTONDUFF

www.maltwhiskydistilleries.com

Miltonduff is one of the two key distilleries for the production of Ballantine's, the other being Glenburgie, which was rebuilt a few years ago and can now be run by just one operator, who can see every part of the production process from his desk. Technology has now reached a point where, were it allowed, a distillery need not be manned at all, but can be controlled by an operator with a laptop. To counteract the obvious deskilling, one whisky company invested in one of its distilleries as a training ground for traditional distilling skills.

Miltonduff 15-year-old 46% ABV

A perfectly palatable and enjoyable Speyside whisky with a twist. It is sweet and fruity for the most part, but it takes an odd salty, nutty turn halfway through. Like finding a knot in a rope.

MORTLACH

www.malts.com

One of Scotland's most enigmatic distilleries and one that produces a whisky that is always worth getting excited about. The distillery is not open to the public, little of its considerable output is bottled as single malt, and what is bottled is either as a 16-year-old or a 32-year-old. But this is a core whisky in Johnnie Walker, and it's a whisky fanboy's dream because the distillation process is unique and includes a triple-distillation process for at least a sizable fraction of the distillation. The distillery has worm tubs—the traditional condensation method, which is thought to ensure a meatier, more robust spirit. It often appears in specialist bottlings as intensely sherried and is unpredictable: oily, meaty, or sulfury.

Mortlach 16-year-old 43% ABV

On one level, this is a street urchin, but get past the unkempt nature of the malt and it is surprisingly sophisticated. There are sherry, spice, oil, menthol, and an endearing, welcome touch of sulfur on both the nose and the palate, with fruit, cocoa, and chili late on. Not for softies.

Mortlach 32-year-old 50.1% ABV

Some light citrus fruit on the nose battles against a wave of sherry and cordite. The palate is grungy—the oral equivalent to the smogs they used to get in industrial cities and which you see whenever a Jack the Ripper film is shown. There is something quite Highland peat about it all, but the taste is so intense that it is hard to know what is caused by oak, smoke, or spice. The taste changes in the mouth, but it is always savory and what little sweet fruit there is gets squeezed by prickle on the palate. It is a total delight—but only if you like rollmops, other Scandinavian salted fish, and chili sauce.

OBAN

www.malts.com

Oban is a port on Scotland's west coast and is the gateway to the Western Isles. The distillery is small and compact, hidden behind the town's main street. Nearly all of Oban's output is bottled at 14 years.

Oban 14-year-old 43% ABV

Another quirky and unique malt, big on fruit and sherry on both nose and palate, but with at least a smattering of west coast and Highland earthiness. Sweet conquers peat here, but there are enough smoke and peat to stop the sweetness elsewhere becoming too dominant in the mix.

Oban Distiller's Edition 43% ABV

The debate about whether you should mess with a special whisky too much is assuredly squelched out of existence by this distiller's edition, which uses sherry casks and adds a spiciness and clean green fruitiness to the sweetness of the standard 14-year-old. It succeeds in pulling off that trick of still being distinctly Oban, but is very much a quality whisky in its own right, with its own personality and character.

OBAN DISTILLERY

5 Stafford Street, Oban, Argyll PA34 5NJ
www.discovering-distilleries.com

If you travel up the west of Scotland on the A82 from Glasgow, it is hard not to feel that you are on vacation, no matter what time of the year it is or the reason for your journey.

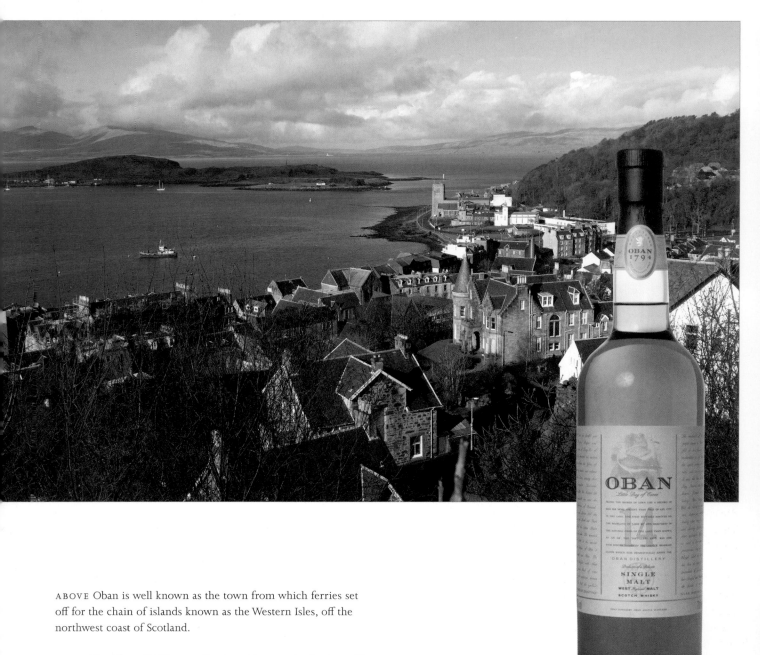

ABOVE Oban is well known as the town from which ferries set off for the chain of islands known as the Western Isles, off the northwest coast of Scotland.

RIGHT The Oban distillery nestles in a side street in the town. The location of the distillery makes expansion very difficult.

You don't want to be in a hurry. The road has a habit of dragging you into Highland time, and the procession of motor homes, travel trailers, and cars pulling boats ensures that progress is slow. Knapsack-carrying hikers line the route, whatever the weather, and to your right-hand side Loch Lomond provides the backdrop for numerous bed and breakfasts, cafés, and water sports centers.

You eventually arrive at the Green Welly Stop at Tyndrum, which is a sort of Highland version of an interstate highway exit services stop, with a café–restaurant, convenience stores, gift and outer clothing shops, a gas station, and a whisky shop that warrants investigation because it often stocks gems that have long been sold out elsewhere.

The road divides here, with the right fork heading off for Glen Coe and Fort William, the left to Oban, a bustling seaside town that serves as a main gateway to the Western Isles and is home to one of Scotland's few town-based distilleries—and one of its quirkiest.

Oban is a relatively small distillery and is nestled in a side street behind the bustling seafront shops, in the shadow of a steep cliff and what looks like the remains of a Roman colosseum. The distillery's location means that it cannot be expanded and, because the standard 14-year-old malt was part of Diageo's original Classic Malts series, it is very rare to find any other expressions of it—although limited stocks of older expressions have appeared from time to time. Such is the demand for it that everything Diageo can bottle it does. So much so that in 2003, exactly 14 years after the distillery was closed and production halted to build a visitor center, Oban malt was all but impossible to find.

There are a few peculiarities about this cramped, characterful distillery, and one of them pertains to the way in which the spirit is condensed.

It is something of a sad whisky-obsessive joke to ask a distillery tour guide whether he or she has worms. Oban has. This is, in fact, a reference to the condensing method used at the distillery. These days, the vast majority of distilleries cool their spirit through a condenser consisting of a pipe within a pipe. The vapor passes through the inner pipe, and cold water through the outer one, in the process condensing the spirit back into liquid.

But there is another more traditional way of condensing spirit liquid. A worm tub consists of a water pool, usually placed externally on a roof, filled with flowing cold water. Under the water's surface, a long copper pipe snakes from

KEY WHISKIES

Oban 14-year-old 43% ABV
Oban Distiller's Edition 43% ABV

one end of the pool and back again. Spirit passes through the coiled pipe and is cooled by the cold water covering it. Very few distilleries have these anymore, but there is a view among some experts that condensation by this method is gentler and enriches the spirit.

Certainly, Oban single malt is like no other, deliciously combining a sweet fruitiness with a hefty peaty base and a pleasant spiciness.

If you are, indeed, passing through Oban on the way to some resort elsewhere, take the trouble to savor an Oban while watching the CalMac ferries heading off to Mull and beyond. The vacation starts right here.

WELL, FANCY THAT . . .

The colosseum building is special to the people of Oban and is called McCaig's Tower. John Stuart McCaig is said to have started work on a family monument in 1895, to provide much-needed employment for local stonemasons and builders. But after spending some £5,000—a fortune at the time—on a model of the Roman Colosseum, he died with the work unfinished. He is remembered by the local people as a caring, altruistic merchantman.

PULTENEY
www.oldpulteney.com

Pulteney is Scotland's most northerly distillery and, if you travel by road, you go so far through the Highlands that you come out the other side and the landscape becomes flat again.

Old Pulteney 12-year-old 43% ABV

This was once described by whisky writer Dave Broom as the ultimate whisky for which you should throw away the cork—and he is spot-on. I know several people who have set out on an (obviously responsible) afternoon or evening session with a group of friends and a bottle of this, and belatedly discovered that they had all but drained the bottle. It is the saltiness in this easy-going citrusy malt that does it, coupled with a spectacularly short finish. As someone pointed out to me, it is a bit like Pringles chips—the whisky seduces you with its sweet and sour combination. You want to resist, but it's futile.

Old Pulteney 17-year-old 46% ABV

Many years ago, the herring were so plentiful around Wick that the sea turned silver—hence the distillery's, and this whisky's, gold and silver theme. You could walk across the harbor by stepping boat to boat. The herring created a buoyant and thriving industry, and at one time Wick had the biggest port in Europe. So great was the trade that the area known as Pulteney was built to house the hundreds of immigrant workers who moved here. Thomas Telford built roads and bridges to service the trade. And the Scottish fishwives followed the herring as they traveled all the way down the east coast and into England. Today, you can visit the Time & Tide museum in Great Yarmouth and learn of the link between Wick and East Anglia, and occasionally you can meet someone of Scottish descent whose grandmother followed the fish and fell in love with the region, one of its inhabitants, or both.

There is nothing left in Wick now, of course, except this distillery. But this whisky is a fitting salute to another lost part of great British industrial history. It is a much more intense version of the 12-year-old, with some oiliness, chocolate, soft toffee, and rich fruit notes.

Old Pulteney 21-year-old 46% ABV

The tide was well and truly in with the 17-year-old and, while this is a wonderful whisky, it is like going back to the 1960s and asking Hank Marvin to follow Hendrix. Lots of honey, just enough wood, and some orange and candy fruit, salt, and treacle toffee. Very good indeed.

Old Pulteney 30-year-old 45.8% ABV

Hard to know what to make of this—it is a very different Pulteney, adding more to the distillery's admirable diversity. This is very delicate and soft, with lemon and grapefruit that belie its age. It is all a little fragile, but more spritely than it has any right to be. The spice is still there, but plays quite a back role.

PORT ELLEN

Increasingly rare now as the last stocks dwindle away, the whisky has taken on iconic status, and the distillery at Port Ellen on Islay has been demolished. So it is hard to decide whether to save it or drink it. My advice? Save for a special occasion, then drink it.

Port Ellen 2nd Annual Release 24-year-old 58.35% ABV

The history of whisky is littered with the remains of closed and silent distilleries. In Scotland, Ireland, and the United States, the winds of economic change have skittled scores of famous distilleries. Where once there were thriving businesses, now there are parking lots and shopping malls. The town of Port Ellen is on Islay, and today you will find maltings there. But there was a distillery once, too.

So why do the likes of Port Ellen, and other closed distilleries Rosebank and St. Magdalene, warrant their own listing in books such as this and scores of others do not? The answer is because Diageo finds enough whisky in its depleted stocks to still put out well-priced special bottlings, partially because there is a highly active market for them. Indeed, there is very little Port Ellen left, and when it's gone, it's gone. Practically the only real guide to the value of what is left is on eBay. So an independent bottle retailing for $150 sells on eBay for $200 and overnight the retail price shoots up to $180. I know of one store where a Douglas Laing bottle went from $120 to $200 through three price hikes in less than 12 months. Now that's a highly investable whisky.

ROSEBANK

I admit that I never really got Lowland malts, but I blame my mother. As a child, I was allowed to dip my finger in her whisky, and I remember vividly the taste of bonfire and smoke. So unsurprisingly my route into malt was through Islay and the islands, with the Highlands not far behind, partially because of the peat that popped up in many of them, but also because I am big on chili and Madras curries, and big, bold flavors work for me.

So pity the poor Lowlands, where nuance and subtlety are key components. Rosebank, though, was a breakthrough. The distillery is demolished, but there is still a fair bit of whisky around. Good expressions, such as those at the Scotch Malt Whisky Society in Edinburgh, are great.

Rosebank 20-year-old Rare Malts 62.3% ABV

Floral and heathery on the nose, with sherry trifle, custard, and Dundee cake on the palate, this has a soft, honeyed, and rounded heart.

ROYAL BRACKLA

Royal Brackla was bought by John Dewar & Sons 12 years ago, but no stock was included in the deal, so only very young malt exists. But the promise is certainly there, so this is one to watch in the future.

Royal Brackla 10-year-old 40% ABV

Youthful, fresh sappy malt with some heather and floral notes, a touch of spice, and a sweet core. It is included here because it is one of the best examples of young and untainted barley.

ROYAL LOCHNAGAR
www.malts.com

This distillery lies close to the Balmoral Estate, Scottish home to Queen Elizabeth.

Royal Lochnagar 12-year-old 40% ABV

Royal Lochnagar is one of only three distilleries allowed to include the word "royal" in its title, thanks to the patronage of Queen Victoria. The distillery is small and traditional, with worm tubs and old wooden washbacks, and it makes a traditional Highland whisky. The 12-year-old provides easy drinking, a rich honeycomb heart, sherry fruits, and a warm finish.

Royal Lochnagar Select Reserve 43% ABV

I happened to be tasting this when my brother called me to say that Bobby Smith had died. That name will mean little to most people, but Smith played soccer for Leicester City in the 1980s (and for Edinburgh side Hibernian for many years, too) and was part of the great Jock Wallace City sides of yesteryear. Years before I fell in love with whisky, Leicester had a special relationship with Scotland. Wallace, who had been a legend at Rangers, gave Leicester one of its greatest spells. He brought in fiercesome fighting Scots such as Gary McAllister, Ally Mauchlen, Iain Henderson, and personal favorite Alan Young. He mixed them up with a bunch of enthusiastic puppies, including one Gary Lineker, future England international player.

I lived in Market Harborough, and our crowd knew one of the players, Andy Peake, so we always felt that we had a direct line to the heart of the club. We went to games home and away, often traveling with the exiled Glaswegians from Corby, whose parents had been moved en masse from Scotland to the English Midlands to work in the steel factories, but who faced mass unemployment and poverty when the industry declined.

Bobby Smith was a journeyman Scot who had a flash of genius. We loved him.

When I am in Scotland talking to taxi drivers, I often bring up Leicester City's Scottish link. Bobby Smith died of cancer in 2010. Just like music, you associate whisky with special moments, happy and sad. So Bobby Smith, this honeyed, rich, and spiced apple whisky is forever yours.

ST. MAGDALENE

Is single-malt whisky a male preserve? There are scores of women who would emphatically say not. Indeed, the likes of Glenmorangie's Rachel Barrie and Annabel Meikle, and French *Whisky Magazine* editor Martine Nouet, are among the very best nosers in the business. Annabel, who was once nicknamed the "Lowland Queen," is responsible for introducing scores of people to the delights of malts such as St. Magdalene, including me.

St. Magdalene is another great and lost Lowland malt. All over the Highlands, there are distilleries that have reopened after being mothballed for years. They were saved because, once they stopped producing whisky, the land they were on was of little use to anyone else, and so they were never knocked down. When the economy picked up, they were reopened.

St. Magdalene 23-year-old Rare Malts
58.1% ABV

It is likely that fine whisky was produced at the St. Magdalene distillery for well over 200 years before its doors were shut forever in 1983 and the land was given over to apartments.

Not surprisingly, there is very little whisky left from this distillery, and you have to be very careful with it—some independent bottlings are on the dodgy side. Diageo still has some stocks, however, and the releases in its rare malts series are worth checking out.

This particular bottling has some vegetal and grassy notes, but develops into a pleasant mix of stewed fruits, clean and sweet damp barley, and some clear honey. Subtle and pleasant.

SCAPA
www.scapamalt.com

Witnessing the resurrection of a whisky distillery is rare, and an experience not to be missed. And so it was that I found myself on the Orkney Isles, clambering over bricks and debris with industry good guy Michael Cockram in driving wind and rain. The roof for the main part of the distillery was off, and birds had taken over the still room to messy effect. But two features stood out: the large window overlooking the brooding Scapa Flow and the black buoy marking where the sunken *Royal Oak* had come to rest, and the big Lomond still in the center of the still room. The Lomond still was a feature of some distilleries in the 1960s.

It fell into disuse, however, because its plates often clogged up and were difficult to clean. Today, the distillery is refurbished and the still room fully functional. The Lomond is in place, but functions as a conventional still these days.

Scapa 14-year-old 40% ABV

This is now a rare bottling because the 16-year-old has replaced it, but it is worth getting hold of. This is an easy-drinking malt that twists and turns on the palate, with light floral and citrus notes and a delicate dosing of salt and pepper. Irresistible. And very quaffable.

SPEYBURN
www.inverhouse.com

Speyburn is owned by Inverhouse and has been used as an entry-level malt. It is not seen very often, but an occasional older bottling suggests that this distillery is an undiscovered gem. Time—and the plans of the parent company—will tell.

Speyburn 25-year-old 46% ABV

This has an unusual aroma, with a slight off note nestled under lemon, grapefruit, and orange, and hints of oak. The taste is soft, honeyed, and rounded, with some oak and spice. The finish is refreshing and really quite fruity.

SPRINGBANK
www.springbankdistillers.com

Once there were scores of distilleries in Campbeltown, which is the peninsula running down the west coast of Scotland. Whisky was exported to the United States from there, but over time the quality of the malt deteriorated, people stopped wanting it, and one by one the distilleries went out of business. Today, there are three distilleries in the region, the biggest and most successful of which is this one.

It is actually three distilleries in one because the triple-distilled Hazelburn and the intensely peated Longrow are also produced here. Springbank itself enjoys iconic status, with serious whisky drinkers attracted by both its unique taste and the rustic boutique nature of the distillery.

Springbank 10-year-old 46% ABV

As complex as a whisky this young gets, with honey, barley, candied lemon, earthy peat, and salt and pepper all contributing to a malt that has an appealing bittersweetness to it.

Springbank 100 Proof
57% ABV

Like the ten-year-old, with the volume turned up. This is an oral orchestra and, although each section is working in harmony overall, it is fun to focus on each component part individually, particularly the peat and spicy notes, which give the whisky its character. There are some vanilla and soft toffee notes in the mix, too.

Springbank 15-year-old 46% ABV

An outstanding rich and full-flavored malt, with a soft and sweet crystallized peach nose, and a full oily, fruity palate that again manages the impressive trick of being sweet and savory all at once. Red and tropical fruits can be found in the taste, and a rustic grunginess provides weight to the whole drinking experience.

Springbank 16-year-old Rum Wood
54.2% ABV

Arguably the best bottling of Springbank there is, with all the exotic fruits, vanilla, and coconut cranked up to the highest level and almost in conflict with big peat and pepper notes, like dueling fencers scampering across your mouth. A big, mouth-coating, and assertive whisky and not one for wimps.

Springbank 18-year-old 46% ABV

The nose here is surprisingly soft and delicate, with grape, some green fruit, and a touch of smoke. The taste, on the other hand, is massive, with an early hit of black pepper, some unripe banana in the center, and some cocoa and smoke toward the end. Peat is most noticeable in the finish. Not much impact from oak for the age, but the overall effect is less sweet than some other bottlings.

Springbank Vintage 1997 54.9% ABV

Toffee, vanilla, peat, and green banana on the nose. The taste is very intense and needs unlocking with water, but when you do so there are oak, smoke, vanilla ice cream with toffee fudge sauce, and tropical fruits.

STRATHISLA
www.maltwhiskydistilleries.com

Flooding in November 2009 forced its owners to give the visitor center a complete makeover. But this is a very pretty distillery, anyway, and one of Scotland's most photographed. It is also home to Chivas Regal.

Strathisla 12-year-old 43% ABV

Another definitive Speysider with a delicate ginger barley and grapey nose and a rich, sweet yellow fruit taste, with some red berries and barley at its core and a wisp of smoke toward the finish.

SPRINGBANK DISTILLERS LTD

85 Longrow, Campbeltown, Argyll PA28 6EX
www.springbankdistillers.com

Springbank is special. Very special. It is one of those distilleries that seems to tick all the right boxes without even trying.

Marketing departments in companies with 100 times the money to throw at image-making cannot touch Springbank for credibility, and must eye it enviously. For no matter how much money you throw at something, it either has that *je ne sais quoi* or it doesn't. In MasterCard-speak . . . New stills: a million pounds. An interactive visitor center: five million. A new brand launch with full marketing and advertising support: ten million. Genuine atmosphere and authenticity: absolutely priceless.

And it is not just its small scale (750,000 liters/198,129 US gallons)—no Edradour, but still a "wee bairn") or the fact that it remains independent, or that it happens to possess a delightful mix of ramshackle disorganization and admirable shrewd professionalism—there is a heroic element here, too.

It is whisky's equivalent to an aging but trusted deep-sea fishing trawler—it operates alone in the harshest of economic swells on the Campbeltown peninsula, the last survivor in a region where once there was a monstrous fleet of distilleries, now alone and buffeted by the swirling waves of economic fortune. Where distilleries in other areas cling to one another and seek solace through shared experience when times get tough, Springbank seems to stand alone. This point was illustrated vividly during the boom of 2008, when the industry did not seem capable of meeting demand worldwide for malt, and seemingly all was good with the world. The demand, however, was matched by shortages of wood and escalating fuel prices. While others spoke misguidedly of the boom to end all booms, Springbank surprised everyone by acting alone in battening down the hatches against the huge seas of spiraling costs and riding out the storm, taking the opportunity to build new warehouses and shape up for the next wave on which it was set to ride.

It is doing that now—and how!

Of all whisky stories, Campbeltown's rapid and hideous decline is among the most tragic. Back in the day, the region boasted the biggest and most important whisky-making region in the world. Its distilleries went all out to satisfy the thirst of the booming industrial heartlands of Glasgow, spewing its waste into the water with little regard for its environment. Then trains arrived and opened up the Speyside region, providing a doorway for the region's

whiskies. The big, heavy, oily, and peaty style of whisky from Campbeltown fell out of favor with drinkers, who turned to the sweeter and fruitier creations from Scotland's northeast. No matter: the region turned to North America.

But the region's distillers had grown bloated and complacent, and they paid scant regard to the spirit they were making and selling. "Campbeltown" became synonymous with "bad malt," and fell out of favor even further and straight into decline. When Prohibition gripped the United States, the end for Campbeltown was fast indeed.

Through it all, Springbank, owned by the Mitchell family for more than 150 years, never once compromised on quality, and survived.

What clinches the deal for this wonderful distillery, though, is the fact that, on the one hand, it is a traditional boutique distillery where there are few nods to modernity and progress. And on the other, someone somewhere knows his onions because the distillery continues to put out exciting and challenging whiskies with the same sense of commercialism as any of the big boys.

Not just under the Springbank moniker, either. This is a three-for-the-price-of-one distillery, bottling heavily peated whiskies under the name Longrow and sweet, rounded triple-distilled malts under the name Hazelburn.

Today, the light is still on for whisky in Campbeltown. Springbank's owners have a hand in keeping Glen Scotia alive in the region, too, and now there is another distillery producing whisky, under the name Kilkerran.

Meanwhile, Springbank goes from strength to strength, its flavorsome and unique whiskies acclaimed across the world.

Yes, very special indeed.

ABOVE Part of the new-look Springbank range, combining a modern marketing approach with traditional production.

RIGHT AND INSET Whisky enthusiasts are drawn to the traditional methods used at Springbank. Here, the malt is being turned.

KEY WHISKIES

Hazelburn 8-year-old 46% ABV
Longrow 10-year-old 46% ABV
Longrow 10- year-old 100 Proof 157% ABV
Longrow CV 46% ABV
Longrow Gaja Barolo 55.8% ABV
Longrow 14-year-old 46% ABV
Springbank 10-year-old 46% ABV
Springbank 100 Proof 57% ABV
Springbank 15-year-old 46% ABV
Springbank 16-year-old Rum Wood 54.3% ABV

STRATHISLA DISTILLERY

Keith, Banffshire AB55 3BS
www.maltwhiskydistilleries.com

Our timing was perfect.

The roads through the Glenlivet valley, many unsurpassable just days before, after the heaviest snowfalls for 30 years, had reopened. Elsewhere, the landscape was dominated by snow, feet of it, turning the region into a stunningly still winter wonderland.

We went up to Tamnavulin, then Braeval, the sun shining across the valley, the snow dazzling and elegant. It was both breathtakingly beautiful and disturbing, the snow and silence intense, reinforcing the desolation of the bens and glens in these parts, the enormity of the snowfall, and the extremes of nature making us feel meek and vulnerable.

There is something very disconcerting about miles of virgin snow where no human has ventured, and something wistful about the occasional trail of footsteps heading out to the hills. It is a miracle that anyone traveled to and manned Braeval distillery through the weeks of snow and ice, and it is hard to imagine a more lonely or isolated workplace.

All very beautiful, yes, but snow comes with a price—and during the winter of 2009–2010 it played havoc with the Scottish whisky industry. A combination of heavy snow, intense ice, and no wind—unheard of in these parts—meant that snow piled up on the roofs of whisky warehouses across the Speyside region, and eventually it exacted its toll.

Chivas—owners of, among others, Strathisla, Glenlivet, Longmorn, and Aberlour—lost 38 of its 67 warehouse roofs. They collapsed onto racked casks of maturing whisky, making the warehouses unsafe to enter and the whisky unobtainable. That, in turn, created a major headache for the Chivas team, who needed mature stocks for Chivas Regal.

"It has been a major problem," says brand ambassador Ian Logan. "They said that when the first roof went down it sounded like a bomb had gone off. And, as others followed, nobody was sure which warehouse would be next, so there was the whole safety issue. They did everything they could to prevent further damage. They brought in helicopters to drop salt onto the roof to shift the snow and ice. Heaven knows

ABOVE Strathisla is one of the prettiest distilleries in Scotland, particularly when lit up at night. It also features on the elegant bottle design.

Strathisla 12-year-old 43% ABV

what it will cost, but it will run into millions to sort it out. The insurance people will pay, but they will also insist that steps are taken to make sure that it does not happen in the future. And it is not just the roofs. There is one warehouse at Glenlivet where walls are leaning by 20 percent."

The logistics of how to move stock to keep the blends flowing is just the sort of problem that the team at Chivas could have done without because nature had already given them one major problem in 2009. In November, the river close to Strathisla burst its banks after heavy rain. The Strathisla team was able to put sandbags across the entrance of the distillery, but the bags simply diverted the water farther down the road, where it flowed into the visitor center. So substantial was the damage caused that the center had to be completely stripped out and refurbished, and was effectively out of commission for five months.

Perhaps a total refurbishment is just what Strathisla needed. The spiritual home of Chivas, it is one of the most photographed distilleries in Scotland, its buildings and pagoda roof almost defining what a Scottish distillery should look like. It is also home to the malts stored for use in Chivas and, although officially no one will tell you what goes into the blend, you have only to look around you to work it out—casks of Laphroaig, Aultmore, Longmorn, and Tomatin are all stored here.

Nor are the casks of ultra-rare 40-year-plus whisky locked in a cage in the corner of the warehouse. One is to be bottled when Prince Charles becomes king; another, filled on the day Prince William was born, will be bottled on the day he gets married or when he becomes king, whichever comes first. The combination of dark aroma-rich traditional warehousing, the presence of such an array of whisky stock, and the collection of iconic and ultra-rare casks make this warehouse almost temple-like. The refurbishment provides the distillery with a fresh start and an environment fit for, if not necessarily a king, certainly a prince.

And it is the future that drives this distillery and the others in the group. Despite all the recent trials, the team at Chivas is bullish, looking forward with confidence. Barring any more catastrophes, the future looks bright. These have been abnormal weather patterns, nature's wake-up call, telling us that time is almost up for our planet. Scotland's whisky distilleries are in the front line, reliant on weather patterns to produce their spirit, vulnerable to the whims of nature. More than most, the industry respects the environment. Perhaps nature understands that and, after such a rough and tumble period, it is about to give Speyside a break.

TALISKER

www.malts.com

You should not trust the Internet. It has no editor, and it can circulate information at an awesome speed, even when that information is wrong. When I first became editor of *Whisky Magazine*, a new James Bond movie portrayed the hero as a Talisker drinker. Judi Dench as M also sipped single malt, so I thought it would be a good cover story. Talisker was, I was told, James Bond's preferred tipple in the Ian Fleming books.

So we did a cover story, after some difficult negotiations with the management of Pierce Brosnan because the actor did not want to be associated with a strong spirit.

A few years later, I was telling a group of people how drinking single-malt whisky had started in the 1970s, when someone asked me how it was that James Bond would have sipped single malt when the Ian Fleming books were written in the 1960s, before Talisker would have been generally available. Good question, so I consulted the Internet.

There are thousands of references to Bond and whisky. Trouble is, they all stem from my original feature. There is no reference to Talisker in the Fleming books. It is not true. By the time of the next James Bond movie, our superspy was drinking Finlandia Vodka. It is called product placement.

Talisker 10-year-old 45.8% ABV

An electric storm of a malt, crackling with pepper and spice, and flickering with cocoa and sweet barley. It has an almost metallic quality, and it bounces around the palate like savory sherbet, as uncompromising, unforgettable, and unique as the island of Skye from where it comes.

Talisker 18-year-old 45.8% ABV

We have opened a bottle of this for Father Christmas for the past three years because, in our house, we know how seriously Santa takes his whisky. No more needs to be said about it. This is one of the world's very best whiskies, richer, fuller, and with more depth than the fiery ten-year-old, but with the pepper and peat still very much to the fore and an intensity to die for.

Talisker Distiller's Edition 45.8% ABV

The extra maturation in sherry casks makes for an intriguing and ultimately rewarding malt, with fruit filling out the flavor over the ten-year-old, but without sacrificing the peat and chili burst so important to Talisker. Like the 18-year-old, this expression is richer and fuller than the standard bottling.

Talisker 57 North 57% ABV

This is a cask-strength bottling that is sailing somewhere between Skye and Islay (which is exactly where I first tasted it), so the trademark pepper and peat are still there, but they are joined by sea breeze and brine, smoke and seafood. This is a rough and rugged malt as big and hardy as a Scottish trawlerman.

Talisker 25-year-old 54.2% ABV

The nose is reminiscent of cracked pepper and salt on lemon-drizzled trout, and on the palate the pepper is still there, but sits snugly alongside citrus, ginger barley, vanilla, and some oak. The tearaway ten-year-old has settled down into an old man that still has some attitude.

Talisker 30-year-old 49.5% ABV

The peat and pepper have calmed down in this whisky and have taken more of a backseat, making it one of the most intriguing and unusual Taliskers that you will ever taste. Oak is unsurprisingly in the mix, and there are some light, even floral notes, alongside the spice.

TAMDHU

www.edringtongroup.com

Most of this sizable distillery's malt goes into blends, including the company's Famous Grouse. Pity, because the malt is quite wonderful. If you like your whisky fruity and sherbety, and you see a bottle of this, go for it. Trouble is, there is that most-of-the-sizable-stock-going-into-blends thing to consider. The distillery has its own commercial maltings.

Tamdhu 40% ABV

No age statement, but this is clearly young, with fresh barley, sweet honey, and a thrilling lemon and lime sherbet core. Outstanding.

Tamdhu 25-year-old

43% ABV

Oily, sweet, plummy, and with enough oak and spice to hold the honey and sweet fruit in check. Very underrated and worth seeking out.

TAMNAVULIN

www.whyteandmackay.com

Tamnavulin is now owned by Whyte & Mackay and was reopened in 2007, but since then it has struggled after being badly damaged by snow in the winter of 2009–2010. Stock is limited, and most of the pre-2007 output tends to be reserved for adding to blends.

Tamnavulin 12-year-old 40% ABV

Another malt that is more often than not destined for blends and therefore hard to find in its own right. Owner Whyte & Mackay does little to support it. The taste is of graham crackers, light spices, and a menthol note, making this the ideal early summer's evening whisky.

TOBERMORY

Tobermory is the only distillery on Mull, one of the few places where you can see both sea eagles and golden eagles, although some local farmers would like to put a stop to that because they somewhat bizarrely claim that the birds are carrying off their livestock. Tobermory is only lightly peated, but the distillery produces the peaty Ledaig (pronounced led-ching) for about six months of the year, although the official bottlings are nothing to write home about.

Tobermory 10-year-old 40% ABV

You expect the big peaty whiskies to divide opinion, but not something as simple and straightforward as this. And yet there are people who choose this slightly salty, very subtly fruity and faintly smoky whisky above all others. Equally, there are just as many who cannot stand it. As with Jura, the reason may lie in the dairyish nose, although the taste is thoroughly fresh and fruity.

Tobermory 15-year-old 46.3% ABV

This is rich in sherry and Christmas fruitcake flavors, with spice and orange dominating the nose and taste. Some oak prevents the malt from being too one-dimensional, but if you do not like sherry you really will not like this.

TOMATIN
www.tomatin.com

You rarely hear much about Tomatin, but in its heyday it could produce more than 12 million liters (3,170,000 US gallons) of spirit a year, making it Scotland's largest distillery. Even today it is one of Scotland's bigger producers, but much of the spirit goes to Japan. The distillery, to the north of the Speyside region, is not the prettiest in Scotland, but it does welcome visitors.

Tomatin 12-year-old 40% ABV

The aroma of this whisky is light and delicate, and the flavor surprisingly rich and robust, with a nutty malt. There are also some noticeable sherry tones and a pleasant, fruity malt finish.

Tomatin 18-year-old
43% ABV

Juicy currants, sweet spice, and vanilla on the nose. The malt is rich, oily, and mouth-coating, with lots of sherry fruit, red berries, and oak. The finish is fruity and woody.

Tomatin 25-year-old 43% ABV

Fluffy apple, vanilla, and lemon on the nose, and the taste is of vanilla ice cream sundae with chocolate and hazelnuts, with a wave of late pepper and an ordered and balanced finish. This was a revelation—a very good whisky indeed.

Tomatin 30-year-old 49.3% ABV

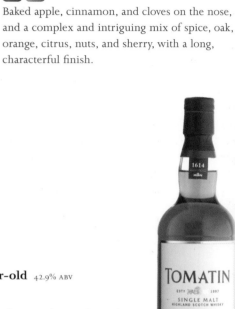

Baked apple, cinnamon, and cloves on the nose, and a complex and intriguing mix of spice, oak, orange, citrus, nuts, and sherry, with a long, characterful finish.

Tomatin 40-year-old 42.9% ABV

A big and bold nose here, with mint Battenberg cake and red apples. The taste is a mix of baked apples with mincemeat filling, nutmeg and cloves, oak and spice. The finish is long and surprisingly zingy for such an old whisky. Another dram straight out of the top drawer.

Tomatin 1997 57.1% ABV

This is young and totally different from what has gone before, with all the sweet fruits and soft banana suggesting bourbon casks, and a very pleasing taste of soft toffee, yellow fruits, and vanilla ice cream. A welcome addition to the family. Not so much the black sheep as the yellow one in the family.

Tomatin 1991 57.1% ABV

Sweet clean barley, and buttery, like corn on the cob dripping with butter. There is also a big wave of caramel, making for a full and enjoyable whisky.

Tomatin 1980 47.4% ABV

Starts off shyly, but eventually blossoms out with a big wave of orange and lemon. On the palate, the fruit theme continues before a wave of paprika draws a curtain over proceedings. Quite delightful.

TOMINTOUL

www.tomintouldistillery.co.uk

Way back before Highland and Speyside whisky went legitimate, the reputation of malt from the region became known as far away as London. There was a thirst for the rich sweet malts in the bars and taverns of Glasgow and Edinburgh, and smugglers would bring whisky on horseback through the Glenlivet valley. The story goes that, on one visit, the king of England asked for a glass of Glenlivet, shocking his Scottish hosts and elevating the reputation of the distillery. Other distillers, keen to cash in on its perceived reputation, added the word "Glenlivet."

Tomintoul still includes the descriptor "Speyside Glenlivet" on its label, and has every right to do so because the two distilleries are sited very close to each other and some distance from other Speyside producers.

Tomintoul 10-year-old 40% ABV

Light, easy-drinking malt and so gentle that it could be from the Lowlands. Perfectly drinkable, but a little underwhelming and with some decidedly sweet toffee notes. This is malt for people who do not like malt whisky perhaps, or whose experience is in blends?

Tomintoul 16-year-old 40% ABV

This one is much, much better, with lemon, orange, and green fruits on both nose and palate, and a pleasant level of spiciness probably from the wood. It does not hang around long at the end, though, but is pleasant and rounded.

Tomintoul 27-year-old 40% ABV

A stocky and rich malt, with orange marmalade on the nose and a pleasing taste that includes fudge, vanilla, and light fruits. Given the age, there is not a great deal of oak coming through, but it is noticeable at the finish.

Tomintoul Peaty Tang 40% ABV

More than just a tang of peat, but not a full-blooded Islay-style whisky, either. This is a two-trick malt, with an earthy, rustic character from the peat and green fruits from the Speyside malt. It all tastes a little like a smoky Irish whiskey (they do exist) or a peaty Bladnoch.

TORMORE

This is a really weird distillery. It is only just over 50 years old and, when it was built, its owners were happy to splash the cash and produce not only a state-of-the art distillery, but an ornate and showy one, too, one that almost begged for visitors to come and marvel at it. It has ornate clocks with moving parts and four different Scottish songs to mark each quarter hour. And yet it is not open to the public and never has been.

Tormore 12-year-old 40% ABV

Another light, unassertive, and gentle toffeeish single malt, this has some straw and yellow fruit notes. Nothing wrong with it, particularly, but you would not miss it if it disappeared. A whisky for those who are not crazy about big-tasting drams.

TULLIBARDINE

Tullibardine was reopened by a consortium in 2003, and since then there has been a flood of different bottlings, as well as extensive tours and the release of other products such as whisky beers. But the distillery's future is uncertain, and there has been talk of a sale.

Tullibardine 1993 40% ABV

A restrained nose complete with floral, almost perfumey notes. On the palate, there are delicate spicy notes, some honey, and oak. The finish is polite and ordered.

Blended whiskies

Single malt might be the John McEnroe, Muhammad Ali, or Meatloaf of Scotch whisky, but the country also produces three other styles of whisky that are happy getting on with what they are doing without shouting loudly about it at every single opportunity.

By far and away the biggest category of these is blended whisky, the category that put Scotland on the map worldwide and which still accounts for the vast majority of whisky sales. One of whisky's greatest ironies is that, while most whisky lovers pay homage to single malt and are dismissive of blends (which they consider inferior), in fact most single malts exist only because of the blended sector. Our ability to enjoy a single malt in its own right is made possible by the economic realities of selling a great deal of blended whisky to fund the single-malt process.

It is quite understandable that single malts should grab the headlines. For single malts, read individuality, variety, unpredictability, and stimulation. For blends, read reliability, consistency, and palatability. Single-malt whiskies are Angelina Jolie or Johnny Depp; blends more often than not are Jennifer Aniston or Hugh Laurie.

To ignore the category, though, is to overlook whisky making at its very best. Blends are like the circus—there is a lot of tired, clichéd, and uninspiring garbage out there, but just occasionally you stumble upon the Cirque du Soleil, a perfect blend of balance, strength, creativity, and grace.

If you buy a bottle of "Clan Sporrantosser" for less than the price of a can of beer from a dodgy convenience store, then expect it to be little more than caramelized vodka, matured for three years and a minute in a cask that has been filled more times than a window cleaner's bucket. Splash out for a special blend, though, and you

get more twists and turns than a season of 24 and more layers than a basketful of onions.

Blends do not have to mean blands and, indeed, at their best they are every bit the match of the very best single malts. Once you have found a favorite, the one that has you oohing and aahing every time you come back to it, then those values of consistency and reliability do not look quite so frumpy, do they?

To make blended whisky, you need grain whisky, which is made in a different style of still than single-malt whisky, one known as the "continuous," "column," or "Coffey" still. The resulting spirit has a less defined taste than new-make malt spirit, but when mixed with malt it smooths and rounds its rough edges. On its own, it can be pretty uninspiring, but it has been described as being like a blank canvas; if you can add enough color through a top-quality oak cask, it is possible to create something that is fresh, new, and vital. The best examples of these are found in the independent sector and are often more than 30 years old.

The final style of Scotch whisky is a mixture of malts from different distilleries. In more sensible times, these were called "vatted" malts, but the term came to be considered as too "industrial"-sounding.

For reasons best known to itself, the Scotch Whisky Association ignored suggestions of alternative names such as "mixed malts," "married malts," "mingled malts," or just "malts whisky," spuriously claiming with a somewhat amazing chutzpah that its research indicated support for a new term: "blended malt whisky." This is a different category than blended whisky because blended malts contain no grain whisky.

Got that? Don't worry—you are not alone. No one has.

100 Pipers 40% ABV

The traditional Scottish song "100 Pipers" was written about Bonnie Prince Charlie and the Jacobite Uprising of 1745, and tells of how the clans marched on England, swimming across the river Esk.

"His bonnet and feathers he's waving high,
His prancing steed naist seems to fly,
The nor' win' plays wi' his curly hair,
While the pipers play wi' an unco flare."

I cannot help wondering whether if they had stopped looking at what his hair was doing and concentrated on fighting with swords, rather than playing with pipes, the Uprising might not have been such a total disaster. The song this blend is named after has survived the centuries, though, and with a symbolic 45 years (the Uprising was called The '45) behind it, the blend is in pretty good shape, too. It is light and toffeeish, and is used by owner Chivas as a good entry blend for new markets.

Antiquary 12-year-old 40% ABV

At 12 years old, this contains a mix of premium spirits and aged grain, and it really is something of a stonker. It is from Tomatin Distillery, a large Japanese producer, and is big, full, and peaty—easily among the best in class for the price. The Antiquary, with its reference to the writing of Sir Walter Scott, used to be a superior premium blend; now, stylishly packaged and immensely pleasant to drink, it is one of whisky's best deals you can come across.

Antiquary 21-year-old 43% ABV

Good golly! Intense, big mouthfeel, the sort of full taste you expect from a Japanese blend, but without the earthiness. There is peat, though, along with lots of sherry and berry. Excellent indeed.

Antiquary 30-year-old 46% ABV

This comes in a deep-blue velvet box that is a bit like the interior of an old Victorian theater: designed to be voluptuous and lavish, but bordering on tacky and dated. Not unlike the blend, actually. This is a whisky that is akin to hitting the crossbar with a 30-yard scorcher in soccer—nearly brilliant, but in the end dropping frustratingly short.

Bailie Nicol Jarvie 40% ABV

This is made by Glenmorangie, and it is another big-bang-for-your-buck blend. The vital ingredients for good-quality malt whisky are: a) good-quality malt; b) a big proportion of it; and c) a skilled blender. You get all of that in this. Look hard enough, and you will find a Scottish road tour in the glass, with Speyside, Highland, and island malt in the mix. This is mainstream malt that stands up on its own, with the citrus notes, in particular, a total delight.

Ballantine's 12-year-old 40% ABV

Years ago, there was a British beer commercial that ended with the slogan: "The pint that thinks it's a quart." This is the whisky world's equivalent, a blend so well made and established that it is produced in a range of expressions in the same way as single malts. This is a honeyed, creamy, and stylish entry-level blend, with some oak.

Ballantine's 17-year-old 43% ABV

There is an argument—supported by this writer—that 17 and 18 years are the ideal age for Scotch whisky. By this age, the cask has given up most of its secrets, the oak has added enough to the whisky's body, but is not beating up the smaller and weaker flavors, and everything has reached a perfect pitch. It is the equivalent of a band at the peak of its powers, playing in perfect harmony.

Ballantine's 21-year-old 43% ABV

This one is almost as good. Here, there is plenty of melody and harmony, but perhaps a little more individuality creeping in. This has some truly scrummy candy bourbon layers, and lots of shifting shadows—smoke, oak, spice, hickory, and red berries.

Ballantine's 30-year-old 43% ABV

This is to whisky what Paul McCartney is to the modern rock scene. It sits on a pedestal, one of the few really great stars, to be treated with the greatest of respect and a degree of reverence.

There are times when a vertical whisky tasting—a tasting of different expressions from one brand—is akin to climbing up a castle on top of a hill. Each time you reach a new level, you gasp at the view in front of you and spend a few minutes immersing yourself in the beauty. You then head on up again, and it gets even better. This is the view from the highest parapet.

SANDY HYSLOP OF BALLANTINE'S

Pernod Ricard, 12 Place de Etats-Unis, 75783 Paris Cedex-16, France
www.ballantines.com

Wentworth, Surrey, winter, and this is England at its very best. It is bitterly, bitterly cold, but the sky is clear blue and a bright wintry sun is casting shadows over the immaculate fairways. A faint hint of wood smoke and damp vegetation hangs in the air.

Over on the seventeenth hole, a convoy of golf buggies is snaking its way up the fairway. In front of them are Graeme McDowell, up-and-coming professional golfer and last year's winner of the Ballantine's Championship in Korea, and Neil Coles, who won the event in 1961 and whose achievements include eight Ryder Cup matches and 28 European Tour titles. McDowell is dressed in 1960s golf gear and is using clubs from that era. We are all here to launch this year's championships.

Among the party is Sandy Hyslop, who is master blender for Ballantine's. Later, he will unveil his latest creation—a Ballantine's 36-year-old developed with golfer McDowell as part of his prize for winning last year's tournament. There are just 20 bottles of it, and some will be auctioned off for thousands of dollars. Hyslop is an amiable and accommodating man, but, like many in the whisky business, he admits that he is not at his most comfortable among the razzmatazz of this sort of marketing event.

"I get invited all the time to do different events, but this is the first one I've done for eight months," he says. "I'm happier being involved with the production side of things. I'm very hands-on and like to be involved. You could easily get wrapped up in all this stuff and perhaps lose touch with what's happening on the production process. I like the fact that, when I walk into the distilleries, I know what's going on and have a relationship with everyone involved with making the whisky."

In some ways, the interest in whisky has grown at such a pace in recent years that jobs such as "master blender" and "master distiller" have gone in different directions in different companies and different distilleries. In some cases, the job title covers a big ambassadorial role.

Not for Hyslop. Now 44 years old, he has been making whisky for 27 years, 19 of them with Ballantine's, which means that a good proportion of the whisky in the iconic 17-year-old was produced during his time with the company. He's a production man through and through, a hands-on whisky maker who likes to be in the distillery and among the casks. He takes his job very seriously, but is delightfully passionate about it, too. And while he is at the helm making Ballantine's, there will be not the slightest compromise in quality. At every stage of the process, he expects as close to perfection as it is possible to get. To this end, he and all his staff have their skills tested annually. Every one of them must identify rogue samples from a batch.

"They can fail for picking out too many rogues, as well as failing to spot the bad ones," he says. "The tests vary for different departments, but we all do them. It sounds tough, but it involves everyone and they feel very much part of the family. They all know that at any time, if they think there is something wrong, they can say so. What I want are people who stay with us. The key to everything is consistency. I always say that it takes years to build up loyalty, but it only takes one rough batch to lose that loyalty. Customers won't complain; they will just stop drinking our brand."

Hyslop says that within his team he has the whisky industry's equivalent of the great white shark, able to smell even the tiniest level of peat or gin aromatic in any given sample. It is a skill honed over years, and for Hyslop the consistency aspect is essential. That, he says, comes from working with the whisky for long periods of time, so that every single member of the team is familiar with every aspect of the blend.

The result is a whisky that continues to enjoy massive success, from the bars of Europe to the golf courses of Korea. Making a limited-edition whisky is quite simply the icing on the cake, he says.

"Ballantine's is all about maintaining a consistently high quality," he says, "so that it delivers every time. Doing a tiny blend like this is a chance to have some fun, and to play about a bit. There are whiskies in the mix going back 50 years. It's all a bit special."

And you just know that he cannot wait to get back into the distillery, where he belongs.

KEY WHISKIES

Ballantine's 12-year-old 40% ABV
Ballantine's 17-year-old 43% ABV
Ballantine's 21-year-old 43% ABV
Ballantine's 30-year-old 43% ABV

Bell's Original 40% ABV

One of the very great names in blends and therefore included here on the strength of provenance and history. But, if I am honest, I am none too sure about this at all. A couple of years back, Bell's eight-year-old was replaced by this, which has no age statement. The company argues that this blend did well in taste tests and has been made to reflect the original Bell's recipe. Two questions then: Was the quality of whisky really better 150 years ago? And, if it was, why was it disposed of in the first place? Truth be told, this is a perfectly acceptable medium blend, in more ways than one.

Ben Nevis Blended at Birth 40-year-old 40% ABV

This is a unique whisky that deservedly picked up a Masters Award in the 2009 Spirits Business Whisky Masters awards. It is different because the grain spirit and malt spirits are mixed together as new make, then matured together for 40 years, as opposed to the usual method of blending the finished whiskies. It is soft, rounded, sophisticated, fruity, with cocoa and oak. Another blend that almost demands a chance to be tasted alone, rather than mixed. Outstanding.

Black Bottle 40% ABV

Pound for pound, quite possibly the best value Scotch whisky on the market. It is a feisty, rugged Islay-soaked blend with whisky from the seven older island distilleries. Now owned by Burn Stewart and, although repackaged, still somehow fails to win the adulation that it deserves. All in all, this is a cracker.

Black Bull 12-year-old 50% ABV

Speyside is much in evidence in this wonderful blend from Duncan Taylor, with green apples, toffee, vanilla, pear, and eventually some sherbety fruit notes that you often get with Tamdhu (which I know is in the 40-year-old, but I am not sure is here). This is a zingy, zippy summer delight of a blend and well worth seeking out if you can.

Black Bull 40-year-old 40.2% ABV

"It's a blend, Jim, but not as we know it." Containing a sort of malt whisky greatest hits, including Highland Park, Glenlivet, Bunnahabhain, Springbank, and Glenfarclas, as well as some zesty Tamdhu, this is 90 percent malt and tastes it. This is a monster of a whisky, with strong apple and pear up front, then a wave of other fruits and spice. The oak is there, but is not in the least bit dominant. Exceptional.

Black & White 40% ABV

Glenrothes brand ambassador Ronnie Cox used to work on Black & White, and was once asked to attend a promotional event in the United States.

"They flew me over on the Concorde, and I went straight to the event," he recalls. "And the bloke organizing it goes, 'We have someone specially flown over from the UK to talk to you now. Ron Cox!' So I get up to talk and have just started when someone stands up and says, 'Are you gay?' 'No, I'm not,' I say. 'I'm as heterosexual as you are.' 'That's my point,' says the man. 'I'm gay, and this brand is a dead horse, but I can sell it to my gay customers.' At this point, the organizer stands up and says, 'Shut the hell up! Just shut up.' So the poor man sits down, and I attempt to carry on. But another man stands up—a big African American. 'This brand is totally dead, but I can sell it, and you know how?' he says. 'I say to the white bartender, give me one of you and one of me. I'm black and you are white, so give me a Black & White. That works.' I knew at that point I had no chance with that crowd." This is a sturdy, old-fashioned blend with a hearty malt core and some well-crafted peat and smoke around it.

Blue Hangar 30-year-old 45.6% ABV

A blend put together by Berry Bros. & Rudd that has been consistently excellent over the past few years and that has also caused a degree of confusion because it is also bottled as a vatted, sorry, blended malt. This unfurls like a good-quality single malt, with oak, oil, and a fruity center. Quite sharp and spiky, too, and therefore a blend for people who do not like blends.

Buchanan's 12-year-old 40% ABV

Buchanan's is a premium blend owned by Diageo that does well in South and North America. This 12-year-old is something of a whisky sandwich, its nose and finish rich and full, its center citrusy and with some grape and sherry notes. Pleasant, though.

Catto's Rare Old Scottish 40% ABV

Catto's is not a household name in the way that some of the old family blends are, but it still has a pedigree stretching back some 140 years. Inverhouse now owns the distillery, and the range has been given a facelift, so we might be seeing more of it in the future. This standard version is fresh and juicy, with distinctive cidery apple and citrus notes in mellow grain.

Catto's 12-year-old 40% ABV

The citrus is still there, and this is refreshing and enjoyable enough, but there is not a great deal of depth and little evidence of the 12 years in wood.

Catto's 25-year-old 40% ABV

Delicious rich and sherried whisky, with burnt fruitcake, dark caramel, oak, and spice. Full and assertive, yet gentle and mellow on the finish. Excellently made—a venerable old whisky.

Chivas Regal 12-year-old 40% ABV

Another of the truly great blends, Chivas is owned by Pernod Ricard and has pretty much worldwide distribution. With Speyside whiskies such as Strathisla and the Glenlivet at its heart, this is unsurprisingly very clean and fruity, and nicely honeyed. Too restrained for this palate overall, though.

Chivas Regal 18-year-old 40% ABV

The distinctive Speyside green fruits are in place here, and there is a honeyed, creamy mouth-coating feel about the whisky, too, with some heather and floral notes. It is nicely balanced, mellow, and polite.

Chivas Regal 25-year-old
40% ABV

Undoubtedly the best in the range, but then you would expect that. Strangely enough, it is the most lively and zingy, too, despite its age—with green, red, and orange fruits, an elegant layer of spices, and clean, chewy barley at the finish.

Clan Campbell 40% ABV

Launched just over a quarter of a century ago, this is a new boy on the block. Owned by Chivas, it contains Aberlour and other Speyside whiskies, and has been successful in some countries where young light and fruity whiskies are popular. A refreshing whisky, begging to be served with ice and therefore suited to warmer climes.

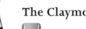

The Claymore 40% ABV

A Whyte & Mackay second-division brand sold in the standard market, but if you take that into consideration it is not bad at all. It is traditional and Highland in style, which means that is full and fruity, possibly because of the inclusion of Dalmore in the mix. A solid "center-back," "linebacker," or "prop forward" of a blend.

Compass Box Asyla 40% ABV

John Glaser set up Compass Box more than ten years ago with a vision to take whisky into new and exciting areas, and he has succeeded in abundance. Many of his creations—call them boutique whiskies, if you want—are blended malts, but this is a blend, albeit not a usual one. It is exceptionally sweet, reminiscent of vanilla slice with squidgy cream, or perhaps the traditional English dessert Bakewell tart.

Crawford's 40% ABV

You do not see Crawford's too often in the major markets, so presumably it is doing license holders Whyte & Mackay a job in developing some overseas territories. This has an intriguing lemon and pepper combination going on.

Cutty Sark Original 40% ABV

There are few more famous or iconic brands than Cutty Sark, and 2010 marked an important crossroads when control of it was handed over to Edrington (owners of Famous Grouse, Highland Park, and the Macallan) and the long-term lease of the Glenrothes was given to Berry Bros. & Rudd instead. Berry Bros. originally introduced the blend for its wine-drinking customers who wanted to drink whisky, but were put off by the prevalent peatiness because it ruined their palates. So Cutty Sark was designed to be fresh and clean, and it was the world's first light whisky. This version fits the bill perfectly, with clean fruit, honey, and vanilla.

Cutty Sark 12-year-old 43% ABV

Don't miss the delightfully tacky Cutty Sark visitor experience. Here, you can visit the Berry Bros. London shop, where Mr. Berry will talk to you, or enter a speakeasy and listen to a World War II American soldier tell you, "You can get a Cutty Sark down the street, buddy, but you'll have to wait in line." Also on display are advertisments used to sell the brand over the years, so you get a strong sense of how big it once was. This version is full and fruity, with honey at the finish.

Cutty Sark 15-year-old 40% ABV

It is possible that Cutty Sark was the impetus for the St. Valentine's Day Massacre. During Prohibition, gangs running the illegal drinking dens and having to make do with poor-quality bourbon mixes welcomed the opportunity to bring in Scotch. One supplier, William S. McCoy, based in Bermuda, supplied Cutty Sark to many parts of the United States. His product was known for quality, and his name is credited with the expression the "real McCoy." Whisky would also travel down the Great Lakes from Canada. And it was after a shipment of whisky was stolen that it is thought that Al Capone ordered the attack as revenge.

Cutty Sark 18-year-old 43% ABV

Oak and sherry notes drift around the edges, woody and honey notes mix at the middle, and there is a nice mix of sweet molasses, some spice, and a sharper lemon note to end. Pure style from start to finish.

Cutty Sark 25-year-old 45.7% ABV

Another classic example of how great blended whisky can be, this includes a good mix of everything, including smoke, all coming together in a perfectly balanced blend. Honeycomb-candy malt and chocolate-like malted milk-ball flavors form the core of the whisky, but there are significant spices, too. A real treat.

Dewar's 12-year-old 40% ABV

The impact that the Dewar family has made on whisky has been considerable, and none more so than Tommy Dewar. He was only the third person in Scotland to own an automobile, was a pioneering champion of whisky, and traveled across the world promoting his brands. He had a less attractive side to his personality, too, as a Conservative MP who campaigned vigorously on behalf of an immigration law aimed particularly at London's East End Jewish community. But he actively supported sport initiatives and was responsible for the building of the Aberfeldy distillery, where today you can visit the excellent and informative Dewar's World of Whisky.

The standard version of Dewar's is pleasant and sweet, with Aberfeldy trademark honey singing through a robust, fruity body. Stylish.

Dewar's 18-year-old 43% ABV

This is a fine and fairly assertive blend, with sweetness from the grain to the fore, and just enough citrus fruit, oak, hints of smoke, hickory, and spice to create a noisy big-band sort of a whisky.

Dewar's Signature 43% ABV

Based around an aged 27-year-old Aberfeldy malt, this is one of my very favorite whiskies and absolute proof to any doubters that blends can feature among the very best Scotch whiskies. Perhaps it is the malty feel of the whisky up front, but it is more than that. It unfurls in the mouth like someone turning over playing cards—a jack of citrus fruit here, a king of spice there, the queen of oak, and an ace of sweet, honeyed, chewy grain. Good heavens—a royal flush of flavor.

Dimple 12-year-old 40% ABV

Now owned by Diageo, this brand was known as Haig Dimple, and it has a long and glorious history as a premium blend. Dimple is a triumph of marketing, and few brands inspire as much sentimentality as this one. The distinctive bottle and the advertising slogan "Don't be vague, ask for Haig," along with some definitive brand advertisements from the 1950s to the 1970s, has created an army of people who all but equate Dimple with quality blends. This whisky expertly mixes dried fruits, spice, toffee, and a little bit of oak.

Dimple 15-year-old 43% ABV

The 12-year-old's big brother is just what you might expect: a full, fruity whisky, with some cocoa notes and hints of smoke. Worthy of the name—and the brand's premium status.

The Famous Grouse
40% ABV

Owned by Edrington, owners of Highland Park and the Macallan, the Famous Grouse is Scotland's number-one blend and has been triumphantly competing with the leading blending houses over the past 125 years. It is a surprisingly full and robust blend and an unexpectedly sophisticated one, with the emphasis on the balance between rich meaty malt and delightful soft and sweet grain.

The Famous Grouse Black Grouse 40% ABV

A fascinating aside for the Famous Grouse, this, with smoky and peaty notes that join a toffee fruit and caramel base. The overall effect is altogether more grungy and chewy. The name refers to a threatened rare species of grouse found on Scotland's west coast islands, and owner Edrington is working with the Royal Society for the Protection of Birds to help conserve the bird via whisky sales.

GORDON MOTION OF THE EDRINGTON GROUP

The Edrington Group, 2500 Great Western Road, Glasgow G15 6RW
www.edringtongroup.com

Distillers and blenders never seem to retire properly.

It says a lot about how much distillers and blenders love their jobs that there are countless examples of whisky men working into their seventies, eighties, and even nineties, rather than hanging up the boots and sitting back with a large glass of something special they created.

That said, though, the whisky industry is at a crossroads, as a whole generation of great whisky makers have stepped down in recent years or are set to do so.

The list is a formidable one: Iain Henderson, Robert Hicks, John Ramsay, Hedley Wright, Jim McEwan, David Stewart, Colin Scott, and Richard Paterson in Scotland; Elmer T. Lee, Jimmy Russell, Parker Beam, and Jim Rutledge in Kentucky. These are all larger-than-life characters who worked their way up from the maltings floor to the very top of their business. When they have all moved on, there will never be another generation quite like them, a generation in which the secrets of the stills and the skills of distilling were learned among the malt and the mash.

The new generation is likely to have been educated in college and have a science background, and there are plenty of people who have concerns over where whisky will go under them. So should we be worried?

Probably not, for a number of reasons. First, knowing more about the science of whisky and precisely why what happens does happen are good things. Secondly, the call of whisky is no less vocational simply because it is pursued through the classroom. Thirdly, many of the new faces may come armed with a chemistry diploma, but they have also benefited from having the best of both worlds, serving under the tutelage of the masters.

And, of course, the new generation is able to hold fast to the traditions that matter, while at the same time looking at new ways to take their whiskies forward. Maintaining heritage

and evolving are not mutually exclusive, as the likes of Dr. Bill Lumsden at Glenmorangie and Chris Morris at Woodford Reserve have shown in recent years.

Then there is Gordon Motion, master blender at Edrington and now the man responsible for The Famous Grouse and Cutty Sark. He comes with the science background and non-distillery background, but he worked alongside previous master blender John Ramsay for close to ten years. Yes, things are changing, he says, but not so you'd notice.

"I learned a great deal from John and know how much integrity he has and how much effort he put into his whiskies," he says. "I have learned from him, so my approach isn't going to be so radically different. I don't have any radical plans for the whisky, though it's natural that I take a more modern approach. I'm starting to use more technology than John did for information gathering, but it won't influence the whisky."

Motion has 13 caps as a small-bore rifleman for Scotland, but says that his hobbies have been put on hold somewhat by the challenges of the job. The modern whisky distiller is expected to produce far more expressions of whisky than would have been the case in the past, and the pressure is constant.

But that is another thing that he has learned from the grumpy old men of the past—being grouchy in defense of your whiskies is ultimately to the benefit of everyone.

"John would never have put out a whisky he wasn't happy with, no matter what the pressure is, and I'll hopefully do the same," he says. "One of the many valuable things I learned from him was that it was acceptable to stand firm and say no to the marketing men from time to time."

Yep, it looks as if whisky is more than safe for some time yet.

KEY WHISKIES

The Famous Grouse 40% ABV
Cutty Sark ABV VARIES
The Glenrothes Select Reserve 43% ABV
Glenrothes vintages 43% ABV

THE FAMOUS GROUSE

SCOTTISH OAK
FINISH

BLENDED SCOTCH WHISKY
A marriage of fine rare Whiskies finished in Scottish Oak casks

The Famous Grouse 12-year-old Gold Reserve 40% ABV

Not sure what the future holds for this expression of The Famous Grouse because it is quite hard to find and its owners were not particularly enthusiastic about supplying samples of it. A shame, really, because the mix of orange and lemon fruits, with some hefty oak, sweet toffee, and wisps of smoke, makes for a winning combination.

The Famous Grouse Scottish Oak Finish 44.5% ABV

Whiskies matured in Scottish oak are exceedingly rare, not least because when they built the Scottish Parliament a few years ago the nation's oak reserves were all but swallowed up. But I cannot think of any of them that were not outstanding, and this is no exception. The effect of the oak seems to be to add a spiciness to honeycomb. Imagine a chili-flavored honeycomb candy bar, and you are getting there. The grain softens the impact in this blend, but nonetheless is pretty awe-inspiring stuff. This is a limited edition and very hard to find. If you find one, though, do not miss the opportunity to try it.

Grand Macnish 40% ABV

With its distinctive, quaint bottle and the fact that there are 40 whiskies in the blend, this makes for a good choice if you are looking to provide the blend drinker in your life with something a little different than their standard tipple—look out for it at specialist whisky shops. It is made by Macduff International and has a sweet, fruity taste.

Haig Gold 40% ABV

Like Mickey Rourke in *The Wrestler*, this blend has seen better days. Indeed, it was a champion once, the leading whisky for a generation. Now it is a bit-part player, part of the vast Diageo stable, and thriving only in some of the remoter southern European markets. It is a perfectly palatable but light blend, with soft touches of fruit, spice, and wispy smoke.

Hankey Bannister 40% ABV

Amazingly, Mr. Hankey and Mr. Bannister's wine merchant business has its roots stretching back more than 250 years to the middle of the eighteenth century. The name is now owned by Inverhouse, and is the umbrella for a range of blends that, at the higher end, are of extremely high quality and continue to win world whisky awards and critical acclaim. This entry-level blend is another good choice if you are looking to break from the norm, with a pleasant and rounded fruity taste and mellow finish.

Hankey Bannister 12-year-old 40% ABV

Speyside United, with fruit, vanilla, honey, a touch of spice and oak, and a balanced and attractive finish.

Hankey Bannister 21-year-old 43% ABV

This is an excellent but surprising blend. Fresh green fruit and a vigorous combination of flavors disguise its age until late on, when malt oak and spice arrive, to give the overall taste a developing complexity. The finish is swanlike—seemingly graceful, but with flavors working hard beneath the surface.

Hankey Bannister 25-year-old 40% ABV

Tastes like the big brother of the 21-year-old, with the same array of flavors, but with the intensity and quality turned up a notch. The oak and delightful vanilla notes make this a standout.

Hankey Bannister 40-year-old 43.3% ABV

This was voted the world's best blend by an impressive cross section of the whisky industry a couple of years ago, and promptly disappeared, although another version has been put out since. It has enough weight and body to appeal to single-malt lovers, with rich oak, malt, and spice. But it is a complex beast, too, with deep orange and yellow citrus notes and an appealing long, rounded finish.

Islay Mist 12-year-old 40% ABV

Another blend from Macduff International, this mixes rich, peaty malts from Islay with some Speyside and Highland ones, and rounds them all up in a smooth grain net. It is a stylish piece of work, though, and pulls off the clever trick of delivering on rich flavor—both medicinal and linctus notes are present here—offering up a "spoonful of sugar to help the medicine go down."

Isle of Skye 21-year-old 40% ABV

The best of a range of Isle of Skye blends from Ian Macleod, this is whisky's Artful Dodger, a street urchin with a cheeky, mischievous streak, and a charming good nature at its heart. Sugar and spice are there, and the malt announces its presence, although how much Talisker is here is unclear. Still, it keeps you interested.

J&B Rare 40% ABV

"J&B" stands for "Justerini and Brooks," but today the company is part of the Diageo empire. It has always been a bit cutting edge, this version having been launched as a light whisky for a new type of drinker in the 1930s, and Diageo has used the brand for a series of innovatory launches. There was a clear version, for instance, aimed at appealing to younger vodka drinkers, while Nox was a triumph of style over substance, packaged to stand out on nightclub shelves. And then there was Ultima, which was just that—a mix of more than 125 whiskies.

This version is hugely popular in many markets across the world and has sweet canned fruits, vanilla, and honey, as well as a very appealing smokiness, all held in check by the grain.

J&B Jet 40% ABV

Wonderfully packaged in sleek black with red touches, this looks the part. Tastewise, there are a distinctive Speyside influence, some assertive notes, and a mellow, rounded finish.

John Barr 40% ABV

If this had originally been produced by anyone else other than the company that became Diageo, there would be a case for "passing off" because everything about it screams Johnnie Walker Red. It was introduced to replace that very brand when Diageo's predecessors DCL got into a dispute with the European Union, and withdrew Red Label. Now with Whyte & Mackay, the blend most likely includes Fettercairn and Jura. A curiosity found only in selected markets.

Johnnie Walker Red Label 40% ABV

Funny what sticks in your mind. I remember clearly my father's indignation at no longer being able to buy this version of Johnnie Walker, and how he was being presented with a choice of paying more for the Black Label, which he did not like (too peaty), or changing brands. It says masses about the power of a top brand that my father seemed genuinely offended that his loyalty could be repaid in this way. I think of him standing in the kitchen complaining to anyone who would listen (me) every time I hear of an American football franchise upping sticks to move cities. He blamed the "gray gnomes of Europe" and I have been cynical ever since about Britons blaming Europe for everything.

Nowadays, this does pop up in British airports and specialist shops. Strangely, the peaty taste my father objected to in Black Label and presumably was not there in the late 1960s is key to the current Red Label.

Johnnie Walker Black Label 40% ABV

As editor of *Whisky Magazine,* a few years back I asked ten blenders to name their favorite blend by a rival company. I recall that eight nominated Black Label, and one of the two blenders who did not was the blender for Black Label.

This really is an iconic blend, a master class in blending, with a touch of everything in the mix, including a delightful wave of spice from Talisker and peat from Caol Ila. I do not claim to be any sort of expert on blending, but I am told Caol Ila is loved by blenders because it is oily and full-flavored, and so makes a successful foundation for a blend.

There is Speyside fruit here, and it is clear that only top-grade 12-year-old-plus whiskies are present. A heavy hitter, for sure.

Johnnie Walker Gold 40% ABV

⭐ 1️⃣ S️

Diwali is the Hindu celebration of good over evil and marks the return of Lord Rama to his kingdom after defeating the demon king. It is known as the Festival of Lights because it is celebrated with the lighting of small lamps, and it is traditional to exchange gifts with loved ones. One of the ultimate gifts a son can give his father at this time is a bottle of Johnnie Walker, and sales to the Indian market during Diwali are huge. In fact, they are so huge that, when a batch of homemade whisky passed off as Johnnie Walker led to the deaths of several people, Diageo put out advertisements across the British trade press written in a number of Indian languages, reassuring South Asian customers that the official bottlings were not tainted.

The Gold label contains whiskies that are at least 18 years old, and you get the impression that someone opened the "very special" cupboard and said, "Fill your boots, boys." No expense has been spared here. I cannot help thinking that, when people moan about the fact that one company owns so many distilleries, they should consider whether this blend would exist if the situation were different and whether the world is a better place for its presence. It most certainly is, and it is worthy of a top place on whisky's highest table—and that's all whisky, not just blends. Initially, this is surprisingly youthful, rich, and zesty, then the full fruit, berry, and smoke notes kick in and kick off. Diageo's marketing people suggest you keep the bottle in the fridge and serve it chilled, then hold it in the mouth, to let it warm so that the flavors reveal themselves one by one. Yep, you could do that. Or just take it as it is, sip it, and enjoy. World-class.

Johnnie Walker Blue 40% ABV

⭐ 1️⃣ S️ 🥃

The British journalist and presenter Piers Morgan annoys a lot of people, but I love him. He is opinionated, brave, and an outstanding journalist, prepared to stand up for his principles and with the uncanny knack of being able to get people to open up to him, and not only tolerate awkward and difficult questions, but answer them as well.

A few years ago, he was approached by Johnnie Walker Blue's marketing people to do some work for them, which was, as he said in one of his books, a bit of a no-brainer—why would he not take money (and, no doubt, some whisky) to say nice things about a blend that he drinks anyway?

As part of his ambassadorial duties, he interviewed the world-famous Italian soccer referee Pierluigi Collina (you know, bald with bulging eyes) in front of an invited audience, the idea being that, if you take different components and bring them together, you create something new—geddit?

Halfway through the interview, Morgan asked Collina what it was like to send off a world-renowned soccer superstar. The Italian gave a lengthy answer about the regret at ending the performance of an artist and depriving the crowd of a craftsman … all very Italian and dramatic.

"Oh, come on," interrupted Morgan after a minute or so, "when you've got that red card in your hand, and you're waving it in his face … well, it must be better than sex, isn't it?"

Priceless Piers.

Beforehand, the guests were invited to numb their mouths with chilled water, then to put Johnnie Walker into the mouth. As the whisky warmed the mouth, its flavors took over.

The most expensive of all the Johnnie Walker range does not have an age statement because the age on the label must refer to the youngest whisky in the mix. Here, there is a proportion of very young whisky, but it is there to pep up some very old grand malts indeed. This is an oral kaleidoscope, with peat giving way to pear and melon, sherbet dip and licorice, and some oak notes. Not cheap, but sublime.

The Last Drop 52% ABV

1️⃣ 🗑️ S️ ❗ ❓ 🥃

Johnnie Walker is a snip next to this. This will set you back some $1,750 minimum, and there is not much of it (hence the name). But if anyone ever tells you that, at the high end, premium whisky cannot match the world's best cognacs, tell them about this. It is another curiosity. There are 12 grains and something like 70 malts in the mix here, and they all date from 1960 or earlier. But they were blended in 1972, when they were a minimum of 12

years old, then returned to the cask for a further 36 years, when the whisky was rediscovered by accident and bottled at 48 years old. Its price comes from its rarity, but it is the most honeyed, rounded, smooth, and wonderful blend that I have ever tasted. Amazingly, every oak note is positive and good, with no sharpness or unpleasant tannin at any point.

If you buy a full bottle, they give you a miniature, so that you can try it and decide whether you are going to keep the big bottle as an investment or drink it. That's not a choice—that's torture.

Lauder's 40% ABV

This does not claim to be anything it is not. In fact, it is a straight-ahead well-made session blend good for mixing. It is made in the heart of Glasgow, and it is a far better prospect than the cheap blends you find in supermarkets and corner liquor stores.

Old Parr 12-year-old 43% ABV

A juicy, fruity, and exceptionally well-balanced blend this, with raisin, toffee, and an earthy underbelly with a whiff of smoke.

Old Parr Superior 43% ABV

I tasted this while listening to Johnny Cash's posthumous album *American VI: Ain't No Grave*. By the time he made the recordings featured on this CD, he was so ill that he was able to record only on certain days. Clearly close to death and struggling to find the strength to sing, you can tell. I defy anyone not to have a lump in the throat or a tear in the eye by the time he sings Kris Kristofferson's "For the Good Times"— "Don't look so sad, I know it's over. But life goes on and this old world will keep on turning. Let's just be glad we had some time to spend together. There's no need to watch the bridges that we're burning."

This whisky is a fitting tribute to the great man—big and old-fashioned, rich and fruity. There's sherry all the way through this. A little rough around the edges, but a class act right until the end. Yep, this is good enough for Johnny.

Pig's Nose 40% ABV

Pig's Nose was part of the same management buyout from Whyte & Mackay as Sheep Dip and, while on the face of it both brands might appear to be novelty acts, they both reflect high-quality whisky-making by Whyte & Mackay's master blender Richard Paterson. Find a stockist for either or both brands, and you will also find a loyal fan base. This is smooth, tasty, gentle, and well constructed.

Royal Salute 21-year-old 40% ABV

Royal Salute is owned by Pernod Ricard and is all about top-quality premium whisky. Lavishly packaged in royal blue and gold, this blend includes some of the company's finest Speyside malts, but don't assume that it will be a soft honey-and-fruit medley. Whether consciously done or not, this occupies a different place than older bottlings of sister blend Chivas Regal; there is some real bite, as well as creamy chocolatey tones that give it an identity all of its own.

Royal Salute Hundred Cask Selection 40% ABV

Another big, big blend that would hold its own in any malt company, not least because it knocks the spots off most malts simply because of its complexity. The chocolate theme remains here, but there are all sorts of twists and turns from fresh and zesty malt notes, and from splashes of spice, oak, and smoke. This is a roller-coaster ride of a blend and delightful on every level.

Scottish Leader 12-year-old 40% ABV

This is owned by Burn Stewart and, like Lauder's, it does not claim to be anything that it is not. Indeed, it is whisky's answer to AC/DC singer Brian Johnson—a salt-of-the-earth, no-frills, honest-to-goodness blend that delivers exactly what you would expect it to.

Something Special
40% ABV

Another Pernod Ricard blend, but this one is aimed at the premium blend market, particularly in South America, and is impressively packaged. It also has Longmorn as its core malt and, as you might expect, there is rich fruit—although soft fudge and vanilla ice cream are not far from the surface. Spice notes add to the pleasant overall experience.

Stewart's Cream of the Barley 40% ABV

Has probably seen better days, but among a certain generation of Scotch drinkers, in Scotland, this remains king. It once enjoyed wide distribution as a "rack whisky" and is surprisingly malty. It is also young, but it captivates because of a touch of chili and smoke in the mix. In fact, it occupies a little niche all of its own.

Teacher's Highland Cream 40% ABV

One of Scotch whisky's old bruisers, this is a heavyweight blend from another era and one that divides opinion. The high malt content and gritty, grainy heart are welcomed by lovers of robust whiskies, but many naturally drawn to blends find it too rough and aggressive. I would argue that it is one of the few blends that can be enjoyed neat, not for the subtleties or nuances of an aged Johnnie Walker or Dewar's Signature, but because of its malty, craggy honesty. Like sitting on rocks by a rugged coastline when the wind is up—not for everyone, perhaps, but for some eminently more preferable than sunbathing on a sunny day.

Teacher's Origin 42.8% ABV

Teacher's was, for a long time, a silent giant and, even when Allied broke up and it ended up as part of the Beam empire, little was heard of it. But that started to change in 2010 with the launch of two new Teacher's products and a general increase in its media profile. The move is long overdue, and I for one am delighted. Of the two new releases, this is the one that is cause for the greatest excitement. Teacher's Origin is genuinely different and a blast of fresh air for blended whisky.

It is based on four principles: a high malt content of about 65 percent, as opposed to many blends that are 40 percent malt or less; a bold and characterful core malt, in this case the savory, peaty, and challenging Ardmore; quality barrels, including the same quarter casks that have produced stunning Laphroaig and Ardmore malts; and a range of aged whiskies, in this case from five to thirteen years. It is not an easy ride—the Ardmore means that here are oily, peaty, fishy, and savory notes to contend with—but give it time to grow on you, and chances are you will be locked in for good. Tasting is like fishing—for every big catch, you have to land a few minnows. This is like finding a monstrous brown trout after a day catching salmon.

Té Bheag Connoisseurs Blend 40% ABV

And talking of unusual fish, this is a west coast sea bass, fat and fleshy, dripping in brine, reeking of sea, oily and slinky, and utterly irresistible. There are some peat, some spice, and some soft fudge. Oh, and if you are wondering, you pronounce it *chay veg*.

VAT 69 40% ABV

My dad's favorite joke in the 1970s was: "What's the Pope's phone number?" And this is what he used to drink once Johnnie Walker Red Label ceased to be an option. Is it still going? A million cases say yes, although only in a few selected markets. This is a medium-bodied and very drinkable blend with a nice one–two between sweet grain and chewy malt.

White Horse 40% ABV

My father's second favorite joke involved this whisky and ended with the punchline: "What? Derek?"

No one has done more work with matching whisky with food than Diageo. Many of the pairings in the early part of this book were put together with the company's help. And a few years ago the company used to stage large dinners with a different malt for each course.

One meal, based around curry, was held at Terence Conran's Bluebird Café in London's Chelsea, especially memorable for me because it was the night when Diageo's Nicholas Morgan introduced me to what is now my favorite pairing, Lagavulin and Roquefort. The evening was also memorable because at the dinner was Charles MacLean, whisky writer, after-dinner speaker, and genial host beyond compare.

This evening, though, he had a bee in his bonnet. He had issues with the way I was editing *Whisky Magazine* as a consumer magazine, rather than a trade one. "That's because that's what it is," I told him.

"Oh, no, it's not," he replied, and thus began a five-hour debate, which started at the restaurant, continued in the taxi, and ended in the hotel bar over several drinks. Gradually, everyone went to bed until it was just us, but still Charlie wanted to continue.

Then suddenly he sat bolt upright and said, "There's a mouse!"

I turned around, but there was nothing there. Five minutes later, it happened again. Same thing. And again. By this time, I was having serious doubts about Charlie's state of mind. But on the fourth occasion, when I turned around there was a mouse, staring intently at us and eating a potato chip.

"Look, Charlie," I said. "Even the hotel mouse has got fed up waiting for us to leave, so let's go to bed and tomorrow send me an email and I'll address your points."

"Tomorrow," says Charlie. "Good golly, man! I won't remember any of this in the morning!"

No email arrived, and the matter was never referred to again.

White Horse is another Diageo blend, and it is a big and busty whisky, with plenty of fruit, honey, smoke, and spice. Spot-on.

Whyte & Mackay Special 40% ABV

Charlie MacLean is a lot of things, but if you asked most people who know him to make a list, "AC/DC fan" would not be on any of them. So I was a bit surprised when Whyte & Mackay's international PR manager Rob Bruce told me that he had tickets to see the band and that Charlie would be coming along. Charlie looks like a World War I biplane pilot, complete with mustache, is a gentleman in the best sense of the word, and is in his element in fine dining rooms surrounded by articulate, wealthy bons vivants But Charlie is also a chameleon, and from the off it was clear that he was going to have the time of his life. The image of AC/DC's Angus Young writhing on his back on a platform underneath a 60-foot-high busty Rosie while Charlie guffawed heartily at the madness of it all will be with me forever—and comes back to me every time I hear the words "Whyte & Mackay."

This is an easy-to-like blend, unchallenging and very palatable, with lots of overripe fruit and a rich, sweet, and pleasantly lengthy conclusion.

Whyte & Mackay The Thirteen 40% ABV

Orange and citrus fruits suggest Dalmore, red berries suggest some sherry influence, and there are yellow fruits, some spice, and a rounded and full grain backbone.

Whyte & Mackay 30-year-old 40% ABV

A big, rich, venerable blend packed with oaky, spicy flavors, good old-fashioned Highland malt, and a substantial sherry hit. One suspects that this is traditional in style, but, whichever way you look at it, this is an impressive blend in an impressive bottle.

Whyte & Mackay 40-year-old 45% ABV

World-class whisky-making by any standards and a perfect balance of all the great ingredients whisky has to offer, not least the rich Christmas fruitcake notes from the sherry cask, full fruit from big Highland and Speyside whiskies, and the most exquisite oaky notes. Another classic example of how blends can, in their truest form, torpedo virtually all other whiskies out of the water.

ROBERT HICKS OF BEAM GLOBAL

Beam Global UK Ltd., Dalmore House, 310 Saint Vincent Street, Glasgow G2 5RY
www.beamglobal.com

Read about Scotch whisky in most books or attend tasting events, and you could be forgiven for thinking that the only type of whisky is single malt.

It is the category that attracts the most attention, provokes all the excitement, and, through its diversity, generates the dynamism that is driving the whisky market forward.

But pity the poor blends. They still account for more than 90 percent of sales of Scotch whisky, most of the recognized brands are made to a high and impressive quality, and at least a proportion of them are not only excellent, but also more than a match for most single malts.

So will the better blends ever get the attention that they deserve? If Robert Hicks has his way, they will. He is a feisty fighter and, since he officially retired from his job as master blender at Allied Domecq in 2005, he has been on a mission to help to get people to look at the blended category afresh. Now working as an ambassador for Beam Global, he is playing a key role in bringing Teacher's, in particular, and blends, in general, back into the public consciousness.

"Nearly all the books and articles over the past 15 to 20 years appear to concentrate on single malts and have relegated blended whiskies to the state of, if not the poor relation, then that of a distant cousin," he says.

"Considering that blended whiskies contain many single malts with all their unique flavors, this does seem very hard, especially when it was blended whisky that kept the industry running for the past 150 years.

"I expect that it's much simpler to write about a specific single-malt distillery which has been producing for many years and where there are numerous stories to be got, while to write about a blend is much more difficult."

Despite the problems, though, Hicks is optimistic that, as knowledge about whisky in general grows, people's attentions will turn toward blends and there will be a renewed interest in how they are put together.

"I really hope that there will be a future resurgence in the popularity of blends," he says.

"If we hadn't started producing and selling blended whisky, and relied solely on single malts, we would still be a cottage industry, if an industry at all. It has been blended whisky that's made the fame of Scotch whisky worldwide, and many people have forgotten this.

"Consumers are becoming more knowledgeable with all the books and articles that have been written over the past couple of decades. The problem is that 99 percent of the books and articles that have been written are about malt whiskies, and that's where the knowledge base is increasing. When I do Teacher's seminars, I am often surprised how low the knowledge about blends is. Over the years, I've received many letters and phone calls from people asking where a blended whisky is distilled and whether they could visit. That still happens occasionally today."

Hicks realizes that the category has a long way to go, but he relishes a challenge, and he has been playing his part of late. Take Teacher's Origin, a groundbreaking blend that may one day be seen as a crucial milestone in the journey back to

KEY WHISKIES

Teacher's Highland Cream 40% ABV
Teacher's Origin 42.8% ABV
Ardmore Traditional Cask
Laphroaig 10-Year-Old Cask Strength 57.3% ABV
Laphroaig Quarter Cask 48% ABV

acceptance. It is a big, rugged, and pulsating peaty whisky that swims against the tide of bland blends.

Hicks agrees. "If you look back at the styles that Teachers have produced in the past, there has always been an emphasis on two main points: the malt content and having a distinct peated style," he says.

"So when I was asked to produce a new style, it was relatively easy to set the baseline: a high, 65 percent malt content with a distinct Ardmore tang. Once I had thought of this, I realized that it could very well have been similar to the styles that would have been produced by the early blenders, especially William himself.

"They all knew and understood malt whiskies, but with grain whisky being a newer style they may have been a bit reluctant to have used large quantities so a high malt/low grain content blend may have been the norm. It was also quite traditional to marry the whiskies in the way we do now. In our case, we marry the malts and grains separately, and from that starting point what other casks could we use for the marrying but quarter casks?

"The difference is that we don't marry for just a couple of months, but for more than a year at Ardmore in the Highlands, in the traditional earthen-floored warehouses, again harking back to the old days. From all these clues, it was then comparatively easy to come up with the brand name—Teacher's Origin."

Hicks is optimistic about the future for whisky in general and believes that blends will be part of the future not simply as the dull and worthy component, but at the cutting edge as well.

"I find it exciting every time I see a new brand or style of blended whisky, whether that be blend or blended malt," he says. "Anything breaking the mold of what's gone before and that stretches the boundaries of aroma and flavor. As has been proved over the past ten years, we've not discovered everything there is to know about whisky, or about distillation, maturation, and blending. That is what interests me the most, trying to come up with something that no one else has tried before, or, if they have tried, they didn't succeed with it."

William Grant 12-year-old 40% ABV

William Grant owns Glenfiddich and the Balvenie, and the company knows more than its fair share about lending. Unsurprisingly, then, even in the relatively young guises, its blends fly. This one is a tango between malt and grain, with the malts showing both the citrus and green fruit zestiness and a creamier, fuller fruit, and the grain all sweet and clean. The result is sweet, rounded, full, and fruity.

William Grant 15-year-old 43% ABV

Basically the 12-year-old with the volume turned up. The extra age adds texture and a fuller oak influence, but essentially everything else is perfectly balanced and in its proper place.

William Grant 25-year-old 43% ABV

Outstanding. A distinct sherry nose, a healthy level of spice, and plenty of oak, but wrapped up in the sweetest, softest grain imaginable, so that the result is a gossamer-like blend that coats the mouth with honeyed fruit, then leaves behind a woody and wonderful aftertaste. It is like a musical concerto in three movements.

William Grant Ale Cask 40% ABV

If you have ever tasted Innis & Gunn beer, then this is where it originated from. William Grant made beer to season the casks for this blend, then threw the beer away. That was until someone in management spotted staff siphoning off the beer and drinking it. It was tasted, found to be excellent, and the rest, as they say, is history. By such happy accidents are some great inventions born.

This is great. The beer takes away a level of sweetness and adds a malty, earthy, and slightly savory level to the blend, leaving all its core characteristics intact. It is the whisky equivalent of a rugby union team playing a rugby league team at league. Odd but fun . . .

Blended/vatted malts

For many, the world of whisky is an intimidating one. The large number of distilleries, the many expressions emanating from many of them, the age statements, special finishes, complex and involved wording on the label—it all adds up to the drinking equivalent of map-reading in Tokyo.

So when a group of friends came up with the idea of throwing out the baggage, presenting whisky in modern and simple packaging, and focusing purely on taste, it offered Scotch whisky a route into the future that would bring on board a new generation of whisky drinkers.

The vehicle to which the friends chose to hitch their idea was the category of vatted malts, where whiskies contain a mixture of malts from different distilleries. Marketed under names such as the Smoky Peaty One, the Rich Spicy One, or the Smooth Fruity One, these new-look whiskies were introduced to a fresh audience at outdoor sport events and food shows rather than the more traditional whisky shows. Although there was nothing new about the category, the new whiskies looked like they had the potential to revolutionize our approach to whisky drinking.

Then the Scotch Whisky Association got involved, imposed a new term for a mixture of malt whiskies from different distilleries on the trade, and in the process caused so much confusion that the progress of the category ground to a complete halt.

The new term—now enshrined in law—for these mixed malt whiskies is blended malt whiskies. This is different from the category known as blends or blended whiskies, because blended malt whiskies are made using only malted whisky, whereas blended whiskies have a large quantity of whisky made with a grain other than malted barley. The new terminology is utterly ill-conceived, misleading, and clumsy because the vast majority of the population know little or nothing about whisky beyond the belief that single-malt whisky is better than blended whisky. Leaving aside the fact that this is in itself wrong, if they do opt to buy a "special" whisky, they tend to bracket the blended malt whisky category with blends.

This is a big shame because some of the most exciting experimentation is going on in this category. Compass Box, in particular, has taken malt whiskies into exciting new areas. At one point, the company launched a series of more than 20 single cask vattings under the collective name Canto, with different territories receiving a different version.

It is a category of whisky worth watching—often offering great value and some seriously fine whisky.

Barrogill 40% ABV

I am no royalist, but it is hard to immerse oneself for eight years in whisky and not grow a sneaking respect for the Prince of Wales. He loves whisky. He has visited a good number of Scotland's distilleries and has casks maturing in most of them. And if he seems stuffy and formal when meeting the suits, that is not the case when he is out among the workers. Talk to a warehouseman or distillery worker who has met him, and you will hear of his genuine interest, his knowledge of whisky, and his enthusiasm for hearing and learning more.

He does not like fuss. Distilleries expecting a visit are instructed to make sure that invited guests arrive well before he does and are given a drink. Guests are told to carry on chatting and not to stop what they are doing when he arrives.

Barrogill is a mix of malts from the northern Highlands and is endorsed by the prince, who is Duke of Rothesay as well as Prince of Wales, and it is liveried in the royal colors. It is a robust, full, and weighty whisky, with some peat, lots of savory tones, and some tingling spice at the finish.

Big Peat 46% ABV

Do not be put off by the somewhat tacky label—it costs independent producers Douglas Laing a fair few sales over Christmas because the whisky comes without a box and looks a bit amateurish. The whisky, however, is amazing, and it deservedly won the best blended malt category in the 2010 World Whisky Awards. It contains Ardbeg, Caol Ila, and Bowmore, and the extremely rare Port Ellen. Big, rich, peaty, and very good indeed.

The Big Smoke 40% ABV

Released by independent bottler Duncan Taylor and another heavy hitter for Islay lovers, with smoke, peat, seaweed, and barbecued fish.

Blue Hanger 4th Release 45.6% ABV

Blue Hanger is made by Berry Bros. & Rudd, and this suggests that whisky maker Doug McIvor was given free rein to produce a whisky worthy of such a respected wine house. He has succeeded. This is a wonderfully intense mix of sherry trifle, tangerine, heavy spice, and some seriously old whisky, with tannins in the mix. It has plenty of dark chocolate and chili, and is not for the fainthearted, but it is excellent.

Blue Hanger 25-year-old 2nd Release 45.6% ABV

In the mid-1980s, I saw the legendary Hüsker Dü at Sheffield's Leadmill, just when they had hit their musical peak. I don't know whether they always played that way or they had misjudged the size of the venue, but they began the set with an unbroken string of five songs in about 20 minutes. By its end, there was a ten-foot gap at the front of the crowd, and people were being scraped off the back wall. It remains the most intense and memorable live performance of my life. This whisky is similar. It marches on, plugs in, and fires a volley of menthol, licorice, hickory, spice, and oak before you can gasp. Awesome.

Clan Denny Islay 46% ABV

A fantastic big, rich, sweet, and peated mix of four great Islay distilleries: Bowmore, Bunnahabhain, Caol Ila, and Laphroaig. If you have ever asked yourself why you would bother buying a vatted malt of your favorite distilleries when you could just as well buy a single-malt bottle of each, this is your answer. I am drawn back to Islay time and time again, and often sit with a dram and debate in my head which is my favorite distillery. This is, in many ways, greater than the sum of its parts, like watching four jazz musicians playing together and bringing out something new and fresh in the other. Sure, if you are in the mood for Coltrane or Davis nothing else will do. Sometimes a medley is enough, though. This is a malt medley, and then some.

Clan Denny Speyside 46% ABV

Like the Clan Denny Islay, but this time substitute peat for fruit. Again big, clean, rich, and tasty, this is every bit the match of the Islay bottling, although more mainstream. Less Coltrane and Davis and more Clapton, Beck, Page, and maybe Jack White of the White Stripes (there is some younger stuff in here, I am sure of it).

Compass Box Flaming Heart 48.9% ABV

Quite close to being my perfect whisky, this is stunning stuff, using the finest mainland and island whiskies. What we have here are black currant, melon, and tropical fruits, all wrapped up in a ball of smoke and peat, and kissed away with licorice, hickory, chili, and cinnamon, and an oiliness that coats the mouth—absolutely the "business." Compass Box makes this in limited batches, and it sells quickly. Hopefully, though, the company will come back to it again and again.

Compass Box Oak Cross 43% ABV

This is another favorite of mine, but for altogether different reasons. Here, the heads of the bourbon cask have been replaced with new French oak (the "cross" reference in the title). The effect is a dusty, dry, fruity, and highly spiced whisky. Late on, there are some Battenberg cake and milk chocolate. Tastes like it should be expensive. It is not. Oh, and, as with all Compass Box products, it is beautifully packaged, too.

Compass Box Optimism 44% ABV

A limited-edition whisky, so it is hard to know whether you can still find it, but this was released as an antidote to all the depression that a recession brings and could be described as "happy juice." It is all bright, zingy, refreshing, and sherbety malts and has a rich, sweet taste, with some delicious peaty notes.

Compass Box The Peat Monster 46% ABV

Does exactly what it says on the can—lots of big and bold smoke and peat flavors, and among the char and oil there are some very pleasant fruit and spice, too.

Compass Box Spice Tree 46% ABV

Every time I write something nice about the Scotch Whisky Association, I receive a wave of negative replies from whisky enthusiasts who despise the organization. Does it have any idea what a large number of whisky enthusiasts think of it? We try to be nice about it, we really do, but the feeling is that it always goes after the little guy, wielding a sledgehammer to crush a nut. This is a case in point. The original version of this was matured in casks where some fresh oak staves were put inside the existing cask. You cannot do that, said the SWA, because you are adding oak. It would have been OK to replace existing staves with new oak, and Compass Box legally replaced the heads of casks with new oak for Oak Cross. But the company could not put in extra staves. Now John Glaser and his team have come up with a new and legal way to bring Spice Tree back. This is another extraordinary whisky, not least because we really do get a spice rack of flavors—from clove, ginger, nutmeg, and cinnamon at one end of the spectrum, to chili, paprika, and black pepper at the other.

Compass Box Lady Luck 45% ABV

Another limited edition that was still available at the time of writing, this is very much in line with what is becoming a Compass Box house style—lots of fresh, open-air fruitiness, wrapped in dense smoky or peaty surrounds. The higher price suggests that there are some rare and older malts in here, but such is the skill of the whisky maker that an irresistible youthfulness is also a dominant theme of the flavor.

The Famous Grouse 10-year-old 40% ABV

If you are an English rugby union fan, turn away now. Ever since I first went to Eden Park in Auckland, New Zealand, in 1988, shared beers with Welsh and Kiwi fans in the gardens of total strangers close to the ground, and watched the best sporting team on the planet, then and since, annihilate Wales, scoring more than 50 points for the second week in a row, I have loved the All Blacks. My love of their way of playing the game has led to countless great shared rugby moments with fans across the world—and to the consumption of far too many whiskies with knowledgeable and intelligent fans of the game. But there is one exception: the English. Maybe they are not the arrogant public school fans of old, but English rugby is dull and their fans remain superior and blinkered. When they win, they crow; when they lose, they whine about the cheating opposition and the poor-quality referee. I am no fan of English rugby, even though former England rugby captain Martin Johnson went to my school. In fact, I am responsible for him playing rugby. When I was a prefect at Robert Smyth in Market Harborough, and he was a new boy, I said to the young Johnson, "No, lad, you can't play netball. Netball is for girls. Go and play rugby with the big boys. And blow your nose."

This might be a lie.

So I was delighted when Famous Grouse invited me up to a Calcutta Cup game in 2006, showed me around the Famous Grouse Experience, and introduced me to this blended malt. Then off we went to the game—or, rather, off to the bar first before the game. It did not kick off until early evening, by which time the Scottish fans had consumed pretty much the entire beer and whisky allocation for Great Britain for that year. And, frankly, the English did not have a chance. The Scots built up to the game by filling up the pitch with bands and pipers, sent on a whole army of fire-waving Bravehearts, and banished the English team to a small corner of the pitch.

When they actually got around to the rugby, the Scots won—a famous victory; remember, this was when the English team was actually very good. I recall sitting in the corridor of my hotel (so as not to disturb the family, who were in bed by the time that I

managed to find my way back from the celebrations) and toasting the day with a glass of this and a big, juicy rare steak. Great memories.

This has blackcurrant and soft fruits in the mix, and is nowhere near as good as it tasted that night. But that's whisky for you.

The Famous Grouse 15-year-old 43% ABV

Lots of vanilla, summer fruits, and soft spices, with a degree of smokiness and a pleasant and easygoing finale.

The Famous Grouse 18-year-old 43% ABV

A whisky-drinking experience can be soured by external forces that have nothing to do with the whisky itself. I first tasted this at a Whisky Live show in Glasgow. The trouble was, the Famous Grouse had a 12-foot-high grouse wandering around the event repeating the tune from the TV commercial. "Duh, duh, duh, duh, de-de-de duhhhh," it went. For two days—two whole days. By the end, several people at the event, both paying customers and other exhibitors, were scouring the city for shooting rifles and organizing a grouse hunt.

This is rich in fruits and has a layer of honey and oak to give it depth and character.

The Famous Grouse 30-year-old 43% ABV

If you have ever wondered what it would be like to drink old Highland Park with old Macallan, this may well be the chance to find out. The rich and full Speyside fruits are at the core of this, with orange in the mix, but there are some honey, oak, spice, and peat notes, too—almost trademark Highland Park. Very well made, indeed, and another example of how a vatting can add up to more than the sum of its parts.

JOHN GLASER OF COMPASS BOX

Compass Box Delicious Whisky Ltd., Chiswick Studios, 9 Power Road, London W4 5PY
www.compassboxwhisky.com

On the face of it, it does not look like much—an incongruous blue building with art deco pretensions in a faceless industrial park off the Chiswick High Road in West London.

Through the doors, though, and you are in a whisky Aladdin's cave. It is a spacious open-plan room, with desks running down the left-hand side, advertising hoardings and posters down the middle, and, bizarrely, keyboards set up in the corner. But the main act is in the middle. Slap bang in front of you is whisky. Bottles and bottles of it, including full demijohns and scores of sample bottles.

This is the home of Compass Box, the United Kingdom's only true boutique whisky maker, and, before company founder John Glaser has even defined the terms for our meeting, he is off, bubbling with enthusiasm and reaching for the sample glasses.

First up is a Laphroaig from 1998, taken out of the wood before its tenth birthday and the product of a wonderful cask, he says, and he is right—it is rich in vanilla and has peat to die for. He follows it up with a quite stunning Glen Elgin, one of the three distilleries he never fails to recognize. I am coming to the end of a 750-plus whisky marathon, but the nose—rich, liqueur-like tropical fruits—is like nothing else I have come across. It turns out it is a vatting of various Glen Elgins he has got his hands on over the years. Five minutes in, and Glaser has offered up two world champions. Surely, he must be tempted to bottle both these outstanding samples as they are?

"That would be so me-too," he says. "What would be the point of that? We attempt to do something a bit different, rather than just do independent bottlings. Better to keep hold of these whiskies just for our friends."

Compass Box was formed at the start of the millennium by Glaser, then in his mid-thirties, to create new and exciting whiskies and present them in stylish upmarket packaging. Compass Box remains small, but it has been punching above its weight for years now, giving whisky enthusiasts such stunning whiskies as Flaming Heart, Oak Cross, Peat Monster, Lady Luck, Spice Tree, and Optimism, all included elsewhere in this book.

Armed with a supply of fine-quality malt from some of Scotland's best distilleries, he has pushed the whisky envelope outward, experimented into new taste channels, and tested the very boundaries of Scotch whisky. Not without controversy: Occasionally, he has fallen foul of the Scotch Whisky Association, but inadvertently he has also become a champion for the small producer and of the craftsman.

"Perhaps it's my background, and I should get on with just making whisky," he says with a shrug, "but it's important that a line is drawn between artisan producers and brands, and the big brands and mass producers speaking the parlance of artisan producers while making industrial products."

Glaser believes firmly that, as whisky drinkers learn more about whisky, there will be more demand for small-scale whiskies from across the world. This in turn will lead to an influx of small companies that will chip away at the dominance of the enormous international drinks companies.

"If you think of the hegemony of French wines over the rest of the world 30 years ago versus the world of wine today, you'll get the picture," he says. "We'll see more people who love whisky cross from avid consumer to whisky producer. We'll see continued growth in small, entrepreneurial whisky-making companies. The consumer perception of what whisky can be, stylistically, will evolve, as new producers push at the envelope of the craft."

The message is clear: Compass Box is doing fine but, if you fancy joining it, come on in. In the meantime, Glaser is living his dream, crafting fine whisky. We lunch at a local pub, but before we leave he asks the barman to pour

Flaming Heart 48.9% ABV
Oak Cross 43% ABV
Optimism 44% ABV
The Peat Monster 46% ABV
Spice Tree 46% ABV
Lady Luck 45% ABV

us a Sipsmith, a small-scale gin produced on a tiny still down the road, in the offices where Michael Jackson used to run his beer and whisky business.

Microdistilling: You can see the temptation in Glaser's eyes.

"We have looked at distilling ourselves," he says, "but we decided against it because we're so small. But it remains a dream, and I'm not against distilling in London or somewhere else in England. We have started filling our own casks with new-make spirit, so we have greater control over the process, so who knows?" Then a cheeky gleam enters his eye.

"If we took a cask of Clynelish and matured it in London, what could we call it? It wouldn't be Scotch if it was matured in England, but could we call it whisky? Or English whisky? Or Scottish malt spirit matured and bottled in England?" He laughs, but I swear I hear something else, too . . .

Not a bunch of Scotch Whisky Association lawyers spluttering into their Scotch on the rocks, perhaps?

Johnnie Walker Green 43% ABV

Green by name and green by nature. Diageo relaunched this as its big hitter in the blended-malt category shortly after the SWA had declared victory for the new terminology well before the votes were metaphorically even in, let alone counted, and just before most of the ballot boxes went missing. I seem to remember we were taken to a big stately home or castle, and played lawn croquet in the pouring rain. And I am still not really sure why. But Diageo's point was that this was an "outdoor malt," the sort of whisky to take hiking through the forest. Spot-on. Whenever I taste this—and I really love it—I am reminded of steep, muddy forest paths by gurgling brooks in the shadow of mountains on a wet spring day. As you would expect from Johnnie Walker, this is a master class in whisky-making and just about as good as vatted malts can get—give or take the odd Compass Box offering (which, interestingly, tends to use a similar range of malts). It is refreshing, clean whisky, with a weighty dose of Clynelish and some to-die-for smoke. Truly outstanding.

Monkey Shoulder 40% ABV

The vatted-malt sector has the potential to bring a whole new generation of drinkers to whisky, and this brand provides the proof. A mixture of malts can come baggage-free, and it does not need to have intimidating labels that many people do not understand, which means that it is possible to present whisky in a totally different way. When the whisky in the bottle tastes like this, that job is twice as easy.

The name sounds slightly offbeat and zany, but it is actually as traditional a reference as you could possibly get, referring to an old distillery affliction that was effectively repetitive strain injury in the shoulders caused by manually turning the malt, causing sufferers to hunch. The whisky in the bottle is a mix of unaged Balvenie, Glenfiddich, and Kininvie, and producer William Grant has deliberately focused on the soft, sweet pear and apple flavors in its malts, making for a light, refreshing, and easy-drinking whisky that tastes great when chilled. It is great neat, but of course, youths being youths, they will insist on mixing it, so the company has created an impressive

and inventive list of Monkey cocktails. So successful has the Monkey Shoulder campaign been that, in some areas, bars apply to become Monkey bars—preferred stockists for this malt. So, in effect, bars are asking to be allowed to sell Monkey Shoulder and to pay William Grant for the privilege of doing so. That's clever and, if it is not the future, I do not know what is.

Sheep Dip 40% ABV

Another wacky name, and another one that has a stronger link to whisky's heritage than at first it might appear. It has been the patriotic duty of Scottish whisky makers over the past 1,000 years to avoid paying tax to the English, and they have demonstrated considerable skill at doing so. One way was to mark casks of whisky as sheep dip, for ridding sheep of vermin and infestations before shearing. If there was duty due on sheep dip, it was far less than it was on whisky. Simple, really. And, again, this is young and fresh, with a range of Speyside and Highland malts brought together without blemish and with the meekest touch of spice. Now marketed independently.

The Six Isles 43% ABV

As the name implies, this blend takes malt from six of the whisky-making islands of Scotland, which when it was launched was all of them, although now there is a new distillery on Lewis. You associate the islands with peaty whisky, but this is not always the case—Tobermory on Mull, Arran on Arran, and Scapa on Orkney all make predominantly peat-free whisky, and Islay has its share of unpeated malt, too.

That said, though, this focuses on the peatier end of the spectrum. The nose does not give too much away, but, boy, does this kick on the palate. There are some citrus notes, a rich, oily undercurrent, and some pepper spices late on.

Wemyss Peat Chimney 43% ABV

Wemyss is an independent bottler, and it has picked up where Dave Mark & Robbo's Easy Drinking Whisky Company left off some years ago, mixing malt together to create a whisky based on a flavor profile. So this is self-explanatory. It is actually not as peated as it might be, but that is not necessarily a bad thing. The unusual tangy and nutty notes, some pear, a sprinkling of pepper, and a mocha-like sheen to the proceedings all make this an intriguing and deliciously different whisky.

Wemyss Smooth Gentleman 43% ABV

I am not totally convinced that "smooth" is quite the right word for this—perhaps "sleazy" is more appropriate. There is something vaguely fishy here (in more than one sense of the word) and, although you get apples and pears on the taste and a pleasant sweetness, it sort of slides in and out without making a huge impression. That said, it is pleasant enough and worth investigating.

Wemyss Spice King 43% ABV

You have to wait for the spices, but they are not necessarily the dominant theme. If this whisky were in the Spice Girls, it would not be Spicy Spice so much as Oily Spice or even Fishy Spice (which is better than Greasy Spice). It is likable enough, like eating canned mackerel with a dollop of soy sauce on it. What do you mean, yuck?

Grain whiskies

There is a view that single-grain whisky is lining up for its place in the sun. If you find an old grain whisky that has been matured in a good-quality cask, it can be quite sublime, bringing the finest elements of Scottish grain together with the rich vanilla and candy notes of an American oak cask—a Scotch–bourbon hybrid to die for.

Aged grains of 30 years and upward can be less expensive than their single-malt whisky counterparts. Independent bottlers include Duncan Taylor and Gordon & MacPhail.

Compass Box Hedonism 43% ABV

Most grain whisky goes into blends, and what little ends up being bottled on its own is mainly produced by independent bottlers, and much of it is very old. This is a vatting of grains, from the grain distilleries Cameron Bridge, Carsebridge, and Cambus. There is nothing younger than 14 years old, and some of the grain is more than 25 years old. By this time, the grain has taken on some of the flavors of the bourbon casks in which it has been matured. This is a delightfully sweet vanilla and coconut dessert whisky, with some gentle oil and oak. A pleasant change.

The Snow Grouse 40% ABV

Unsurprisingly from the Famous Grouse family, although you would be hard-pressed to make any real connection. This is another one of Edrington's experimental releases, and is a whisky designed to be kept in the fridge and served chilled. It is a refreshing-enough drink, has a sweet two-dimensional taste, and has very little to do with whisky as we know it. Make of that what you will.

U.S.A.

United States of America

Of all the great whiskey regions of the world, the United States is potentially the most exciting.

LEFT At the Maker's Mark distillery in Louisville, Kentucky, workers dip the tops of the bourbon bottles in red wax by hand, to produce the signature glossy seals for this classic bourbon.

Not only is U.S. whiskey in good health as we enter the second decade of the millennium, but it is sitting on the brink of a whiskey revolution as well. All sorts of weird and wonderful whiskeys currently maturing across the country are set to revolutionize our perceptions of the nation's spirit.

The United States has form in this area. A few years back, a new wave of microbreweries did for its beer industry what punk rock music did for bloated corporate rock: shook it by the throat, scornfully cast it aside, and replaced it with something altogether more vibrant and exciting. Now, it seems, the same might be happening to whiskey, albeit on a smaller scale. In the United States, whiskey has tended to

mean bourbon and a few add-ons, and bourbon has tended to mean Kentucky. These days, though, new microdistilleries are starting to pop their heads above the surface, unfettered by tradition and convention, and not afraid to take whiskey in whatever direction they see fit. They are just starting to pick up awards domestically, and in time their reputation will spread overseas.

So a classic case, then, of out with the old, in with the new? Actually, no. They are built of sterner stuff than that down in Kentucky. You know that song that goes, "I get knocked down, but I get up again ..."? That's Kentucky. It is a state littered with the crumbling remains of fallen

Y
S
IL
NY MA
VA
KY
NC
TN
A
I C

ABOVE Although Kentucky and Tennessee dominate the whiskey distilling scene, whiskey production also takes place in eight other states within the continental United States.

distilleries, its history books packed with great whiskey-making names that have been battered and broken, but still have a habit of popping up again within the portfolios of the surviving distillers. Economic tornadoes and social hurricanes have battered Kentucky's whiskey industry, but this is a state built on limestone rock, and it will take much more than a few upstarts in Portland, San Francisco, Colorado, or New York to rock it off its axis.

Indeed, Kentucky has risen to the challenge. Across the state there are casks made of maplewood, ash, and hickory filled with maturing spirit; there are barrels containing single malt, pure wheat, and rye whiskey, and spirit made

with oats and even white (sweet) corn. And then there's the more traditional bourbon: rich, flavorsome, magnificent—and in as good a shape as it has ever been.

Only Islay in Scotland can match this wonderful state for its cohesive sense of purpose, its intensity, the quality of its whiskey, and its empathy with—and understanding of—grain spirit. Just as single-malt whisky will be dominated by Scotland for generations to come, so, too, will Kentucky dominate American whiskey—and, aided by the new wave of exciting new distilleries elsewhere, play a key role as it moves forward to a new level on the world stage.

LOUISVILLE ● **6** FRANKFORT ● **1**

CLERMONT ● **4** VERSAILLES ● **2,9**
LAWRENCEBURG ● **2,8**

BARDSTOWN ● **3,7**

LORETTO ● **5**

K E N T U

When you think of Kentucky the state, you tend to picture green pastures, glistening chestnut geldings, fields of corn, and white-painted fences—and, in part, this is true. The distilleries of Woodford Reserve, Maker's Mark, Four Roses, and Wild Turkey are situated in deepest rural Kentucky, and Tom Moore, Kentucky Bourbon Distillers, and Heaven Hill are all a stone's throw from the historic town of Bardstown.

But there is another Kentucky, too. Louisville lies to the very north of the state, the historic and symbolic Ohio River that separates north and south flowing through its heart. It is a growling, vibrant city, a mix of old down-and-dirty industry and modern skyscraper-based business,

faceless retail malls and independent student-dominated suburbs. Whiskey first reached out to the world from here. Today, Brown-Forman and Heaven Hill have their biggest distilling operations in the center of the city, and the historic Distiller's Row, bourbon's historical trading front line, is still in evidence. In the battered rough-and-tumble Shively, spirit still sleeps in large industrial whiskey warehouses and the brooding but long-closed distilling giant Stitzel-Weller is a monument to the past. It smells of another era.

But regeneration is in evidence, too. The urban bourbon trail boasts world-class restaurants and bars such as Revue and Proof, where bourbon is served in salubrious

ABOVE, LEFT TO RIGHT
Jim Beam, Maker's Mark, and
Buffalo Trace distilleries are some of
Kentucky's most interesting whiskey
tourist destinations.

surroundings alongside the state's finest cuisine. In just a
few short years, the producers of bourbon have given the
drink an image overhaul. While bourbon is still very much
a people's drink, its big-name brands no longer occupy the
bottom shelf in liquor stores.

It is in this context that you realize that bourbon is
looking forward and not back. Its distilleries might still
be monuments to hospitality, history, polite manners, and
gentle country ways, but here in Louisville the business men
are finding new ways to sell their whiskeys and marketing an
increasingly diverse portfolio that includes everything from
newly bottled White Dog to 25-year-old rye.

Bourbon

The United States' native spirit must contain at least
51 percent corn, although it would usually have considerably
more, and it must be matured in new white oak barrels,
which may be toasted and charred. Straight bourbon must
be matured for at least two years, and the drink is bound by
strict rules on distilling strengths and the strength that it can
go into the barrel. Nothing can be added at all beyond grain,
yeast, and water, meaning that the rules for bourbon are
stricter than those governing Scottish single-malt whisky.

Ancient Age 10-year-old 40% ABV
www.buffalotrace.com

"Ancient Age" is the old name given to what is now
Buffalo Trace. The site, on the banks of the Kentucky
River and close to the state capital, is where the
traditional world of Native Americans and that of
the new settlers met head to head. Buffalo Trace
is so named because it lies on an old buffalo
(bison) trail. The vast herds had to slow and
stop in numbers to cross the river, providing
plentiful opportunity for the Cherokee. But
the region offered the settlers much, too, and
their arrival and eventual settlement was not
without bloody incident. Frankfort is named
after Stephen Frank, who was killed by a Native
American party while camping with other settlers.

This bourbon is a delicate balancing act of soft corn,
spicy rye, and chunky fruit, particularly citrus ones,
all held together by some delightful oils.

Baker's Aged 7-year-old 53.5% ABV
www.jimbeam.com

One of four whiskeys in Jim Beam's small-batch
collection, Baker's is named after Baker Beam, Jim
Beam's great-nephew and a master distiller in his
own right. This is made using a 60-year-old yeast
strain and is matured for seven years, an age at
which some would argue that the bourbon has
taken all it can from the wood in terms of fruit,
vanilla, and sweetness. The recipe is the same
as the standard Jim Beam, but this spirit comes
off the still at 125 proof. This strength gives a big,
upfront bourbon flavor with anisette and licorice
notes and a crisp, fruity heart, while the seven-
year maturation gives it a chunky fullness.

Basil Hayden's 8-year-old 40% ABV
www.jimbeam.com

When Basil Hayden traveled to Kentucky from Maryland, the state had been in existence for just four years and George Washington was still president. The marketing material reckons that this bourbon is made to a recipe perfected back then, which is, of course, fantasy. What is true, though, is that the recipe is that of Old Grandad, which was originally distilled in the 1880s by Richard Heydon—note the different spelling—who named it after his granddad Basil. It was Basil's picture that appeared on the old Old Grandad label. What you will find in the bottle is a healthy amount of tasty rye, as much as a third of the mashbill. The spirit is taken off the still at 120 proof, much lower than Old Grandad, and is casked with no water. There is a distinctive pepperiness about this, but the lower strength means more fruity flavors, particularly citrus, and the eight years' maturation ensures some delicious woody notes.

Benchmark Old No. 8 40% ABV
www.buffalotrace.com

A curiosity, this. The bourbon has appeared as just Benchmark, and as Benchmark Old No. 8. Some but not all bottlings have the word "McAfee's" before the name. That's the case here. It is said that the McAfee brothers traveled to Kentucky as early as 1773, identified a site near Frankfort, then left surveyor's benchmarks for subsequent settlers to find. This bourbon was part of the Seagram stable before its demise, and has ended up at Buffalo Trace near Frankfort—not far from where the McAfees laid down their markers. This version of the bourbon is an easy-drinking and inoffensive tipple, with strong, sweet vanilla and some soft toffee notes.

Blanton's Single Barrel No. 209 46.5% ABV
www.buffalotrace.com

Arguably the first single-barrel bottling and therefore the very first drops of what has become a torrent toward premium bourbon. Bottlings of this sort are to official whiskeys what bootleg CDs are to the music industry. Every barrel is different and, certainly in the case of Blanton's, differences between them are significant. That is where the fun lies, of course.

This particular series of bottlings was started by former distiller Elmer T. Lee, now in his nineties. To this day he has free rein to seek out fine casks for future bottlings. He is one of a number of people still associated with the Buffalo Trace distillery who worked with Colonel Albert Blanton, who dedicated more than 50 years to making fine handcrafted bourbon. Most bottlings are taken from casks stored high up in warehouse H, but they vary in age and so the bottle carries no age statement.

This one has a soft nose with exotic fruits upfront. Next follows a big wave of spicy rye, with a dark treacle undertow, ending with a honey and licorice combination that is to die for. Excellent.

Booker's 6-year-old 63.5% ABV
www.beamglobal.com

Number three in Beam's small-batch quartet and arguably the best—but what a great argument to have. Booker Noe died a few years back and is sorely missed by anyone who came across him. His son Fred still works with Beam, and a few years ago he was forced, against his better judgment, to speak to a group of festival visitors while the PR people replaced some faulty samples that had been poured out. For ten minutes he spoke about his father, about the special qualities that made him so loved, and about his legendary generosity. Finally, he told how they went to him one night as he lay sick and offered him a whiskey, but he declined. "That's when we knew he was leaving us," said Fred. "Because he no longer cared for a bourbon."

This is a fitting tribute to him. It is a big, characterful bourbon just like Booker, rich in vanilla, fruit, and spice, and with a honeycomb-candy heart that is battered, but withstands, the influence of the oak. All in all, this is everything that a sledgehammer bourbon should be.

Buffalo Trace 45% ABV
www.buffalotrace.com

Ever had an experience that you will always associate with a particular whiskey?

For me, it's this bourbon—and the day I interviewed Jon Bon Jovi and he referred to our chat on stage in front of 12,000 people.

It was in Sydney, Australia, during the Keep the Faith tour. I was working for the *New Zealand Herald* and had seen the first of three Sydney shows the night before the interview. He was a journalist's dream. He spoke of how he had nearly tripped over a dead body as he jogged through Sydney's Kings Cross district that morning. He spoke about how much he missed home life while he was on the road. And he spoke about how he'd trade his rock-star status for a few nights playing guitar for one of his—and my—heroes, Southside Johnny, as a member of the Asbury Jukes, in front of 200 people.

That night he referred directly to our conversation on stage and mentioned me by name, and at the after-show party I toasted him with Buffalo Trace. Two weeks later, he rang me to say he'd gone on the road with Southside Johnny and the Asbury Jukes. What a star.

This bourbon is, like Bon Jovi, pretty damn good. It rocks when it wants to, but a sweet fruitiness makes it pretty mainstream, too. Easy on the palate, but that doesn't mean that there isn't greatness here.

Bulleit 40% ABV
www.bulleitbourbon.com

A few years ago, Tom Bulleit, great-great-grandson of original Bulleit distiller Augustus Bulleit, held a party for journalists in the suburbs of Bardstown. One small group of journalists arrived to find that Tom was not there yet, so they went back to the Bourbon & Cigars event happening elsewhere, planning to return later. When they came back two hours later, they walked into the house where the party was, to find no one there. After some moments wandering about, they heard laughter and talking in the neighboring garden. They had entered the wrong house.

"That could have gone either way," one of the Bulleit entourage said later. "In Kentucky, if the householders had found you, they would have pulled a gun—or offered you dinner."

Bulleit is made at the Four Roses distillery, and the fruitiness suggests so. The recipe is said to be based on Augustus's original one. This is populist bourbon with lots of honey and vanilla.

Eagle Rare Single Barrel 10-year-old 45% ABV
www.buffalotrace.com

Eagle Rare is another single-barrel bottling and, while there are big differences between each bottling, you can be pretty confident that what you are going to taste will be outstanding. Originally launched by Seagram and now part of Buffalo Trace, Eagle Rare was arguably the first super premium bourbon. A new version is released every fall, but demand tends to outstrip supply; you have to move fast to get hold of it because it is hard to find. When you do, you will encounter a citrus and orange nose with an almost liqueur-like quality. Exotic fruits, floor polish, and sweet grain make it an easy-drinking bourbon with just enough oak to give the overall experience shape and structure.

Eagle Rare 17-year-old 45% ABV
www.buffalotrace.com

Named after the great American symbol the Bald Eagle, Eagle Rare is meant to epitomize similar values—the pursuit of life, liberty, and happiness. When it soars, the 17-year-old is up there with the very best bourbons. But there is considerable variance. This one has the trademark woodiness and substantial rye spice, but there's also a grassy and almost floral thing going on, too, making it an unexpectedly soft and gentle version of Eagle Rare. That should not be seen as a criticism, but it is slightly surprising.

BUFFALO TRACE DISTILLERY

113 Great Buffalo Trace, Frankfort, KY 40601
www.buffalotrace.com

Distilleries are to whiskey writers what children are to teachers—you know you should not have favorites, but sometimes you just can't help it. And even by Kentucky's exceptional standards, the visitor experience at Buffalo Trace is special. No matter which of the three tour options you take, you are in for a world-class whiskey treat.

ABOVE Past, present, and future: The stylish Buffalo Trace bottle is a perfect example of old meeting new in bourbon's quest to appeal to a broader market.

RIGHT Buffalo Trace distillery has traded under various names since it was opened. It backs onto the Kentucky River, once used to ferry resources and whiskey.

If you have the time, though, and are in good health, make sure that you take the Hard Hat Tour. It does exactly what it says on the can, and is a delightful trek up and down ladders and rickety staircases, into the heart of the distillery and through its warehouses.

Buffalo Trace occupies an immense site on the edge of Frankfort, the state's capital, and it is another of those places with links to some of the great names of bourbon. Formerly called Ancient Age, the roll of honor at this distillery includes George T. Stagg, William Larue Weller, Colonel Albert Blanton and Thomas H. Handy. Tennessee whiskey-maker George Dickel was based here for a while, the Van Winkle range of old bourbons is maturing on site, and bourbon legend Elmer T. Lee, now in his nineties, still pops in regularly to check on stock. They, of course, make Buffalo Trace here, but also Sazerac Rye, Eagle Rare, and Hancock's.

If you think that once you have seen one distillery you have seen them all, then Buffalo Trace and its amazing guides will make you think again. Strange artwork, stunning views, a quirky microstill, now used to create all sorts of single-barrel experimental whiskeys—all add to the color. Recent additions to the tour include a visit to the barrel room and a meeting room that looks like a classroom in a nineteenth-century schoolhouse.

"You might think that what a distillery fears most is fire, but it's not," says Freddie Johnson, who, like his fellow guides at the distillery, is a gushing font of bourbon knowledge. "The biggest fear is a bad cooper. You get the barrels wrong or end up with leaks, and it can wipe out your whole profit."

At the back of the meeting room is a bookcase that turns out to be a secret door leading into warehouse C. It is whiskey's answer to Harry Potter's Room of Requirement and, once through it, you will find all manner of mini casks and strange creations as the distillery team test new whiskeys for future release.

But the best part of the tour is the visitor center, which tells the story of the distillery and includes some stunning photographs stretching back 150 years. On one wall there is a list of every distillery ever opened and/or closed in Kentucky, including scores that never reopened after Prohibition. Close by, there is a full-size picture of a worker inspecting barrels for leaks with a torch. This is Jimmy Johnson, Freddie's father.

"He's in his nineties now, but the distillery still involves him in celebrations and events, and it makes him feel wanted," says Freddie. "They brought him in to roll out the six-millionth barrel since Prohibition, and it's thought that

he is the only man alive who touched the millionth barrel all those years go, and the second-, third-, fourth-, and fifth-millionth since."

Freddie's grandfather also worked at the distillery, alongside Colonel Blanton, and the distillery has several other families in which generation after generation has helped to pour out the spirit and roll out the barrels. No other distillery quite captures such a sense of history. When you look at the black-and-white photos on the visitor-center wall, at the workers from 140 years ago, and you read the list of great distilleries, many of which are now reduced to rubble, you feel as if you are passing through history on a conveyor belt that was here before you stepped onto it and will continue to roll on by when you step off.

A special place. If you only ever visit one U.S. distillery, try to make it this one.

LEFT Behind the imposing red-brick walls of the distillery's warehouses in Frankfort are housed many a fine bourbon.

WELL, FANCY THAT . . .

Buffalo Trace is so named because the distillery is sited at a point where once-great buffalo herds, following a traditional migration route, slowed down to cross the Kentucky river at a natural ford, making them perfect targets for local Native American tribes.

Elijah Craig 12-year-old 47% ABV
www.heaven-hill.com

The nose is surprisingly wispy and subtle, with traces of cherry and mint, and some pine and forest flower notes. Given its age, this is nowhere near as bold as it might be, but the oakiness holds in check the sweet vanilla heart; the overall taste is rounded, smooth, and moreish. With its traces of candied cherry and spearmint, this is very much a band effort, with no soloists.

Elijah Craig 18-year-old 45% ABV
www.heaven-hill.com

Is it only age that makes this bourbon significantly more assertive than the 12-year-old? Or could it be that it is made with whiskey distilled and matured at the old distillery, while the 12-year-old is made with stock from the Bernheim plant? Time will tell. Let's hope nothing happens to this, though—it puts up a strong argument against those who say bourbon does not work older than ten years. You should be a fan of oak in your whiskey to appreciate it, but this is no wooden battering ram, with plenty of spicy rye, peach, tangerine, and licorice notes, and a squelchy, oily base to carry it off. Stunning.

Elmer T. Lee 45% ABV
www.buffalotrace.com

Elmer T. Lee is a bourbon legend. After serving in the armed forces for four years after Pearl Harbor, he returned to university in Kentucky, before starting work in 1949 at what was then known as the George T. Stagg distillery. There he worked with two bourbon recipes that have remained largely unchanged, as well as a rye recipe.

We tend to think of single-barrel and small-batch bottlings as relatively recent developments, but Elmer T. Lee can be credited with starting the trend 25 years ago.

This one has lemon, orange, and sour apple notes, then a wave of spice, before a smooth finish marked by a perfumey quality and some soft fudge. Dangerously quaffable.

Evan Williams 43% ABV
www.heaven-hill.com

Heaven Hill's Heritage Center on the outskirts of Bardstown was built a few years ago and is a good introduction to bourbon in general and the Heaven Hill story in particular. A large barrel-shaped tasting room is the ideal place to sample the distillery's bourbons, and a well-stocked shop ensures that you can take one of the iconic brands away with you. Here you will find the stories of Evan Williams and Elijah Craig. But make sure that you maintain a healthy dose of cynicism when you read them. Williams was born in Wales, settled in Virginia, and moved into the unchartered territories within the state during the 1780s, some years before they were renamed Kentucky. Whether he was the state's first distiller is questionable, but he was certainly among its pioneers, providing the United States with a rich and evolving distilling heritage that stretches back 220 years.

This standard black-label bottling is a big seller and as good an entry-level bourbon as you will find. But it is bourbon for people who have discovered Jack Daniel's or Jim Beam, and want to move on—this is easygoing, sweet, and toffeeish, with some pear and apple flavors. Unchallenging and pleasant enough—the bourbon equivalent of mainstream country singer Garth Brooks perhaps?

Evan Williams 12-year-old 50.5% ABV
www.heaven-hill.com

Twelve years old is a weighty age for a bourbon, and the strength of this bottling is just above the traditional industry standard strength of 100% ABV. This is made up of casks specially selected by Parker and Craig Beam from Heaven Hill's ironclad warehouses at the Bardstown site and is not widely available.

It is a bold and assertive bourbon, and drier than many of its competitors. There is a juicy berry fruit aspect to it, as well as just enough tannins to keep everything in check, moderate vanilla notes, and a delightful wave of spices courtesy of the rye.

Evan Williams 23-year-old 46.75% ABV
www.heaven-hill.com

The Watson Twins, from Louisville, record torch-song country and blues songs. The perfect way to enjoy their music is to pour a glass of something such as Evan Williams 23-year-old, dim the lights, and let the music and bourbon dazzle your senses. This is therapy of the highest order; after 30 minutes, no problem seems too great.

This whiskey is hard to find, but great to savor. You will encounter kiwi fruit, guava, then hickory, and finally sweet chili and cayenne pepper. As delightful, complex, and varied as the twins themselves, this is a heaven-made match.

Evan Williams Single Barrel 2009 43.3% ABV
www.heaven-hill.com

These special bottlings from Heaven Hill are released annually and have been consistently excellent. But a couple of years ago the distillery began using nine- or ten-year-old whiskey from the new Bernheim distillery rather than from the pre-fire Bardstown site. Despite this major change I can't agree with those hankering back to a "no longer an option" past, nor do I think that the changes have taken these releases downhill. This has lots of exotic fruit, some caramel, chewy candy, nutmeg and sandalwood, plus the right level of oak and spice. Pretty faultless really.

Four Roses 40% ABV
www.fourroses.us

The sentimental story of how this bourbon received its name involves a marriage proposal from the distillery founder to a Southern belle being accepted by the symbolic wearing of four roses on a ballgown. More interesting is the fact that it stands out from more assertive bourbons like a ballerina in a rugby scrum. It is very fruity, with orange in the mix, some fruit peel, cinnamon, and creamy vanilla. You have to look for it, but there is enough rye there to provide a solid backbone. Bourbon's equivalent to Annie of "Get Your Gun" fame—quite feminine, but pretty feisty, too. Often accompanied by a rendition of "My Old Kentucky Home" at the annual Four Roses Let's Talk Bourbon breakfast.

Four Roses Small Batch 45% ABV
www.fourroses.us

There is nothing wrong with the standard yellow label, but when you move to the single-barrel and small-batch versions you start to realize how very good this bourbon is. Four Roses uses two recipes and five different yeasts to create ten different whiskeys within its walls. Just three of those are used for the Small Batch version.

The citrusy notes from the standard version remain, but this is like mixing alcohol with fruit jellies and is far removed from big woody and ryed bourbons. This is bourbon's answer to Scotland's Monkey Shoulder, bringing a new generation to this world of bourbon.

Four Roses Single Barrel 50% ABV (VARIES)
www.fourroses.us

For many years, you could not buy Four Roses bourbon in the United States beyond the regions where the workforce lived. Its rollout in the past three years has therefore been dramatic. But people still need convincing that this is a very different whiskey from the blend that dominated liquor-stores when the Bronfman family and Seagram took over. It was not an uncommon sight to find distiller Jim Rutledge handing out samples in malls most Saturdays.

Blanc blend this most certainly isn't. This is Four Roses at its sharpest and cleanest, with all the grains playing an active part, the fruits giving it the chewiest of centers, and with just enough oiliness to hold it all together.

Four Roses Mariage 58% ABV
www.fourroses.us

Based on the French wine concept of taking two different wines and blending them to create something new and better, this Mariage from 2009 is bottled at a weighty 58% and is arguably the fruitiest bourbon ever made. It's like chewing on alcohol-soaked orange jelly candies, with a liqueur-like intensity. Also present are a charry, toasty aspect and plenty of oak tones to calm the sweetness. Best of all, there is a gloopy oiliness that coats the mouth, so the flavors linger long after swallowing.

FOUR ROSES DISTILLERY

1224 Bonds Mill Road, Lawrenceburg, KY 40342
www.fourroses.us

Every September, the historic town of Bardstown hosts the Great Kentucky Bourbon Tasting and Gala, a weeklong celebration of all things bourbon, culminating with the prestigious Gala.

One of the best-attended events, however, is Let's Talk Bourbon, held early on the Friday morning, miles away from the Gala, south of Lawrenceburg at one of the state's most remote distilleries.

Four Roses distillery is like no other. Its butterscotch-yellow Spanish bodega-style buildings complete with bell tower and terra-cotta awnings suggest that it should be making wine, not bourbon. This pretty, delicate distillery is surrounded by ugly and imposing warehouses that are now filled with Wild Turkey bourbon, distilled down the road. It is as incongruous as a Madonna in a mudflat.

Every year, as the humidity rises and summer mist drapes the distillery lawns and surrounding trees, guests gather under a large gazebo to hear master distiller Jim Rutledge explain how bourbon is made. Beforehand they tuck into crisp bacon, grits, and eggs, and sip freshly squeezed orange juice and strong rich black coffee.

"But I must be a pretty lousy teacher because the same folk come back year after year," Rutledge says about his seminar with a chuckle.

And, of course, no one's there for the science. They are there to see friends whom they have not caught up with since last year's Gala, to partake in what is becoming a Gala institution, and to wait for those golden nugget moments when Rutledge breaks from any pre-prepared script and indulges his 200 guests with anecdotes and stories that reflect his deep love of bourbon in general and this historic distillery in particular.

These are heady times for Four Roses. Five years ago, you could barely buy the bourbon in the United States. Now it is available in close to 40 states and rising. New distribution deals in Europe suggest its future is healthy there, too. The change in fortune stems from Japanese company Kirin's purchase of the distillery in 2002, after years as part of the Seagram stable.

"The problem with Seagram was that the Bronfman family were into blends," says Rutledge. "Four Roses was sold as a blend in America, and the bourbon was removed from the shelves. Way back it was not only the most recognized whiskey in America, but also probably its most recognized distilled spirit. But it was a totally different type of whiskey. So we have a big job to do, not only to re-establish Four Roses in America, but also to show people who remember it that this is something totally different—a good-quality bourbon. Thankfully, there is a new generation coming through who do not remember the old Four Roses at all."

Four Roses is unique among bourbons in that the pretty distillery operates more like a Japanese operation than an American one. It creates ten different whiskeys within its walls, based on two recipes and using five different yeasts. The whiskeys are then mingled together to create the standard Four Roses bourbon. Of those ten, four recipes are selected for the Small Batch, and one for Single Barrel.

Where Four Roses is really making up lost ground, however, is through its annual special and limited releases. Started in 2007 to mark Rutledge's fortieth year in the industry, it was followed in 2008 by Mariage, a bourbon built around the wine concept of combining two very different wine styles to create something new and better. Since then a limited-edition bourbon has been launched each year at the festival, and they have all been consistently outstanding.

"We're genuinely creating different whiskeys here, not just taking from different warehouses or from different parts of the warehouse or from different years," says Rutledge. "We're making bourbon of fine quality as part of the Four Roses stable, but also offering a range of styles and tastes. People are starting to understand this, and it's very exciting for us."

It's exciting for everybody. Four Roses is definitely one of the distilleries to watch.

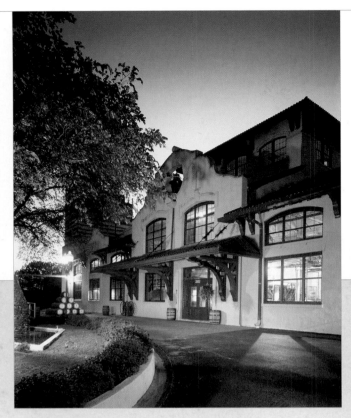

KEY WHISKEYS

Four Roses 40% ABV
Four Roses Small Batch 45% ABV
Four Roses Single Barrel 50% ABV (VARIES)
Four Roses Mariage 58% ABV

ABOVE AND BELOW The Four Roses distillery now
and then. Its distinctive facade makes it unique in
the world of whiskey.

OPPOSITE The Four Roses are a symbol of acceptance
of a wedding proposal made by the distillery's founder.

George T. Stagg 70.7% ABV
www.buffalotrace.com

George T. Stagg is one of those characters who ducks and dives through early bourbon history. The whiskey bearing his name today is fittingly distilled on the site that he once owned and which bore his name. But he also appears in the history of Labrot & Graham, and within the Jim Beam empire through his links with Colonel Edmund H. Taylor.

The bourbon that carries his name today is part of the Buffalo Trace Antique Collection and is, frankly, the star quarterback. Each fall a new bottling is put out, and each fall there is a mad rush to get hold of it. Little makes its way into Europe and what does is considerably more expensive than in the United States. But if ever there was a bourbon worth shelling out for, this is it. One of the world's truly great whiskeys, the Big Brown of bourbon is a true thoroughbred with no obvious weaknesses whatsoever.

So take your pick of the flavors—Stagg is rich in honey, oak, cinnamon, cloves, orange peel, marzipan, cocoa, sandalwood, tobacco pouch, and candy stick. For me, though, it is all about cherry in dark chocolate, hickory, red licorice, and pepper dust. Sip and savor it without water. For the ideal accompaniment, play Whiskeytown's *Faithless Street* CD—perfect Americana for an all-but-perfect bourbon.

Hancock's Reserve Single Barrel 44-45% ABV
www.buffalotrace.com

This expression has an oily, slightly winey note at first, almost Scotch-like, but it gives way to a spiky, spicy note and some vanilla. The palate is dominated by the rye, and could just about pass for a rye whiskey, but then a wave of sweet vanilla, some cocoa, and dark chocolate notes arrives before an astringent, oaky finish. It is the oral equivalent of one of those fireworks that goes through the colors of a traffic light. If Elmer T. Lee selected this, then he sure is a complex individual.

Heaven Hill 40% ABV
www.heaven-hill.com

Bourbons such as Heaven Hill are matured first, then charcoal-filtered before bottling. In this case, the bourbon process of distillation and maturation is unaffected. Jack Daniel's, on the other hand, cannot be called a bourbon because it is put through a wall of maplewood charcoal to mellow it after the still and before being casked. In this case, the bourbon process of distillaton and maturation is unaffected.

This whiskey is mellow, as well as inoffensive and underwhelming. Best served as an early-evening apéritif bourbon on a summer's night.

Henry McKenna Single Barrel 50% ABV
www.heaven-hill.com

Single-barrel, so nothing is guaranteed when you buy a bottle, but if it's anything like this you are in for a treat. It has an applejack nose and is liqueur-like, with pruney rumtopf notes. Intense. The taste on the palate, too, is full, concentrated, and intense, with baked apple and concentrated syrup. The ideal music to accompany it? Try Kentucky's Broadfield Marchers, comprising brothers Mark and Dustin Zdobylak. They play jangly post-Byrdian pyschedelic rock reminiscent of REM at its best. Their mix of exuberant youthfulness and respect for tradition is a perfect foil for this wonderful whiskey.

Hudson New York Bourbon 46% ABV
www.tuthilltown.com

For more than 200 years, the gristmill at Tuthilltown used water power to grind grain into flour. About ten years ago, a small group of whiskey aficionados acquired the property and converted one of the mill granaries into a microdistillery and set about learning the craft of distilling. It took them a couple of years to negotiate the legal hurdles put in their way, but by 2004 they were making spirits and today the range includes vodka, brandy, rum, fruit infusions, and several whiskeys.

Tuthilltown's main achievement has been in getting some of New York's trendier drinkers to take a fresh look at rye and bourbon.

I. W. Harper 43% ABV
www.fourroses.us

Some whiskeys are for sipping, some for slugging—but only responsibly, of course. Some are for daytime, others for evening or late at night. Some are reflective, some raucous; some passive and subdued, others edgy and active. I. W. Harper, if you can find it, is smooth and elegant, and one that should be sipped while listening to something special. For this whiskey, my suggestion is the CD *Face a Frowning World*, a tribute to Estil Cortez Ball, an Appalachian country and folk singer from Virginia who sang both secular and gospel songs. Sixty minutes listening to these country greats with the complex I. W. Harper: now that's a classy night in.

Jefferson's 8-year-old 45.1% ABV (VARIES)
www.mclainandkyne.com

Some non-distiller producers refer to a distillery where one does not exist. McLain & Kyne, now part of Castle Brands in New York, implies that it makes bourbon in Bardstown. It doesn't, but that does not mean that it is not buying good-quality bourbon; this small batch uses just eight to twelve barrels for each bottling. This is perfectly palatable, with hickory, rye spice, and a pleasant sweetness. Tastes mature without being overly oaky, and has a delightful fruity finish.

Jefferson's Presidential Select
Fall 2009 47% ABV
www.mclainandkyne.com

Rare as hen's teeth, but this may well be one of the last chances to taste bourbon from Stitzel-Weller. It is 17 years old and is taken from the last casks ever filled at the old distillery. Some of the final Stitzel-Weller inventory went with Weller to Buffalo Trace; some went with Old Fitzgerald to Heaven Hill. Diageo, which uses the distillery for storage now, may have retained some. No one really knows what's left, but they need to think about bottling it. This is woody and wilting, and another couple of years in the barrel might stamp out the grain notes entirely. After the oak is soft wheat, plummy fruit, and rich fudge.

Jim Beam 40% ABV
www.jimbeam.com

Like Jack Daniel's, Glenfiddich, Famous Grouse, Teacher's, and Jameson, the standard Jim Beam suffers from contempt because of its familiarity. This is grossly unfair. World-class whiskies become world-class for a reason. Next time you walk into a bar and you realize that your whiskey choice is limited to the above, make a point of going for one of them anyway. It will be then that you remember just how good each is—and how you'd forgotten about it. With Beam, you'll get brown sugar, a significant alcohol bite, and a sweet corn center that is not so obvious in many other bourbons.

Jim Beam Black 8-year-old 43% ABV
www.jimbeam.com

Proof if ever it were needed that big does not necessarily mean bland. This is aged for twice as long as the standard white label version, and it is premier-league stuff, capable of holding its own in a blind tasting against any mainstream bourbon younger than ten years old. Rich fruitcake, ginger drizzle and licorice come into play here; juicy berry fruits and raisins dip in and out of the mix; and there are just enough wood and rye notes to make this a complete experience. Complex and well balanced, this is exhibit A for those who think eight years is the perfect age for bourbon.

Johnny Drum 43% ABV
www.kentuckybourbonwhiskey.com

A bit of a curiosity comes from the Kentucky Bourbon Distillers, which bottles for a range of other brands. Johnny Drum varies in strength, is usually bottled at four years old, and is rare. But it is a jolly bourbon, made, we are told, from small batches of top-quality barrels, and it is rich, fruity, spicy, and zesty.

Johnny Drum Private Stock 50.5% ABV
www.kentuckybourbonwhiskey.com

This has an intense and fruity flavor with hints of strong candy stick, leather, tobacco pouch, and overripe fruit, together with a pleasant woodiness.

HEAVEN HILL DISTILLERY

PO Box 729, Bardstown, KY 40004
www.heaven-hill.com

Visit California, Louisville, when it's raining, and you cannot help thinking that whoever named it had a sick sense of humor.

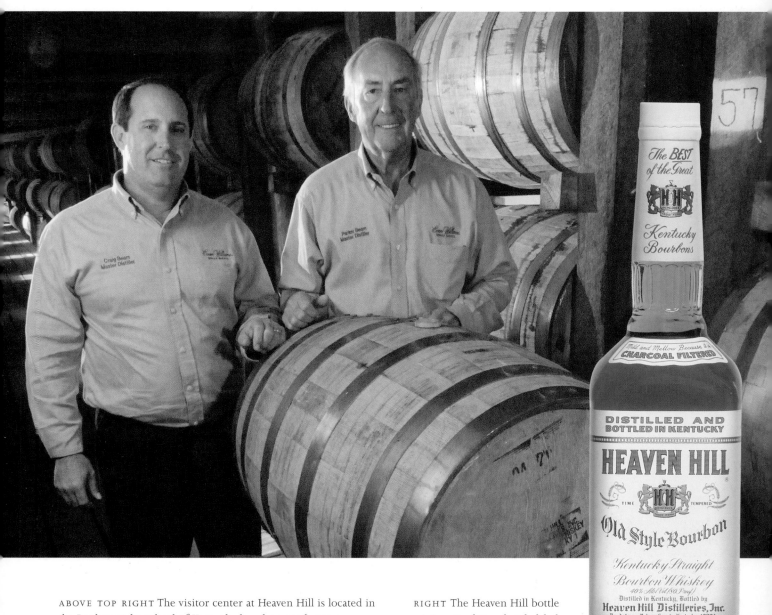

ABOVE TOP RIGHT The visitor center at Heaven Hill is located in the Bardstown heartland of Kentucky bourbon production.

ABOVE Like father, like son: Craig and Parker Beam, continuing the family line, in one of the distillery's warehouses.

RIGHT The Heaven Hill bottle retains a traditional-style label that fits perfectly well with its traditionally produced Kentucky bourbon.

It's a grim, run-down inner-city suburb that has nothing in common with the Sunshine State on the West Coast, and there are few reasons to stop by. But it is home to Brown-Forman's big distillery and the Bernheim plant where Heaven Hill now produces its spirit—not without incident. The plant flooded a couple of years ago, and more recently some local youths opened fire on it with a gun.

"They had been over at Brown-Forman, and the security guys had chased them off," says Heaven Hill's head of corporate affairs Larry Kass. "They came down here and fired two bullets into the fermenters. They were caught by the police, but the fermenters had to be emptied to be repaired because they were leaking. The slugs were never found.

"Now that's what you call bullet bourbon!" he adds, and lets out a barking laugh in distinctly Kass-like fashion.

Life at Heaven Hill is not usually as lively. Nevertheless, it is hard to imagine a whiskey distillery more removed from the standard country image on show throughout Kentucky. Heaven Hill moved here about 12 years ago, after its distillery was destroyed by fire. It bought the site from United Distillers, who were merging with spirits giants UDV to form Diageo, and it inherited a distillery that is both huge and high tech. And there's something distinctly incongruous about finding a check-shirted Craig Beam, broad Kentucky accent and all, seated in an office surrounded by computer screens and automated production equipment.

Craig and his father Parker's role within the company is to ensure that the passage from grain delivery in Louisville to whiskey maturation out at Bardstown, then back for bottling is a smooth one, and that all the traditional values of brands such as Evan Williams, Elijah Craig, Rittenhouse, and Henry McKenna are maintained. They oversee the second-biggest quantity of aging bourbon in the world.

They do it by bringing the old production skills and methods into the modern environment. It is a classic case of old meeting new and hopefully taking the best from both. For instance, across from Beam's office is the refrigerated room where the yeasts are kept. There is always an air of mystery about yeast because it is at the heart of whiskey-making magic, and it contains a whiskey recipe's deepest secrets. That applies just as equally in a high-tech monster plant as it does in a farm-hut microdistillery. At Bernheim, two buckets on the floor contain the raw yeasts. But, in the refrigerator itself, there are scores of packets of dried yeast. Made in Belgium.

"I'm not too sure how Craig and Parker feel about dried yeast, but it works for the plant," says Kass. "The original yeast is sent all the way from Belgium because this place is considered the best. Only Parker and Craig know the exact yeast strain, though. It was handed down by Parker's father, Earl, from the old days, when they would have to weigh it

down and drop it to the bottom of the lake to keep it cool in summer. Earl would make up the yeast in a bucket and then cover it with a cloth and put a monkey wrench on top to hold it down. And that monkey wrench always faced the same way. You didn't mess with the monkey wrench."

The way in which distilling skills and habits are handed down through the generations is much in evidence here. Craig shares his grandfather's obsession with cleanliness, too, even in the new plant. That's how it all started for him, he says.

"There was this old building which needed cleaning down, so I got to do that with some friends," he says. "Pigeons had been roosting in there for years, so we had to wade through the muck to clean it out. We'd come out as black as coal miners."

Craig represents the eighth generation of family distillers and his great-grandfather was the brother of James, better known as Jim. He is immensely aware of the dual responsibility of carrying such a famous bourbon name and being responsible for some of its most famous brands.

"But that's why we take such great care doing what we do," he says.

Kass agrees: "Heaven Hill has strong family connections through the Beams and through the Shapira family that owns it. It's important for everyone to keep the old traditions alive, not just with bourbon, but with rye, wheat, and even corn whiskey—no matter where it's made."

JIM BEAM DISTILLERY

526 Happy Hollow Road, Clermont, KY 40110
www.jimbeam.com

If you're in a fighting mood and feel like kicking up a storm while downing a few whiskeys with bourbon lovers at the Talbott Tavern in Bardstown, bring up the issue of small–batch bourbon.

On paper, it would seem to be a simple-enough concept. Small batch, in theory, is exactly what it says it is—bourbon made from a small amount of bourbon, with the emphasis on using only whiskey of the highest quality.

Problem is, there is no legal definition of the term. And one man's small shack is another man's castle.

At the big distilleries such as Jim Beam, they probably make in a minute what Maker's Mark makes in a day, so how small, exactly, is small? Are distilleries such as Maker's Mark, by definition, small batch? And if a distillery makes 10 million liters (2,641,720 U.S. gallons) of spirit a year and directs 10% of it—one million liters (264,172 U.S. gallons)—into its "small-batch" range, can that really count? Indeed, so vague is the whole concept that one respected whiskey writer has even declared: "There is no such thing as a small batch."

He's wrong—because there is. Or, more exactly, there are. Smaller volumes of specially selected bourbons that are superior to their standard versions do exist. It is just that they exist under a number of different definitions.

The confusion arises from the fact that many assume that the term "small batch" refers to the size of the production run, but this is not the case. If it were, Maker's Mark and Woodford Reserve (if stock taken only from the new distillery were bottled) would qualify as small-batch distilleries.

At Four Roses, they have their own definition. The distillery produces ten whiskeys from two recipes and five different yeasts, and marries them together to produce its standard bourbon. For its small-batch runs, Four Roses selects just four of the ten. That may still well be a massive amount of whiskey.

The term "small batch" was introduced back in 1988 by Jim Beam as a way of describing a special whiskey Booker Noe had created to set it apart from standard Jim Beam. This was at a time when there was no great market for premium bourbons as there is now, and when single-barrel selections were few and far between.

Jim Beam has two huge distilleries producing millions of liters of spirit every year, and, although the company website is not above some smoke and mirrors when it talks of returning to small-scale handcrafted bourbon with its small-batch range, the company's whiskey professor Bernie Lubbers is more forthright.

"We have big distilleries and production is 24/7, and so in this sense production could never be small batch," he says. "But that doesn't mean we can't make a small-batch bourbon." The issue here is over barrel selection. "If you pre-plan what you are going to mature as single batch before you start maturation, and put a part of your spirit production in a set number of casks in specific areas of your warehouse, then that constitutes small batch."

It makes sense, particularly in Kentucky, where temperature extremes mean that there are areas that will produce honey barrels—ones producing spirit of particularly high quality.

"It's not just a marketing trick," continues Lubbers. "In 2008, we ran out of Knob Creek and there were shortages of it. If you look at the figures from the Kentucky Distillers' Association for that year, you'll see we had 23,000 barrels of nine-year-old bourbon, but we didn't pull any of it out and call it Knob Creek because those casks weren't part of the planning for the small-batch run."

Perhaps we should not get too hung up on definitions, anyway. The likes of Jim Beam, Brown-Forman, Tom Moore, and Heaven Hill may be big, but they produce bourbon to the same exacting standards as even the smallest producers. Are Booker's and Knob Creek mighty fine bourbons? Yes, sir, they sure are.

And, as someone put it while sipping moonshine at a barbecue a while back: "Don't matter if it's one barrel or one thousand. Fine bourbon's fine bourbon, and rotgut is rotgut. No marketing man can ever change that."

Then he smiled and refilled my glass—with fine, very small-batch bourbon.

ABOVE RIGHT Visitors to Kentucky can visit the Jim Beam American Outpost close to the distillery. It includes a tasting room housed in a traditional clapboard building.

KEY WHISKEYS

Booker's 6-year-old 63.5% ABV
Jim Beam 40% ABV
Jim Beam Black, 8-year-old 43% ABV
Jim Beam Rye 40% ABV
Knob Creek 9-year-old 50% ABV

WELL, FANCY THAT . . .

A version of Jim Beam has been sold in one form or another since 1795. Today, it is the world's most popular bourbon, and the company's two distilleries have the capability to make 40 million liters (10,566,882 U.S. gallons) of spirit per year.

Kentucky Gentleman Straight Bourbon 40% ABV
www.heaven-hill.com

The nose here is soft and fruity, like canned pears, with soft fudge in the mix. The makers claim that rye is higher in the mix than is sometimes the case, and certainly the overall volume of the other blended grains is turned down. This whiskey is fine, but it won't kick or punch, preferring to make peace in the mouth, not war. Greener and fresher than classic bourbons, and with shades of eucalyptus, it is still very drinkable and ideal for sultry summer evenings.

Kentucky Tavern 40% ABV
www.bartonbrands.com

If you want a great Kentucky tavern, head on over to the Talbott in Bardstown. It is as old as the state of Kentucky, puts on great live music from time to time, serves some fine beer, and has a marvelous selection of bourbon. Easygoing and fun, and a great place to meet bourbon folk (especially at festival time), this was my nomination for inclusion as one of the world's great whiskey bars in *Whisky Magazine*. They say that Jesse James held court here.

The whiskey, which is actually named after a totally different tavern, is quite endearing. Sweet apple and pear on the nose, not unlike Kentucky Gentleman; some very gentle spice on the green fruit palate—bizarrely, it is not dissimilar to some of the stuff they are bottling at Bladnoch in the Lowlands of Scotland, or at Cooley in Ireland.

Knob Creek 9-year-old 50% ABV
www.knobcreek.com

There are two Knob Creeks in Kentucky. One is found next to a gun range; the other is the creek running through the farm where Abraham Lincoln grew up. His father made whiskey, too.

The bottle is designed to look like a bootlegger's version, with newsprint on the label to ape the old newspaper that the distillery used for wrapping.

The oldest and best of the Jim Beam small-batch range, Knob Creek is full of flavor, with endearing cocoa and dark chocolate notes, honey sweetness, and rye and oak as well.

Maker's Mark 45% ABV
www.makersmark.com

This is one of the most distinctive and softest of all bourbons, and so it should be, as it is designer-made and aimed to appeal to people who do not like bourbon. It is the creation of William Samuels, who bears the name of one of the great bourbon families, but had retired from whiskey-making in the 1940s. When he decided to come back into the business, he wanted to do something new and different and consulted Pappy Van Winkle, and hence he settled on a high-wheat recipe. The story goes that it was his wife who persuaded him to drop the family name from the bottle, to go for a distinctive wax seal, and to model the product on the jewelry industry, with a stamp representing the maker. William's son Bill is still the brand's figurehead, but these days the distillery is part of the Jim Beam empire. Only Maker's Mark is made in relatively small batches. Nevertheless, bottlings tend to be pretty consistent, probably because this is the only Kentucky distillery that rotates its casks during maturation. This is an angel's delight of a whiskey, with soft bread and custardy notes.

Bill Samuels claims that every member of the bottle-dipping team has his or her own wax "signature" and that he can tell who dipped each bottle just by looking at it.

Noah's Mill 57.15% ABV
www.kentuckybourbonwhiskey.com

The Willett distillery has a long and checkered history in Bardstown, and news that it was being restored was greeted with enthusiasm. But its owners agreed that they would not get into debt reconstructing it, so over the past few years they have been building a new still house brick by brick. Now it seems the project is complete, and the new Willett distillery is accepting visitors again.

Over the years the company has bottled bourbon for a number of companies and has had its own bottlings, too. This one is an award-winner and arguably the best from the Bardstown stable.

Another small-batch whiskey bottled by hand and containing some rare and special bourbon, Noah's Mill is a robust and full-tasting bourbon that is aged for about 15 years and has strong woody notes. A dash of water opens up an Aladdin's cave of flavors, however—banana caramel pie, vanilla ice cream with hot fudge sauce, and crumbly fruitcake.

Old Charter 8-year-old 40% ABV
www.buffalotrace.com

This is another great, iconic bourbon brand with a history that stretches back close on 140 years. In that time, the company has been buffeted by economic fortune and circumstance, with both the owner and the recipe changing more than once. Now it is a bit like an old steam engine—you keep it on the tracks for sentimental and historical reasons, but it does not really cut the mustard anymore in terms of performance and style. That said, if you are looking for a sweet, honest, and unsophisticated whiskey, you could do a lot worse.

Old Charter 10-year-old 43% ABV
www.buffalotrace.com

Two years and a few units more alcohol, and this steps up a division. There are lots of rye, some grapefruity citrus notes, and a nice slab of oakiness to this—although it doesn't taste as if it is anywhere near ten years old.

Old Crow 40% ABV
www.beamglobal.com

One of the greatest names in bourbon, Old Crow was given a new lease of life in 2010 when its owners, Jim Beam, relaunched it as a four-year-old, gave it new packaging, and pitched it up against Evan Williams. For some years before that it had been neglected, available in limited quantities as a not-particularly-exciting three-year-old, although there was something to be said for its youthful exuberance.

James Crow was a physician who became a leading figure in the development of bourbon, developing many of the techniques employed by bourbon-makers today to ensure consistency and quality. He was a skilled and charitable doctor, spent more than two decades at the Labrot & Graham distillery, and is remembered as one of the pioneers of modern bourbon. However, he never owned his own distillery, and the Old Crow distillery sited on Glenn's Creek was not constructed until several years after his death.

The new version of Old Crow has some strong licorice notes, retains its freshness, and is clearly aimed at the mainstream, but it works as a session bourbon and is one to look out for.

Old Fitzgerald Prime 43% ABV
www.buffalotrace.com

Most bourbons that feature a name in their title tend to take it from a particular distillery owner or distiller. But not in this case, according to Sally Van Winkle. This is named after a security guard who used to help himself to bourbon from select casks to give to friends. He had excellent taste, and his reputation for identifying good casks became well known. So when a good-quality bourbon went down to the blending room, it would be known as a "Fitzgerald." Eventually, it was applied to a brand. There is fudginess here, plus sweet pepper and cinnamon.

Old Forester 43% ABV
www.brown-forman.com

Old Forester's roots lie in the very earliest days of distilling. This was the whiskey—then spelled "Forrester"—that George Brown made at the distillery he founded in Louisville and that today is at the heart of the Brown-Forman empire. The whiskey's claim is that it was the first bourbon to be bottled. Before this time, whiskey was sold in barrels to wholesalers and retailers. This tipple is a bit of an A–Z of bourbon flavors and covers everything from fruit-and-nut chocolate bar and vanilla ice cream to nutmeg, cinnamon, sandalwood, and chili spices. Class in a glass.

Old Forester Birthday Bourbon
2009 Edition 48.5% ABV
www.brown-forman.com

A special limited-edition Old Forester Birthday Bourbon has been released each September since 2002 to mark the birthday of George Gavin Brown, a founder of Brown-Forman, and each release has become something of an event because the quality has been consistently good.

This release, tasted in Proof on Main earlier this year, and not under strict tasting lab conditions, did not disappoint. It is the bourbon equivalent of a Muse gig—a three-pronged assault on the senses, breathtakingly ambitious, and with the volume up. There are peppery rye qualities; chewy corn; and some fresh green fruit notes to give a stylish drinking experience.

MAKER'S MARK DISTILLERY

3350 Burks Spring Road, Loretto, KY 40037
www.makersmark.com

As you travel through Kentucky from Louisville to Loretto, you pass a number of houses that have statues of the Virgin Mary standing in upturned bathtubs.

The story goes that a bathtub salesman visited these parts a few years back, but could not get the local folk interested in investing in new washing facilities. But he found out that this region of Kentucky is devoutly Catholic, so assuming the locals were more into spiritual than personal cleansing he hit on the shrine idea, sold his entire stock of bathtubs, and retired a wealthy man.

Loretto is home to both the Maker's Mark distillery and some of the world's most expensive Thoroughbred horse-breeding facilities. That's no coincidence, either: The whiskey and the horses are here for the same reason. Kentucky is rich in limestone that enriches the grass with vitamins, making it ideal for developing healthy and strong bones in the horses. And it hardens the water and makes it ideal for distilling top-quality bourbon.

One of Kentucky's smallest and prettiest distilleries, Maker's Mark is very much at home among the wealth and beauty of the region.

It was launched some 65 years ago, but distilling has been carried on at the site next to Hardin's Creek for more than 200 years, making it the United States' oldest working distillery. It was established on farmland deep in rural Kentucky, and when you arrive there you are struck by how sedate and tranquil the neighborhood is.

The distillery is a sedate and calming place, too, even when it is in full production. That is partly because everything is done on such a small scale. While the debate rages as to what constitutes "small-batch" bourbon, it remains a fact that at Maker's they produce as much bourbon in a month as sister distillery Jim Beam does in a day.

The whiskey-making process is more gentle than at other distilleries, too. The corn is crushed, not by hammer as elsewhere, but by roller because Maker's owners believe that the heat generated by hammering scolds the grain and makes it bitter. The grains are cooked for longer, too, and brought to their cooking temperature over a longer period of time, and a higher proportion of wheat and lower proportion of rye are used than for other bourbons, giving the whiskey a softer, sweeter, and less spicy flavor.

Traditionally Maker's Mark produced only one expression of bourbon, and it is about six years old. The distillery has argued that this is the perfect age to bring out the full flavour of the bourbon.

Once the bourbon is matured to the distillery manager's satisfaction, the barrels are dumped on site and bottles filled in a small bottling hall. Each bottle is then dipped into the red wax to give it its trademark cap, labeled, and boxed by hand.

ABOVE Bill Samuels, the quirky founder of Maker's Mark. He has played a key role in the renaissance of the bourbon category in the United States.

Maker's Mark 45% ABV

RIGHT Maker's Mark
Distillery, set in countryside
in Loretto and a National
Historic Landmark, is one of
Kentucky's longest-established
sites for bourbon production.

Maker's Mark Distillery

Old Forester Signature 50% ABV
www.brown-forman.com

Old Forester with the volume turned up, this is an intense and robust version of the standard bottling made up from a number of specially selected casks.

Old Pogue 45.5% ABV
www.oldpogue.com

Old Pogue is produced by another non-distilling company, despite the fact that the website displays a lovely old photograph of a Kentucky distillery and its home page claims that the bourbon is bottled in Bardstown by the Old Pogue Distillery. Pogue is an old bourbon name, and the people behind this bottling are descendants of the original distilling Pogues. A mainstream bourbon launched a few years ago, this manages to find a niche all of its own—and that's because it is thinner and less sweet than many other bourbons, having an almost apéritif-like dryness and unusual barley meadow quality.

Old Rip Van Winkle 10-year-old 45% ABV
www.oldripvanwinkle.com

Sounds like a character from a nursery rhyme, and indeed "Rip Van Winkle" is the name of a short story by Washington Irving. It tells of Rip Van Winkle, who escapes his nagging wife by wandering off into the Catskill mountains and encounters some strangely dressed men who are playing ninepins and drinking liquor, which Rip shares with them. Doesn't sound so odd if you have downed a couple of glasses of this bourbon, and maybe this bourbon is meant to be the liquor in the story. It is aged to perfection and uses the distinctive Van Winkle wheated recipe, so it is soft, mellow, and rounded, with a rich, creamy toffee flavor to it and perhaps some chocolatey notes. There is a stronger 53.5% ABV version of this available, too.

Old Taylor 40% ABV
www.jimbeam.com

I reckon that, if you asked 100 movie buffs to name their favorite stars, Jeff Bridges would not figure very highly. Over his career, though, he has produced some absolutely storming performances—*Arlington Road*, *Thunderbolt and Lightfoot*, *The Fabulous Baker Boys*, *The Last Picture Show*, and *The Contender* are all great movies. The Dude, Bridges's character in *The Big Lebowski*, has reached cult status.

In his most recent offering, *Crazy Heart*, he is exceptional as a washed-up country singer who slugs whiskey while watching his former band partner hit the big time with country and western slush. The soundtrack is by T-Bone Burnett, Stephen Bruton, and Ryan Bingham, the movie is a study in Americana, and, if you are a fan of the new country genre, this hits all the right buttons.

I like to think that Bridges's drink of choice in the movie is based on Old Taylor because it's every bit as wizened, honest, genuine, traditional, and soft at its center as Bridges's character is. A lovable old rogue of a bourbon, perhaps out of kilter with the smarter-marketing whiskey world in which we now live, but one to look out for and to savor at least once. It reminds me of Battenberg cake—all jam and marzipan. Good old bourbon as it should be.

Pappy Van Winkle's Family Reserve 15-year-old 53.5% ABV
www.oldripvanwinkle.com

Julian P. Van Winkle was born in 1874 in Danville, Kentucky, and he did not come from a whiskey-making family. But he fell into the industry, spent more than seven decades in it, helped to shape the modern world for bourbon by putting emphasis on quality over quantity, and in the process started a whiskey dynasty. If it has the name "Van Winkle" on it, you are assured that the whiskey is going to be of the highest quality. There's a good chance, too, that it's going to be woody—these whiskeys are a challenge and are not for everyone.

Pappy Van Winkle's Family Reserve 15-year-old is an oddball when it comes to flavor; it's intense, toasty and oaky, but with a rumtopf-like rum-and-raisin heart and some citrus fruits in the mix. It is the whiskey equivalent of a Mad Hatter's tea party, with so much going on that you may miss it all the first time around. So, a perfect excuse to go around again, then.

Pappy Van Winkle's Family Reserve
20-year-old 45.2% ABV
www.oldripvanwinkle.com

Van Winkle's lovely old labels picturing Pappy with a cigar provide a rosy view of Southern life back then. Take the new offices built in 1949. Instead of a door knocker to gain entry, there were five heavy brass keys, one for each stage of the bourbon-making process. They also served as "a link between Stitzel-Weller and the old Southern traditions of warmth, hospitality, and enjoyment of the finer things in life," writes Sally Van Winkle.

This is not for the fainthearted. There are some green fruit and red berry notes, but also sharp burnt wood and astringent spice.

Pappy Van Winkle's Family Reserve
23-year-old 47.8% ABV
www.oldripvanwinkle.com

As you progress up the ages of the Van Winkle range, it is a bit like running a marathon. If you're running, then by 23 miles all the clowns and part-timers have been left way behind and it is only the serious contenders that are left. After 23 years of maturation, you have to be pretty serious about your bourbon, and here wood is a big part of the mix. For this reason you can't talk about balance because there isn't any—but this is a worthwhile, iconic bourbon, providing an important link to a different time.

Parker's Heritage Collection 64.8% ABV (VARIES)
www.heaven-hill.com

The growth of new microdistilleries across the United States has perhaps created something of a dilemma for Kentucky's distillers. On the one hand, there has been a clear and growing need to respond to the fleet-footed creativity of the new boys; on the other, you do not want to be throwing the baby out with the bathwater. What makes bourbon great will always make bourbon great and, anyway, they have seen it all before in these parts. So what do you do? Increasingly, Parker's Heritage Collection, like Woodford Reserve's Master's Collection, is being used for experimental and frontline whiskeys, giving bourbon fans an annual treat to look forward to. Each one has been a Godzilla, a roaring oversized beastie.

Rebel Yell 40% ABV
www.rebelyellwhiskey.com

Once sold only below the Mason–Dixon line, Rebel Yell had a brief flirtation with international stardom some 20 years ago when it made its way to Europe accompanied by a free rock tape. Yep, before CDs were the main musical vehicle. Now you don't see it so much, but it is still palatable enough and the one to choose if you want to tear it up with some Southern boogie. Right now your best option for that comes courtesy of Kentucky boys Black Stone Cherry, who strut with the panache of Skynyrd and insult anyone who does not buy in to their brand of good-time Southern rock: "Roll with Elvis in his Cadillac, Rode with Jesse on horseback, Slingin' guns and raisin' hell, Livin' our life with a rebel yell!" they sing in *We Are the Kings*. For those of us who don't buy into the Confederate thing, we take that as a reference to bourbon. Way to go.

Ridgemont Reserve 1792 46.85% ABV
www.bartonbrands.com

The launch of this bourbon a few years ago signaled that times were a-changin' at what was the Barton distillery. It is a premium bourbon, aged for at least eight years, and when launched its modern packaging was a clear statement of intent. Its birth was not without controversy, however. Originally called Ridgeford Reserve, it attracted the wrath of Brown-Forman, owners of Woodford Reserve, and its owners had to change its name.

The date refers to the year when Kentucky broke from Virginia and became a separate state, although a sizable number of settlers had already arrived in the region by then and whiskey was already being made. While the name and packaging might have attracted accusations of plagiarism, the bourbon itself is something else again. It's a full-bodied and highly tasty whiskey with just enough rye and oak to give it weight, but it is the creamy center with vanilla pod and stewed apples that really delights. Some chicory coffee and hickory are in the mix, too. If it were a sports star, it would be the tennis great Roger Federer—immensely powerful and hard-hitting, but charming, soft, and likable, too.

J. P. VAN WINKLE & SON

2843 Brownsboro Road, Louisville, KY 40206
www.oldripvanwinkle.com

When Eli Boone Van Winkle was born in the last week of 2009, a new chapter started for two of Kentucky's most famous families.

Eli is the first child of Preston, who has taken up the baton of the illustrious bourbon-making Van Winkle family, and his wife, Whitney, who is a descendant of Daniel Boone, the pioneer and folk hero who established the state of Kentucky in the late eighteenth century.

You would struggle to find a more famous name in this part of the world than Boone, but the bourbon-makers are giving it a go. No family name excites bourbon fans more than that of Van Winkle. No family name more evocatively recalls the highs and lows of bourbon history or the struggle for survival endured by the bourbon dynasties in a changing world. And no name better symbolizes the link between the old bourbon industry of 50 years ago and the modern one geared up for the challenges of the twenty-first century. With good reason.

In her excellent book *But Always Fine Bourbon* about her grandfather the legendary Julian "Pappy" Van Winkle and the Stitzel-Weller distillery he founded, Sally Van Winkle quotes a sign that hung at the distillery: "We make fine bourbon. At a profit if we can, at a loss if we must. But always fine bourbon." This is as true today as it was more than 75 years ago, when Prohibition ended and the Stitzel-Weller distillery was founded and started producing what is still some of the world's finest whiskey.

These days Van Winkle bourbon enjoys a special status in Kentucky. The company is run from a couple of small offices in a suburb of Louisville by Julian III, Sally's brother and grandson of Pappy, and increasingly by Preston, who is yet to reach his mid-thirties, but is already close to celebrating his tenth year in the business.

They do not distill anymore. Stitzel-Weller shut its doors many years ago, and today only the warehouses are used for maturing spirit owned by Diageo. But the magic remains, and it is created in the cask, not the still.

RIGHT The Pappy Van Winkle labels feature old photographs that are both nostalgic and classic, summoning up a past era when most bourbon distilleries were family-run.

What sets the Van Winkle portfolio apart from the competition is its age. Van Winkle whiskeys range from 12 to 23-year-olds—monster ages for bourbon, especially when you consider that Very Old Barton, for instance, is only six years old and that very few bourbons pass the ten-year mark.

Maturing bourbon to this age is no mean skill. Kentucky's traditional metal-clad warehouses of seven storeys or greater, sweat under the baking Kentucky sun in summer and are iceboxes during its sharp, brutal winters. On a hot day, temperatures from top to bottom can vary by 27°F (15°C), and in the crow's nest at the very top it is not unusual for the thermometer to pass 113°F (45°C). Effectively, the spirit cooks here, and maturation is rapid.

There are other factors, too. It is often stated that, while the alcohol strength of whiskey spirit will decline during maturation in Scotland, it rises in Kentucky. This is only part of the story. Higher up in the warehouse, the spirit does indeed get stronger as water in the cask evaporates out toward the hot, dry air outside at a faster rate than alcohol vapor does. But at some point farther down there will be a "neutral" floor, and at the lowest, moister, and cooler levels bourbon may behave just as malt does in Scotland—it will decline in strength. There are even anomalies found within each floor of the warehouse.

To successfully steer selected casks past 10, 15, 20, or more years without turning their contents into stewed wood or losing them altogether is an impressive skill. Today, the Van Winkles have their stock scattered across the lowest floors of the warehouses at Buffalo Trace, with whom they are in partnership. They are using a Weller whiskey made with a wheated recipe similar to the one that Pappy used to make.

Fine whiskey, all right, but the elitist status of the Van Winkle range lies partly in its rarity. After 15 years, each cask contains little liquid. Few casks make the marathon journey.

"So it's our oldest problem," says Julian while sipping on Van Winkle 12-year-old in Louisville's Proof on Main. "We don't have enough whiskey, and we spend much of our time having to disappoint people or trying to justify to one bar account why they haven't got any Pappy and the bar down the road does."

As drinkers learn more about bourbon and seek out its heritage brands, it is not likely that the problem will go away soon. The plus side, though, is that with the involvement of a giant such as Buffalo Trace at least some supply is guaranteed and the future for Van Winkle looks secure.

He doesn't know it yet, of course—but that's good news for little Eli of the next generation.

RIGHT Julian III, grandson of Pappy, and his son, Preston Van Winkle, still run the family firm. While no distilling takes place here now, plenty of spirit is matured in the warehouses.

KEY WHISKEYS

Old Rip Van Winkle 10-year-old 45% ABV
Pappy Van Winkle's Family Reserve 15-year-old 53.5% ABV
Pappy Van Winkle's Family Reserve 20-year-old 45.2% ABV
Pappy Van Winkle's Family Reserve 23-year-old 47.8% ABV
Van Winkle Family Reserve Rye 13-year-old 47.8% ABV
Van Winkle Special Reserve 12-year-old 45.2% ABV

Sam Houston 42.8% ABV
www.mclainandkyne.com

Sam Houston is one of the most amazing characters in American history. He is the only man ever to be governor of two states, and he made a remarkable impact on the state of Texas. He has no obvious links with Kentucky, having been born near Lexington in Virginia and spent his life in Tennessee, Texas, and Mexico. He was a slave-owner and anti-abolitionist, but like the state of Kentucky did not want to secede from the Union and refused to sign for the Confederacy. He spent time with the Cherokee nation and married into it, then emigrated to Mexico before becoming the leader of the Texas Revolution. And, of course, the city of Houston was named after him—as is this whiskey. A ten-year-old premium small-batch whiskey, it is a robust big hitter, with plenty of rye and oak, a delicious raisin heart, and caramel and toffee notes at the finish.

Ten High 40% ABV
www.bartonbrands.com

In Kentucky, many of the warehouses used to mature whiskey are tall, ugly buildings that dominate the skyline. They contain seven floors or more, and are wooden constructions. Given the huge weight of the scores of full barrels that they contain, they are feats of engineering.

Each floor will differ from the next, with the hottest and most active ones at the top of the building and the cooler ones lower down. At Tom Moore, the warehouses have three ricks (or stacks) per floor, and the bottom three floors are not used for bourbon at all. So the first rick used for whiskey is ten-high (the first rick of the fourth floor)—hence the name of this bourbon. But, of course, the folks at Tom Moore are well aware of the incidental gambling pun, too.

"I'd like to bottle a bourbon using barrels from the crow's nest at the very top of the warehouse," says Greg Davis. "We could call it Black Jack because it would come from the twenty-first rick."

No doubt it would be nearly black in color, too.

This bourbon is a delight—very easy to drink, fruity, and sweet. Great with ice and a perfect example of what some people refer to as a sippin' whiskey.

Tom Moore 40% ABV
www.bartonbrands.com

Tom Moore is perhaps not as well known as some other historical distillers; now that Barton has restored the old Tom Moore name to its Bardstown plant, this may change. Moore was a successful businessman who set up the Mattingley & Moore distillery in 1876, a couple of hundred yards from where the Tom Moore distillery sits today. By the time the first whiskey was bottled, however, he had already set up his own distillery, and it has been producing quality bourbon for 120 years.

Moore was a devout Catholic and a keen horseman who at one time owned the Talbott Tavern in Bardstown. A newspaper article of 1889 said of him: "Tom Moore is one of the cleverest distillers in Kentucky, and makes a whiskey fine enough to set before a king."

I am not sure that the current bottling could justify that claim, but I do have a real soft spot for it—there are fluffy red apples on the palate to start with, some marzipan and stewed pear in the center, and a dusting of white pepper over caramel at the end.

Van Winkle Special Reserve
12-year-old 45.2% ABV
www.oldripvanwinkle.com

Prohibition, introduced in 1920, was part of a moral crusade that ended up nearly destroying a Kentucky bourbon industry employing good, honest, and steadfast men, while creating a skilled and exploitative class of bootleggers, moonshiners, and gangsters. Bizarrely, a number of distilleries were allowed to stay open to make bourbon for medicinal reasons, and at the same time the number of people being prescribed bourbon by their doctors grew massively. Whiskey may well have been the cause of the St. Valentine's Massacre in 1929, when five members and two associates of Chicago's North Side Gang were shot dead by members of Al Capone's notorious gang. To replace his bourbon empire, Pappy Van Winkle went into business selling farm parts for a while—not very successfully.

This is the most accessible of the Van Winkle stable, a perfect after-dinner whiskey with a distinctive orange marmalade and sweet taste. There is also summer pudding with cream, with some paprika and cinnamon spice in the mix.

Very Old Barton 6-year-old 50% ABV
www.bartonbrands.com

A few years back, whiskey writer Charles Cowdery and I were invited to a barbecue held by Bettye Jo Beam. She is well known in whiskey circles, and has been a keen competitor in the barrel-pushing competition at the annual bourbon festival. She married a Beam and her maiden name is Boone, so she is linked to two of Kentucky's most famous families. On hearing that we were coming, she asked Chuck if she could tell all her friends.

"No, Bettye, because that would be half the state of Kentucky," replied Chuck. "OK, then, what about family?" she inquired.

"That, Bettye, would be the other half," said Chuck.

That barbecue was some event, but before we went I asked Chuck, who knows masses about bourbon and whose opinion I respect greatly, what bottle I should take with me. He suggested this one because it enjoys the respect of almost everyone.

"Very Old" in this case is just six years, and strangely the whiskey is bottled at three separate strengths. If you can get it, though, this is the one to go for. It is complex and challenging, but never sharp or overaggressive, and has a distinctive berry fruit center in a pepper and candy wrap. Another solid backliner of a bourbon, this is as steady and reliable as a Swiss watch.

W. L. Weller 7-year-old Special Reserve 45% ABV

William Larue Weller was one of the great early pioneers of bourbon. He was particularly noted for two things: using wheat in the grist rather than rye, creating a softer and more rounded bourbon, and long aging of his whiskey. Weller and later the Stitzel-Weller distillery became synonymous with aged and top-quality bourbon, and all of the current bottlings from Buffalo Trace live up to the name.

This is the youngest expression of Weller, and it has a soft, fruity nose and a soft, rounded honeycomb-candy center, together with gently ebbing and flowing waves of mild chili. It is as soft and delicate as bourbon gets, but none the worse for that.

Weller Antique 53.5% ABV

This bourbon is all about contrasts, with the soft honeyed and wheaten notes associated with Weller whiskeys meeting their match from an elephant-size chunk of oily corn and oak flavor. There is no obvious winner between the two sides, but the effect in the mouth is captivating and, as it slips down the throat, it is tempting to pour another drop so that you can go through the boxing match experience again.

Whenever I have a glass of this, I also toast the late, great Keith Weller, who is something of a legend among Leicester City soccer fans and who was my hero and role model. He is remembered most for playing an English cup game wearing white tights—an act that echoes this bourbon with its confusing mix of macho brawn and effeminate gracefulness. He was something of a pioneer in American soccer, too, playing and/or coaching in a number of places, including Fort Lauderdale, New England, Tulsa, Houston, Dallas, and San Diego. He died of cancer in 2004 at just 58 years old.

William Larue Weller 67.4% ABV

Every fall, Buffalo Trace releases a group of special whiskeys under its Antique Collection series, and they are snapped up within days. They are all exceptional. This year's offering from William Larue Weller is significantly stronger than usual and, unlike the George T. Stagg release, requires water to truly reach its heart. Even with a considerable dash of water it is X-rated stuff; the soft wheaten notes are swatted aside by huge high-cocoa-content dark chocolate, hickory, molasses, and espresso coffee notes. Work with it and you will find some mint notes, and some plummy fruit. But you cannot escape the fact that it is to bourbon what the Indianapolis Colts are to American football— tough, uncompromising, ruthless, and thoroughly brilliant in equal measure.

TOM MOORE DISTILLERY

300 Barton Road, Bardstown, KY 40004
www.bartonbrands.com

Kentucky's bourbon distilleries are scattered across the state, but the industry's heart is in Bardstown, about 40 miles south of Louisville.

ABOVE TOP The world's biggest whiskey barrel. And, no, it doesn't have any whiskey in it.

ABOVE The parkways in Louisville, near Bardstown, typify the pleasant landscape found in the state of Kentucky.

Bardstown is a sleepy, traditional Kentucky town that hosts the annual bourbon festival each September, and it is also home to the Oscar Getz Museum, which tells the history of Kentucky's famous spirit. Most of the year, though, there is little evidence that this is bourbon's capital.

Once the region boasted dozens of distilleries. Today, bourbon production barely figures here. Close by, Heaven Hill stores its bourbons in vast warehouses and has a state-of-the-art visitors facility that is well worth the journey, but the distillery was destroyed in an infamous fire some 15 years ago, and production now takes place in Louisville. Close to Heaven Hill on the site of the old Willett distillery, the Kentucky Bourbon Distillers company is rebuilding a distillery brick by brick. But the only proper distillery is on the other side of town.

These are good times for the Tom Moore distillery. Until a few years ago, it was known as Barton Brands. It did not welcome visitors, and it tended to trade on its former glories. Latterly, though, the distillery's owners launched a premium bourbon called Ridgemont Reserve 1792. Sometime later, the decision was taken to revert to its original name, it was sold to Sazerac, and it joined the Kentucky Bourbon Trail, allowing visitors to get up close and personal at one of the bigger industrial-like facilities.

With the affable Greg Davis at the helm as master distiller, and the tireless champion of bourbon aficionado Pam Gover fronting up the visitor experience, Tom Moore has had a face-lift—at least in terms of perception and attitude it has. Its problem, though, is that what really needs a face-lift is the distillery itself: it is old, grimy, and ugly. How do you sell that to the bourbon tourist?

Easy. By telling it like it is. You make a virtue of the fact that it is an old, working distillery. So when you go to Tom Moore, be prepared: You are about to get a definitive nuts-and-bolts tour. Literally.

And it is fascinating. Pam takes small groups by minibus around the sizable estate, commentating as she goes. It is an engineer's dream, this place, a mass of pipes welded together in improbably complicated patterns, all linked by dozens of faucets, spigots, and tanks. The huge column stills down which the fermented beer runs before meeting a blast of high pressure and scalding-hot steam are a particularly impressive sight.

LEFT Barrels of spirit mature at the Tom Moore Distillery in Bardstown, Kentucky. It is now on the Kentucky Bourbon Trail and well worth a visit.

RIGHT This eponymous bourbon is one of several expressions produced at the distillery.

KEY WHISKEY

Tom Moore 40% ABV

The warehouses are run-down, too, their white exteriors covered in black fungus.

"We could paint them, but that would affect the way the whiskey matures because the heat would be absorbed in a different way," Pam explains. "The fungus is totally harmless, but it's produced by the evaporating spirit—the angels' share—so it's part of the process. That's how they used to catch moonshiners. They just looked for where the trees had turned black."

She points out the little hills around each warehouse, giving each building in effect its own moat. This is a legacy from the great Heaven Hill fire in the 1990s.

"The reason they lost so many warehouses is because burning whiskey spirit flowed from warehouse to warehouse. These hills would help stop the contents flowing if ever there was a fire."

To be fair, the Tom Moore site is not without some attractive parts. You can go down close to the distillery entrance and see the old spring where the original Mattingley & Moore distillery once was, and there is a point where you can see the spring water that serves the distillery flowing through limestone to nearby Teurs Lake. Overall, though, the distillery is like most of the whiskeys it produces—solid, dependable, and unglamorous. It is, like the people who work within it, bighearted and honest.

"In 1945, there was a fire here, so when they refurbished this place in 1946 they spent a lot of money on it and made it a state-of-the-art distillery," Pam Gover explains. "And today it's still state of the art. We're still using state-of-the-art equipment from 1946."

And she laughs heartily. They make whiskey the way it should be made here, warts and all. I think people respect that. And for this reason Tom Moore is a welcome addition to the Kentucky Bourbon Trail.

Wild Turkey 40% ABV
www.wildturkeybourbon.com

The story goes that Wild Turkey was named after the sport of hunting wild turkey, which is one of the most dangerous sports in the world. Not because wild turkeys are extremely vicious—although you would not want to mess with one, especially when it finds out that the sexy bird cooing at them is actually a human dressed up as Thanksgiving and about to blow its head off. No, the problem comes from "friendly fire."

To steady the nerves, you could do worse than this. It is uncluttered, unchallenging, and sweet. Nice with ice.

Wild Turkey 101 50.5% ABV
www.wildturkeybourbon.com

Wild Turkey 101 is the ultimate rock-and-roll bourbon, and to enjoy it fully you need to crank up Lynyrd Skynyrd's "Tuesday's Gone" or Blackfoot's "Good Morning," sit back in your favorite chair, close your eyes, and wallow in nostalgia. This is also the official passport to good times and friendship south of the Ohio, certainly. If anyone in a flannel shirt asks you if you'd like a bourbon, just say, "101." Nothing else. Can't fail.

The bourbon is a big and balanced mix of spice, candy, overripe yellow and orange fruits, dark chocolate, vanilla, and cigar box, all held together by some chewy and oily undernotes.

Wild Turkey American Spirit 15-year-old 50% ABV
www.wildturkeybourbon.com

This is way out in the wilderness agewise, but it is not what you might expect. Wood is there, certainly, but it is not overdomineering and is not the taste that you will take away. That comes from the rich fruitcake and almost floral fruity heart, the daggerlike rye hit, and the gentler vanilla heart. A departure for Wild Turkey, this bourbon is certainly not to everybody's taste, but it is an interesting diversion nevertheless.

Wild Turkey Kentucky Spirit 50.5% ABV
www.wildturkeybourbon.com

There may well be a few bourbons from Kentucky that are not what they claim to be, but when Wild Turkey's owners claim that Jimmy Russell personally selects the casks that go into this single-barrel offering, you can bet your last dollar he did. His nose for great bourbon is undiminished and this is a gem. It has trademark citrus notes, rugged rye, and lashings of sweet vanilla and spice.

Wild Turkey Rare Breed 51.4% ABV (VARIES)
www.wildturkeybourbon.com

To catch a wild turkey, you need to get close enough to it to shoot it. The best way to do this is to disguise yourself, strap yourself to a tree, and summon a male turkey by impersonating a female. If you are good enough, it will strut toward you and start showing off. But turkey calling has become a sport in its own right, and there are televised competitions, where you can win big bucks. There are various categories, and sounds include clucking, and cackling. Competitors take a nickname, and the one who told this used the name "motherclucker." Really.

This is a total fruit bowl of flavors mixed with butterscotch, vanilla ice cream with toffee fudge sauce, licorice root, and methol.

Wild Turkey Russell's Reserve 45% ABV
www.wildturkeybourbon.com

Jimmy Russell is one of the world's true great whiskey personalities, and he's a bit like his bourbons—pleasant, soft, and gentle on one level, but hardy, determined, and with a great sense of purpose on the other. He does not believe that bourbon gets better after ten years of maturation, hence the age of this beauty. But his preferred bottling strength is 101 proof—51.5% ABV. Odd, then, that this is 45%. No matter because it's a corker—an oral roller-coaster that takes you slowly up and up, the flavors building, then whoosh—a crash of vanilla, citrus fruit, waves of sweet spices, and some polished wood in the mix. Very lovable.

Woodford Reserve Distiller's Select 43.2% ABV
www.brown-forman.com

The Kentucky Derby is not just one of the world's greatest sporting events, it is the highlight of the social calendar in Kentucky. The race itself is short and sweet, particularly for a country that likes to drag out its sporting events, but the pomp and ceremony that surrounds the Churchill Downs race would be hard to match. The drink most associated with the event is the mint julep, and revelers raise their glasses of it while singing "My Old Kentucky Home" with a religious fervor. According to Wild Turkey's Jimmy Russell, though, you can spot true Kentuckians from visitors as soon as the singing is finished. While visitors drink their Mint Juleps, he says, local folk reach for their favorite bourbon.

High on the list is Woodford Reserve, used to make Mint Juleps, but it stands apart as a fine straight drink, too. With higher-than-average rye content, a triple distillation process, and about eight or nine years in the barrel, this is a full and rich fruity bourbon with delightful spiciness and enough oaky astringency to prevent cloying.

Woodford Reserve Four Grain 43.2% ABV
www.brown-forman.com

In recent years, the makers of Woodford Reserve have taken to launching an unusual annual release under the name Master's Collection. Each one is effectively small-batch, using barrels taken just from the Woodford Reserve distillery (unlike the standard version, which is mixed with spirit from Brown-Forman's Louisville distillery), and each is a twist or take on standard bourbon. Each is rare.

Four Grain was the first and effectively second release in the series. Most bourbons are made using three grains—predominantly corn, but with a proportion of other grains, most often some malted barley because it is an efficient catalyst in the process of converting sugars to alcohol, but also rye, wheat, or unmalted barley.

Here four grains are used, and the resulting bourbon is intriguing and very different. The first version was sappy and oily, with grains battling against one another. Another year on, though, and the oily corn and spicy rye have made friends, there is an earthy but highly attractive base to the whiskey, and a delightful linseedy note sets it apart from any other bourbon.

Woodford Reserve Seasoned Oak 43.2% ABV
www.brown-forman.com

Ah, that's much better. The best of the Master's Collection, so far, by some considerable distance. This is a punchy, sharp, well-shaped bourbon with a delicious spiciness from the oak. There is a muskiness to it, too, and the oils make sure that it coats the mouth and stays there, alongside a suitable amount of the trademark Woodford rye, too. A classic in the making?

Woodford Reserve Sonoma-Cutrer Finish 43.2% ABV
www.brown-forman.com

Not strictly a bourbon because the final part of the maturation process is carried out in a cask that has been used previously for wine. The technique of using wine casks is common enough in Scotland, but does it work with bourbon? Well, of all the Master's Collection series so far, this is the one I struggle with most. That's probably because it does not taste very much like a bourbon, and its grapiness takes it into a whole new place. I'm not convinced, but it raises some interesting questions and might be a signpost to the future.

Woodford Reserve Sweet Mash 43.2% ABV
www.brown-forman.com

One of the cornerstones of bourbon-making is the sour-mash process. At the end of distillation, there is a stillage made up of liquid and spent grain, with all the sugars stripped out and converted to alcohol. This stillage is known as "backset" and is the soured, sugar-free remains of this mash. By adding this backset to the next mash, it is possible to prevent bacterial infection and to ensure a consistency in the solution's pH levels and therefore consistency in the mash—and eventually the new spirit. It follows, then, that every time a distillery is shut down and restarted, the first run will be a sweet mash, and it is rejected.

This is one example of what it tastes like. If you are a bourbon geek, then it is an interesting exercise. As you might expect, it is sweeter than the standard Woodford, but it is also flabbier, blander, and less complex, too. It's a sort of Woodford Lite.

WILD TURKEY DISTILLERY

1525 Tyrone Road, Lawrenceburg, KY 40342
www.wildturkeybourbon.com

Nobody rushes in Kentucky and, when it comes time to retire, there seems to be no hurry to hang up the boots and head out onto the porch for a well-earned cigar and a bourbon or two.

In fact, if you want proof that bourbon-makers live for their work and love what they do, just look at how many of the industry's senior citizens are still turning their hands to making whiskey.

Elmer T. Lee celebrated his ninetieth birthday last year, but still comes in to check on stock at Buffalo Trace, while Parker Beam and Jim Rutledge show no signs of letting up in their posts at Heaven Hill and Four Roses anytime soon, even though both have passed the 40-year service mark.

And then there's Jimmy Russell at Wild Turkey. He's been making bourbon for more than 50 years and is moving into his late seventies. When his beloved distillery was sold by Pernod Ricard a couple of years ago, you would have thought that would be the perfect time to call it a day. Not a bit of it.

"The owners have got plans, and they want me to go to New York, Chicago, and San Francisco in the coming weeks," he says when we meet at the distillery visitor center. "This is what I like to do, meet people who enjoy my bourbon, see the pleasure it brings them, travel to places to talk.

"Mind you, you know you're getting old when you start working with your grandchildren, and I sometimes wonder when we fill the casks whether I'll still be around to see the whiskey being bottled."

Russell is on site almost daily when he is not traveling, and splits his time between greeting visitors—"I try to personally say hello to everyone who visits here," he says, and playing an active role in producing spirit, which he now does with his son Eddie.

There are few people anywhere in the world who understand their spirit the way Jimmy Russell does. He can tell how long the mash has been fermenting by the size of the bubbles, for instance, and he knows instantly if a batch of bourbon has strayed from the correct recipe or is the wrong strength. He also has a very precise idea of what great bourbon is. He does not care for spirit that has been aged for more than ten years, for instance, and his preferred bottling strength is 101 proof, not the more common 100 proof, which was the industry standard for a good while. According to him, the bourbon's name and its strength are interrelated.

"The distillery was once owned by the McCarthy family, and Thomas McCarthy was a keen wild turkey hunter," he recalls. "They used to go on shoots, and everybody would contribute something to the food and drink for the trip. The story goes that Thomas McCarthy took a barrel of his bourbon one time, and it happened to be at 101 proof strength and everybody enjoyed it very much.

"The next time they asked him to bring some more bourbon, so he found some the same strength and he referred to it as the 'wild turkey bourbon.' Finally, he christened it that way."

Wild Turkey 101 remains one of the great old bourbons, but the distillery has not sat back and let progress leave it behind. Certainly, 101 is still going strong, but over the years the distillery has released a single-barrel bourbon, a rye, a liqueur, and a number of special bottlings including Tradition and Rare Breed. At the heart of everything, though, is big-flavored Wild Turkey whiskey because, says Russell, sooner or later everyone comes back to it.

"A few years ago they started experimenting with light whiskey, and I never thought it would work," he says. "If I had not been wrong then, I would not be sitting here today. It's good that new things come along and keep people interested, but what goes around comes around, and folk always come back to proper well-made bourbon."

Exactly what new owner Campari plans for Wild Turkey next is anyone's guess, but, whatever it may be, you suspect that Jimmy Russell will be involved right at the very center. "For sure," he says.

"I'm in good health and I've got the energy," he says. "As long as that's the case, I'll be here."

ABOVE Wooden bourbon barrels are stamped with identifying information while they are left to mature on racks at the distillery.

A distillery fire at Wild Turkey at the start of the millenium sent burning spirit into the Kentucky River, and this was blamed for an environmental disaster soon after. More than 200,000 fish were killed by a blanket of algae, which was thought to have fed on the alcohol and drained the river of oxygen. Wild Turkey was faced with a bill for nearly half a million dollars.

KEY WHISKEYS
Wild Turkey 40% ABV
Wild Turkey 101 50.5% ABV
Wild Turkey American Spirit 15-year-old 50% ABV
Wild Turkey Kentucky Spirit 50.5% ABV
Wild Turkey Rare Breed 51.4% ABV
Wild Turkey Russell's Reserve 45% ABV
Wild Turkey Russell's Reserve Rye 45% ABV
Wild Turkey Rye 50.5% ABV

ABOVE Legendary bourbon maker Jimmy Russell, who has been making bourbon for more than 50 years, keeps an ever-watchful eye on the maturing whiskey.

LEFT Wild Turkey Kentucky Spirit—one of the fine bourbons produced at Wild Turkey's remote distillery—also has one of the most distinctive bottle designs.

WOODFORD RESERVE DISTILLERY

7855 McCraken Pike, Versailles, KY 40383
www.woodfordreserve.com

At the pretty Woodford Reserve distillery, situated in Kentucky's famed bluegrass country, they are ringing in the changes and looking firmly to the future.

History seeps from every pore here. James Crow carried out some of the pioneering scientific work into bourbon on this site. He may not have invented the sour-mash process, but he mastered it and laid down the blueprint for consistency that is still maintained today. This was home to Elijah and Oscar Pepper, too. Major history.

That may well be the case, says master distiller Chris Morris, but Woodford Reserve is a premium bourbon that looks to the future rather than the past.

"Sure this distillery is associated with Oscar and Elijah Pepper, and with James Crow. But whatever they were making then wasn't what we know as bourbon now. We make Woodford Reserve here, so we've taken down some of the displays about the past and replaced them with information on Woodford Reserve, and we're focusing more on what we're doing now. That's what's important."

Maybe, but it's not just Crow and the Peppers who haunt the distillery. George T. Stagg is said to have distilled here, as well as Colonel Edmund Taylor, who was to later create Old Taylor at a distillery he built just down the road. The remains of distilleries are scattered around this part of Kentucky,

known as Versailles, a few miles from Frankfort. Some of them, such as Old Crow and Old Taylor, have taken on legendary status among bourbon enthusiasts.

It is like a ghostly bourbon hall of fame here. Combine this with the sublime charm and beauty of the place, and there are few distilleries on the planet as magical and mystical, few so entwined in such a rich tapestry of history.

Woodford Reserve is situated close to Glenn's Creek, and to reach it you must venture into the heart of Kentucky's bluegrass country, negotiating tree-lined country lanes and fields containing gleaming chestnut brown thoroughbred horses. In summer, birds of prey circle overhead, wild turkeys strut nonchalantly, and red cardinals, the state bird, frolic from white-painted fence rail to white-painted fence rail. In winter, chilly mists create eerie shrouds across the hills, and icy rain helps to cast a pall over the terrain. This really is the heart of rural Kentucky, and nothing can quite match the marriage of culture, history, and beauty found at the new Woodford Reserve Distillery. But such a heady combination can be a swamp, and you cannot blame anyone for trying to break free of the ghosts of history.

What Morris and his team are keen to stress is that this is a new distillery making a sophisticated and stylish premium bourbon ideal for the twenty-first century. It might be built from the ruins of Labrot & Graham, but owner Brown-Forman spent a small fortune on renovating this site. It does not even use the old name anymore.

Woodford Reserve is Kentucky's smallest distillery—and its least typical. Instead of the standard industrial-like column-still method of production, for instance, it has pot stills from Scotland. It distills three times, too. There is only one standard expression of the whiskey, but even then the distillery cannot make enough bourbon to meet the demand, so the new distillery's output is mixed with a significant—some would say high—proportion of nine-year-old whiskey made to the Old Forester recipe at Brown-Forman's Louisville distillery.

But the real draw for bourbon fans is the Master's Collection series. Each year for the past five years a limited-edition bourbon has been made purely with pot-still whiskey from the Woodford distillery, each one testing out a new

ABOVE Brown Forman's Wayne Rose checks the quality of a new bottling at the Woodford Reserve distillery.

Woodford Reserve Distiller's Select 43.2% ABV
Woodford Reserve Four Grain 43.2% ABV
Woodford Reserve Sonoma-Cutrer Finish 43.2% ABV
Woodford Reserve Sweet Mash 43.2% ABV
Woodford Reserve Seasoned Oak 43.2% ABV

angle. The first used four grains, for instance, one was finished in a wine cask, and another dispensed with the sour-mash process. Not all of them have worked, but they are always interesting.

"The last one was a big, weighty oaky bourbon after a couple of lighter ones," says Morris. "So in 2010 we went with a sweeter bourbon finished in maplewood. We have 100 percent rye whiskeys and single malts maturing, whiskeys made with white corn and oats, and whiskeys maturing in hickory and ash. Some won't work and we won't do them; some will be outstanding."

At their best, the special releases are enhancing an already greatly respected bourbon reputation. Morris and his team are tinkering on the margins, testing and experimenting as they look for new channels in the future.

They are looking forward rather than back. But you know what? James Crow would surely have approved of what is happening now.

LABROT & GRAHAM
WOODFORD RESERVE
DISTILLER'S SELECT

OPPOSITE ABOVE The visitor center includes a room devoted to distilling methods and history.

ABOVE The Woodford Reserve Distillery, with its smart visitor reception area and well-maintained buildings and grounds, is a highlight of any whiskey lover's trip to Kentucky.

Tennessee whiskey

It is one of American whiskey's greatest ironies that the brand most people would cite as its most famous bourbon is not a bourbon at all.

Jack Daniel's is a Goliath of a brand and the whiskey world's most accomplished grifter, able with ease to bottle and sell millions of gallons of spirit while fooling its audience into believing that a few good ol' boys in Lynchburg, Tennessee, are making and bottling whiskey exactly as Mr. Jack used to. In fact, this is a huge operation, with close to 200 million liters (52,834,410 U.S. gallons) maturing on the vast site at any one time, and three bottling plants in operation. Not that you would know it from visiting—as millions do because no other distillery enjoys an iconic status quite like this one. You know it's vast, but this is Disneyland for whiskey drinkers and a million miles away from the hard-hat tours up North at Barton or Buffalo Trace.

Jack Daniel's is made in almost exactly the same way as a bourbon, but it does not qualify as one. Not because it is from Tennessee, but because at the end of the distillation process its producers break bourbon's strict rules by pouring the new spirit through a wall of maplewood charcoal. This process is a form of filtration and is known as the "Lincoln County process," thus defining the whiskey as a Tennessee one and not a bourbon.

Some people say that Jack tastes like bourbon and the technicalities do not matter. They do, though—especially to the people in Tennessee and Kentucky. Jack is not the only distillery in the state. George Dickel is a relatively large operation in its own right and produces whiskey using the Lincoln County process, but with a small difference—it chills the spirit before passing it through the charcoal, a process that allows even more mellowing.

George Dickel No. 8 40% ABV
www.dickel.com

This lighter version of Dickel is probably aimed at the mixing market, but it is pleasant enough with ice. It is a smooth, easy-drinking whiskey with a balanced but laidback mix of fruit, vanilla, rye, and burnt oak. A lazy summer afternoon of a whiskey.

George Dickel Superior No. 12 45% ABV
www.dickel.com

The Dickel distillery is only a short drive from Jack Daniel's and is now owned by Diageo, although the drinks giant seems to have a problem with American whiskey and has struggled to establish a foothold for this in the international arena. This is a perfectly decent whiskey, with floral and vanilla notes, soft sweet corn, and toffee and chocolate in the mix. It also has a big mouthfeel and a surprisingly long finish.

Jack Daniel's Gentleman Jack 40% ABV
www.jackdaniels.com

The problem with spending years telling the world that Mr. Jack got his whiskey right the first time and you don't mess with a winning formula is that you leave yourself no room for maneuver when it comes to brand extension. So this version of the famous whiskey divides the room like no other. While Single Barrel is just regular Jack unplugged and acoustic, Gentleman Jack is a different expression because an extra level of mellowing has been introduced. This is the alcohol equivalent of Diet Pepsi.

Jack Daniel's Old No. 7 40% ABV
www.jackdaniels.com

Whiskey enthusiasts get sniffy about this, but really they shouldn't. It is quite remarkable that a strong-tasting dark spirit of any sort, let alone whiskey, should have established itself as the world's biggest spirit. Bland it most certainly isn't. It is true that most people mix it, but, next time you get the opportunity to do so, sip it neat or mixed with a little ice. The vanilla, oak, and licorice triple whammy is impressive whichever way you cut it. This, then, is the Harley-Davidson of the drinks world—a big, growling, rugged, and iconic symbol of blue-collar working man's America.

Jack Daniel's Single Barrel
www.jackdaniels.com

If Jack Daniel's is a Rolling Stones tour—a huge, glitzy worldwide greatest-hits package that delivers just what its audience expects—then Single Barrel is a Keith Richards solo gig—recognizably from the Stones, but altogether rootsier, rougher, more intense, and less predictable. It offers you the chance to get up close and personal. Each barrel not only differs from the next, but also differs significantly, and every barrel is chosen from the best parts of the best warehouses and every batch reinforces the view that Jack is a very well made whiskey indeed.

It would obviously be impossible to provide notes for a large number of different single-barrel bottlings, but here is a snapshot:

Jack Daniel's Single Barrel 8-15-08 8-2886

Licorice allsorts on the nose, with hickory, red licorice, glacé cherries, and orange and grapefruit marmalade. The palate has anisette, licorice, and a big dollop of orange marmalade, before an intense wave of pepper and spice. A big, growling monster truck of a whiskey, with all its lights on high beam.

Jack Daniel's Single Barrel 9-30-08 8-3531

The nose is dusty and powdery, almost flighty, with some grapefruit and lemon, caramel, and faint spearmint. The palate is quite gentle, with banana skin and green melon. The citrus notes give it freshness, and there are some late spice and oak notes toward the end.

Jack Daniel's Single Barrel 8-29-09 8-0267

Less masculine than some other expressions, with sweet tobacco and saddle leather on the nose, some floral notes, and mincemeat pie filling in the mix. There is toffee on the palate at first, then some sharp apricot and orange fruits, traces of cocoa, and some late chili.

Rye whiskey

Rye has a long and proud history in American whiskey, but until relatively recently its popularity had declined and it had been marginalized. Over the past couple of years, it has been enjoying a new wave of popularity, rediscovered by whisky enthusiasts and bartenders who see it as an ideal base for several different cocktails.

In actual fact, there are three very different types of rye. Canadian whisky, which for a long time was actually referred to as rye, is often made up of several ryes produced in Canadian distilleries, but these are blander and less spicy than American rye. American rye whiskey is made in the same way and to the same regulations as bourbon, but must contain at least 51 percent rye in the gristbill. There are also a few examples of 100 percent rye whiskey. In this case, the rye is malted, so it is effectively a single-malt rye.

Cougar Rye 37% ABV

This is a curio. Cougar is distilled by Foster's, the Australian beer-maker, but, although a rye has existed in the past, it is rarer than the brown-ringed blue-spotted cougar after which it is named. Those who swear they have tasted it talk of it as a stunning elixir. For this reason it warrants inclusion here. I, however, have been unable to track it down. And even those close to the subject admit that it seems to have gone to ground of late.

Devils Bit 47.7% ABV
www.mcmenamins.com

McMenamins is a small pub and hotel company that runs its establishments in a quaint and old-fashioned manner, including its own microdistillery that produces a range of spirits. It is exactly this sort of whiskey that shows the future is very bright indeed for the new wave of U.S. distillers. What makes rye such a stunning drink is the way it packs spikes and spices at its heart, but delivers on a crest of oil and oak, as is the case here. It is bold, assertive stuff. No drink can match it on its day.

Hudson Manhattan Rye 46% ABV

www.tuthilltown.com

New York was once famous for its rye, which was the whiskey used in the original Manhattan cocktail. So it is fitting that, now that small-batch distilling is taking place in the city once more, the whiskey makers should turn their hand to a proper, edgy rye.

This has an odd nose—aromatic wax candle, floral, and with floor polish notes—all quite pretty. On the palate, it is initially rootsy, with linseed oil coming before some orange jelly notes. This is all a bit odd until the spices arrive to pull it back on track.

Jim Beam Rye 40% ABV

www.jimbeam.com

This is not Beam's best bottling, but it has its place because beyond the tough, robust, and grainy nature of the core drink there are aromatic and floral notes. As a result, it is a good starting point for anyone wanting to get to grips with rye. Very reasonably priced, too, and I understand that Beam is upping output after some initial supply problems.

Old Potrero 18th Century Style Whiskey 62.55% ABV

www.anchorbrewing.com

According to Anchor, single-malt rye made back in the eighteenth century called for heated oak wood chips to be used to heat the staves to bend them. The heat would have toasted but not charred the inside of the barrel. That's what is done with the barrels here. This is another amazing and totally incomparable whiskey. What a big nose you

have, Grandma! Sort of Campbeltown with licorice. The taste is bold and mouth-coating, with oily hickory and cloves, and lots of peppery spice. I reckon this would not only numb a toothache, but would go some way to curing it, too. The medicinal notes are balanced by anisette, treacle toffee, and apricot. Complex.

Old Potrero Hotaling's Single Malt Whiskey 50% ABV

www.anchorbrewing.com

The great San Francisco earthquake of 1906 destroyed 28,000 buildings and claimed countless lives. Some religious leaders blamed the entire event on the city's wicked ways. Oddly, although a number of churches were destroyed, Hotaling's distillery survived, despite the fact that there were thousands of gallons of flammable liquid on site.

Old Potrero is the whiskey wing of Anchor Brewing, the cutting-edge San Francisco brewery headed by brewing genius Fritz Maytag, and its intention is to re-create whiskey as it used to be. To do this, it takes malt rye and uses it as the only ingredient—a 100 percent single-malt rye. And this is, quite simply, incredible. The nose is spiky and pithy, with a touch of water kick-starting waves of aromatics. Tastewise, it has a peatlike intensity of earthy spices mixed with chocolate honeycomb candy followed by floral notes, then finishing off with some orange and lemon candy chews.

Old Potrero Single Malt Straight Rye Whiskey 45% ABV

www.anchorbrewing.com

Over time, whiskey-makers learned that, if they left the oak chips to continue to burn the inside of the barrels, the charring would allow even more flavor into the whiskey. This, then, is Anchor's attempt to re-create that style.

It has an oily, puttyish nose, with some meaty almost kebablike notes. On the palate, it's like mixing Talisker with Jamaican fruitcake, a delightful mix of berry fruits in soft cake, plus sweet red pepper. It is delicate, too, with aromatic and floral notes. A total delight.

Pappy Van Winkle Family Reserve Rye 13-year-old 47.8% ABV

www.oldripvanwinkle.com

This is all old polished wood-paneled office in feel. It is as uncompromising as whiskey gets, with dark chocolate and espresso notes fighting against hickory, sharp pepper, and orange fruit and plum. It is to other whiskeys what Them Crooked Vultures are to rock music: an edgy and challenging experience, but ultimately a rewarding one.

Pikesville Supreme 40% ABV
www.heaven-hill.com

While we tend to think of Kentucky as the center of American whiskey production, it was not always that way. Tennessee clearly has a strong whiskey tradition, but so did Virginia, Pennsylvania, Indiana, Idaho, and Maryland. Pikesville is named after the last rye to be made in Maryland and is meant to be based on that recipe. Even so, it has been made in Kentucky for 30 years and is part of the Heaven Hill empire. This is clean and zesty, with apple and pear sours, some rich candy chew, and spice notes.

Rittenhouse 40% ABV
www.heaven-hill.com

Rittenhouse's time seems to have come. Once one of the few brands keeping the rye style alive when everyone seemed to have turned their backs on it, Rittenhouse has not only survived, but also started picking up the very highest international awards. What makes it particularly special for me is the fact that the three most available expressions of it are so different from one another. This is probably the poorest of the three, but that does not mean it is not a great whiskey. A 40% ABV means that it works as a good entry-level rye, although it is quite spiky.

Rittenhouse 23-year-old 50% ABV
www.heaven-hill.com

This is a monster: a dusty, damp, oaky, and musty room with a treasure chest packed with color and flair. You have to work your way through the woody and spicy intensity to unlock the delights within, but, boy, is it worth it. Ancient by American whiskey standards, but undoubtedly a wonderful world-class whiskey.

Rittenhouse 100 proof Bottled in Bond 50% ABV
www.heaven-hill.com

Arguably the best of the three bottlings on offer here because fruit has a bigger say in the mix and, when battering against the rye, it makes for oral fireworks. This is complex because a fruit bowl of flavors each make their case one by one. Impressive stuff.

Sazerac Rye 6-year-old 45% ABV
www.buffalotrace.com

Sazerac Rye's big brother is the weighty 18-year-old, which is part of Buffalo Trace's Antique Collection and a superstar. A bit like having Muhammad Ali for a big brother. But this is no wimpy kid, or Sazerac Lite—the mouthfeel is big and assertive, and there is lots of spice and oak. It is not particularly complex and far less challenging than many others in this category, but that is actually no bad thing. Very well balanced, too.

Sazerac Rye 8-year-old 45% ABV
www.buffalotrace.com

This is a linebacker in a skirt. One of the truly great American whiskeys, this would seem to be almost overwhelmingly muscular and brawny in terms of oak, spice, and deep, dark fruit. But it is also surprisingly feminine around the edges—almost floral and honeyed at the heart. The peppery notes are a delight, and weave in and out of the oak and fruit unpredictably—which means that every sip is an adventure.

Templeton Rye 40% ABV
www.templetonrye.com

The makers of this are based in Chicago, but claim that this rye is made to the same recipe as one that a town in Iowa produced during Prohibition. Its owners claim that the rye the town produced was so good that it commanded premium prices on the black market and became the drink of choice of Al Capone himself. It was sold in speakeasies in Chicago, Des Moines, and as far afield as San Francisco.

It's a good marketing pitch, but this version has been available for only four or five years, and is a bit of a curio—well made and enjoyable, it is sweeter and less spicy than most ryes and has a distracting smoothness. Definitely worth seeking out because it stands apart from other ryes.

Thomas Handy Sazerac 63.8% ABV
www.buffalotrace.com

The Sazerac was invented by Antoine Peychaud, who made it at his pharmacy in New Orleans's French Quarter. Originally, it was made with brandy, absinthe, and a secret mix of bitters. It became popular and was copied across coffee shops in the city. But its whiskey link came courtesy of Thomas H. Handy, who bought the Sazerac Coffeehouse and added rye whiskey instead of brandy.

He would have been proud of this. Big and bold, it has more ups and downs than a baby in a bouncer. There are boiled candy fruits and sharp ryes battling one another, oak and alcohol punching in and out, then traces of nutmeg, tarragon, chili, and mint.

Wild Turkey Russell's Reserve Rye 45% ABV
www.wildturkeybourbon.com

Six years old but surprisingly set at a slightly lower strength than the favored 101, this is nevertheless another giant. There is some unexpected honey, nuttiness, and mint in the mix, some distinctive woodiness, and lots and lots of spice.

Wild Turkey Rye 50.5% ABV
www.wildturkeybourbon.com

This is the most bourbon-like rye on the market, but is no worse for that. The trademark rye pepper is all present and correct, but a wave of vanilla, licorice, and aniseed, and some orange fruits, make this rye easy-drinking and palatable.

Bottled at Jimmy Russell's preferred 101 proof, there is enough weight and richness to make this worth seeking out.

Wheat whiskey

Wheat whiskey is made in the same way as bourbon, but the wheat content must account for at least 51% of the grist. Wheat is not a particularly common ingredient in bourbon, but it was what Bill Samuels Sr. used to give Maker's Mark its softer, more female-friendly personality. Wheat whiskeys are also rare, but Heaven Hill has had significant success with Bernheim, and some of the new generation of microdistillers are turning to the style, most notably Dry Fly. The style is softer and sweeter than bourbon, more in keeping with a pure grain whiskey.

Bernheim 45% ABV
www.heaven-hill.com

For many years, Heaven Hill stood apart from the other distillers in Kentucky as the lone producer of both wheat and corn whiskeys. Now, though, as the United States wakes up to the potential of different whiskey styles, a new wave of both styles is upon us.

Wheat whiskey is notoriously difficult to make. The grain is more delicate and requires delicate handling. But as this bottling shows, the results can be remarkably impressive. This is the American drinking equivalent of wrapping yourself in a soft down comforter, a melt-in-the-mouth orange and lemon sorbet with a vanilla overcoat, and honey and spice in the finale.

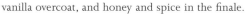

Dry Fly Wheat Whiskey 40% ABV
www.dryflydistilling.com

I have not tasted this, but it is included for three reasons: 1) because wheat whiskeys are so rare that any release in the category is a news story; 2) because in early 2010 this beat Bernheim in an Internet-based awards event, suggesting that the company behind it means business.; and 3) because it seems that this is a 100% malted wheat whiskey, making it pretty special. Dry Fly also produces other spirits using only local ingredients and is based in Spokane, Washington. By all accounts, this is not easy to find at all, but is well worth the effort.

Corn whiskey

Corn whiskey breaks all the rules when it comes to American whiskey production. It must include more than 80 percent corn; does not require aging; and, if it is matured, the barrels must be either virgin oak or used—they cannot be new and charred or toasted as with bourbon production. This is the style of whiskey most usually associated with moonshine—and the marketeers certainly do not shy away from this fact when they are considering such things as packaging and labeling.

Moonshine was produced on homemade stills and barely matured in casks, and the whole idea of drinking it young is part of the experience. That is at least partly due to the fact that corn makes for good sweet whiskey, like an alcoholic corn on the cob. If a drink genre ever reflected its culture, it's this one—it is no-frills hillbilly whiskey and damn proud of its history and heritage.

Dixie Dew 50% ABV
www.heaven-hill.com

NASCAR racing is one of the biggest commercial draws in the United States, and it has its roots firmly entwined with the days of whiskey-running. Cars would be converted to maximize storage space for moonshine, and the engines would be customized to ensure that, if the law did try to catch up with the whiskey-makers, they could outmotor them and race to cross a state line where legal jurisdiction changed. Cue the long-running U.S. television series *The Dukes of Hazzard*.

Dixie Dew has a rough-gut youthfulness about it, some sweet liqueur notes, and entertaining corn notes—corn on the cob in vodka, perhaps. An acquired taste and a basic one.

Georgia Moon 50% ABV
www.heaven-hill.com

The amateurish label, the jug-style packaging, and the proud boast that maturation took only days should forewarn you that this is going to be a cross-country motorbike ride, as rough around the edges as drinking whiskey gets. This is almost winey and vegetal, everything about it is short and sweet, and it is about as subtle as bare-knuckle boxing. Nonetheless, it feels and tastes pretty authentic.

Hudson New York Corn 46% ABV
www.tuthilltown.com

New York Corn is smooth and sweet, and, while lacking some of the bite and aggression of most Kentucky bourbon, is a pretty good entry-level whiskey. The smart packaging has ensured a smooth passage for the whiskeys into some of New York's cooler bars, and Tuthilltown can be credited with helping to change the attitudes of many urban drinkers toward the bourbon category.

J. W. Corn 50% ABV
www.heaven-hill.com

Searching for rare corn whiskeys should be declared a sport. This seems to have just about fallen off the map, but does turn up very occasionally. Older bottlings of it exist that contain eight-year-old whiskey originally distilled in Indiana. More recently, it has been bottled as a four-year-old, and the younger version is sweet and much fruitier than Georgia Moon and with less oily corn notes. Almost certainly, it is produced by Heaven Hill. The "J. W." refers to James Walsh & Co.

Mellow Corn 50% ABV
www.heaven-hill.com

If Georgia Moon comes across as a good impression of moonshine, this is at the other end of the spectrum. It is a soft, sweet, and full-corn whiskey with rounded and smooth edges, a gentle landing, and green apples and treacle toffee on the palate. This is easy-drinking whiskey and tastes significantly softer than most bourbons.

Other American whiskeys

Contrary to popular belief, bourbon does not have to be made in Kentucky, nor is it the only style of whiskey made in the United States. For many years now, a small number of distilleries have operated in other parts of the country making malt whiskey. Now a new generation of microdistillers is experimenting with wood types, grains, special finishes, groundbreaking blends, and hybrid products that mix production techniques from both single-malt whisky and bourbon production. It's all reminiscent of what happened with beer a few years back, albeit slower and smaller. It would be impossible to cover them all here— some produce at the tiniest of scales or intermittently—but this is a dynamic and exciting category all the same.

Catdaddy 40% ABV
www.catdaddymoonshine.com

Piedmont Distillers is based in Madison, North Carolina, and this is a triple-distilled flavored moonshine. It is made by New Yorker Joseph Michalek, who came to North Carolina and spotted an opportunity to reproduce the taste of some of the great illegal moonshine that was available at public events in the state. He will not say what spices and fruits are added to the mix, but technically this is somewhere between whiskey and flavored vodka.

A sister product that I have not come across is called Junior Johnson's Midnight Moon, named after a famous moonshiner, and is described as: "Smoother than vodka, better than whiskey. Best shine ever." Mmm . . .

Charbay Hop Flavored Whiskey 64% ABV
www.charbay.com

Not strictly a whiskey at all because hops are used in the mashbill, giving a distinctive hoppy and floral aspect to the taste. But this warrants inclusion because it is one of several examples that shows where U.S. microdistillers might head—effectively creating new whiskey-infused drinks categories and potentially setting the world of whiskey on fire. This is made in St. Helena, California, and is big, bold, and impressive.

Early Times 40% ABV
www.brown-forman.com

Another whiskey that is bending the distilling rules, Early Times is produced at Brown-Forman's Louisville distillery and disqualifies itself from being called bourbon because some of the spirit is matured in used barrels. The result is perfectly acceptable—a light, sweet vanilla ice cream with maplewood syrup and crushed nuts.

Edgefield Hogshead 46% ABV
www.mcmenamins.com

McMenamins is a hotel and pub company in Oregon and prides itself on originality and authenticity. It has been brewing its own beer for 25 years now, making it an easy forerunner of the recent microbrewery insurgency, and it now has an impressive 24 breweries producing 200 new recipes a year. It makes its own wine, roasts its own coffee, and, as of 12 years ago, started distilling. This big, soppy monster of a whiskey is proof that someone knows what they are doing. It is a toffee-rich and full-fruited single malt with a unique character and an unsubtle, uncompromising mouthfeel. Some honeycomb candy and wood enter the mix, too.

Kessler 40% ABV
www.jimbeam.com

This is an American blended whiskey, which means that it is a mix of bourbon and unaged or grain-neutral spirit. As a style, it has fallen from popularity, but Kessler is one of the category's biggest labels. It is named after Julius Kessler, who sold whiskey in the late 1800s, and the whiskey's motto is "Smooth as silk." It certainly lives up to its claims, although some licorice, citrus, and spice notes ensure that the experience here is far from bland.

McCarthy's Oregon Single Malt 47.5% ABV
www.clearcreekdistillery.com

If ever a distillery sounded as if it were in Kentucky, it is Clear Creek. And if ever an American whiskey tasted less like bourbon . . .

This is a single malt that is a smoky monster, with engine oil, barbecued fish, and a charriness on the nose. Tastewise, it is very sweet and rich in peat, but delightfully balanced by the grain. This is the drinking equivalent of American soccer—it appears to be very like the European game, but has been tweaked to give it a personality of its own.

Stranahan's Colorado Whiskey 47% ABV
www.stranhans.com

The result of an unlikely alliance between a Colorado spirits connoisseur and a part-time fireman who helped to save his barn from burning down, Stranahan's is a single malt dressed in a Kentucky colonel's finery. So you get candy stick, vanilla, honeycomb candy, leather polish, spice, and oak, but the whole mix has a barley malt heart. A bit like drinking very old grain whiskey matured in bourbon casks—arguably providing the best of both worlds.

Rogue Dead Guy 40% ABV
www.rogue.com

Oregon-based Rogue is part of the new wave of great North American beer-makers, and it makes some of the most exciting and tasty beers in the world, selling them in irreverent, almost punk-like packaging. Dead Guy was released by the company some years back to mark the Mexican Day of the Dead, and its rich flavors are the result of four different malts. This whiskey is distilled from that beer and is every bit as quirky as the ale. There is a delicious spiciness, as well as youthful fruitiness.

Triple Eight Notch 44.4% ABV
www.ciscobrewers.com

Triple Eight distillery is part of Sisco Brewers on Nantucket Island, Massachusetts. The company makes a range of spirits and was at the vanguard of the microdistilling revolution when it was formed in 1997. The company's single-malt whiskey was created with the support of former Morrison Bowmore distilling consultant George McClements. The whiskey is finished in ex-Merlot casks—potentially risky—but the result is impressive, with soft canned fruits and vanilla in the mix. It has been given the name "Notch" because it's not Scotch. Geddit?

St. George 43% ABV
www.stgeorgespirits.com

Made in Almeda, California, this is a single malt that so impressed a couple of members of my whiskey club that they made a detour while on vacation in the United States just to visit the distillery. St. George is made in very small quantities, and each batch differs from the next, but it is distilled from a smoky brown ale, due to the barley being heavily roasted. Some malt is dried over alder and beech. The spirit is matured for three to five years, mainly in bourbon casks, but also in French oak and port casks. Sound good? It is. It has been a while since I tasted this, but the batch we had was sweet, very fruity, and quite complex, with some cocoa, milk chocolate, toasted oak, and a touch of mint at the finish.

Wasmund's Rappahannock Single Malt 48% ABV
www.copperfox.biz

The Copper Fox distillery sits beneath the Blue Ridge Mountains of Virginia, and distiller Rick Wasmund is on a mission. He learned his trade by spending some time working at Bowmore, but returned to the United States with a burning desire to use all he had learned, taking it to a new place. Some of the malt here is dried over apple and cherry wood, and it shows in the end product. Wasmund's is made barrel by barrel, so there will be some variety in taste. But expect to pick up some oak and smoke, and some unusual yellow fruit notes. Bizarrely, this is exported to Liechtenstein, which, as described elsewhere in this book, has just started bottling its own whisky.

THE WORLD'S BEST WHISKIES

CANADA

Canada

Several years ago, the late whisky and beer writer Michael Jackson was invited to Canada to visit a distillery, so he extended a trip to the United States and headed north.

But when he arrived at the Canadian border, he was refused entry and quizzed about his reasons for entering the country.

"I'm a journalist, and I want to write about a whisky distillery in Canada," he announced.

Not good enough, he was told, to justify giving him an entry visa.

"Canada has journalists of its own," he was told. "Why would we let a foreign journalist come and do a job that a Canadian could do?"

Perhaps because an unbiased international whisky writer stating that Canada had great whisky to discover would have more authority in overseas whisky circles than if one of their own sang its praises, Michael pointed out.

In the end, the Canadian authorities relented, but the story goes some way toward explaining Canada's disjointed relationship with the rest of the world of whisky. To be fair, it has less to do with Canadian whisky and more to do with the overofficious and outdated protective nature of the country's authorities. Even so, Canadian whisky does not attempt to sell itself in the same way as Irish whiskey or bourbon does.

Or at least not in Europe, anyway. With Scotland dominating the world of whisky today, and Ireland providing it with much of its historical context, there is an assumption that other whisky markets should kowtow to the "old" markets. Not Canada. It has a proud whisky tradition of its own and knows which side its bread is buttered on—and that side is known as the United States. Canadian whisky still sells by the oceanload in the United States, and much of it is owned by international companies with large U.S. interests. Beyond some key brands such as Canadian Club and Crown Royal, there is simply not that much of an incentive for Canadian brands to seek out markets elsewhere.

The American connection has helped to define Canada's whisky. Although Canada is associated with rye, whiskies from the country are nothing like the fierce, spicy, and flavorsome American ryes that are exciting whisky enthusiasts across the world.

ONTARIO

● VANCOUVER

QUEBEC ●

CANADIAN DISTILLERY PROFILE

1 Kittling Ridge PAGES 210–211

TORONTO ●
GRIMSBY ● 1

Canada's whiskies have been lighter in style, easy-drinking, easy-mixing whiskies made through a complex process of combining many different whiskies, which are produced using an array of grains. Most Canadian whisky is blended, although there are a few grains and a notable exception at Glen Breton in Nova Scotia where, unsurprisingly, the local folk look to Scotland's single-malt whisky for inspiration. The distillery achieved international fame (or notoriety depending on your point of view) when the Scotch Whisky Association went to war with it and, in the eyes of many, made an ass of itself in the process.

There are other reasons that Canada stands alone. Its liquor sales are controlled by the state, and its whisky-making industry, once characterized by hundreds of small distilleries, has in recent years been the story of drinks giants such as Schenley, Seagram, and Hiram Walker. Some Canadian brands are owned by Kentucky bourbon producers, and some even include bourbon in their recipe due to a somewhat bizarre law that permits a fraction of a Canadian blend to be made up with another liquid, which can often include fruit juice or foreign whisky.

So it should come as no surprise that some parts of the Canadian whisky industry have an identity crisis and other bits appear complacent, satisfied, and smug.

The final part of the picture, however, is made up by the small number of innovators and trendsetters within the country. Unfortunately for many of us, they are too small to make too much of a mark internationally, but they provide enough evidence that Canada as a whisky market is not finished quite yet. It just needs to get better at opening its doors to the world and telling us its story.

Single malt

Glenora distillery is in Nova Scotia, and unsurprisingly folk there are proud of their links with Scotland. So when they decided to make malt whisky, they imported Scottish barley Glen Breton and turned to Scotland for their stills.

They have been producing whisky on and off for 20 years now, but it has been a bumpy journey. Lack of funds threatened to unseat them, and they also attracted the ire of the Scotch Whisky Association, which made few friends with its heavy-handed approach toward the distillery. Thankfully, despite this, the whisky is still flowing.

Glen Breton 10-year-old 43% ABV

The nose here is slightly doughy and oily, with a trace of orange and some honeyed sweetness. Tastewise, there are toffee and fruit, and a gentle wave of prickly peat. Comparisons with Scottish single malt are inevitable. This is slightly lower down the soccer league, more of a Hibs or Hearts than a Rangers or Celtic.

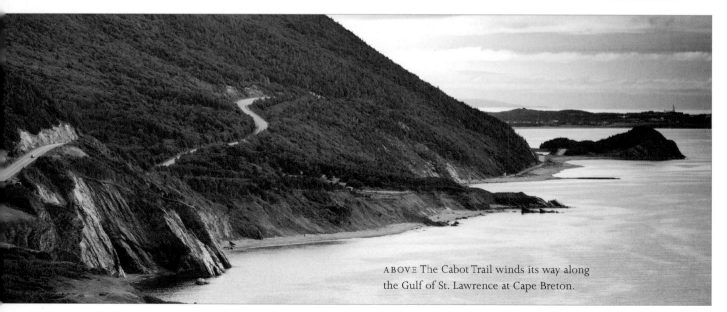

ABOVE The Cabot Trail winds its way along the Gulf of St. Lawrence at Cape Breton.

Blends

The dominant style of Canadian whisky is a combination of several different whisky styles, including a number of different rye recipes, often from the same distillery and mainly produced in column stills. Sometimes Kentucky bourbon is used in the mix.

Alberta Premium
40% ABV

A complex and challenging whisky, with orange and lemon, and vanilla on the nose, and a chewy toffee and rich fruit heart. It is nicely balanced, perfectly palatable, and is subtle and nuanced.

Alberta Springs
10-year-old 40% ABV

If you have a sweet tooth, then this is for you. It is a rye-dominated whisky and a perfect starting point to understanding how different the Canadian version is to the American one. This is all about vanilla and caramel on the palate, with some pepper in the mix.

Canadian Club 6-year-old 40% ABV

This may well be the brand that caused Chicago's St. Valentine's Day Massacre because it was shipped in huge quantities by Al Capone down the lakes from Canada and into the United States during Prohibition. Undoubtedly, the brand was established as a big player at that time, and it has maintained its position as one of the world's best-known whiskies. The whiskies are mixed after distillation and before maturation, and there are a number of expressions available.

This is oily and spirity, with a fruity base. It is stereotyping the whisky, I know, but this really does show its truest colors when mixed.

Canadian Club Classic
40% ABV

Vanilla, yellow fruits, and honey on the nose; raisin, berries, overripe banana, and vanilla ice cream on the palate; and confectioners' sugar and cinnamon spice to top it all off. This is a real treat.

Canadian Club Reserve 10-year-old 40% ABV

Arguably the best expression in the Canadian Club range. Here, the oiliness works alongside green fruits and some white wine flavors, there are some wood and spice in the mix, and considerably more body than you might expect.

Canadian Mist 40% ABV

An oddball whisky from an oddball distillery that has achieved big sales in the United States. It is made using corn and malted barley, then transported to Kentucky, where it is mixed with a proportion of Kentucky rye. And for what purpose, exactly? A whisky that whispers, an innocuous, mild, sweet, and fruity nothingness. Like any winner of *The X Factor* (with the exception of Leona Lewis): pleasant enough, but easily forgotten.

Crown Royal 40% ABV

Now part of the Diageo empire, this whisky was originally created by legendary drinks boss Sam Bronfman when he was head of Seagram, and it has a long and illustrious history. It is a thoroughbred blend, too, flowing with juicy grains, rich and delightful fruit, and some stunning peppery notes. Unlike some of its national rivals, it is not oversweet, either.

Crown Royal Special Reserve 40% ABV

It is hard to remain focused on the job in hand sometimes, and the mind wanders, especially when you are faced with some pretty ordinary whiskies that, hand on heart, you know will not make the cut.

Before getting to this, for instance, I had three samples that will remain nameless, and while tasting them I found myself wondering what odds I would get on Eddie Izzard becoming Britain's first transvestite prime minister. If you are reading this and wondering who on earth I am talking about, that would suggest pretty good odds. If you are thinking he is just an oddball comedian and would never get elected as a politician, you are probably right.

But my reasoning goes like this: He is very intelligent, much loved, has a social conscience, and is debating standing as a Labour candidate in the future. He is an Internationalist and respectful of other cultures. I once took a French girl to see him on stage, and such is the nature of his comedy that she spent the entire performance asking me to explain his jokes, so that being there was a waste of time for both of us. Weeks later, she rang to say that she went to see him again in Paris, and he did the whole performance in French. And in 2010 he pulled off the almost impossible feat of running 43 marathons in 51 days, and raised more than £1 million for SportsAid—a quite awesome achievement made all the more so by the fact that he is chubby and he has bad feet from wearing high heels. This makes him a British national treasure.

Yep, definite long-term prime minister potential I would say. But perhaps I am just delirious after too much bad Canadian whisky. Thank goodness we are back on track with this one, then—lots of fresh tropical fruits, traces of spice, and rich, oily rye. Quite possibly my favorite Canadian whisky.

Forty Creek Barrel Select 40% ABV

The nose does not do this whisky any favors. It is young and spirity, and not great, to be honest. Thankfully, the taste picks up the pace, with an intriguing layered attack. On the surface, it is as flat as a summer pond; underneath, there are some grungier, meatier notes among the fruit.

Forty Creek Double Barrel Reserve 40% ABV

Soft, fruity, and candied, with strawberry and sweet lime present early on, then a mix of fruits, some spice, and some oil from the grain as this complex whisky opens up.

It is like going on the latest ride at the theme park, one that is like nothing that has gone before. But whether you will like the experience or not is another matter. All credit to Kittling Ridge for daring to be different, though.

Forty Creek Portwood Reserve

45% ABV

Bold, winey nose that is almost liqueur-like. The mouthfeel is rich and oily, and you can taste a battle between the Canadian rye and the port and fruit influences. It is almost chewy in its intensity, and opens new doors for whisky from this part of the world.

Seagram's 83 40% ABV

The number refers to 1883, the year in which the Seagram company was founded. This is a classic Canadian blend, with a sharp grainy core, some lemon notes, and a rich and smooth taste that provides the perfect platform for mixers.

Wiser's Deluxe 40% ABV

One of the fruitiest whiskies to come out of Canada and one of the most pleasant: The oil-paint nose that characterizes a lot of Canadian whisky is a turnoff, but the soft grains, the honeycomb-candy heart, and some attractive vanilla and oak alongside the rich fruits all work in this whisky's favor.

KITTLING RIDGE ESTATES WINES & SPIRITS

297 South Service Road, Grimsby, Ontario L3M 1Y6
www.kittlingridge.com

In some parts of the world, making innovative and exciting whiskies is akin to climbing a mountain without a map—and you have to be a bit crazy to do it.

Take the case of John Hall, the man behind the Forty Creek whiskies produced by Kittling Ridge in Canada.

The Canadians will hate it being said, but Canadian whisky has stagnated and failed to keep up with the pace of progress in other parts of the world. Canadian whisky is still a player—it sells more than Scottish, Irish, and American whisky put together in North America—but its whiskies are owned by big companies and, unlike virtually every whisky-making country, Canada has few innovators or exciting and dynamic new whiskies. In the nineteenth century, Canada had more than 200 independent whisky makers. Now, there are hardly any.

John Hall, though, is proving that Canada can produce whisky of the highest standard, and since 1992 when he set up his distillery he has been doing it by tearing up the rule book and experimenting with tastes and flavors. A winemaker by trade, he came to whisky-making with no baggage.

"I am a first-generation whisky maker, so I have no restrictions as to how I paint my canvas," he says. "I have often thought that, if I was a twelfth-generation whisky maker, it would be a really boring job having to make whisky exactly the way it had been made for 12 generations. I am not bound by tradition; I am inspired by it."

He started by throwing away the test book that explained how he needed to put the mashbill together, then turned to the way the spirit was distilled.

"I followed my intuition," he explains. "After all, I didn't make wine by mixing all the varieties together. At breakfast time, I don't mix my cereals together. Corn doesn't taste like barley, and rye doesn't taste like corn, so why would you mix them together at the start of the process? So I treated each of my grains the same way as a noble grape variety, trying to bring the best taste characteristics of each varietal grain.

"This meant I would make my whiskies

as single grains, bringing out the fruitiness and spiciness of the rye, the nuttiness of the barley, and the heartiness of the corn. Each of these grains has unique taste characteristics, and to me it was important to define them and bring them out as singular whiskies.

"In Canada, all whiskies are column-distilled. It wasn't like that in the 1800s. Back then, whisky makers used copper pot stills, but whisky makers moved to column stills because it was cost-effective. I use copper stills because they capture not just the alcohol, but also the flavor."

Hall has taken a radically unusual approach to maturation and barrel selection, too, and has even gone as far as to make his own sherry to fill casks that would later be used to hold whisky.

"The first thing I learned as a whisky maker was that I needed more patience and passion," says Hall. "As a wine maker, I could have a wine out on the market within a couple of years. As a whisky maker, I would have to wait ten years. If you are truly passionate, then the tedious preparation of the barrels must be done. It's very time consuming, but it has to be done."

Hall's approach has resulted in a range of whiskies that taste like nothing else on earth and are taking Canadian whiskies into new and exciting areas. He has not abandoned his country's whisky traditions, and his whiskies are distinctly Canadian, but they are rich with new and exciting flavors. His efforts have been recognized across the world, and all the signs are that there is plenty more to come. He is climbing up the mountain when everyone else seems to be getting off it because the conditions are so bleak.

"I am very humbled to be acknowledged by the industry, by fellow whisky makers, customers, and whisky writers," he says. "These accolades have reinforced my quest to continue to follow my dream. And I hope that my passion for creating handcrafted Canadian whisky will encourage many others to follow."

KEY WHISKIES

Forty Creek Barrel Select 40% ABV
Forty Creek Portwood Reserve 45% ABV
Forty Creek Double Barrel Reserve 40% ABV

ABOVE TOP The Kittling Ridge Distillery in Grimsby, Ontario, was founded in 1992.

ABOVE John Hall, founder of Kittling Ridge, inspects one of his new, highly regarded Canadian whiskies.

LEFT The distillery's distinctive copper column stills.

THE WORLD'S BEST WHISKIES

IRELAND

Ireland

Until spring 2007, Ireland's whiskey industry was like a big old dusty museum. You could visit a whiskey distillery in the Irish Republic all right—you were just not able to experience whiskey being made.

There is plenty for the whiskey tourist to do. The Jameson visitor center is plush and stylish—but free of the aroma of fermentation and distillation. There is the stunning old distillery at Midleton, where you can all but hear the laughter of the workers, but today it is a mass of open space and unused distilling equipment. And most depressing of all is Tullamore, a distillery in a rural backwater, where you can walk around the museum exhibits, then sit by the canal that once took the casks away to the ports and off to the rest of the world, and now sits idle, its banks overgrowing and the midges dancing in the summer sun. There are ghosts to be found everywhere.

Until spring 2007, you could have added Locke's Museum at Kilbeggan to the list of ghost distilleries. That was until owners Cooley fired up one of the old stills and started distilling there once more. In 2010, the company bottled its first whiskey at the site.

Ireland does produce whiskey, of course. It is just that, certainly in the south, whiskey is produced where people are not permitted to visit. The only two large fully operational distilleries are Irish Distillers' huge and impressive Midleton plant at Cork, which towers over the old distillery and is probably the most advanced distillery in Europe, and Cooley, which occupies the site of an old industrial alcohol plant and is hidden away in foothills on the east coast.

Cooley is looking at the possibility of allowing visitors there, too, but for the time being it means that Ireland does not celebrate its whiskey in the same way that Scotland, America, Japan, and Canada do.

"It is true," says Cooley's managing director, Jack Teeling. "Ireland's still got plenty of pubs, but no distilleries to visit."

The good news, however, is that Ireland does have whiskey—very good whiskey. And with Jameson opening the door for Ireland in more and more markets, Diageo giving some much-deserved support to Bushmills, a single-malt distillery in the north, and Cooley playing the role of maverick by shaking up the industry and giving drinkers a diverse and unusual range of whiskeys to choose between, Irish whiskey is in pretty good shape. Ignore all the blarney about how Ireland has the oldest whiskey, and how none of it is peated and all of Scotland's is, and how it is all triple-distilled and none of Scotland's is. The repetition of such inaccuracies sounds like a nation clutching at straws.

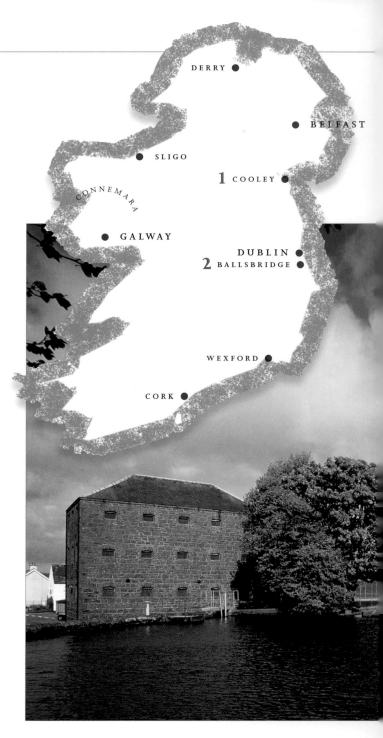

Instead, get yourself a glass of something special—an older Bushmills, a rare Midleton, a vintage Jameson, a peated Connemara, or a stunning Tyrconnell, perhaps—and enjoy Irish whiskey for what it is: first-class spirit perfected over generations, and still as relevant as ever.

ABOVE Bushmills is Ireland's oldest whiskey distillery, located just a few miles away from the spectacular Giant's Causeway. It is now owned by the drinks giant Diageo.

RIGHT Noel Sweeney, master distiller at Cooley Distillery, northeast of Dublin on the Cooley Peninsula, noses a sampling next to the still.

Irish single-malt whiskey

Until the launch of Cooley a few years ago, Irish single-malt whiskey had become something of a novelty, a tradition kept alive at Bushmills, north of Belfast. But Ireland once had scores of distilleries, many of them making whiskey using only malted barley. Cooley has resurrected some of the lost names and given Irish single-malt whiskey a new lease on life through award-winning single malts such as Connemara and Tyrconnell. Cooley has also started emulating some of the diversity found in Scotland by introducing peated whiskies, as well as whiskies finished in a range of cask types.

Bushmills 10-year-old 40% ABV

This is summer fruits in a glass, with orange, yellow, and green fruit wrapped up with honey in the nose, while sweet grape, summer fruits, and red apples appear on the palate, before dark cocoa and pepper arrive to give the whisky some shape. A definitive Irish whiskey.

Bushmills 16-year-old 40% ABV

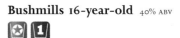

The extra few years in the cask give this expression an extra weightiness, with oak and spice adding an extra dimension to the malt. Beautifully crafted, and elegant on the palate.

Connemara 40% ABV

Gentle smoke, twiggy and dry leaves, then a heady mix of apple, fresh barley, green fruits, and just enough smoke to keep it all interesting. The peat and savory notes get stronger toward the end.

Connemara 10-year-old Sherry Finish

46% ABV

A strange journey indeed, this. Early on, this is like cooking a cob of corn on an open fire—you get rootsy embers and musty flavor, but then, on the palate, peat and plum grapple with each other and sherried notes march through the middle. But the peat wins out. Extraordinary.

Connemara 12-year-old 46% ABV

This is a wicked mix—a bit like hip-hop band Run DMC covering an Aerosmith single, or Lemmy, lead singer of heavy rock band Motorhead, appearing with Britney Spears—not quite what you might expect, but it has the potential to be quite wonderful. This is soft, rounded, and gently smoked, but with gooseberries, oak, and unripe green fruits dominating before a strong and spicy conclusion.

Connemara Cask Strength 60% ABV

Here, you will find an aroma of Hornby train set, oily burnt dust on the nose, with some polished wood notes. The palate is quite sublime: canned soft fruits, wood fire, and some sweet milk chocolate and cocoa. Smoke stays in the conclusion.

Locke's 8-year-old 40% ABV

This tastes young, with fresh cereal and some lemon and orange notes on the nose, while later on some sour lemon and lime, cutting chili pepper, and a degree of astringency appear.

The Tyrconnell 40% ABV

Anybody who tells you that Irish whiskey cannot offer variety needs to line up a Locke's, a Connemara, and this. It is all sherbet fruits and Starburst candy on the nose, some apple and pear, orange, and mandarin on the palate, and some oak. Refreshing, summery, and full of flavor.

The Tyrconnell 15-year-old Single Cask 957/92 46% ABV

Lemon, bitter orange, and melon on the nose here, while the palate is rich with demerara sugar, sweet fruits, some wood and spice, and nutty almonds. The finish is pleasant and medium-sweet.

The Tyrconnell 15-year-old Single Cask 1850/52 46% ABV

Sweet melon, yellow fruits, vanilla, and clean grain on the nose, a dash of chewy spearmint, then toffee apple. Late on, you will encounter other green fruits, with a bit of pepper at the finish.

The Tyrconnell 10-year-old Madeira Finish 46% ABV

This is an extraordinary, world-class whiskey by anybody's standards. The nose is a wonderful mix of fresh exotic fruits, with sweet lime and fruity and sherbety elements. It tastes like canned fruits covered in Jell-O, and it goes on, with fruity ice cream on canned pears at the finish.

The Tyrconnell 10-year-old Port Finish 46% ABV

Here is another one that reaches for the stars, but just falls a tad short of the Madeira finish. This has some rum and raisin notes and richness, thanks to the port.

The Tyrconnell 10-year-old Sherry Finish 46% ABV

Dusty lemon-polished wooden office notes on the nose, then sherry fruits, red and black berries, and some wood. Pleasant, balanced, but just a tad directionless, given this brand name's very high quality standards.

The Wild Geese Single Malt 43% ABV

If you have ever been around a brewery or, better still, a cider maker, you will know the unusual aroma that is a mix of yeast, malt, and slightly stale ale. It is not unpleasant, just unusual, and you get it on this whiskey, at least initially. Toffee then takes over, and there are some fresh apple notes. The taste is actually quite meek after the intro, but perfectly pleasant, with apple and pear, and some spice.

Irish blended whiskey

Irish blended whiskey is the signature whiskey style from Ireland, but it is a different drink entirely than the blends produced by Scotland. In Ireland, a blend is a mix of pot-still whiskey and grain whiskey, and, unlike in Scotland, the various whiskeys are blended before going into the cask for maturation. Irish blends were traditionally regional, so that in Dublin it was Guinness and Paddy; in Cork and the southwest, Murphys and Powers. The two main distilleries in the south—the mighty and massive Midleton, and the smaller but flexible Cooley—are complex in that they produce grain and malt whiskies, then blend them all under the same roof, using different combinations of pot-still and column-still whiskeys to make different brands.

Bushmills Black Bush 40% ABV

Black Bush is an old and iconic whiskey—a fine example of what the country is capable of when it comes to full-bodied blended Irish whiskey. There is a mountain of fresh fruits in the taste, but juicy golden raisins and a clutch of savory and sweet spices ensure that this twists and turns from start to finish.

Bushmills Original 40% ABV

If Bushmills is a prizefighter of a whiskey, this is the street equivalent, a bare-knuckle bruiser trained at Ryan's gym and as rough and ready as you would expect. You can almost see the tattoos. That said, the grain at the core is vintage Ireland, and it is good value for money. File with Powers and Paddy in the "unreconstituted" section. . . .

COOLEY DISTILLERY

Riverstown, Cooley, County Louth
www.cooleywhiskey.com

Until a few years ago, Ireland's whiskey industry found itself floundering on the margins, increasingly becoming a bit player, with a couple of solid brands.

No longer. While it would be exaggerating to say that Irish whiskey has undergone a revolution in the past decade, it has certainly been transformed; although still relatively small, it is more dynamic than it has been for many a year.

There are three reasons for the turnaround: the success of Jameson on the world stage, and with it the desire by Irish Distillers to launch expressions of the brand into the premium whiskey category; the new life given to Bushmills since it was sold to Diageo and came out of the shadow of Jameson; and, most of all, the arrival of Cooley to provide Irish whiskey with a much-needed shot in the arm.

Cooley is the brainchild of John Teeling, a somewhat larger-than-life figure who has made his money in mining, including for gold and diamonds. The day-to-day running of the business has now been placed in the hands of his two sons, Jack and Stephen.

The company's importance to the Irish whiskey story cannot be overestimated. Its arrival just about doubled the number of whiskeys on offer to the customer, and has provided real choice. For a while, virtually all Irish whiskey from south of the border was made at Irish Distillers' Midleton plant—from Jameson to Paddy, Powers, and Redbreast, through to whiskeys such as Green Spot and Tullamore Dew.

Worse still, you had to travel north of Belfast to see a working whiskey man. Midleton does not allow tourists, and the only places you could visit—Tullamore, Locke's, and the Old Jameson distilleries in Dublin and Midleton—are museums. Or, in the case of Locke's, were; Cooley has been bringing the distillery at Kilbeggan back to life.

"It's true enough that Ireland has always had more than its fair share of pubs, but no distilleries to visit," says company managing director Jack Teeling. "It makes it hard for the whiskey enthusiast to share the experience as they can in Scotland and America. It's something we have been very aware of and have tried to do something about."

With a determination bordering on craziness, Cooley set about trying to produce whiskey at Locke's. No easy task because, while the equipment there was beautifully preserved, it was, quite literally, from another era. In 2007, however, the company started distilling on the site; in 2010, it bottled its first whiskey from it.

Cooley has brought a fresh impetus to Irish whiskey. The peated but fruity Connemara is a reminder that peat did play a role in Irish whiskey's past, and is a bottled poke in the eye to all the Irish tour guides who claim that Irish whiskey never uses peat, while all Scottish malts do. Tyrconnell is world-class premium whiskey by any standards, and Greenore is a quality grain whiskey, demonstrating another aspect of the nation's distilling past.

Cooley has battled hard to survive and prosper through difficult times, but now, armed with a clutch of awards for its brands and a solid portfolio that is becoming better known by the month, the future is looking bright.

"Perhaps we need to inject some of the fun back into Irish whiskey," says Teeling.

"Jameson has kept the door open for Irish whiskey and is finding new markets. We have some great whiskeys for those who want to explore further.

"But other countries are offering a whiskey experience which we need to match, and it is within the Irish character to do it well. If we get that right, Irish whiskey can prosper. It's win–win for everyone."

Indeed, it is—and with the three Irish rivals competing with one another, but all working for Irish whiskey, the comeback is set to continue. That's good news for all of us.

ABOVE Cooley is helping to bring some of Ireland's more neglected and dilapidated whiskey museums back to life.

RIGHT This may be a case of smoke and mirrors, but the Kilbeggan distillery is at last enjoying a new lease of life under Cooley.

KEY WHISKEYS

Connemara 40% ABV
Connemara 10-year-old Sherry Finish 46% ABV
Connemara 12-year-old 46% ABV
Connemara Cask Strength 60% ABV
Greenore 15-year-old 43% ABV
Kilbeggan 40% ABV
Kilbeggan 15-year-old 40% ABV
Locke's 40% ABV
The Tyrconnell 40% ABV
The Tyrconnell 15-year-old Single Cask 957/92 46% ABV
The Tyrconnell 15-year-old Single Cask 1850/52 46% ABV
The Tyrconnell 10-year-old Madeira Finish 46% ABV
The Tyrconnell 10-year-old Sherry Finish 46% ABV
The Tyrconnell 10-year-old Port Finish 46% ABV

Jameson 40% ABV

This is a world trailblazer right now, single-handedly burning a path for Ireland into new and exciting territories as the world once more realizes that Ireland can produce world-class whiskey. This may be a standard and ubiquitous whiskey, but do not let familiarity breed contempt—it is a beauty. All the rounded fruit content is there and present, but there are some luscious red berry notes from the sherry, some oiliness from the pot-still whiskey, and some spices and oak. This is the work of distillers at the very peak of their craft—and a total delight.

Jameson 12-year-old Special Reserve 40% ABV

The years in wood give this a richer and fuller sherry content than the standard bottling; there are more pepper and spice, and a noticeable and delightful toasted oak content.

Jameson 18-year-old Gold Reserve 40% ABV

For many years, Jameson employed a man named John Ryan as a brand ambassador. His sophisticated and cultured accent gave little indication of his Irish roots, but he loves his country and knows its history and culture inside out—including its fractious relationship with Britain.

His approach to promoting Irish whiskey to journalists was simple: Do not force it on them, or try to market it. Just give them a wonderful Irish experience that happens to include whiskey, and they will naturally fall in love with it. Some years ago, we were put up at a hotel near Cork, where it was required that a suit and tie be worn for dinner. The entertainment was the sort of plastic Paddy diddle-ie-ay-do stuff, and John Ryan was so appalled by it that he decided to take us to a "real" pub in Cork. Before he went in, he told us that we should leave when he told us to.

So we walked through the door in suits and ties, and the pub fell silent. A group of leather-jacketed youths just stared at us. It turns out that we had gone in to a staunchly Republican pub.

Ryan ordered a bottle of Jameson, produced an acoustic guitar, and headed off to a back room, where he proceeded to regale us with IRA and

Republican songs. He offered the bottle around the bar and, within minutes, the regulars had joined our table for a whiskey and some rousing versions of songs about freeing Ireland from the Brits.

John Ryan insisted on ordering another bottle, then challenged us English to sing a song. There was only one volunteer, and all he could muster was a weak version of "On Ilkla Moor Bah T'at," to general amusement among our hosts. After some more IRA songs, Ryan announced we were leaving. The locals insisted that their new Brit friends stay, but Ryan was adamant. So, to loud applause, pats on backs, and shakes of hand, we left. That is whiskey for you.

Another wonderful example of aged Jameson, with the fruity green fruit flavors mingling with oak, spice, and some quite delicious sweet honeycomb candy. Some red berries are in there, too, and it is all held together by the rich oiliness provided by the pot-still whiskey. Outstanding.

Jameson Rarest Vintage Reserve 46% ABV

Nobody can throw a party quite like the Irish. When they launched this most special of Irish whiskeys, Irish Distillers brought journalists from around the world for a hoolie and a half. They put us up in a new hotel near Cork that was so big it took 20 minutes to walk to your room. This made the round trip 40 minutes—and that is my excuse for making the decision in the early hours to ensure that I did not miss an early morning departure by sleeping in the bar. The party included an exclusive concert by the amazing Sinead O'Connor, who not only performed a surprisingly hit-friendly set, but also sat on my table. Watching her sing "Nothing Compares 2U" in a small venue while drinking this rare whiskey is up there with my best memories.

The whiskey is stupendous, made with the finest, very old whiskeys, and with a price tag to match. But it is the fruitiest, tastiest, oiliest, spiciest, and fullest Irish whiskey you will ever taste. Best of all, its strength has been boosted from 40% to 46%, giving it the muscle power to compete with the top whiskies of Scotland, Japan, and the United States.

Kilbeggan 40% ABV

A value-for-money whiskey that puts up quite a showing. There are cereal notes and some fresh barley, but plenty of green fruit and the odd hint of lemon at the finish.

Kilbeggan 15-year-old 40% ABV

The man behind Cooley, which makes this whiskey, is not a natural whiskey maker. He made his money in, among other things, diamond, gold, and copper mining, and, bizarrely, he mined zinc in Limerick, Ireland. He is just a little crazy, and opened Cooley in 1987 because he thought it would be fun. One of his crazier ideas was to get Kilbeggan up and running again, but in 2007 he did just that. Kilbeggan sits on the main route from Dublin to the west coast; when the economy was booming, Friday nights through the region was one long traffic jam as affluent Dubliners headed off to their boats. So imagine their outrage when they found the road blocked by a pot still. Cooley brought traffic to a standstill for hours as it tried to put new stills in place. But whiskey is being produced again at the site. If it matures as well as this has, it will be worth waiting for. This has cereal, honey, and rich oak notes, as well as the trademark fruit.

Locke's 40% ABV

If you have a sweet tooth, then this should be right up your street. It is a solid, chunky honey monster of a whiskey, with a pleasant and balanced mix of malt and grain.

Midleton Very Rare 2008 Bottling 40% ABV

Midleton is the name of the big Irish Distillers'–owned distillery near Cork, and this is a small-quantity annual release, so it will vary from batch to batch. On the whole, though, the standard is pretty good. This one starts off with soft, fluffy apples, then is taken over by a sharp razor-edged wave of oak and spice, suggesting that some very old whiskeys are in the mix, and concludes with a honeyed oiliness. Great stuff.

Paddy 40% ABV

This is included here because Paddy is in the memory banks, a throwback to a different, quieter, more naive Ireland, when every village had at least one pub that looked like someone's living room and where you were made to feel completely at home, whoever you were. Every one of those pubs had an old boy nursing a pint of stout and a whiskey chaser, studying the racing form. Give him the chance, and he would tell you amazing stories from his past and offer sound advice. Paddy was that old boy. I am sure that pubs like this still exist in Ireland, but there have been huge changes over the past 30 years. As a brand, this is going nowhere and it is an acquired taste—but it is a taste of history, an everyday blend with some pleasant pot still–induced moments, a straight-ahead maltiness mostly, then a twist of pepper to finish.

Powers 12-year-old 40% ABV

A blend dominated by rich, mouth-filling, oily, grainy, pulsating pot-still whiskey and another traditional classic Irish whiskey. This time, though, this is relevant in the way that a big old Triumph Bonneville motorcycle is relevant, powered on the twin engines of hard solid grain and the pot-still whiskey. Big, rich, fluffy green fruit and a sharp and incisive wave of spice.

Powers Gold Label 40% ABV

There is an argument that with some whiskies, particularly peat ones, years in the cask integrate the flavor, but dull the impact—a bit like when you add curry powder to meat. While young, all you get from the curry is chili burn; only over time does the spice become integrated and balanced. Thing is, if you like a big chili hit, younger is best. This is what has happened here. It is much mellower, smoother, and more rounded than the original version, so the oily pot-still and pepper spice is more balanced and pleasant, but nowhere near the roller-coaster ride. Better than standard Powers? Debatable. I am a raw chili man, myself.

IRISH DISTILLERS PERNOD RICARD

Simmonscourt House, Simmonscourt Road, Ballsbridge, Dublin 4
www.irishdistillers.de

There is no doubt that this is a golden age for Irish whiskey.

If you take Irish Distillers' three wise men—master distillers Barry Crockett, Billy Leighton, and David Quinn—include retired maestro Brendan Monks, maverick whiskey maker Barry Walsh, Cooley supremo Noel Sweeney, and Bushmills' gifted Colum Egan, then we are truly looking at the whisky world's Magnificent Seven.

Ireland's whiskey world is small but perfectly formed, and it is starting to gain international accolades once more. Without doubt, a great part of this is due to the dedicated and focused efforts of Irish Distillers. It is unusual to find three master distillers at one distillery, of course, but Midleton—the futuristic and somewhat enigmatic super-distillery that

produces Jameson, Redbreast, Midleton, Powers, Green Spot, and Paddy—is no ordinary distillery. The very nature of Irish whiskey demands that it be treated in a special way.

"We simply cannot make blended whiskey the way that the Scots do because we do not have the portfolio of whiskies here from which to work," says Crockett. "We have to create different styles of whiskey within the one distillery, but we're reaping the rewards from investing in the finest wood back in the 1980s and with trying different things during the distillation process."

In recent years, Irish Distillers has been faced by some real competition, after decades of having events pretty

Green Spot 40% ABV
Jameson 40% ABV
Jameson 12-year-old Special Reserve 40% ABV
Jameson 18-year-old Gold Reserve 40% ABV
Jameson Rarest Vintage Reserve 46% ABV
Midleton Very Rare 40% ABV
Paddy 40% ABV
Powers 40% ABV
Redbreast 12-year-old 40% ABV
Redbreast 15-year-old 46% ABV

much all its own way. But it must be commended for the way in which it has not only stayed ahead of the pack, but also excelled, opening up new markets for Irish whiskey and playing a crucial and fundamental role in establishing a premium for the category by creating higher strength, older, and rarer whiskeys that are every bit the match of the very best Scottish output. Jameson has been the battering ram to knock down doors, and the brand has helped the whole Irish category, providing the platform for Cooley to thrive. That very point, though, is why Jameson cannot become complacent, according to Crockett.

"We think we are doing well and we are, but then we hear other companies say we are providing them with a way in for their brands. We must make sure that we do the same thing with our other whiskeys."

It is a very good point. If there has been a criticism of Irish Distillers in recent years, it is that it has not paid as much attention to other whiskeys in its stable, such as the wonderful pot-still whiskey Redbreast, as it might have done. That is all set to change, with plans by the company to put some proper investment behind the rest of the portfolio, including the Redbreast and Powers brands.

The skill will be to bring on such whiskeys while maintaining the growth of Jameson. That is going to

happen, predicts Billy Leighton. "We are operating close to full capacity now, and we are plowing additional money into building new warehouses," he says. "But we need to expand significantly by adding more pot stills, and new brewing facilities. Plans are in place. No one is quite sure how big the expansion is going to be, but we might be looking at building up the distillery and doubling the production capacity within ten years."

That is exciting, positive news and further proof that Irish whiskey is well and truly back from the brink. A golden era, indeed—and, with so many distillers performing at the top of their game, it can only get better.

FAR LEFT The old distillery manager's accommodation at the Midleton distillery.

ABOVE The impressive waterwheel at the old Jameson distillery, now a popular tourist attraction.

LEFT The smart and stylish Jameson range—putting Irish whiskey back in the front line of the world's top distillers.

Tullamore Dew 10-year-old 40% ABV

Pretty mainstream Jameson-like blend, with apple and pear fruits, some nice grain and pot-still notes, plus polite levels of oak and spice. It is not going to set the world on fire, but is perfectly drinkable and well put together.

The Wild Geese Fourth Centennial 43% ABV

And just to make the point about 400 years of hurt, this is a special bottling that is light, honeyed, and rounded. It is slight and delicate, a tad fey. If you look carefully, however, all the classic Irish whiskey traits are here—fruit, vanilla, grain, and malt all make a showing.

The Wild Geese Rare Irish 43% ABV

The "Wild Geese" in the name refers to the huge number of people who have left Ireland over the past four centuries and built Irish communities in all parts of the world. The whiskey is a relatively recent addition to the Irish offering and has been effectively designed to service what is perceived to be a demand for premium whiskey. It is made at Cooley for an independent company and, although the brand does not have much in the way of provenance, it is extremely well made. There is a great interplay between grain and malt, along with some fierce, shard-like spicy notes and some hints of honey, lime, and oak.

Irish pot-still whiskey

You would think that this does exactly what it says on the can—or, more accurately, copper—but you would be wrong. In fact, it sounds like a bad joke: When is a pot still whiskey not a pot still whiskey? When it is made just in a pot still.

If ever there was a territory that needs to sort out its definitions, it is Ireland—and thankfully that is exactly what it is doing. The problem comes from the fact that there are some who have claimed that, if an Irish whiskey is distilled in a pot still, it is a pot still whiskey. This is not only wrong, but hugely damaging to the Irish whiskey category as well. After all, that would mean that all Scottish single malt is pot still whisky.

Pot still whiskey is a style unique to Ireland, and contains a mix of malted barley and another grain, often unmalted barley, in the initial grist. This is then mashed, fermented, and distilled in a pot still, and makes for a rich, oily whiskey.

Green Spot 40% ABV

A few years ago, *Whisky Magazine* had an event called Best of the Best. Every two years, they would take their best scoring whiskies from the tastings pages, divide them into flights—Irish, Scottish blends, bourbons—and tour them around the world, to Tokyo, Bardstown and soon, Kentucky, Dublin, Edinburgh, and London, where representatives of the industry would taste them and score them, awarding one in each category and one overall winner Best of the Best.

Judges were asked to give them a minimum of five out of ten, and to be generous with their marks because these were already high-scoring whiskies. Judges could also write comments.

In Kentucky, the Islay single-malt category had them flummoxed. One by one, the score sheets came back with every whisky scored five, and the comment "peaty" or "smoky." In Scotland, they didn't get bourbon. But being Scotland they ignored the scoring advice and gave them scores between zero and two, with the supporting comments "crap" and "s**t."

There are two reasons for mentioning this. One, because the tasting in Dublin was held at the wonderful old shop of Mitchell & Son, which owns this brand. And two, time and again, this whiskey would score well at Best of the Best, seemingly able to appease the palates of both flummoxed Kentuckians and grouchy Scotsmen.

Not surprisingly, this is arguably the cleanest, sharpest, fruitiest whiskey known to humankind—on one level, bursting youthful exuberance and with a sweet heart; on another, a complex whiskey with oily pot-still traits, some white pepper spice, and traces of licorice, menthol, and cocoa.

Oh, and in case you are wondering, the Irish judges did not "get" either peaty whiskey or, surprisingly, bourbon.

Redbreast 12-year-old 40% ABV

Redbreast is another classic Irish whiskey, a marvelous example of rich, full, and tasty pot-still whiskey, with the grains and oils coating the mouth and refusing to let up. The spices dance across the mouth, sherry bobs in and out, the oily pot-still whiskey bursts out for a solo spot from time to time, licorice and coffee have cameos, and on it goes. Have you seen a Cirque du Soleil performance? This is the whiskey equivalent—so much going on you have to try it all again. Awesome.

Redbreast 15-year-old 46% ABV

A limited edition and a rarity for Ireland—a whiskey weighing in at 46% ABV and with a solid 15 years behind it. The nose has a grungy, tough, sulfury note to it at first, but this is merely a bit of macho posturing and a statement of intent. Give it a couple of minutes and it goes, like early morning mist giving way to warming sunlight. The nose is fresh, clean, floral, and fruity all at once, but the magic lies in the taste. Crisp red apples, underripe pears, some citrus notes, and pepper form the center of the taste, then something wipes everything to the side to leave a long, fruity, and spicy finale. This would be a contender for a top 20 place in any definitive list of the world's best whiskies, let alone the top 750.

Grain whiskey

As is the case in Scotland, the term "grain whiskey" in Ireland tends to refer to whiskey that is made with a grain other than malted barley, and in Ireland it is also taken to be a category distinct from pot still whiskey. There are plenty of people who believe that this style of whiskey has great potential and is underrated.

Some Scottish companies are actively promoting grain as a style. Irish and Scottish grain whiskey are very similar, and although Ireland does not produce much of it, Greenore has picked up awards around the world and is a leading player in the category.

Grain whiskey is most often produced in a continuous still as opposed to a copper pot still. Quality casks play a major role in the development of good grain whiskey and Greenore has achieved its success by double-distiling then maturing its grain whiskey in bourbon casks for at least eight years.

Greenore 15-year-old 43% ABV

Elegant, rich, sweet, and chewy, this is proof if ever you needed it that grain on its own can still make for a significant and impactful whiskey. This won the award for World's Best Grain in the 2010 World Whisky Awards, and no wonder. This style of whiskey will never have great depths, but there is an interesting interplay between sugar and spice, a great sweet grain core, and some woody notes to prevent it all from becoming too cloying at the end.

THE WORLD'S BEST WHISKIES

JAPAN

Japan

I have long held the view that, as we move toward a more homogenized and globalized world, there will be a counter-reaction by consumers. We are already growing sick of traveling intrepidly to a remote tribal village in darkest Peru, only to find Carlsberg, Guinness, and Bacardi on sale in the ramshackle bar.

Increasingly, we will seek out products with a serious heritage and a traceabale provenance, drinks with a proper story to tell and a unique way of telling it. All this is very good news, indeed, for single-malt whisky, which has provenance and heritage by the bucketload.

But woe betide any drinks company that dresses its brands in the clothing of heritage and provenance. When the public discover that they are looking at a Sears suit and not an Armani one, they will be uncompromising in their rejection of it. All those claiming to distill whiskey in Bardstown, Kentucky, but who are not part of Heaven Hill or Tom Moore, please take note. American owners of Canadian brands containing small amounts of American bourbon should pay heed. And Ireland needs to watch itself, too.

But most of all, Japan's two biggest whisky-making companies, Nikka and Suntory, need to get their act together. There is a strong argument that Japanese whisky has already been held back in some countries by its questionable approach to making blended whisky, which has often included a significant proportion of Scotch whisky. In the future, as people take a greater interest in what they are drinking and where it comes from, they will take a dim view of hybrid brands with no meaningful story to tell.

Japan's problem in this area is created by the fact that the country has relatively few distilleries and a work culture that pretty much rejects the concept of cooperating with rival companies. The best blends contain a large number of different whiskies, and in Scotland producers pool their resources to everyone's benefit.

They do not do that in Japan, so they have only two options: to create a number of different styles of whisky in each distillery or to buy in whisky from other countries. Both options are in play.

Thankfully, no such problem exists with the country's single malts, and it seems that the word about exactly how good Japan's malts are is well and truly out. For some years now, whisky writers have written glowingly about them, and they have scooped a clutch of major awards. But growth has been relatively slow, partially because supply has been patchy.

All that, though, is changing. When The Whisky Shop opened a branch in Norwich, England, four years ago, it requested large stocks of Japanese whisky and was told that there was little of it anywhere across the 15-shop estate, and no demand for what there was. So it gathered in all that was available and sold the lot within the first month—Norwich is in the Far East (of England), after all. Now the Suntory brands are not only available across the whole group, but they are selling well—even in the Scottish outlets.

I know it is a terrible pun, but you could sum up the situation for whisky from Japan in the phrase: "The land of the rising Suntory." The company dominates the country's whisky export market, although Nikka has some excellent whisky, too. Also, although it is operating from a small base, the Number One Drinks Company (also in Norwich—what a place!) is bringing Japanese whisky from smaller distilleries to the attention of whisky enthusiasts in Britain.

Traditionally, Japanese whiskies have emulated the single malts of Scotland and are closer in style to them than the whiskeys of Ireland, the United States, and Canada are. In recent years, however, they have increasingly developed their own style and character, and many have distinctive mushroomy/fungal notes. It sounds odd and may require a taste recalibration, but these notes add distinctive and attractive characteristics to the whisky in the same way that the savory and arguably discordant flavors contribute to the overall taste of olives or blue cheese.

Most importantly for Japan, its whiskies are growing in popularity, and people are buying into their provenance, history, and heritage. As drinkers continue to explore farther afield, it all augurs well for Far Eastern whisky.

NAGASAKI ●

ABVOE AND ABOVE RIGHT
The gleaming stills at Suntory *above* and Ichiro *above right*.

Japanese single-malt whiskey

The Japanese have done with single malt what they have done with cars—taken the model, stripped it down, worked out how to make it, and rebuilt it, not only matching much of the competition in the process, but surpassing it as well. Japan does not pretend that it looked any farther than Scotland for its whisky inspiration; its two biggest companies, Suntory and Nikka, were both effectively set up by an individual who learned his trade in the Highlands. Japan has been making malt whisky for a long time now, but widespread critical acclaim and a clutch of awards suggest that it has now passed Canada up the league table and is giving Ireland a run for its money as whisky's third most important market.

Fuji Gotemba 15-year-old 43% ABV

A strange nose that is part dry shredded wheat, part dough ball. The taste is sweet and clean, with honey on vanilla ice cream and an escalating mouthfeel, before a wave of sweet spices and some oaky notes arrive late on.

Hakushu 10-year-old 40% ABV

Sometimes you taste a whisky, and you taste a color. A lot of Japanese whiskies are russet or autumnal brown. This one, though, is spring-like and green, with a wonderful crispness to it. Imagine pear crumble and custard, followed by toffee apples. The palate has some earthiness underneath and is like a Scottish Bladnoch or an Irish Connemara.

Hakushu 12-year-old

43% ABV

This has a very unusual and complex nose, with freshly cut leaves, clean and chewy barley, some citrusy notes, and a touch of peat. The peat is noticeable on the palate, but is not dominant. Among the fruits are some pleasant licorice notes. All in all, a little gem.

3 ● YOICHI
SAPPORO

MIYAGIKYO ●

N

P
A
J

1 ● CHICHIBU

TOKYO ●

KYOTO ●

2 ● OSAKA

JAPANESE DISTILLERY PROFILES

1 **Ichiro's Malt** PAGES 232–233
2 **Suntory** PAGES 236–237
3 **Nikka** PAGES 240–241

Hakushu 18-year-old 43% ABV

1

In terms of the contribution from the cask, the tide was in with the 15-year-old. Indeed, for many, this whisky will be a step too far. Right from the first aromas—big polished church pews, sawdust, and some smoke—you can tell what is coming, and it does. But before that, it is like the sun making a brief appearance on a cloudy day—as bright apple and pear flavors, and some enticing and tantalizing sherbety notes shine through for a while. Then the big, dark, and brooding oaky clouds roll over again and, by the finish, the astringency is mouth-puckering...

Hakushu 1989 60% ABV

1 !

A big, grouchy bullfrog of a whisky that gives little away on the nose, but is uncompromising in its concentrated sherry attack on the palate. It comes into its own, however, when water is added. Rich stewed plums, toasted oak, lemon and grapefruit, and some incense-like fragrance all contribute to a big, bold, and complex whisky.

Hakushu 25-year-old 43% ABV

1 ?

After the oaky intensity of the 18-year-old, you approach the 25-year-old with something that borders on trepidation. It is a big sherry trifle of a whisky, and it seems as if a big dollop of fruity jam has pushed the wood back to the fringes. Oak is still there, as are pepper and spice; this is a whisky in which flavor fluctuates successfully.

Hanyu Single Cask 1991 57.3% ABV

1 !

By Japanese standards, this has a surprisingly delicate and floral flavor, with sweet toffee and citrus notes on the nose, and a big mouthfeel, with intense fruits, spices working their way through, and some menthol and licorice notes. The finish is quite long, sweet, and spicy.

Hanyu 1988 55.6% ABV

1 !

If you have ever heard Deep Purple performing "Highway Star" on the band's live masterpiece *Made in Japan*, you will have a good idea of what to expect from this whisky. No messing around, everything turned up to 11, and ... bang! We're off ... This is the full aged sherry shooting gallery, with wave after wave of power chord marmalade up front, a wicked solo from dark cocoa, and a pulsating spice and oak rhythm section. Alltogether now "Ooh, it's a killing machine, it's got everything."

Hokuto 12-year-old 40% ABV

1

This is the whisky equivalent of one of those disturbing television thrillers that you cannot quite decide whether you are enjoying watching or not, but cannot bring yourself to turn off. A curious and unusual whisky, with stewed fruits, oak, and some dusty wood shavings on the nose, petal water and sherbet on the palate, and a stewed prune heart, with pepper and oak late on. The finish is long and spicy.

Ichiro's Malt Eight of Hearts 56.8% ABV

1 !

Finished in an oloroso sherry butt, the Eight of Hearts looks as if it should have a bark and a bite, to go with its bold coloring. The nose is all dusty old principal's office, but the taste is surprisingly fresh and jolly, with pepper, ginger, nutmeg, and cinnamon all making an appearance, and some juicy currants in the finale.

Ichiro's Malt Five of Spades 60.5% ABV

1 !

Very sherried trifle, with strawberry flan and vanilla custard on the nose and a bold, nutty, sherry-rich taste, with some oaky and peppery notes on the palate. A traditional, tweed-jacketed sort of a malt.

Karuizawa 17-year-old 59.5% ABV

Stewed apples filled with fruit mincemeat on the nose, with some nuttiness and dry sherry notes. But it is a complex and evolving nose, and after a while it becomes zesty and sherbety. The whisky has a big, full flavor, but is nonetheless surprisingly gentle and rounded, with a nice balance, the right amount of oak and spice, plus lots of soft fruits, almost like a cordial. The finish is long and warming.

Karuizawa 1985 Single Cask 60% ABV

A big rich fall woodland of a nose, with musty mushroom, rich prune fruits, and oak. Nothing quite prepares you, however, for the intense and fruity taste of this big whisky, with plum, prune juice, and intense red fruits and oak. With water, added sherry comes to the fore. The finish is rich and sherried—Japan's answer to Scotland's A'bunadh, without a doubt.

Karuizawa 1986 Single Cask 60.7% ABV

At first, this whisky is shaped by damp, rootsy fungal notes, with celery and truffles. With time, some lemon and grapefruit notes appear, and the refreshing citrus notes extend to the palate, which flip-flops and is altogether a lot less grungy than the nose suggested. It has a big, rich mouthfeel, with orange barley in the mix. The finish is chewy, with clean barley notes to the fore.

Karuizawa 1976 32-year-old Single Cask 63% ABV

Slow to open out, but when it does there is an almost lemony quality to it, but there are also redcurrant, raspberry, and raisins in the mix. The taste is thick and concentrated, with blackcurrant to the fore, but also some menthol, overripe melon, and delicate wafting smokiness. But just when you expect everything to free-fall into an astringent and sharp conclusion, a puffy pillow suddenly appears, and you are left with an exquisite soft and rounded conclusion.

Karuizawa 1971 Single Cask 6878 64.2% ABV

This is to whisky what the Australian rock band Wolfmother is to music—a monster-sized, roaring "amps up to 11" throwback to another era, but still very contemporary and relevant. This is a serious burnt fruit and nut case, all served up with rich fruitcake and wrapped up in oak. Want a malt to relax with at the end of a hard day? Do not go for this one. This is for surfers—some of the time, you go with the flow; at others, you have to battle the currents and rips, and all the time it is a white-knuckle ride. Just like listening to Wolfmother. And, if you have a rock-and-roll heart, then both band and whisky will have your head banging and leave you exhausted and contented by the end.

Karuizawa 1967 42-year-old Single Cask 58% ABV

Same age as my wife at the time of tasting and, while nowhere near as beautiful or elegant, it is nearly as spritely and wearing quite well all the same. In fact, there is a youthful zestiness about the nose, with grapefruit marmalade and clean, sweet fruit. The taste is very much an all-or-nothing one. If you can get past the astringent oaky barricade at the entranceway, there is much to recommend this, with rich orange and grapefruit, and some nuttiness.

Miyagikyo 10-year-old 45% ABV

This does not start very well, with a dull score draw of a nose, but it kicks into life when you taste it, with an intense duel between sweet fresh fruit and savory spices. The fruit just about wins it.

ICHIRO'S MALT

Chichibu, Japan
www.one-drinks.com

In a country where the whisky industry is so totally dominated by two companies, Ichiro is a rarity—an independent and free-spirited whisky maker taking an individual approach to the industry.

KEY WHISKIES

Ichiro's Malt Eight of Hearts 56.8% ABV
Ichiro's Malt Five of Spades 60.5% ABV

ABOVE The purpose-built distillery at Chichibu was completed at the end of October 2007 and has been busy ever since.

That does not mean that Ichiro is new to the alcohol business, however—far from it. His family has been making sake in Chichibu since 1625, and his grandfather, who represented the nineteenth generation of the family in the drinks business, built the Hanyu distillery in 1941.

When his family's business ran into problems at the start of the new millennium, Ichiro saw it as his duty to pick up the baton and run with it.

"We sold the business, including the Hanyu distillery, at that time," he says. "But the new owner was only interested in quick business and had no desire to continue maturing whisky. I rescued the last 400 casks from the distillery before they were redistilled. Whisky is in my blood."

Having taken the step into the whisky business, Ichiro set about doing things a little bit differently. He has been bottling his whisky stocks in small batches, with each one bearing a playing card on its label. A gimmick? Not at all, he says.

"When I visited bars in Japan, I was struck by how difficult it is to remember the years and the numbers of single casks on the bottles," he says. "I wanted to find something distinctive which would look good on the back of the bar, but would also be easier to remember. That's when the card series came to me. There will be 53 releases in total, so I will finish off the series with the joker."

Selling existing stocks of whisky is one thing, making it is another. But Ichiro is going down that route, too. He has built a new distillery at Chichibu, and the first fruits of his labors, young malt spirit, have been released to critical acclaim. Among the standard ex-sherry and ex-bourbon casks are some made with Japanese oak, and Japanese barley is also being used.

"Ultimately, I want our whisky to be uniquely Japanese," he says. "Chichibu distillery is very small, and I want the whisky to be handmade. I would like all my experience, and that of my ancestors, to be appreciated in each bottle from Chichibu. I have carefully studied every aspect of the whisky-making process first-hand. As well as working at Hanyu, I have distilled spirit at Karuizawa and at BenRiach, and I want this to show."

Chichibu is producing three different types of spirit: a non-peated medium-bodied one, a non-peated heavy one, and a heavily peated one. Ichiro is excited about the arrival of his first whisky, but is already looking forward to producing 10-year-olds, 20-year-olds, and 30-year-olds.

"The intention is to release six casks from Chichibu annually, three from the domestic market and three for export," he says. "It's a small operation, but, when I travel and see many people enjoying whisky, it fills me with hope for the future. I see young people enjoying whisky, and I am pleased that Japanese whisky is being recognized. It makes me very hopeful and optimistic about the future."

ABOVE LEFT New casks used in the distilling process are made from American oak and Japanese Mizunara oak.

ABOVE RIGHT Reused casks are also integral to whisky production at Chichibu, and include American, Japanese, French, and Spanish oak examples.

LEFT The Ichiro's Malt collection is a series of bottlings based on a complete pack of playing cards.

Miyagikyo 12-year-old 45% ABV

Gooseberry, rhubarb, and cocoa on the nose, then the softest and sweetest of starts when you taste it. Do not be fooled, though, because pretty quickly a razor-blade wave of sharp spiciness arrives and takes you through to a peppery conclusion.

Miyagikyo 15-year-old
45% ABV

The aromas here are of rich Christmas fruitcake, raisins, sultanas, and sweet spices, while the taste is mouth-coating, with plummy fruits, raisins, and a pleasant malty core.

Miyagikyo Single Cask 1989 61% ABV

The nose is reedy, with green salad, chestnuts, and some mustiness. Tastewise, this is a big hitter, with sherried raisins and red berry fruits, damp oak, and fall leaves—all very intense and savory. The finish is long, chubby, and warming.

Nikka Single Cask 1991 58% ABV

A light and breezy whisky, this has candy, vanilla, banana, and toffee on the nose, and a taste of sweet fruity soda and black currant Starburst. The finish is clean and sweet, with a touch of spice.

Yamazaki 10-year-old 40% ABV

Lots and lots going on here, and surprisingly complex for what is effectively the distillery's standard flag bearer, with sweet spice and fluffy apples on the nose, and fresh sweet lemon, melon, and apple in the taste. Very clean and fresh; an easy-drinking delight.

Yamazaki 12-year-old
43% ABV

Starts off with aromas of polished wood and pine, then opens out with summer fruits on the nose. The whisky marches into the mouth and occupies it. The word that springs to mind here is "luscious"—this is as juicy as whisky gets, as if someone has made a redcurrant, raspberry, blueberry, and blackcurrant smoothie, and mixed it with alcohol. The fruity finish is long and very warming.

Yamazaki 18-year-old 43% ABV

I tasted this while staying at Center Parcs, and it seemed totally appropriate because the aroma is like damp leaves and an early morning stroll in the forest. There are also some juicy raisin notes on the nose. The palate is astounding—lots of sherry and wood, dark chocolate, and rum and raisin. Lurking under the surface are some meaty, grungy notes, probably from sulfur, but this only adds to the fun and festivities of this whisky, and it is effectively a defiant two-finger salute to anyone who deducts marks from all sulfur-tinged whisky as a matter of principle. There are a few thoroughbred whiskies in this Japanese section, and more than one from this distillery. This, though, is arguably the pick of the bunch.

Yamazaki 1984 48% ABV

This whisky has an almost liqueur-like quality, with sweet barley and orange fruits on the nose, and with watermelon and grapefruit. The taste is big, full, and unusual, but quite appealing, with menthol, orange, and cherry-flavored cough lozenges. The finish is long and sweet, with some medicinal notes—daringly different.

THE YAMAZAKI SINGLE MALT WHISKY DISTILLED IN 1984 "YAMAZAKI"

Yamazaki 25-year-old 43% ABV

Like a dusty old polished office—stately and imposing at the same time, with full, rich sherry, raisins and berries, and some dustiness and mustiness, with a trace of mushroom. The taste is rich and mouth-filling, with plum chutney and orange rind. The finish is long and fruity, with a nice balance of oak and spice.

Yamazaki 1993 62% ABV

Hah! Just as you are coming to grips with this wonderful distillery, and you are well and truly focused on your target, they go and move the goalposts. Completely. All the way to Islay, in fact. This has barbecued fish, white pepper, and smoke on the nose, and a taste that bobbles about like a rowboat in a swell, with oil, peat, and fishy boathouse notes on the one hand, and buttercups, sweet lemon, and hickory on the other. The peat holds out longest and dominates the finish.

THE CASK of YAMAZAKI 1993 HEAVILY PEATED MALT

THE CASK of YAMAZAKI 1979 JAPANESE "MIZUNARA OAK"

Yamazaki 1979 Mizunara Oak 55% ABV

Mizunara oak usually imparts a strong spiciness to whisky, and that is definitely the case here. There is also a strong woodiness to it—and not much else. Certainly, there is little in the way of balance. Not for everyone, then. If you enjoy hot chili sauce and charcoal-grilled steak, however, it is worth a try.

Yoichi 10-year-old 43% ABV

We live in safe times. Nobody dare has an opinion on anything for fear of losing their job or being reprimanded. Which is why the live album *White Stripes* released in 2010 is so important—it sounds as if it might fall apart at any moment, but never does, making for a thrilling ride. This is the whisky equivalent—the sherry, toffee, peat, and vanilla should not work together at all, but they just about do.

Yoichi 12-year-old 45% ABV

Another intriguing mix of sherry and peat, although the sherry is by far the senior partner, with dried fruits and golden raisins very much to the fore. There are some vanilla and candy flavors here, too, and a rich sweetness, making for an outstanding, complex malt.

Yoichi 15-year-old 45% ABV

This is an absolutely fantastic whisky if you cannot resist peaty, smoky whiskies with a rich, chewy fruit heart—and I can't. This is an extremely difficult distilling trick to pull off, and only a handful of whiskies manage it. But Yoichi excels in this area and would give any whisky of this type a run for its money. What makes this such a sublime experience is the way that the sherry and smoke are battering rams; once they have gained access, there are all sorts of flavor nuances to savor—like dipping an orange in a pepper pot, with lots of citrus.

Yoichi 20-year-old 52% ABV

Holds up well for its age, and definitely another to put in the credit box. In fact, Yoichi has a perfect score in that respect. Musty but captivating all the same, with burnt toffee and raisin, nut cluster and treacle on the nose. The taste is soft and rounded, with peanuts and honey, and paprika toward the finish.

SUNTORY

5-2-1 Yamazaki, Shimamoto-cho, Mishima-gun, Osaka
www.suntory.com

When Suntory's Dr. Koichi Inatomi speaks about his company and the whiskies it makes, he does so with pride.

ABOVE The Suntory distillery, built in 1923, sits in the vale of Yamazaki and was the first malt-whisky distillery in Japan.

LEFT On the outskirts of Kyoto, where the climate is extremely humid and the water pure, the environment is perfectly suited to the successful maturation of Suntory whisky.

ABOVE RIGHT Copper stills are used to create a superior Suntory. Only the middle cut of the second distillation is used for the whisky.

Dr. Inatomi is something of a whisky legend. He is responsible for creating some of Suntory's finest whiskies, including the Hibiki range. Hibiki 21-year-old was awarded the title of world's best blended whisky in the 2010 World Whisky Awards.

Now retired, but still a brand ambassador for Suntory's Yamazaki and Hakushu single malts and its Hibiki blends, he is the perfect spokesperson for a company that has not only put Japanese whisky on the map, but has also established it as a major and growing force in world whisky.

"These are very good days for Japanese whisky," he says, when we meet in Glasgow, Scotch whisky's heartland. "You can now find Suntory whiskies in whisky shops around the world and even in Scotland. It has made huge progress."

Meeting in Glasgow is no coincidence. Dr. Inamoto is based here, and in the Glasgow suburb of Springburn you will find the headquarters of Morrison Bowmore, owners of Auchentoshan, Bowmore, and Glen Garioch distilleries, and a company now owned by Suntory—a sign of just how big the company is.

Japanese whisky might be relatively new in many international markets, but it has a history stretching back to the 1920s, and Suntory goes back even further than that.

"The company was formed by Shinjiro Torii as a wine importing business," explains Dr. Inamoto. "The name is taken from Torii and the symbol of the sun, which is very important to Japanese culture. Then in 1907 he launched a sweet wine called Akadama, and it became very successful. The company still makes it. It provided the money to allow him to build Japan's first whisky distillery, Yamazaki."

To help him to make fine-quality whisky, Shinjiro Torii turned to Masataka Taketsuru, who had spent some years in Scotland perfecting the techniques of distilling whisky. The rest, as they say, is history. Today, Suntory has two distilleries, producing very different malt whiskies: Yamazaki between Kyoto and Osaka, from where both Yamazaki and the Hibiki blends emanate; and Hakushu, a giant and complex distillery that produces the Hakushu range.

Suntory's whiskies were hugely successful in Japan and remain very popular with, in particular, older Japanese drinkers. But one of the whisky world's greatest ironies is that, while the rest of the world has caught on to the high quality of Japanese malt, younger Japanese drinkers have fallen in love with Scottish single malt.

"But this is often the way," says Dr. Inamoto. "Younger drinkers in the bars of Glasgow do not often drink Scottish single malt But one of the jobs we have to do is win over the next generation."

In the meantime, Suntory is putting time and effort into bringing its whiskies to new territories. The huge critical acclaim they have had from whisky experts around the world is ensuring that they are getting a fair hearing and, along with other Japanese whiskies, they are now regularly picking up top international awards.

"It does make me very proud," says Dr. Inamoto. "I have seen Suntory whiskies go from nowhere to the very top of the whisky world. These are very exciting times for our Japanese whiskies."

Japanese blends and others

Only the most blinkered would question the validity of Japanese single malts, but blends are a different story altogether. To make a great blend, you need a large number of whiskies to play with, and the small number of Japanese whiskies coupled with a culture that discourages intercompany cooperation means that the country's whisky makers simply cannot match Scotland for variety and

choice. One of the ways around the problem was to bring in Scotch whisky—which, in these days of provenance and authenticity, is a hard sell as a story. Japan has another route to pursue, though. Its distilleries are complex and capable of producing a range of whiskies by using different yeasts and different production techniques. Certainly, the country is now producing world-class blends.

Hibiki 12-year-old 43% ABV

On the nose, there are plum liqueur and exotic fruits. The taste is extremely gentle and sweet, with zesty fruit and lots of vanilla. It is a refreshing summery blend and very drinkable. Some spices give the overall experience some depth.

Hibiki 21-year-old 43% ABV

This was chosen as the world's best blended whisky in the 2010 World Whisky Awards, and it is not hard to see why. The flavors here are all bold, precise, and irresistible. Orange marmalade and Christmas fruitcake are on the nose, with glacé cherry, raisins, and currants all perfectly balanced and in tune.

Hibiki 17-year-old 43% ABV

Unripe banana, red berries, and vanilla on the nose, and the green bananas extend to the palate first. This is a big whisky and it coats the mouth, with other fruits arriving, some oak and spices having a say, and a degree of stringency appearing toward the end. Big, full, and rounded—very nice.

Nikka Rare Old Super 45% ABV

This is a brave whisky. There is no age statement, but it claims to be old and rare, and it is veritably buzzing with aged oaky whisky. The nose is beguiling, but it is little more than a curtain-raiser for the taste—it bursts with rich grain, big peat, and sharp spice flavors. It says on the bottle that it is a smooth whisky—claptrap. This is a feisty, prickly wee beastie, with few blunt edges. A truly delightful blend that is right up there with the very best in its category.

Japanese blended/vatted malts

In Scotland, the major whisky producers work together by swapping their malts with those from other companies so that each of them has a comprehensive choice of whisky styles with which to make its blends and blended/vatted malts. A blended malt is not a blend—it contains no grain whisky, just malt whiskies from different distilleries. Japanese companies tend not to work together in this way, so historically whiskies in this category have tended to be a mix of malts from the distilleries of just one company.

Nikka Pure Malt 12-year-old 40% AEV

If you are of the view that there is little point in mixing malts, then you ought to try this because it is definitely greater than the sum of its parts. The nose is all sweet fudge and soft toffee, but the taste is altogether different, with bitter dark chocolate, some chili spice, and a peppery finish.

Nikka Pure Malt 17-year-old 43% ABV

By Japanese standards, this is a surprisingly neutral whisky. You would never guess that it was 17 years old, for a starter, with little coming from the cask. Instead, it is sweet, smooth, and pleasant. I was going to say that it is a bit like listening to Coldplay, but it is not that bad, and the peatiness in the tail is a treat.

Nikka Pure Malt 21-year-old 43% ABV

The distinctive Japanese earthy mushroom is present and correct on the nose, while the taste reveals a master class in whisky-making. There are rich juicy fruit, over a delicious peaty base, enough oak to give proceedings shape, and some bitterness for balance. The whole shooting match is soft and rounded. All in all, this is a cracker of a whisky.

Nikka Pure Black 43% ABV

This has an intense and savory nose, with fall forest, horse chestnut, damp leaves, and dark treacle. The palate is complex and evolving, with cherry throat lozenges, some earthy peatiness, soft orange fruits, canned peach and mango, and some spice. After such a wave of flavors, the finish is relatively slight, with some fruit and traces of spice.

Nikka Pure Red

43% ABV

This flip-flops from an initial burst of luxurious cocoa-rich dark chocolate and exotic fruits over an oaky base into something you might find in a delicatessen. Imagine one of those very expensive handmade chocolates presented in a little polished wooden box, then pickle it with olives and German sausage. It does not sound great I know, but, when you take the plunge, it provides a tangy taste sensation.

Nikka Pure White 43% ABV

Not quite sure about this color coding, but I do know a good peaty whisky when I taste one, and this is a belter—lots of rich oil, grilled trout, and intense peat, all wrapped up in a sugar-and-spice blanket, with a saltiness of which any Islay distiller would be proud. All the controls are set to high for this one and, if peat and smoke rock your boat, it is not to be missed.

NIKKA WHISKY

Hokkaido Yoichigun Yoichimachi Kurokawacho 7-6
www.nikka.com

What is the difference between the rock band Status Quo and the Japanese whisky company Nikka? Status Quo has been rockin' all over the world for years; Nikka is just about to.

Or at least that's how Nikka's Naofumi Kamiguchi light-heartedly puts it when he talks confidently about the future for his company's whiskies.

"Yes, we're going to be rocking all over the world," he says. "The sales of Nikka outside Japan are now starting. The first reaction is superb; we're confident it can spread further in the future."

He has every reason to be confident. The growth in interest in Japanese whisky in recent years has been phenomenal, the number of whiskies finding their way to all parts of the world is growing apace, and, most important of all, the quality is mind-blowingly high. Tasting Japanese whisky for this project was one of the true highlights—and no other country can boast such a consistent and uniformly high standard across the board. Every whisky tasted has been included, and there were no duds. Remarkable.

Nikka is Japan's second-biggest whisky maker and is dwarfed by Suntory. But it was founded in 1934 by Masataka Taketsuru, the same man who had brought whisky-making skills to Suntory ten years before. Taketsuru learned his trade in Scotland and had a vision for Japanese whisky. He set up the country's first distillery in 1924, but ten years later found what he considered an even more perfect site for a distillery. To build Yoichi on Hokkaido, he had to set up his own business,

and so the company that was to become Nikka was formed. A second distillery, Miyagikyo, was built in 1969.

Although widely accepted and increasingly praised by the whisky-loving community, Japanese whisky is still relatively small, albeit growing rapidly. But Naofumi Kamiguchi believes that Japan has the quality of whisky to continue growing into the future.

"Over three years, the sales of Nikka have exploded in France," he says. "The whisky's reputation is growing across Europe and the sales are coming, and the next step is America and Asia. Our friend Suntory is investing aggressively in its expansion, and in that sense Nikka is the follower. But we're proud of the quality of our whisky, and we think it is unique. We think, for instance, that our distinctive coal-fired distillation at Yoichi is helping us to make the world's best whisky.

ABOVE The Nikka Miyagikyo distillery.

RIGHT The Nikka Yoichi distillery.

Although Japan's whiskies are modeled on the whiskies of Scotland, what's exciting whisky enthusiasts the most about Japan is the way in which its malts continue to evolve and are heading off in their own direction. Japanese whiskies are designed to be consumed with food, and with that comes a distinctly Japanese way of drinking. Mizuwari-style means adding ice and water to dilute the whisky as a long drink, and may become increasingly popular as understanding of Japanese whisky grows.

One thing's for sure—we are going to hear a lot more about Japanese whisky, and the malts from Nikka Whisky will certainly be in the front line.

"Our main issue is making sure younger people drink whisky," says Naofumi. "We have to recruit a new generation for the future, but we can do that. Certainly, we are keeping up the high tradition of whisky-making, while never forgetting the need for innovation and improvement."

No doubt about it, Nikka is on a roll. Maybe it is time to get out the air guitar.

THE WORLD'S BEST WHISKIES

EUROPE

Europe

You'd expect countries with a tradition of making alcohol from grain to make whisky, and ones in which the grape is the main source for alcoholic beverages to have little interest in it.

This is not the case at all. Outside the traditional whisky territories of Ireland and Scotland, there is no long whisky-making tradition in Europe. You would expect beer-making countries such as Germany, Belgium, and the Netherlands to have distilled their products into whisky. Instead, they traditionally made either jenever or distilled fruits for fruit liqueurs.

There has been an explosion in distilleries making whisky across Europe in recent years, however, and some of it is very good indeed. Most of it is based on a pot-still production system, but much of it is made on small and unusually shaped stills, and some of it tastes radically different from Scottish single malt. A proportion of it, though, is outstanding, and there are at least five distilleries that are making a case for promotion to the whisky world's premier league.

3 VALBO ●

SWEDEN

ENGLAND

WALES

4 PENDERYN ● **5** ROUDHAM ●

NETHERLANDS

GERMANY

BELGIUM

1 GRÂCE HOLLOGNE ●

2 EGGOLSHEIM ●

LIECHTENSTEIN

AUSTRIA

FRANCE

SWITZERLAND

CORSICA

SPAIN

TOP RIGHT A distillery tour at Blaue Maus in Germany.

MIDDLE RIGHT Rolling out the barrel at the Whisky Castle, run by the Käser family, in Switzerland.

BOTTOM RIGHT Sweden's Mackmyra Distillery is making world-class whisky from its base in Valbo.

EUROPE DISTILLERY PROFILES

BELGIUM

The Belgian Owl 2/2009 46% ABV
www.belgianwhisky.com

Single malt

A tad too young and underdeveloped
this, but with enough to recommend it
nevertheless. The nose is sweet and toffeeish;
the taste is zesty and sherbety, with some
licorice notes. It has a spicy finish, with citrus
fruits and green fruits emerging from the sweetness.

The Belgian Owl 10/2009 46% ABV
www.belgianwhisky.com

Single malt

This is between three and four years old,
and vanilla has joined the toffee on the
nose. But it is the flavor that impresses—
pear dessert mixed with apple crumble.
The finish is short and dies away quickly,
but that just makes it moreish. Proof that
this distillery knows what it is doing.

The Belgian Owl 10/2009 74.2% ABV
www.belgianwhisky.com

Single malt

Nearly four years old,
this is a monster cask-strength whisky, but with
trademark sweet pears and apples, vanilla, marzipan,
and some spices. A potential award-winner, this.

THE NETHERLANDS

Dutch Rye 5-year-old 40% ABV
www.zuidam-distillers.com

Rye whisky

Not as assertive as its U.S. cousins, but the
rye is distinctive and the whisky is very well
made. It includes 100% pot-still rye, not the
easiest grist to work with. A spicy and prickly
nose with some raspberry, plus hickory and
spearmint flavors, and some vanilla candy.

Millstone 7-year-old 40% ABV
www.zuidam-distillers.com

Single malt

The Dutch angle to this malt is that the
malted barley is ground by machinery
powered by a traditional Dutch windmill.
Merely a gimmick? Not necessarily. The
process is slower than commercial mills,
but as a result little heat is generated so
there is no scalding of the grain. Over in
the United States, Maker's Mark would
back this approach because it does a similar
thing, arguing that scorched grain has a
bitterness to it. Certainly, this is a beautifully balanced whisky, with
a soft floral, black currant, and honey core, and
some vanilla and coconut—one more wonderful
discovery made while researching this book.

Millstone 8-year-old French Oak
40% ABV BOTTLED NOV. 2009
www.zuidam-distillers.com

Single malt

The distillery says that the warm
and dry conditions in which this
whisky is matured account for its
rapid maturation and a large annual
evaporation of 4–5%. This might explain
the malt's aggressive nose and its pinelike
characteristics. But so might the fact
that at least some new
oak is used, French oak, in
particular, is capable of giving whisky a spiciness.
There is plenty going on here, and the finished
malt steers its way, in an excellent manner,
through a myriad of interesting flavors.

Millstone 8-year-old American Oak
40% ABV
www.zuidam-distillers.com

Single malt

This is quite lovely—a big, creamy vanilla-
and honey-dominated whisky, with some
delicious creamy coconut notes. There are
distinctive bourbony, candy, and leather
notes, then late on it gets winey. It is
strange and complex, but utterly beguiling.

FRANCE

Armorik 40% ABV
www.distillerie-warenghem.com

Single malt

This is French whisky's version of its national rugby union team—it looks ugly and brutal on first appearances, but is in actual fact a delightful mix of ruggedness and beauty. There are lots of spices in this, but some sweeter notes, too.

Breizh 42% ABV
www.distillerie-warenghem.com

Blend

This is a smooth Breton blend that is made up of 50% grain and 50% malt. It tastes sweet and delicious, with lychee and sweet pear.

Eddu Gold 43% ABV
www.distillerie.fr

Buckwheat spirit

This really walks the line. Buckwheat might be called *blé noir* in French (and *eddu* in Breton), but it is not a grain; it is a pulse, and so you have to question whether we have whisky at all. But Brittany is a fascinating whisky-producing region, and this is no slouch. There are fluffy apples and overripe pears in both nose and palate, some slushy melon comes into play, and the whole ball game is sealed off with a spicy finish. A very pleasant experience.

Eddu Silver 40% ABV
www.distillerie.fr

Buckwheat spirit

There is nothing subtle about this whisky, but that is no bad thing. It is rich in fruit and honey, the oak and spices slap you around the mouth a bit, and the finish is pleasant and intense.

Eddu Grey Rock
40% ABV
www.distillerie.fr

Blend

Surprisingly assertive and grungy for a blend, with plenty of fruit, but also a coastal tang and some smoke. The appley notes mixed with the earthiness give this whisky a distinctly different and attractive character all its own. Impressive.

Glann ar Mor 46% ABV
www.glannarmor.com

Single malt

There are many things to get excited about at this distillery in Brittany, not least its judicious use of casks and the way in which even its young whiskies are balanced and complete. There are grassy, haylike notes on the nose here, and the salt-and-pepper flavors are not totally in balance with the fruit; however, the beautiful big apple and pear flavors and gorgeous rich oak suggest that this distillery is well on the way to producing some whisky classics.

THE BELGIAN OWL DISTILLERY

Rue Sainte Anne 94, 4460 Grâce Hollogne, Belgium
www.belgianwhisky.com

It is easy to get confused about Etienne Bouillion's whisky–making operation. He might know exactly what he is doing when it comes to malt, but the naming of his distillery is something else.

For a while it went under the name Pur.e, until someone advised him that "pure" was likely to be a no-go area for European malt whisky. Then some confused his whisky with his fruit liqueur business, Lambicool.

So let us get this straight. This wonderful, charming, haphazard, and utterly unique distillery in and around Liège is called the Belgian Owl Distillery. And it makes great sweet apple- and pear-flavored malt whisky that, even in its youngest versions, was clearly of the highest quality.

I say "in and around Liège" because the production process for whisky here has been carried out at three sites. Barley was grown at a farm in the rolling Belgian countryside, before being sent away to be malted. It was then fermented at the farm, before being transported by tanker to Etienne's distillery, where it was distilled in portable French brandy stills. And from there it was transported to the suburbs of Liège, to the sort of industrial and garishly lit storage warehouses where you expect to find cardboard boxes, not whisky casks. Such are the warm and dry conditions in the warehouse that the alcohol strength increases quite dramatically during maturation.

It was clearly not the most ideal or efficient way of making whisky, but bizarrely it worked. Note the past tense, though. Finance allowing, the whole operation is to move to the farm. It is a move fraught with potential problems. While, in theory, the new distillery setting will enhance the whisky, you change your production techniques at your own peril.

Only time will tell, but what is without doubt is that Bouillion is a whisky maker of the highest order, and he has had the good sense to take what distilling knowledge he does have and to seek out the very best source of information for malt whisky production in the form of Bruichladdich's maestro distiller Jim McEwan.

The whisky is well packaged, too, and at last Bouillion has gotten the name right.

ABOVE TOP RIGHT The local and unique barley variety from which the Belgian Owl whisky is made.

RIGHT The Belgian Owl whisky range.

OPPOSITE TOP LEFT Whisky maker Etienne Bouillion.

OPPOSITE FAR RIGHT The entrance to the farm courtyard where the Belgian could be based if plans fall into place—complete with little pagoda.

The Belgian Owl 2/2009 46% ABV
The Belgian Owl 10/2009 46% ABV
The Belgian Single Malt 10/2009 74.2% ABV

Guillon No. 1 46% ABV
www.whiskyguillon.com

Single malt

Guillon brings a touch of France to
the whisky party by maturing its malts
in wine casks. This has the potential
to topple into the disaster zone, but
in this case it never does, and this
whisky is a revelation. There are rich,
sweet orange and citrus notes at play,
sponge cake and malt in the center, and
swirling, whirling red fruits late on,
with a touch of earthiness in there, too.
A complex and impressive whisky.

Meyer's Alsacien 40% ABV
www.distillerie-meyer.fr

Single malt

The nose is rustic and youthful, and
on the palate there are soft barley and
the most delicate of fruits. No real
assertiveness, but this is very pleasant.
Just when you think that it is going
to sneak away quietly, a
very late burst of spice
provides a finale.

Uberach 42.3% ABV
www.distillerie-bertrand.com

Single malt

If you do not like sulfur notes in your whisky,
look away now. Uberach is from Alsace and is
from a distillery specializing in fruit liqueurs
and brandy. If you are expecting a clean, sweet
fruity whisky, however, think again. There is
a gritty, industrial side to this that divides
drinkers. I suspect, though, that they know
exactly what they are doing here. Germany's
just around the corner, and this sort of thing
goes down well with the German palate. It
works for me, too, in the same way as the new
wave of lively Glendronachs work.

CORSICA

P&M Pure Whisky 42% ABV
www.brasseriepietra.com

Hybrid whisky

Certainly not pure and arguably not a whisky, but this has a delicious
and totally original taste. P&M is made from a beer containing
chestnuts as well as grain, so strictly this is not whisky. But there are
attractive liqueur-like flavors, soft fruit notes, and toasty cereal.

P&M Blend Supérieur 40% ABV
www.brasseriepietra.com

Blend

A bold-flavored blend with lashings of citrus and yellow fruits, and
a soft mouth coating, but with a gentle palate.

SPAIN

DYC 50th Anniversary 40% ABV
www.dyc.es

Single malt

Released in 2009 to mark the fiftieth
anniversary of the distillery's opening,
this single malt is lighter and safer than
the cask-strength version. It has a clean
and crisp green fruit
taste, a nice balance
between spicy and sweet
notes—from bourbon
casks—then heather and
grass.

DYC Pure Malt 40% ABV
www.dyc.es

Blended/vatted malt

DYC is owned by Beam Global and is a
malt and grain distillery, blending plant
packaging, store, and electricity power
station all in one. This whisky includes
Spanish and Scottish malt, including some
Laphroaig, but is smoother in flavor.

GERMANY

Austrasier Single Cask Grain 40% ABV
www.fleischmann-whisky.de

Single grain

This is a delight—unlike any whisky I have ever tasted. With fudge and licorice on the nose, the palate is soft, gentle, and honeycombed, with some spices that stay firmly in the background. Bourbon, candy, vanilla, and hickory also make an appearance.

Blaue Maus 40% ABV
www.fleischmann-whisky.de

Single malt

There is some off-putting linseed oil on the nose, but get past this and you will discover the most gentle honeyed and fudge-like taste, then finally a significant but not harsh level of spice.

Blaue Maus 1983-2008 40% ABV
www.fleischmann-whisky.de

Single malt

There are some quite delicate flowery notes on the nose here, with Parma violets and blueberries. The taste is like bourbon liqueur, with intense candy, honey, nutmeg, licorice, and pepper. A big, beguiling whisky.

Blaue Maus Fasstarke 58.9% ABV
www.fleischmann-whisky.de

Single malt

Treat this one carefully—it is capable of biting. The nose is oily and pruney; the taste liqueur-like, with intense fruits and a fierce, un-Fleischmann-like wave of pepper. But it is a pleasant experience, with a malty heart.

Grüner Hund 40% ABV
www.fleischmann-whisky.de

Single malt

This has soft fudge and honey on the nose, with polished wood and beeswax making an appearance. The taste is liquid honey—soft and rounded, beautifully put together, and delivered on a palate of very delicate, gentle spice.

Grüner Hund Fasstarke 51% ABV
www.fleischmann-whisky.de

Single malt

The most bizarre whisky in the entire Fleischmann stable, this has lots and lots going on. On the nose, there are pistachio nuts and rich fruit liqueur notes. This takes you out of your comfort zone, but ultimately rewards you with a smorgasbord palate of camp coffee, burnt treacle, and a wave of spice.

Old Fahr 40% ABV
www.fleischmann-whisky.de

Single malt

Nougat and roasted nuts on the nose, with some fresh wood polish, then chocolate chip and nut ice cream, fresh runny honey, and traces of cherry. Another gossamer-like whisky experience from the mighty Fleischmann whisky empire.

BLAUE MAUS DISTILLERY

Bamberger Strasse 2, 91330 Eggolsheim, Germany
www.fleischmann-whisky.de

I know a German whisky writer who is extremely well respected in the industry. He is a Keeper of the Quaich, a recognition by the Scottish industry of the contribution he has made to the promotion and celebration of Scottish whisky. He is a good man.

But he refuses—point blank—to accept that any good whisky will ever be made in central Europe, and particularly in a German-speaking country.

"If they were meant to have produced whisky, they would have done it centuries ago," he rages. "Germans are meant to make beer and fruit liqueurs. They simply cannot make whisky."

I like my friend, but he is wrong. We have discussed holding events where we each present the arguments for and against Europe to an audience, while tasting some of the whiskies from Belgium, France, Austria, Germany, and Switzerland.

I have always been confident that I could win these debates on any territory, including in Scotland. But now I know without doubt that I would win. I could even do it by using whisky samples from just one German distillery: Blaue Maus.

There are not many European distilleries outside Scotland and Ireland that can boast that they have a 25-year-old malt, but Germany's Blaue Maus is a pretty special distillery altogether.

Let's start with the name. It means "blue mouse," and it is not the only wacky whisky name being produced by the company. Other whiskies include Grüner Hund (Green Dog) and Schwarzer Pirat (Black Pirate). Then there is the whisky itself. Let's get something straight. This is not Scottish single-malt whisky and is not trying to be, nor is it bourbon or Irish whiskey—but that does not mean it cannot be great.

And Blaue Maus does make great whisky. Adjust your taste buds, throw away your prejudices, and approach these whiskies as if they were a brand-new drinks category all of their own, and you may find yourself enjoying a roller-coaster ride. Taste is subjective, of course; however, if you find the right wavelength, then this is malt nectar—honeyed, toffee, milk chocolate delights, each one of the range (and there are more than ten of them) a soft and subtle delight.

Robert Fleischmann set up the Blaue Maus distillery in 1980, on the same site as the original family grocery and tobacco business in Eggolsheim, to make brandy. In 1983, it made its first whisky. The distillery says that the first attempts were poor, but Fleischmann took the view that practice made perfect. Interestingly, a 25-year-old malt released in 2008 is very good, so either the early efforts were not so bad or maturation has worked wonders.

Since then, the distillery has blossomed, developing a maritime theme reflected in its Spinnaker whiskies. It started selling whisky commercially in 1996 and has expanded its range, which now also includes Austrasier and Old Fahr.

Now run by Robert's son and daughter-in-law, Thomas and Petra, it bottles single-cask whiskies under a range of names. Every one of my samples was a total treat. Not just great German whisky, but great whisky period. Now, Bernard, my old German friend—put that in your pipe and smoke it.

ABOVE TOP RIGHT The Fleischmann family has been making whisky for 25 years.

THIS PAGE The distilling equipment at Blaue Maus produces malt nectar that is honeyed and chocolatey.

Schwarzer Pirat 40% ABV
www.fleischmann-whisky.de

Single malt

Some oddball nutty and fruit notes on the nose, then fruitcake, jam sponge cake, and a dusty, oaky, and spicy ending. Not the usual distillery fayre—but none the worse for that, all the same.

Slyrs Bavarian Single Malt 43% ABV
www.slyrs.de

Single malt

Both beautifully packaged and beautifully made, with sweet pear and apple, honey and toffee strutting along merrily and being buffeted by the warmest oak and milk chocolate notes. There is an attractive bittersweet thing going on here, too. World-class whisky by any standards.

Spinnaker 40% ABV
www.fleischmann-whisky.de

Single malt

I am not sure it is possible to get malt whisky any softer or more rounded than this—and not in a dull way. It's more like eating alcoholic honey-combed chocolate bars. Even by this distillery's remarkable candy standards, this is the oral equivalent of falling onto a feather mattress.

Spinnaker Fasstärke 48.2% ABV
www.fleischmann-whisky.de

Single malt

Not the greatest of noses—too much like oil paints. But the taste is intriguing, a strange mix of bourbon and malt, with ginger liqueur and a touch of schnapps to add body. Chewy and chunky, too. An altogether different and very impressive-tasting whisky.

Spinnaker 20-year-old 40% ABV
www.fleischmann-whisky.de

Single malt

Another oily and not too distinctive nose, and yet another from this distillery that redeems itself on the palate, starting out with trademark demerara sugar and honey, some chewy barley, and a late wave of delicious spices. Some oak as well, but there is nothing here that is too sharp or abrasive. Excellent.

AUSTRIA

Reisetbauer 7-year-old 43% ABV
www.reisetbauer.at

Single malt

The nose on this is a nightmare, stodgy and oily, with linseed and paint—a typically off, European nose. The palate is altogether better—I guess we are not in Kentucky anymore, but reset the taste buds and there is plenty to enjoy, including some cereal and straw notes, and what is the oral equivalent of intense church incense.

Reisetbauer 12-year-old 50% ABV
www.reisetbauer.at

Single malt

One of Austria's oldest distillers, Reisetbauer double-distills its spirit in pot stills and matures it in Austrian wine oak casks. The distillery makes fruit liqueurs, and traces of fruit in the cask find their way into the final whisky. This has been matured for 12 years and bottled at high strength, and is rounded and cerealy, with some toasted oak and nutty notes.

SWITZERLAND

Säntis Edition Dreifaltigkeit
52% ABV
www.santismalt.ch

Single malt

The whisky equivalent of one of those big European smoked cheeses. This is like barbecuing peppered trout over charcoal embers. There is some oiliness to this, but it is robust, well balanced, and thoroughly enjoyable. Brauerei Locher in Switzerland mostly produces beer, but this is another most pleasant new discovery made during the course of this book.

Säntis Swiss Highlander 40% ABV
www.santismalt.ch

Single malt

Matured in beer oak casks, this has a soft and easy straw nose. On the palate, it is gentle and honeyed vanilla ice cream and soft fruit, then some peppery spice later on. It is clean and sweet, elegant and sophisticated—and very refreshing.

Swissky 40% ABV
www.swissky.ch

Single malt

A clean and crisp nose here, with a sweet and barley-drenched palate. This is as refreshing and crisp as the chill Alpine air, with a weighty malty core.

Whisky Castle Double Wood
43% ABV
www.whisky-castle.com

Single malt

Not for the fainthearted, this is big-boy whisky, but very different and intriguing, too. The savory flavors are bold and aggressive, but there is a distinctive corn-on-the-cob taste and texture, with buttery oiliness that coats the mouth.

Whisky Castle Smoke Barley
43% ABV
www.whisky-castle.com

Single malt

Everyone has their breaking point. This is mine. The only alcoholic concoction I can think of that would present a bigger challenge would be olive-flavored tequila. Lots going on—cereal, rootsy vegetables, some oiliness—but overall this is a whisky for S & M fans.

Zürcher Single Lakeland 42% ABV
www.lakeland-whisky.ch

Single malt

Zürcher is a brewery relatively new to whisky-making, but all the signs from this are that it is learning the game very fast indeed. This is matured in sherry casks and is surprisingly complex for a malt that is just three years old. Lots of spice, some smoke, some vanilla, and sweet honey make for a satisfying and enjoyable whisky.

LIECHTENSTEIN

Telsington 42% ABV
www.telsington.com

Single malt

Liechtenstein's two biggest exports are apparently false teeth and sausage skins. It may well be that whisky will be up there before too long, too. This bottle looks different from anything else on the market, coming as it does in a wooden wraparound that makes it look like an oversized giraffe in a coffin. The nose does not give much away, but this is a traffic light of a whisky on the palate—it starts off with a distinctly Germanic/Swiss resinous and winey beginning, then changes to a softer, malty sweet center, and finally mutates again so that it is all go, into a spicy salty and dark chocolate–tinged conclusion. This is triple-distilled and matured in Pinot Noir casks, and tastes like nothing else in the whisky world. Great fun and the last whisky I tasted for this book. I am happy with that.

SWEDEN

Mackmyra Preludium:05 48.4% ABV
www.mackmyra.se

Single malt

Mackmyra has done its growing up in public, launching some of its earlier releases under the name "Privus," and some under the name "Preludium," to make it clear that the distillery recognized that the whiskies were not the finished article. Some earlier releases showed great potential, but were difficult, the fruit squeezed out by saltiness, by earthy peat, and by a wave of spices running riot. Not the best release from the distillery, but the first to truly announce that here we have a major player. An oily malt but sweet, with chocolate, vanilla, and sweet citrus fruits.

Mackmyra Preludium:06 50.5% ABV
www.mackmyra.se

Single malt

E-i-e-i-e-i-o, up the whisky league we go … And we have takeoff. This is complex and immense, with sweet lemon, melon, and pear all dressed smartly and proudly representing fruit; oak, salt, and pepper providing the deli counter; and cereal and barley showing off the whisky's agricultural roots. Sweetness abounds, but there is enough growling smokiness to keep everything interesting.

Mackmyra The First Release 46.1% ABV
www.mackmyra.se

Single malt

The public dress rehearsals are over, but compared to the older bottlings it is as if they have turned the serious drama we have watched so far into a musical. At first, it is sweet, with some orange liqueur-like notes, then sweet medicinal notes arrive, plus tangerine, and eventually it is rounded off with earthy spice. An unmitigated joy.

Mackmyra Special:01 51.6% ABV
www.mackmyra.se

Single malt

Rich in fruit. and a delightful journey down a clean and sweet pear-and-lychee pathway. It has a big mouth-coating, and concentrated flavor, some almond notes, confectioners' sugar, and pepper to finish.

Mackmyra Special:03 50.6% ABV
www.mackmyra.se

Single malt

A tangy taste sensation, with salt and pepper turned up high, but the melon and citrus notes battle gallantly, and the barley at the core of the malt is solid. This is big, oily, and with a chunky and weighty level of peat, but it is an utterly pleasant and rewarding malt whisky–drinking experience nevertheless.

U.K.: ENGLAND

St. George's Chapter 6 46% ABV
www.englishwhisky.co.uk

Single malt

Respected Scottish whisky maker Iain Henderson was charged with producing England's first new malt spirit for more than 100 years, and he did an outstanding job. The distillery bottled the spirit at various stages of its development, but the real excitement came at the very end of 2009, when English whisky was launched. It is, of course, young and immature, but maturation is faster in the east of England than it is in Scotland, and even at three years there are a few feinty, cerealy notes and, while not complex, this fruity whisky has all the signs of a major malt in the making.

U.K.: WALES

Penderyn 46% ABV
www.welsh-whisky.co.uk

Single malt

Penderyn's owners set out to make a unique-tasting malt whisky, and they have succeeded. Each batch of Penderyn varies, but there are some consistent threads. There is a sweet, almost liqueur-like wine flavor to this that is probably the result of the high proportion of Madeira casks used in maturation. There are plenty of sugary raisins and some spice, but no peat or oak at all.

Penderyn Peated 45% ABV
www.welsh-whisky.co.uk

Single malt

A very small amount of Penderyn has peat in it. The story goes that this expression was discovered by accident, when some casks sent to Penderyn from Scotland were not peat-free as ordered. In other words, the peatiness comes from the wood and not from the barley. The plus here is that the peat adds more depth. The downside is that grizzly peat and sweet grape are not the best match.

Penderyn Sherrywood 46% ABV
www.welsh-whisky.co.uk

Single malt

This is the whisky equivalent of removing your elegant throwing quarterback from the game, and replacing him with a running quarterback. Not better or worse—just a different way of playing. The Madeira influence is much reduced, and a grittier, spicier alternative appears in its place. The busier, more fruity, and nutty characteristics are closer to a single malt.

MACKMYRA DISTILLERY

Bruksgatan 4, 818 32 Valbo, Sweden
www.mackmyra.com

**Trust the Swedish to give the world its most
democratic whisky distillery—and, while we're
at it, one of its most unusual ones.**

ABOVE Mackmyra Distillery is making unique malt whisky with a
distinctive Swedish flair.

LEFT Charring the casks—Swedish oak is very different from other
European or American woods.

FAR RIGHT Mackmyra uses an old mine to store some of its
maturing spirit, 150 feet below the surface.

Mackmyra was set up by a group of friends who had hired a chalet for a skiing holiday. Each was asked to bring a bottle of something to furnish the bar, and each brought a bottle of Scotch. Which got them to wondering—several whiskies later—why it was that Sweden did not have its own distillery and whether they might provide one.

As with most late-night whisky-fueled ideas, this one went to bed when most of the party did. But two of the group got up the next day and continued dreaming the dream. Now Mackmyra is a dynamic and thriving business with some of the most attractive whiskies outside the traditional regions.

So how did the dream become reality? The distillery's marketing manager, Lars Lindberger, takes up the story.

"This was at the time of the dot-com boom, so no serious investor was going to look at this project," he says. "So the group agreed to give up their next holiday or a new car, and put the money into distilling one batch of whisky to see how it went. If it worked, they could try making some more; if not, well they would each have some Swedish whisky of their own."

Then someone came up with the idea of advertising the project on the Internet and offering shares and a right to have a say in how the whisky was made, in return for a small amount of investment. They struck a chord with the Swedish public, attracting scores of investors and establishing a bond that has meant that lines form at the state-owned liquor store every time that Mackmyra releases a new whisky.

And the whisky is distinctively Swedish. The barley is Swedish, Swedish oak is used where possible, and a unique peat that is salty from years under the Baltic Sea has helped contribute to a distinctive flavor. Juniper twigs, used as a smoking agent in traditional Swedish cooking, have been used for drying malt.

Early malts from the distillery were something of a struggle, but they have improved by the year and hit their stride, and have been consistently good for a while now. Should you want to, you can buy your own quarter cask and choose from several sites where you would like to mature it.

Whisky of the people, by the people, for the people—or something like that. It is very Swedish, very eccentric, and very good. What more could you ask for?

KEY WHISKIES

Mackmyra Preludium:05 48.4% ABV
Mackmyra Preludium:06 50.5% ABV
Mackmyra The First Release 46.1% ABV
Mackmyra Special:01 51.6% ABV
Mackmyra Special:03 50.6% ABV

ST. GEORGE'S DISTILLERY

The English Whisky Company, Harling Road, Roudham, Norfolk NR16 2QW, England
www.englishwhisky.co.uk

PENDERYN DISTILLERY

The Welsh Whisky Company, Penderyn, Mid Glamorgan CF44 9JW, Wales
www.welsh-whisky.co.uk

In whisky terms, we have a United Kingdom once more—for the first time in well over 100 years, England has joined Scotland, Wales, and Northern Ireland as a whisky-producing nation.

Scotland has, of course, produced malt whisky consistently for nigh on 1,000 years, and in Northern Ireland Bushmills can lay claim to being the world's oldest licensed distillery, having registered to produce malt whisky in 1608—although, amusingly, and some would say typically of the Irish, the media was invited to a 400-year anniversary party in early 2009. All that time to plan ...

So Scotland and Ireland have the form, but Wales and England are not without a little bit of previous form of their own, either.

England made whisky more than 100 years ago, but it was mainly for export to Scotland, to be used in blends, and whisky-making struggled to compete with the distillation of gin. The English, history shows, have always enjoyed getting drunk, and had little time for any notion of waiting for spirit to mature in casks, preferring to drink it straight off the still, its unsavory flavors made more palatable by aromatics. Thus gin was born and, with it, the infamous drinking palaces of old London town.

English whisky distilleries were therefore victims of economics. The last one to close was in Stratford, East London, and is under the 2012 Olympic stadium.

Welsh whisky was also well established way back, but its demise was as a direct result of the Temperance movement, whose members considered alcohol an evil curse and sought to banish it from their communities. Stories abound that distillery workers worked at night, leaving their houses under the cover of darkness so that their neighbors did not know what they did. Eventually, though, they were driven off, and many emigrated, which was good news for U.S. whiskey—among the descendants of Welsh immigrants to the United States were the parents of Evan Williams and Jack Daniel.

There was a feeble attempt to reestablish Welsh whisky a few years ago, but it ended in criminal proceedings. The company involved basically bought up cheap Scotch, added a load of spices bought from local supermarkets, and called it Welsh whisky. Visit Penderyn today, and ask them about the rugby balls full of "Welsh" whisky ...

Penderyn, though, is the real McTaffy. It is not just a genuine attempt to put a distinct and original Welsh whisky on the map, but it's a successful one, too. The distillation process takes place on an innovative still unique to the company, and it employs an unusual method of maturing its spirit in Madeira casks, Buffalo Trace bourbon casks, and used Scottish casks—mainly unpeated, but there is a small-scale smoky Penderyn created by old Islay casks in existence.

So popular has Penderyn become that every batch created has to be bottled, and there is now only a small amount of stock maturing for the future.

While the Welsh are heading off on a route all of their own, the English have played it safer.

St. George's Distillery in Norfolk, England, is modeled on a Scottish malt distillery, complete with a pagoda roof. It bought its stills from north of the border, and employed whisky-making legend Iain Henderson as its first distiller, the malt equivalent of non premier–league Norwich City soccer club signing David Beckham.

I happen to live on the distillery's doorstep, so I have been able to monitor its progress closely since the distillery started producing spirits in late 2006. Now a young whisky in both peaty and non-peaty form, it is maturing far faster than Scottish malt does, and it is very well made indeed. Drinking it is like watching a high-school football player make his debut for a senior team. You can see the talent is all there, and you would bet that there is a star in the making, but there is some bulking to be done, some refining is in order.

The signs are all good, though. And a United Kingdom of whisky looks on course for a long and prosperous future.

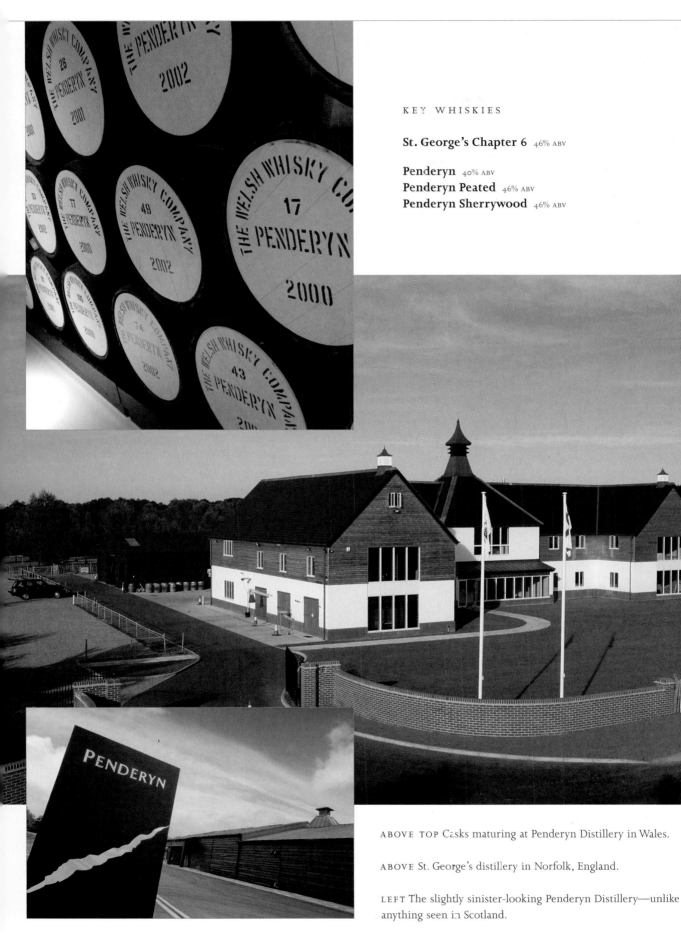

KEY WHISKIES

St. George's Chapter 6 46% ABV

Penderyn 40% ABV
Penderyn Peated 46% ABV
Penderyn Sherrywood 46% ABV

ABOVE TOP Casks maturing at Penderyn Distillery in Wales.

ABOVE St. George's distillery in Norfolk, England.

LEFT The slightly sinister-looking Penderyn Distillery—unlike anything seen in Scotland.

REST OF WORLD

Rest of world

Given how long it takes to make and mature great whisky, changes to whisky's natural world order have been remarkably swift in recent years.

For decades, whisky was pretty much the domain of just four territories: Scotland, Ireland, the United States, and Canada. Other countries—most notably India and Japan—did make whisky, but mainly for consumption in local home markets.

While Japan has made whisky since the early part of the twentieth century, it remained, to a great extent, a world secret. But, boy, how that's changing.

As recently as the beginning of the new millennium, whisky writers started to get excited about the innovative whiskies coming out of Japan and, very soon after that, those whiskies began winning awards.

Now Japan has not only been elevated to the whisky world's premier league, but has also arguably moved above Canada and Ireland into third place as the most productive and exciting whisky maker on the planet. Japan's success may have played a crucial role in encouraging other countries to step up their efforts to make good whisky and sell it beyond their national boundaries. Some countries are natural candidates—Australia and New Zealand, for instance, have big expatriate communities from Ireland and Scotland. But whisky is starting to emerge from all sorts of other interesting places, too. Taiwan, already a major consumer of whisky, now has a distillery, which suggests that it could

easily follow Japan onto the world stage. India has a world-class whisky producer in Amrut, and its 2009 releases were among the world's very best.

What makes the rest of the world intriguing is that the producers operate outside any clearly defined view of what whisky is. The definition of what whisky and single-malt whisky are in Europe, for example, is prescribed under European law. In the United States, whiskey categories are defined in U.S. law. So what has that got to do with someone in Wellington or Delhi? "Whiskies" exist that are made with molasses and not grain, for instance. There are plenty of so-called whiskies that have never met copper or oak, and are effectively colored vodkas.

Under European law, malt spirit must be matured for three years before it can be called whisky. Three years in, a new oak cask results in a spoiled, wood-dominated drink. But what if you live in a hot, humid country where maturation is faster, and the rules do not stop you from using new oak for, say, 18 months? There are grounds for experimentation here, new flavors to explore, and exciting new "whiskies" to create.

AUSTRALIA

Bakery Hill Classic 46% ABV
www.bakeryhilldistillery.com.au

Single malt

You might assume that Bakery Hill distillery is named after David and Lynne Baker, who run it, but it is not. The label on the whisky features a miner's pick and shovel, and the name comes from the name of a hill where a miners' rebellion started in 1854. For years, there had been growing unrest among miners who were denied the right to vote, had to pay for costly equipment and licenses, and were forced to use some of their paltry income to buy a small piece of land from which they could keep any gold or valuable stones they found, but invariably yielded nothing. About 10,000 miners gathered at Bakery Hill and, after a few days' standoff between the miners and the authorities, the miners set up the Eureka Stockade. The uprising was suppressed brutally three weeks later, with scores of miners killed and many others fleeing to die lonely deaths in the wilderness. But the rebellion was a watershed because it prompted political reform and the granting of rights to the workers, excluding Aborigines.

This is further proof that the Australians are coming—the fruit and barley are perfectly balanced, there are some nice milk chocolate notes, and the overall taste is pleasant and fruity, with apples and marzipan in the mix.

Bakery Hill Classic Cask-Strength Malt 60.1% ABV
www.bakeryhilldistillery.com.au

Single malt

Born Sandy Devotional by Australian band The Triffids is one of the finest albums ever made. Released in the 1980s when Australian sporting prowess meant that Australia was soaked in its own cockiness, the album revealed a more sensitive side to the country, and hinted at its insecurities and fears. It captures perfectly a sense of desolation in Australia's vastness. I listened to it again while tasting whiskies from Bakery Hill, and the combination is perfect. Like that album, this whisky is about nuance and detail, almost the opposite of the brash experience you may associate with Down Under. There are some strong citrus notes, clean, fresh apple and pear, and a layer of sweet vanilla. Songwriting genius David McComb died from heroin poisoning following a car crash just before his thirty-seventh birthday. This one is for him.

Bakery Hill Cask-Strength Peated Malt 60% ABV
www.bakeryhilldistillery.com.au

Single malt

This is a chunky, chewy, and classy malt that displays a concentrated mix of lemon and bitter orange, and dusty, smoky peat. Hickory and licorice are at the whisky's core, but then it just melts away with the softest of peaty endings—extremely impressive.

Bakery Hill Double Wood 46% ABV
www.bakeryhilldistillery.com.au

Single malt

A mix of bourbon and French oak wine casks makes for a busy and playful malt, with vanilla and coconut mixing with Christmas fruitcake and stewed fruits. It is as rich and unpredictable as Richard Branson, but utterly captivating.

Bakery Hill Peated Malt 46% ABV
www.bakeryhilldistillery.com.au

Single malt

Surprisingly refined, with a soft and sweet vanilla-dominated core and gentle smoke notes. A touch of both pepper and wood are in the mix, but nothing too heavy.

Lark Distillery Single Malt 43% ABV
www.larkdistillery.com.au

Single malt

A sure sign that things are moving swiftly forward for this wonderful distillery can be seen from the fact that, these days, Bill Lark's daughter Kristy is in charge of distilling. You cannot see the joins because, after some over-young malt in the past, the whisky has continued to move forward. This is crisp and clean, like the Tasmanian air. Fresh green fruits and cocoa are held together by mouth-coating oils.

Lark Single Malt Cask Strength 58% ABV
www.larkdistillery.com.au

Single malt

Melbourne band Wedding Parties Anything was described as the Australian Pogues, and one of the band's best tracks is "A Tale They Won't Believe," based on a true story from Robert Hughes's excellent history of Australia, *The Fatal Shore*.

It tells of how a group of convicts escaped from prison in Tasmania when Australia was a penal colony, in the hope of finding a boat and sailing back to England. When one prisoner was caught sometime later, he told how the desperate men had eaten first a prisoner who had died, then the weaker members of the group, until finally there was just him left. The authorities did not believe him, deciding that he was using the story to cover up the other prisoners' escape. He was returned to prison, only to escape again with one other man. And the authorities started to believe his original story when they recaptured him again—with body parts of his fellow escapee in his pockets. . .

Ever since I befriended a Tasmanian girl named Alison Kille and she spoke of her island with such affection, I have wanted to go there. After hearing this song—real boy stuff—that desire became even stronger. And this distillery is yet further reason for a trip Down Under one day. It is top-quality malt whisky by anyone's standards. It is not the most welcoming of malts first up, with some distinctive linseedy oiliness, but later you are in for a big, fruity treat, with apples and pears, and some chocolate and pepper. A corker.

Lark Distiller's Selection 46% ABV
www.larkdistillery.com.au

Single malt

Talk to anyone involved with the Australian whisky industry, and he or she will talk about boutique whiskies and how small-still producers are giving the Scottish a run for their money because most of Scotland is sacrificing quality for quantity. It is not as black and white as all that, but undoubtedly the small distillers from Germany, Belgium, the Netherlands, France, and Australia who are getting it right have all brought some small-still qualities to their whisky.

This is a case in point. There are some chunky oily notes, some rustic notes, and some sharp and crisp green fruit notes. Very good indeed.

Limeburners Barrel M27 43% ABV
www.distillery.com.au

Single malt

If there were a special award for most improved whisky, this would win it hands down. Just 12 months before this version was bottled, Limeburners was a mighty challenge, bottled far too young and with a vicious and unpleasant linseed oil and eucalyptus mix. This is by no means perfect, but it has come on in leaps and bounds, and it suggests without a shadow of a doubt that Australia has another superstar in the making. Some of the linseed notes are still there, but now they are joined on the nose by some pineapple, melon, and treacle notes. It is still very young on the palate—the distillery was set up only in 2007—but the fruit is getting greater and, when the wood and some depth kicks in, well. . .

Sullivans Cove 40% ABV
www.tasmaniadistillery.com

Single malt

Sullivan's Cove has played a pioneering role in the story of Australian whisky, and was one of the first to get its malts into the European market. The distillery is one of several in Tasmania. Like so many distilleries across the world, however, its earlier efforts were immature, unbalanced, and unpleasant. The distillery does not get it right all the time even now, but nevertheless it has come forward exponentially. This standard bottling is pleasant, easy-drinking, and unchallenging, with some oiliness and rich fruit.

Sullivans Cove 6-year-old 60% ABV
www.tasmaniadistillery.com

Single malt

Matured in port casks, this is an unusual and a little grouchy whisky, with toffee, loose and untamed fruit, and a wave of spice. This is not an easy ride and will be too much for some people, but it is ambitious and ultimately falls into the credit column.

Sullivans Cove Cask Strength Bourbon Cask 60% ABV
www.tasmaniadistillery.com

Single malt

If you are wondering what sort of country produces whisky such as this, then take a listen to the album *So Much Water So Close to Home* by Paul Kelly. Based on a Raymond Carver short story, it tells of a group of friends who go away on a fishing trip. Once there, after a long trek, they discover a young woman's body in the water. They debate going back to report the find, but have looked forward to their trip so decide not to. This is perfect for such a grim scenario. Big, and gutsy, it has plenty of oak, honey and spice battling against the barley.

Sullivans Cove Double Cask 40% ABV
www.tasmaniadistillery.com

Single malt

A mix of malts from both bourbon and port casks, and it makes for a weird combination, although not unpleasant. The chocolate and honey are still there, but winey, intense berry fruits join the mix. Unusual.

NEW ZEALAND

Mackenzie Blended Malt 40% ABV
www.hokonuiwhiskey.com

Blend

Surprisingly feisty, this: prickly and spicy, with strong rich savory notes on both the nose and palate. There are some honey and sweet vanilla in here, but the overall experience is more challenging than you might expect. Not entirely sure what this is—it is described as a blended malt, but there is talk on the website about a mix of malt and grain. That is the new labeling for you—at best, a mess; at worst, a bunch of old baubles.

Milford 10-year-old 43% ABV
www.milfordwhisky.co.nz

Single malt

It is possible that New Zealand has one of the biggest small-time private distilling industries in the world. When it comes to commercial and official stills, however, well, they are rarer than the weta, a scary-looking beastie unique to Aotearoa.

But New Zealand has a significant Scottish population and ought to have a whisky industry, and the hope is that it is on the way back. The owners of this whisky are set to start production at a new distillery in the South Island, and there is a growing interest in producing malt elsewhere in the country. This is an oddball malt.

Milford 15-year-old 43% ABV
www.milfordwhisky.co.nz

Single malt

Good golly, what an oddball whisky. For starters, you struggle to find any great influence from the cask after 15 years, which suggests that the wood has not been top rate—and yet it works. It is softer, more rounded, and more palatable than the 10-year-old, so age has worn down the edges in some ways. And then, just when it seems to be wandering off harmlessly, it heads off in a sharper, more citrusy direction.

Milford 1989 19-year-old 43% ABV
www.milfordwhisky.co.nz

Single malt

That we can still taste and enjoy whisky of this quality is due to Warren Preston, a man with a passion for whisky and a man on a mission. He has set up a little whisky world around his business in New Zealand's South Island, and this particular whisky is proof that the country can offer something genuinely special to the world of malt. This lovely whisky tastes salty, but there is more zesty and youthful fruit than any of the younger expressions. Simply delightful.

LARK DISTILLERY

14 Davey St, Hobart, TAS 7000, Australia
www.larkdistillery.com.au

If you fancy a wager from time to time, then how about a bet on Australian whisky to be as accepted by 2025 as its wines are now?

Crazy? Not if you are old enough to remember back to the 1970s, when the concept of Aussie wine was an international joke. Now, look at it.

The progress of its whisky industry in the first ten years of the twenty-first century has been nothing short of remarkable, and already some of its malts are good enough to be picking up international awards. Others are young and wayward like a teenage Shane Warne, cricketer extraordinaire, but you just know that, once they get their line and length right, they are going to be at the top of their game for years. Australians seem to excel at whatever they turn their hands to, and whisky is proving to be no exception. I am a big fan.

There are two distinct sides to Australian whisky. One is the concentrated whisky region emerging in Tasmania, which is Australia's answer to Islay, and the other is a scattering of distilleries on the mainland. But wherever you look for whisky in Australia, you will come across Bill Lark.

Bill Lark is the Che Guevara of whisky. He does not look much like a revolutionary, but behind the Santa-like white beard and affable personality lie a shrewd planner and a canny businessman, and he is leading an Australian uprising in the world of whisky.

He runs the Lark distillery with his wife and daughter in the pretty port of Hobart. Lark, along with Sullivans Cove nearby, is the most established distillery in the Antipodes. But there are several others at varying stages of development,

and most of them have had help from Bill Lark. It seems that, with every passing year, new projects are coming on line, and Lark is refreshingly enthusiastic about them all.

"It's all great news for Tasmania and our attempts to establish it as the whisky state of Australia," he says. "The latest project is by a farmer called Peter Bignall, who has constructed a 500-liter copper pot still to produce Tasmanian rye whisky. He grows rye grain on his farm at Kempton in Tasmania. This will be the only rye whisky in Australia, and he is going to brew the wash himself.

"I have also been having discussions with another chap who has bought property in southern Tasmania near Port Arthur, with a view to establishing a small distillery to produce malt whisky and other fruit spirits. His point of difference will be that he will use a Holstein still, rather like most of the craft distilleries in the U.S.A."

Lark has also set up a distillery school for would-be distillers, covering everything from how to make whisky to legislation. Interested parties have attended from across Australia and New Zealand. And Lark offers visitors the Ultimate Whisky Experience tour.

"It includes a day trip to our peat bog in the central Highlands, where they are treated to a Tasmanian trout, whisky-cured and smoked over a peat fire," says Lark.

"Mind you, that's only if they dig enough peat to bring back to the distillery for peat smoking the malt for the next day's production. It's a full hands-on experience, lightened by trips to gourmet wine luncheons and haggis-whisky dinners."

Exciting times for Tasmania, then, but Lark has not forgotten that he has a core business of his own to run. He has succeeded in establishing a distribution deal for Europe through Maison du Whisky in France, is exporting into Asia through Singapore, and has some distribution in the United States; Lark products are now available throughout Australia.

"Yes, it's heads down, bums up for all at Lark just keeping up with production and looking after the many new visitors being attracted to whisky in Tasmania," says Lark in typically Australian fashion. "It just seems to get busier and busier."

Outstanding Australian whisky? Maybe you won't get such good odds. Bookies rarely give money away on dead certs.

LEFT Lark's first copper still was sourced at an antiques auction.

LEFT BELOW Tasmania's peat bogs and pure soft water are perfect for creating world-class whisky.

KEY WHISKIES

Lark Distiller's Selection 46% ABV
Lark Distillery Single Malt 43% ABV
Lark Single Malt Cask Strength 58% ABV

THIS PAGE Bill Lark, founder of the Hobart-based Lark Distillery— one of Australia's leading spirits distilleries.

Milford 20-year-old 43% ABV
www.milfordwhisky.co.nz

Single malt

Bizarrely, this one is the fruitiest of the entire batch, with some oak and spice. If you had told me this was 12 years old, I would have accepted it, but 20 years? Really?

That said, it is a match for some very good 12-year-old Speyside malts, and the fruitiness of it is really very attractive indeed.

INDIA

Amrut Single Malt 40% ABV
www.amrutdistilleries.com

Single malt

Amrut has come on an amazing journey. From the early days, when it turned heads at Whisky Live London, to distribution through a number of British curry houses, the company has built up a reputation for high-quality whisky. This is where it started—a balanced malt, with clean barley, toffee, and vanilla at its center, plus hints of oak and spice to finish.

Amrut Cask Strength 61.9% ABV
www.amrutdistilleries.com

Single malt

An intense, outstanding roller-coaster ride of a malt. There are lemon and citrus on the nose and an intense bittersweet battle going on in the taste. Astringency from the casks gives an added depth, then there are some honeyed, dusty spice notes and a sweet, rich barley core.

Amrut Fusion 50% ABV
www.amrutdistilleries.com

Single malt

In a moment of exuberance, I wrote in my notes: "Is this the most exciting distillery in the world at the moment?" Maybe a slight exaggeration but you get the point. I defy anyone to go from Two Continents to Fusion and not conclude that Amrut is competing in whisky's upper echelons, with its intense and wonderful fruit notes, and lashings of oak, smoke, and dark chocolate. It is called Fusion because both Scottish and Indian barleys, some of it peated, are used to make it.

Amrut Peated 40% ABV
www.amrutdistilleries.com

Single malt

This is an intriguingly different take on the usual peated whisky model, with youthful barley and fruit holding their own well in the mix, but the smoky component gives the whisky a smoked-fish flavor. The elements of smoke drift in and out, making for a strange but captivating drinking experience, ensuring that this whisky has an identity all its own.

Amrut Peated Cask Strength 61.9% ABV
www.amrutdistilleries.com

Single malt

There have been some wonderfully defining moments at Whisky Live London over the years, but some of the best have been when a company from outside the recognized whisky-making world has not only dared to set up shop among the finest Scottish, Irish, and American distillers, but have flourished in the company as well. A few years back, there was a buzz around the show when this whisky was unveiled. Not surprising: It is a gem, with peppered smoked fish dancing around the fruit and barley. It has found a niche of its own, while retaining recognizable flavors for hardened Scotch fans. Very classy.

Amrut Two Continents 46% ABV

www.amrutdistilleries.com

Single malt

This is extremely hard to find because, when word filtered out about how good it was, it practically flew off the shelves. It is an intense flavor experience—with an almost Ardmore-like savory peatiness, then the most attractive rounded and balanced fruitiness to it. It gets its name from the fact that it is matured first in India, then Europe. If you have any lingering doubts about the world-class quality of this distillery, this will well and truly banish them.onderful.

SOUTH AFRICA

Bain's Cape Mountain 43% ABV

www.distell.co.za

Single grain

This is produced at the James Sedgwick distillery in Wellington, South Africa, and is a captivating and somewhat feisty number for a grain whisky. Indeed, it starts off aggressively, with a distinctive sharp and fiery bite, before softening up into a soft and honeyed tipple, with an apricot heart and the gentlest of spices. Grain can be too sweet and soft for my palate, but this is a robust and intriguing dram.

Three Ships 5-year-old 43% ABV

www.distell.co.za

Blend

The company website says that this is a blend of Scottish and South African whiskies. The result is perfectly acceptable and pleasant. Certainly, there is enough flavor, particularly from some sherry casks, and a distinctive oakiness to hold the attention. The real winner, though, is the peat, which gives the whisky a smoky base off which to hang.

Three Ships Bourbon Cask Finish 43% ABV

www.distell.co.za

Blended whisky

This is the latest and best release from the Distell company. Blended from South African malt and grain, then returned to bourbon casks for a further period of maturation, it has the sort of honey and vanilla heart that you get from real ice cream–truck ice cream.

TAIWAN

Kavalan Solist Cask Strength Ex-Bourbon Cask 57.3% ABV

www.kavalanwhisky.com

Single malt

As surprises go, this is as big as it gets. Each year, judges for the World Whisky awards are sent samples marked only with a country of origin and an alcoholic strength. In the 2010 awards were samples marked "China." They were all excellent, and this one, a quite incredible Taiwanese whisky—only two years old—reached the very last stages of judging.

From a large distillery—the King Car, with ambitious plans and a world-renowned whisky expert, Dr. Jim Swan, as a consultant—this whisky has a rich creamy flavor, with sweet exotic fruits and sugary spices. Truly delectable.

Kavalan Solist Cask Strength Sherry Cask 57.3% ABV

www.kavalanwhisky.com

Single malt

If the bourbon sample was all bright summer and sunlight, this is all winter and night-time, with a huge blast of sherry, some distinctive winey notes, and a mix of toasted raisins and dates that suggests several years of aging. Maybe there is a clue to the whisky's youth in the fact that all the flavors are up front and there is no great depth, but the deep flavors—capped by remarkable spicy undernotes—make for a very enjoyable ride.

AMRUT DISTILLERIES LTD.

Kambipura, Bangalore-560074, India
www.amrutdistilleries.com

It would not be quite right to describe Amrut whisky as an overnight success—the distillery that produces it was founded in 1948, and it has been making whisky since 1980.

The reputation of the company's malt has been increasing at a fast rate in recent years, and now there are plenty of people who will argue that the whisky from here is not only good, but also among the finest in the world. Taste the 2009 bottling Fusion—if you can find it because since it started earning plaudits it has been in very great demand—and you will discover an exceptionally fine, luxurious, and complete malt. When you add Amrut's Two Continents to the equation, it is pretty clear that something very special is emerging.

Amrut is based in Bangalore and primarily uses Punjabi barley. But for Fusion, it mixed Indian barley with Scottish, and distilled it in Bangalore. So good was the whisky that the first batch sold out in weeks, and a second batch sold out on pre-order, before it even reached international markets—not bad going at all for a distillery that had to overcome some natural prejudices.

"It was not easy for us to begin with," says the company's international sales manager Ashok Chokalingam, "mainly because we're not a traditional whisky country and some of India's whiskies are not noted for their quality, though to be fair that is to do with pricing and consumer behavior. I find equally poor-quality whiskies in Britain, too.

"But now consumers are starting to believe that we can produce good-quality single malts and therefore the trend will grow for sure."

Amrut always intended to establish a malt whisky that was distinctive and different than those from Scotland and, from the earliest days when the brand was targeted mainly at curry houses, the identity of the whiskies has grown stronger and stronger. In particular, two cask-strength whiskies—a peated and a non-peated one, launched in the early part of the millennium—had whisky experts enthusing about the superior quality.

"We never had any intention to copy anyone else or adopt a particular style of whisky that was being produced anywhere else," says Ashok. "We wanted to produce something different, and you get that with the licorice taste our whisky has. There are a few elements which contribute to Amrut having a distinctive style—the strength at which we distill, for instance, the flavor of our homegrown barley,

LEFT Much care is taken over the labeling and presentation of Amrut's fine collection of single malts.

LEFT BELOW Amrut is named after a golden pot, taken from Indian mythology, purported to contain the elixir of life.

BELOW The Amrut distillery, founded in 1948, is based in Bangalore in the state of Karnataka.

and, perhaps most importantly, the pace at which the whisky matures in the cask."

Not everybody is convinced—root around the Internet for long enough, and you will find people who just will not accept that single-malt whisky can come from anywhere apart from Scotland, let alone from India. But, frankly, they are wrong, and the pure quality of the whisky on offer from this distillery means that such people are becoming a dwindling minority. Ashok's aware of the naysayers, but you suspect that he could not care less about them.

"We're cautious about where we send our whiskies for review, and we will not send samples to some organizations which are just acting for some specific territory," he says.

"But a lot of the serious whisky writers have been very positive, as have the likes of the Malt Maniacs. And, most importantly, it doesn't matter about reviews as long as whisky drinkers acknowledge the quality they find here. And that is most certainly the case."

Yes, it most certainly is. Amrut is one of the most exciting distilleries on the planet.

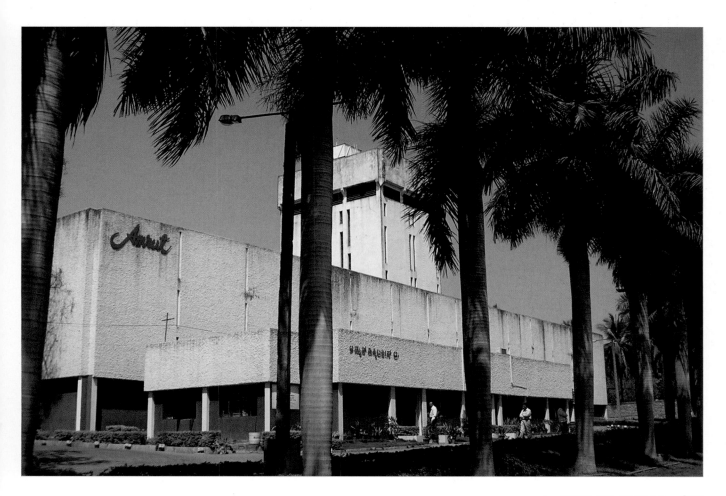

Independent bottlers

Wander into a whisky shop and you will find a whole range of bottles on the shelves that are listed not only by distillery name.

These bottlings are ranged under banners such as Connoisseurs' Choice, Old Malt Cask, or The Vintage Collection, and contain malt of different ages and from different distilleries. Many of the bottles are limited in number and contain whisky from just one cask. When they're gone, they are gone forever, but there will always be new ones on the way. This is an evolving and dynamic end of the market, the part that really excites whisky enthusiasts.

The limited-edition bottles are marketed by companies known as "independent bottlers." They buy up stocks of surplus malt, often a single cask or a handful of casks, and bottle them. Some independents are fastidious about what they do and go in search of quality whisky, bottling only what they consider to be of the highest standard. Others buy whatever ingredients they can get their hands on via the Internet, and bottle them without asking too many questions.

So the world of the independent bottler is a hit-or-miss affair, and the bottlers tend to enjoy a love-hate relationship with the rest of the whisky industry. Producers do not particularly like them because they have no control over the quality of the malt that is being bottled under their name—a single cask may taste significantly different from an official distillery bottling, and might well be considered by the producer as of only good-enough quality for inclusion in a blend, and not good enough to be bottled in its own right.

Some companies go out of their way to ensure that their whiskies do not end up being bottled by independents. Glenmorangie, for instance, adds a small amount of malt from another distillery to its casks so that they cannot be sold on, as either Glenmorangie, or as single malt. Some bottlers in the past have reached an agreement whereby they do not mention the distillery from where the malt is sourced, and instead use labeling such as "Speyside's finest," though this now falls outside the laws governing bottle labels. And you can always tell when the world of whisky is thriving and malt is in short supply, because the whisky producers refer to the independents as "parasites."

Truth be told, though, the independent sector plays an important and necessary role in the world of whisky. It provides a demand for excess malt when there is a glut, and it plays a crucial role in fueling the passion of whisky fans, who are constantly in search of something new and exciting, and who would quickly get bored and frustrated if restricted only to proprietary bottlings.

What is more, the great independent bottlers have histories as long, or longer than, many of the whisky producers, and have access to some of the world's rarest and most cherished malts. They employ the finest warehousemen and seek the best wood to ensure that they are producing the very best whisky, so you may have every chance of finding your dream malt. You may equally, however, pay a considerable amount of money for a malt that is just not that good.

So two pieces of advice: Seek out as much information about your independent purchase as you can, and if you can taste it before purchasing, do so. If you do find your dream dram, buy as much of it as you can afford. Chances are it will not be around for long.

Here is a list of some—but by no means all—of the top independent specialists in Scottish malts, with a couple of recommendations from each.

LEFT The Connoisseurs' Choice collection, bottled by Gordon & MacPhail, is highly collectible.

Adelphi

Based in Argyll, Adelphi specializes in single cask and cask-strength single-malt whisky.

Choice:

Breath of the Isles 1993
Glen Garioch 1990 19-year-old

Berry Bros & Rudd

London-based wine merchant that sells an excellent range of whisky and is the custodian of Glenrothes.

Choice:

Berry's Own Selection 1989 Mortlach
Berry's Own 1989 Girvan Grain

Blackadder

Placing a particular emphasis on Sweden, Blackadder specializes in single-cask whisky bottled at cask strength. Whiskies from this bottler tend to get snapped up very quickly indeed.

Choice:

Blackadder Raw Cask
Blackadder Smoking Islay

Cadenhead

Scotland's oldest independent bottler, with more than 260 years' experience under its belt.

Choice:

Authentic Collection Aberfeldy 1996 13-year-old
Ardmore 1997 11-year-old

Dewar Rattray

Dewar Rattray has been selling whisky for more than 200 years, and now specializes in unusual and exclusive malts.

Choice:

Cask Collection
Glencadam 1990
Glenallachie 1990

Douglas Laing

Glasgow-based company Douglas Laing is run by brothers Stewart and Fred Laing, and has access to a broad range of exciting whisky. It specializes in bottling whisky of an unusual age, and its labels include Old Malt Cask and Provenance. The company has shown an admirable degree of creativity in recent years, mixing malts from different distilleries to create new whiskies.

Choice:

Big Peat (four Islay malts including Port Ellen)
Double Barrel (combinations including **Glenrothes** and **Ardbeg**, **Highland Park** and **Bowmore**, **Laphroaig** and **Macallan**, and **Caol Ila** and **Braeval**.)

Duncan Taylor

Based in Huntly in Speyside, Duncan Taylor has a spacious treasure-laden grotto of a store in the town and consistently bottles great whisky. Some of its aged grain whisky is particularly wonderful.

Choice:

Rare Auld Caperdonich 37-year-old
Peerless Glenlivet 40-year-old

Glenkeir

The independent bottling arm of the Whisky Shop chain, which has 15 outlets across England and Scotland. The range includes a number of whiskies available from the cask in the company's stores, and a number of limited-edition bottlings at cask strength. Many are available for sampling before purchasing.

Choice:

Springbank 17-year-old
Glenfarclas 40-year-old

Gordon & MacPhail

One of the oldest and most established independent companies, Gordon & MacPhail owns Benromach distillery and has a wonderful store in Elgin, in the heart of Speyside. Its independent labels include Connoisseurs' Choice. In 2010 it revealed just how rare and special malt owned by independents can be, when it bottled the world's oldest whisky, a 70-year-old Mortlach.

Ian MacLeod

Owners of Glengoyne Distillery and bottlers of some outstanding blends and blended/vatted malts.

Choice:

Smokehead (a peated independent bottling of Caol Ila)
Six Isles (containing malt from six different Scottish islands)

Scotch Malt Whisky Society

A membership club that bottles cask-strength whisky and has won a reputation for high quality. Traditionally it has not named the distillery from which the malt comes. Instead, it refers to the distillery by number, and provides a large clue through an on-label taste description.

Choice:

Tamdhu
Rosebank
St. Magdalene

Signatory

The independent company owned by Andrew Symington, who also owns Edradour Distillery.

Choice:

Laphroaig 1990 17-year-old

Whisky festivals & events

You can talk and write about whisky all you like, but the only proper way to experience it is of course to drink it. So how can you go about trying a number of different whiskies without blowing the budget?

The most obvious way is to go and visit a distillery or two. Whisky tourism is big business these days, and many distilleries now offer a visitor experience. Others will show you around if you call in advance. The pick of them, in the main whisky markets, are listed on these pages.

There are also a number of whisky festivals and tasting events held across the world. Events come and go, but there is now a number of well-established shows, some of which tour large cities each year. The key ones are listed here.

FESTIVALS

Kentucky Bourbon Festival
www.kybourbonfestival.com

The Kentucky Bourbon Festival is usually held during the third week of September in and around Bardstown, Kentucky. It is a week of events celebrating bourbon, including a cigar and bourbon evening, events at individual distilleries, and the prestigious black-tie gala on the final Saturday night.

Feis Iie
www.theislayfestival.co.uk

The Islay festival is a celebration of music and whisky held on the island during the second May bank holiday weekend. Events are held at all eight distilleries and on Jura.

Spirit of Speyside Whisky Festival
www.spiritofspeyside.com

An annual celebration of the distilleries of Speyside. This takes place over the first bank holiday weekend at the end of April/beginning of May.

Autumn Speyside Whisky Festival
www.dufftown.co.uk

This is normally held annually in late September, and is based in and around Dufftown.

EVENTS

Whisky Live
www.whiskylive.com

Whisky Live events are organized by *Whisky Magazine* in England and they are now held all over the world. The events vary from territory to territory but, in essence, they offer whisky drinkers the chance to try different whiskies, to meet the people who made them, and to learn more about their whiskies by attending masterclasses. The events attract some of the industry's biggest names.

The principle destinations are:

New Delhi, India	January
Tokyo, Japan	February
Brussels, Belgium	February
London, England	March
New York, USA	April
Shanghai, China	May
Taipei, Taiwan	May
Glasgow, Scotland	September
Paris, France	September
Sydney, Australia	September
Los Angeles, USA	October
Fort Lauderdale, USA	October
Toronto, Canada	October
Barcelona, Spain	October
Leiden, Netherlands	November
Cape Town, South Africa	November
Johannesburg, South Africa	November

WhiskyFest
www.maltadvocate.com/docs/whiskyfest

Organized by the leading US whisky magazine *Malt Advocate*, WhiskyFest is a whisky show that is held in three American cities and features more than 200 whiskies, gourmet buffets, and seminars by distillery managers and master blenders.

The events are held in:

Chicago	April
San Francisco	October
New York	November

Whisky Luxe
www.whiskylive.com/luxe

Whisky Luxe is a new event created by *Whisky Magazine*. It aims to be a niche show that puts premium whisky alongside some of the world's most prestigious luxury brands. Tickets are extremely limited and guests are pampered with luxury travel to the event and treated to the finest cuisine. Events tend to be held in 5-star hotels, and other exhibitors have included Canali, Versace, Ducati, and Remy Cointreau.

Events lined up include:

New Delhi, India .... *January*
Shanghai, China.. *May*
Singapore.. *May*
Madrid, Spain .... *May*
Taipei, Taiwan .... *August*
Moscow, Russia .... *September*
Sydney, Australia.. *September*
Glasgow, Scotland .... *September*
Paris, France .... *September*
Barcelona, Spain .... *October*
Los Angeles, USA .... *October*
Toronto, Canada .... *October*
Fort Lauderdale, USA .... *October*
Cape Town, South Africa ....*November*
Johannesburg, South Africa....................................*November*
Leiden, Netherlands..*November*

Other whisky shows include:

The Whisky Show
www.thewhiskyshow.com

This show was launched in 2009 at the Guildhall in London. It is a luxury whisky-tasting event focused on premium and higher-end whisky brands, and is aimed at the connoisseur. It takes place in late October.

Whisky Fringe
www.royalmilewhiskies.com

This event is held around the time of the Edinburgh Festival in late August/early September, and is organized by Royal Mile Whiskies. It features more than 200 different whiskies.

Whiskies of the World Expo
www.whiskiesoftheworld.com

Held annually each March in San Francisco, this show features whisky, bourbon, and a range of other artisanal and craft spirit products.

Whisky Fair at Limburg, Germany
www.festival.whiskyfair.com

The Whisky Fair has grown into one of the world's most popular whisky events, and attracts thousands of visitors to Limburg, Germany, each April.

Whisky Show Budapest
www.whiskytumbler.tumblr.com

Hungary's first whisky event was launched in April 2010.

Toronto Annual Whisky Gala
www.spiritoftoronto.ca

Held each April, this is a well-established and highly respected whisky event, and includes live jazz, gourmet food, cocktail bar, and tutored tastings.

Whisky directory

MAGAZINES

Whisky Magazine

This is a UK-based magazine that is published eight times a year, in English, French, and Japanese. The magazine's website hosts a forum.
www.whiskymag.com

Malt Advocate

A US-based quarterly magazine that also hosts an Internet forum, and the very informative "What Does John Know?" feature.
www.maltadvocate.com

Whiskeria

Published by The Whisky Shop in the UK, and edited by the book's author, *Whiskeria* is a magazine aimed at entry-level whisky enthusiasts and has a circulation of 30,000. Also published in digital form.
www.whiskyshop.com

Unfiltered

This is the magazine of the Scotch Malt Whisky Society (see Whisky Experiences).

BOOKS

Michael Jackson's Malt Whisky Companion

fully updated 2010 edition, by Dominic Roskrow, Gavin Smith, and Will Meyers
The sixth edition of the world's bestselling whisky book has 550 new tasting notes, and new chapters on Japanese, world and vatted/blended malt whiskies.

The Whisky Bible

by Jim Murray
Here you will find frank, funny, direct—and occasionally offensive—tasting notes for hundreds of world whiskies from the industry's answer to Jerry Sadowitz. Updated annually.

The Malt Whisky Yearbook

edited by Ingvar Ronde
This book is updated every year, with new features written by the whisky world's leading writers, and is an essential annual purchase. The author has been a contributor for four years and provides tasting notes for each new edition.

WHISKY EXPERIENCES

Distillery Visits

Distilleries across the world offer tours to varying degrees. Many have dedicated visitor centers and offer a range of tours from novice-level to a lengthy and involved VIP version. Some do not have visitor facilities as such, but will be happy to show people around if the visit is planned in advance. Check on individual websites for whether visitors are permitted, and for opening times.

The Scotch Whisky Heritage Centre

The SWHC is situated on the Royal Mile in Edinburgh and is the perfect gateway in to the world of whisky, offering guided tours and an introduction to whisky as well as useful information about distilleries.
www.whisky-heritage.co.uk

CLUBS AND ORGANISATIONS

The Scotch Malt Whisky Society

Members can buy exclusive cask-strength whisky, receive its excellent magazine, and take guests to the society's properties in Leith Edinburgh, Queen Street Edinburgh, and London. The society also holds regional tastings.
www.smws.co.uk

The Whisky Tasting Club

This an online club that offers members the chance to taste special whiskies from around the world and then comment on them at the club site. The club also aims to be a one-stop store for whisky aficionados, with blogs, forums, the latest whisky news, and opinion.
www.thewhiskytastingclub.co.uk

There are many whisky websites and blogs, and their numbers grow by the day. Here are a few that I enjoy.

Dr. Whisky
Dr. Feelgood! This is likeable and laidback.
www.drwhisky.blogspot.com

The Whisky Exchange Blog
The live arm of the Whisky Exchange in London.
www.blog.thewhiskyexchange.com

The Whisky Grotto
No frills and not fancy, but comprehensive and worth
checking out.
www.whiskygrotto.com

The Scotblog
Kevin Erskine's site is the one that everyone else's has to
match up to. Excellent.
www.inebrio.com/thescotchbog

Whiskyfun
This is my type of site. A bit rock-and-roll, a bit kooky, and
undoubtedly written with authority by Malt Maniac Serge
Valentin.
www.whiskyfun.com

Caskstrength.net
One of the better up-and-coming sites. Pitched perfectly.
www.caskstrength.net

Edinburgh Whisky Blog
Written by 20-something-year-old students—and done
extremely well. Nice and irreverent.
www.edinburghwhiskyblog.com

What Does John Know?
The boss! Malt Advocate's publisher, John Hansell, brings his
considerable expertise to this blog. Essential reading.
www.whatdoesjohnknow.com

Nonjatta
Independent and intense Japanese-facing site.
www.nonjatta.blogspot.com

The Malt Madness Blog
Another awesome mix of frighteningly knowledgeable
information and delightful zaniness, this time from Malt
Maniacs mainman Johannes van den Heuvel.
www.maltmadness.com

Whisky index

The whisky index is organized by whisky name, then distillery owner, and country of origin.

Index

Figures in italics refer to captions.

Acknowledgments

AUTHOR'S ACKNOWLEDGMENTS

Although this is not my first book project, it is very much a culmination of the last 20 years as a drinks journalist, and nine specializing in whisky. There have been many shared drinks, many great moments, and lots of happy times. Perhaps unsurprisingly, therefore, there are far too many for me to remember, and I couldn't start to thank all the people who have played some part in getting me to this point. However, some deserve a special mention for services beyond the call of duty.

Let's start with this book. A huge thank you to my amazing editor Jo Copestick, who not only offered me the chance to write it, but pretty much gave me free license to do with it what I wanted. Or at least, allowed me to think she did. Jo reined in my wilder editorial indulgences (really!) while steering the good-ship whisky book through all sorts of obstacles during what have been the three most intensive writing months of my life. If any of this is any good, then it is down to her composure and good sense.

A special thank you to the "Burt Bacharach" of book design, Robin Rout. Time and time again I sent him works in progress, and he sent me rich, sophisticated, and beautifully produced completed gems; to Jacqui Small, for backing me from the offset, offering advice as necessary, but trusting me by leaving me to it; and to the rest of the Jacqui Small team, especially Kika "rottweiler" Sroka Miller, who went in search of pictures from across the world and, amazingly, found them. Respect. Perhaps my biggest thanks of all should go to Marcin Miller, who started all this off by taking me on as editor of *Whisky Magazine*, and who has been a friend and co-conspirator ever since. And a big thanks to Rubyna Sheikh, who works in Marcin's office, makes miracles happen, and has consistently supported me over the years.

I'd also like to thank Damian Riley-Smith and Rob Allanson of *Whisky Magazine*, for giving me access to Whisky Mag's whisky cellars, and to John Hansell and Lew Bryson at *Malt Advocate* for being thoroughly good guys. A massive thanks to Ian Bankier, for being a friend and sounding board as well as a business partner, and to all the team at The Whisky Shop, but particularly Chris Rodden in Norwich and Peter Semple and Catherine Service in head office, for constant support.

A special thank you to Dave Broom for being a friend and mentor ever since we first debated Uncut's Albums of the Year over a dram or two back in the day, and to Jim Murray, whisky writer extraordinaire. I made it a point of principle that I didn't refer to other whisky books when I wrote this. But I'd be a liar if I didn't acknowledge two: Murray's Whisky Bible, which I carry everywhere, and his book on American bourbon, rye, and Tennessee whiskey. I hope my American section updates and does justice to the work Jim has done in the past. And while on the subject of America, a big thank you to Susan Dallas and all at the Louisville Convention and Visitors' Bureau for all the wonderful support and hours of driving round ol'Kentucky.

I'd like to thank the Norwich VIP Whisky Club massive, who have been listening to this book for the past three years—Derek, Susie, Mark, Mary, Peter, Andrew, Sue, and Geoffrey. Also thanks go to my new business partners in the Norwich Whisky Tasting Club, Pat, Tony, and Michelle.

I'd like to thank my mum, who started me on my whisky journey many, many years ago by letting me have a taste of her peated whisky when I was very small; my little brother Ben and his family who have provided a home to me on many occasions over the years.

And most of all, thanks to my long-suffering wife, Sally, who is my very own Flaming Heart, and my children: Jules and Louie, my wee men who are just realizing how weird it is to have a dad who drinks for a living, and adorable Maddie, who keeps it all real.

I'd like to thank Dr. Oetker for his whole grain peach yogurts —and grapefruit-juice manufacturers everywhere, as well as my sporting heroes who have given me hundreds of good and bad moments to reach for the whisky bottle over the years—Leicester City, the mighty All Blacks and the Dallas Cowboys.

Finally to those "missing in action": my father, a good man who I think of every day and who taught me that strong doesn't mean tough or physical; Peter, the best friend I ever had or ever will have; and Lewis, wherever or whoever he is now—I wouldn't have got in to drinks journalism let alone whisky writing without him.

And I'd like to thank every one of my distillery friends across the world for so generously sharing their world with me; anyone anywhere who enjoys a whisky; and the scores of enthusiasts everywhere who make the world of whisky such a dynamic one.

This has been, without doubt, the best experience of my life and I never want it to end. If you're ever in Norwich, pop in to The Whisky Shop in Swan Lane, the Rumsey Wells in St. Andrews Street, or Franks Bar in Bedford Street, and ask for me. I'd be delighted to make your acquaintance.

PUBLISHER'S ACKNOWLEDGMENTS

The publisher would also like to thank the following people who helped in the production of this book:

Pat Roberts of malts.com; Tim Forbes of The Whisky Exchange; Marcin Miller and Rubyna Sheik of the Number One Drinks Company and Ann McMichael.

Chris MacLean of The Whisky Shop and Michael Hopert of Royal Mile Whisky for the loan of whisky and glasses for photography; Riedel for the loan of glassware for photography; Patricia Michelson of La Fromagerie for the loan of cheese boards and knives; Stewart McCarroll for the loan of two oak quaiches for photography.

For cocktail recipes: Esther Medina Cuesta of Bureau Club; Stuart Hudson of Viajante; Nidal Ramini of Brown-Forman Spirits, Alistair Malcolm of Lab, Soho, London; Vamsi Putta of Salt Whisky Lounge and Dining Room.

PICTURE CREDITS

The publisher wishes to thank the many distilleries from around the world that kindly provided images of their whiskies and distillery facilities that are reproduced here.

Special photography by Simon Murrell:
Cover image; pages 1–33, 36–51, 162–163, 204–205, 212–213, 226–227, 244–245, 264–265, 286–288.

All other images are credited to their respective distilleries, excluding the following:
Page 34 food shots malts.com; 35 food shots malts.com; 60 Arran The Whisky Exchange; 70 Blair Athol The Whisky Exchange; 85 Glen Elgin 16 Year The Whisky Exchange; 92 Glen Garioch 15 Year The Whisky Exchange; 94 middle Louise McGilviary – fotolia.com; 103 background Brian Stewart-Coxon – fotolia.com; 104 Hazelburn 8 Year The Whisky Exchange; 111 Laphroaig 30 Year The Whisky Exchange; 112 C. Spreiter; 113 C.Spreiter; 114 Longmorn 17 Year The Whisky Exchange; 117 Miltonduff 15 Year The Whisky Exchange; 118 background Louise McGilviary – fotolia.com; 123 Spring Bank Vintage 1997 The Whisky Exchange; 129 Tamdhu, Tamdhu 25 Year The Whisky Exchange; 146 Te Bheag The Whisky Exchange; 188 top, bottom Ann McMichael middle Melissa Farlow/Getty Images; 192 top Ann McMichael; 193 portrait Ann McMichael; 202 Charbay Hop Flavoured Mitch Rice; 207 bottom istockphoto.com/Pgiam; 250 top Thierry Mariot; 251 top left, bottom right Thierry Mariot; 268 all Bakery Hill Andrew Ashton.